Shula:
Code Name The Pearl

Shula:
Code Name The Pearl

AVIEZER GOLAN & DANNY PINKAS

Delacorte Press/New York

PUBLISHED BY DELACORTE PRESS
1 DAG HAMMARSKJOLD PLAZA, NEW YORK, N.Y. 10017

Manufactured in the United States of America
First printing

DESIGNED BY LAURA BERNAY

Published by arrangement with Michaelmark Books, Israel

Library of Congress Cataloging in Publication Data
Golan, Aviezer.
Shula, code name the Pearl.

1. Kishak—Cohen, Shula.   2.   Spies—Israel—Biography.
3.   Espionage, Israeli—Lebanon.   4.   Israel—Biography.
I.   Pinkas, Danny, joint author.   II.   Title.
DS126.6.K57G64   327'.12'0924   [B]   79–23315
ISBN 0–440–01516–2

Shula:
Code Name The Pearl

The Bartered Bride

1 Twilight and the piercing chill of the Jerusalem winter combined to give the thick-walled room the severe look of a boarding school. The sparse furniture helped to bear out this impression—an old cupboard, two cots separated by a tightly shut window, a simple wooden table, and a single chair. There was no heater in the room, but the slight disorder helped to soften the Spartan atmosphere. The bedcovers were crumpled and textbooks and notebooks lay open on the table. There seemed to be a deliberate, although disorganized, effort to make the room cheerful: a knitted blanket served as a rug, a multicolored poncho hung from one wall, pictures of film stars cut from magazines decorated another, several dozen books haphazardly lined a bookshelf, and on the cupboard a simple glass filled with yellow wild flowers stood next to an Argentinian gaucho doll.

The two girls sat cross-legged, each on her own bed, covered with blankets to ward off the cold. They were sisters, very much alike in their features, yet very different from each other.

Shula, the elder of the two, was fifteen but looked older. Her tight-fitting blouse outlined a well-developed figure and the serious look in her steel-blue eyes suggested a woman used to responsibility rather than a girl who had only just cast off her childhood. Yet remnants of childhood remained; when she was relaxed, she looked almost like a young child.

Naomi, who had black hair and dark eyes, was one year younger, but her thin, pointed face and boyish figure and the spark of rebellion in her deep eyes were ageless.

As Naomi sat on the bed wrapped in the blanket, nothing in her appearance suggested the limp, caused by a childhood disease, which severely restricted her movements. It had prevented her from participating in the games of her peers and had turned her into a homebody. Her thirst for excitement was slaked by vicarious identification with her sister's adventures. Naomi's feelings for Shula were little short of hero worship, moderated by a hint of cynicism.

Shula, with some pride, told her sister what had happened to her that morning on the way home from school: "Then Eli asked me if he could see me home and I said I wouldn't mind. On the way he began to talk—and guess about what? About the Haganah. He said they had checked up on me and found that I could be trusted. He said he was told to ask me if it would be okay to put my name up for recruitment into Gadna. . . . It was so insulting. If Mathilda and Rosa weren't just in back of us, I would have walked away then and there."

"What's with you?" Naomi cried out in agitation. "Joining the Haganah? That's fantastic. You agreed, I hope. . . ."

"I said no. You know father would never allow . . ."

"Shula!" A note of disappointment and rebuke crept into Naomi's voice.

"Father has so many problems as is," Shula replied gravely. "I just can't add any more."

"You're impossible with that sense of responsibility of yours," Naomi pounced on her. "It's always the same—what will father say, how will mother react? You've got a life of your own to lead, haven't you? And to join the Haganah? If anybody asked me, I wouldn't hesitate for a second."

In their neighborhood—Mekor Baruch—as well as in the other Jewish quarters of Jerusalem, people were ambivalent about the Haganah, the illegal Jewish defense organization. The young people held it in great respect and admiration, particularly since the Arab riots of 1929, when the Haganah had saved some of the more remote and isolated neighborhoods from pogroms and mass killings. People were increasingly coming to the realization that the two national movements, the Jewish and the Arab, were trapped in Palestine, advancing along an inevitable collision course, and that the Jews could look for no aid from the British mandatory government. Even though the British had promised to "take a favorable view of the establishment of a Jewish national home," they were inclined to support the Arabs. That being the case, the only defense for the Jews was an independent military force of their own. For the young people the greatest attraction of all lay in the romantic experience of belonging to an underground organization. The secret meetings, the exchange of passwords and codes, the clandestine training in the use of weapons—all these were both a fascinating game and a challenge to the traditional way of life of a society set firmly in its ways. And herein lay one of the major reasons for the objections of the older generation to the Haganah.

But there was more to it than that. For the inhabitants of these quarters—both those from families whose ancestors had settled in Jerusalem generations before modern Zionism brought over the first idealistic young revolutionaries from Europe, as well as those more recent immigrants from Arab lands who had been attracted to the Holy Land for its sacredness rather than by its promises for a better future—for both these groups the armed, clandestine organization was not only criminally subversive, undermining law and order, but also a contravention of divine decree. Jews had always lived in danger of their lives yet had always known how to stave off disaster—whether by buying the favors of rulers or by cowering low until the storm abated. To take up arms and fend off attack was not the Jewish way.

Worried parents warned their children against joining the Haganah and ostracized those who did.

The girls chatted away in their room and when the sun had fully set, Naomi absentmindedly reached for the light switch at the head of her bed.

"Don't turn on the light, it isn't dark yet," Shula said automatically. Naomi drew back her hand resentfully.

"You sound just like mother," she replied.

"But mother is right," Shula responded firmly.

At that moment Shula looked like a little girl pretending to be mother.

"We've got to go easy on the electricity. You know that as well as I do."

"Yes," Naomi said, curling up in her blanket, "but I'm tired of being told how poor we are. You know, sometimes I think to myself that it's really too bad father came home. Is that really awful of me?"

Shula made no reply but admitted to herself that the unspeakable thought had crossed her mind more than once. Seeing her father's constant frown and listening to her mother's interminable grumblings, Shula, too, had looked back longingly to the time when her father had spent most of the year far from home, kept overseas on business. Then, at least, the atmosphere at home had been relaxed— and there was always the eager anticipation of his homecoming.

Her father, Meir Arazi-Cohen, was born to a wealthy merchant family in Egypt. As a young man he emigrated with his older brother to Argentina, where they entered the clothing business. Within a few years they were well established and operated a successful chain of retail stores in Buenos Aires. But when the time came for him to marry, he returned to Cairo and turned the matter of finding a bride over to his family and professional marriage brokers. After a long and careful search they presented him with Allegra, the daughter of the prominent Jerusalem rabbi Shimon Harush.

It was a successful match. They had twelve children, and Shula was their fourth. Allegra had great difficulty adjusting to life away from Jerusalem and Meir, who had only seen the city for the first time during his engagement, was enthralled with its magical splendor. He came from a religious family and was deeply moved by its holiness. It did not take very much pleading to convince him to make Jerusalem their home.

It was not, however, possible to transplant the business from Argentina to Palestine, and Meir Arazi was forced to divide his life. For nine months of the year he worked in Buenos Aires. Then, just as the autumn rains would begin to fall on the Argentine pampas, he would turn the business over to his brother and set sail for the East.

In years to come Shula would remember her childhood as one of the happier periods of her life. She never had a moment's time for idleness. Even when she was very young, she had to help her perennially pregnant mother with the housework and with the care of her younger brothers and sisters. And she enjoyed the responsibility and the role of "little mother." She attended the Evelyna de Rothschild School for Girls—the same school her mother had attended—and was considered an excellent student. She received top grades with little effort and made friends easily. She was popular among teachers and students alike and was always the one chosen to welcome important visitors to the class.

She accepted her father's long absences as a matter of course, although she did at times envy her friends whose fathers were at home more. Even so, the great rejoicing that accompanied her father's arrival was more than adequate compensation.

Father would arrive from the railroad station in a taxi or, in the days before taxis, in an *arabiya hantur*, a two-horse coach with an Arab driver. First he would stand silently in front of the coach, inspecting the family "tableau" on the balcony. Then he would kiss his wife and become acquainted with any new offspring born during his absence. Only then would the other children approach to be kissed. Finally he would enter the house with the family in tow. The two eldest sons had the honor of carrying his luggage.

They all gathered in the spacious living room, where Shula and her mother served Turkish coffee and lemonade. And while their father slowly sipped his coffee, one by one the children would approach and hand him a report card. While he rigorously examined their school achievements, their mother would report on their behavior at home. Shula could not remember her father ever raising his voice in anger at any of them. Even so, the air was filled with tension, as though they were being examined at school.

At last the tension would break. As though reminding himself of what was expected of him, he would let loose a broad smile and contentedly announce, "Very nice. You've been good children!" And then he would motion to his eldest son, who would drag over the heavy suitcase.

It was present time.

Once the excitement of receiving and comparing gifts and new clothes was over, the children would run out to play with their friends and to show off their bounty. But the tranquillity within the house would be short-lived. News of Meir Arazi-Cohen's arrival would spread quickly and throngs of visitors would begin to drop by—relatives, friends of the family, strangers in search of information about relations in South America, others interested in obtaining visas to Argentina, rabbis, women's groups, and representatives of *yeshivot* soliciting donations. The procession would last throughout the holiday, and Shula and her mother were kept close to the kitchen, cooking and baking, and serving the multitude of guests.

Before the holiday, her father would go to the *suk*, the open-air market, to buy provisions. He would buy lavishly, and at least two Arab porters—each carrying an oversized wicker basket brimming with food—would accompany him home. A resplendent *seder* table was Meir Arazi-Cohen's pride and joy; that and standing at the neighborhood synagogue surrounded by his progeny all aglow in their holiday clothes as the members of the congregation came to shake his hand and congratulate him on the newest addition to his family.

Passover was a joyous time for the Arazi-Cohens, and the holiday spirit would last well into the next two months. But then the large leather suitcase would be brought down from the attic; the Kurdish laundress, brought in for an entire day, would hover near the hot-water stove bubbling over in the courtyard; and Shula's mother would spend long hours bent over the ironing board, her feet swollen and her eyes puffed. Then mother and father and the older children would climb into the coach for the trip to the railroad station.

Father was off again on his long journey.

In the summer of 1932, at the age of twelve, Shula was chosen to accompany her father to Buenos Aires. She had been promoted twice at school and was already in the eighth grade.

Despite the excitement of the journey and of living in a strange country, Shula did not have pleasant memories of that year. She was terribly lonely, even though her uncle and his family lived nearby. It took her a while to learn Spanish, and only then did she begin to make a few friends at the Jewish girls' school she attended. She was homesick for her family and friends in Jerusalem, and she spent much of her time writing letters. She wrote to her sister Naomi more than to anyone else. Shula was closer to her than to any of her other brothers and sisters.

Just as she was beginning to grow accustomed to life in Buenos Aires, the year was over and she and her father boarded the ship for home.

A seemingly unimportant incident occurred during their voyage that was to remain buried in her subconscious until many years later. Several days after the ship had departed, when the passengers had become adjusted to life on board and were no longer complaining of seasickness, Meir Arazi-Cohen began to stuff his pockets with rolls and sandwiches or any scraps that were left over on the table in their second-class dining room. When a curious passenger commented on his behavior, he announced, "I suffer from a stomach ulcer. I have to eat every few hours to alleviate the pain."

Shula knew her father was lying, but it never occurred to her to expose him or to question his actions. One cloudy afternoon when most passengers preferred the warmth of their cabins to the rough weather outdoors, she saw her father walking about strangely, stealthily making his way to the main deck. He seemed to be looking about him in all directions, making sure he was alone. When he seemed certain that no one had seen him, he headed toward one of the lifeboats, lifted its tarpaulin cover, took a paper bag from his pocket, and threw it into the boat.

That evening Shula mustered up the courage to ask her father about the strange goings-on. He was so shocked at being discovered, he confessed the whole story.

"There's a stowaway hiding in the lifeboat," he said. "A Jew. He was forced to leave Argentina."

She did not question him any further and became an accomplice to her father's deeds. Until the ship anchored in Genoa, she prepared the sandwiches herself and constantly reminded her father: "Don't forget to take this to our cabin. You'll want it later, when the pain comes. . . ."

She never saw the stowaway. They disembarked at Genoa, traveled by train to Trieste, and there boarded a ship sailing to Jaffa. During the trip she asked about the man's fate.

"He got off in Genoa," her father replied. "We may get to see him in Jerusalem. I lent him the fare."

When he noticed Shula's curious, innocent look, he added: "We have to help Jews. If he had been caught in Italy, they would have put him in jail. The greatest of God's commandments is the ransoming of prisoners. . . ."

The past year had not been a good one in Argentina, not even for Meir Arazi-Cohen. The country was in the throes of an economic depression and business was slack. He was also beginning to feel the pressure of his years. The long journeys had become a burden and he was eager to spend more time with his family. While gloomily reviewing the company books with his brother, he hinted that should "something good" be offered to him in Jerusalem, he might consider dissolving the partnership. His brother acceded, but cautioned that it was not a good time to withdraw capital from the business.

However, it took him two more years before he achieved his ambition and settled in Jerusalem for good. But by then he had missed out on the prosperity in Palestine. In October, 1935, Italy attacked Ethiopia, and the skies of the Middle East were overcast with clouds of war. Potential investors were reluctant to risk their capital in such troubled times. The situation grew steadily worse and a local economic depression set in.

For a while the Arazi-Cohen family did not feel the strain and their life-style remained much as it had been. But the money Meir Arazi had brought from Argentina began to dwindle and was not replenished by any new source of income. The bad times had begun and by winter's end, in 1936, the austerity program Shula's mother had enforced had reached the height of severity. Shula was all of sixteen and was completely absorbed in her lead role in the end-of-year school play. But even she could not help notice the anxious expressions on her parents' faces as they pored over the household bills in the evenings.

They had good reason to worry. Passover was approaching and the more Meir Arazi-Cohen inspected his accounts, the clearer it became that this year's holiday would be very unlike its predecessors. But he found it difficult to accept the verdict that reality was enforcing upon him. Passover was the high point of his year, the symbol of his material and social success. This year it would only symbolize his dismal failure. He felt disgraced and humiliated, and when he thought of the grim future, he felt hopeless and depressed.

For Shula the focal point of the family economic crisis was a red dress she had seen in a shop window on Jaffa Road. She needed a new dress. She had grown taller in the last year and her figure had filled out. Last summer's clothes no longer fitted her. As spring approached, she eagerly awaited the semiannual ritual when her mother would gather the older girls for the trip to Grazia, the neighborhood dressmaker. But Purim had passed and her mother had said nothing. Shula was well aware of the reason. As a result, she could not muster up the courage to ask her mother about new clothes for Passover. In another week the situation would be hopeless. Even if the money could be found, Grazia would never be able to sew the new dresses in time for the holiday. All her hopes focused on what she herself knew was an unrealistic dream—that her mother would agree to spend even more money and buy her a ready-to-wear dress in a store. Without fully comprehending her own actions she began window-shopping in the center of town on her way home from school. Until she discovered the red dress. There was no price tag on it, but Shula knew it would be terribly expensive. It was almost as though she had decided, if there is to be a miracle, then let it be a great one. . . .

Maurice Batash returned to Jerusalem ten days before Passover and went directly to the home of his good friend Meir Arazi-Cohen. Batash was a traveling salesman and conducted most of his business in Syria and Lebanon. Recently he had been contemplating the possibilities of expanding to Egypt and hoped that Meir would introduce him to his relatives in Cairo.

Shula served them cold lemonade and sesame cakes. As she was about to go to the kitchen to brew the Turkish coffee, Maurice discovered that he had run out of cigarettes. He asked her to run down to the grocery to buy him a pack of Matosian. Her father offered him cigarettes from his own pack, but Maurice was adamant. Shula went out on the errand.

By the time she returned, coffee had already been served and her mother was busy with something else in the kitchen. Shula offered to help, but for once her mother declined. "Aren't you supposed to visit Mathilda?" she asked. Mathilda was Shula's classmate and they often did their homework together. Shula replied that Mathilda could wait, but her mother did not let up. "If you promised, then you must go."

She returned two hours later, just as Maurice Batash was at the door saying good-bye to her parents. He pinched her cheek affectionately, then turned to her father and said, "With God's help everything will work out well."

Her mother echoed piously, "With God's help," but she avoided looking into Shula's questioning eyes.

Maurice called the following day and once again a pretext was found to send Shula out of the house. By the time she returned, Maurice had left and her parents were sitting at the large dining-room table, lost in thought. It was an all too familiar sight. Her heart ached every time she saw them there, poring over their bills. She was about to go to her room when she noticed that their usual downcast expression had changed. And then she heard what her mother was saying:

". . . then four chickens, and fish and meat, of course. And mutton?"

"A fresh lamb," her father replied with a burst of pride that reminded her of the old days. "Make that two lambs—"

"All right, but let's not get carried away. And Shula needs a new dress."

Shula held her breath when she heard her father matter-of-factly say, "Well then, take her to Grazia tomorrow."

Her heart beating furiously, she ran to her room. The miracle had happened!

The following day she woke up very early but her father had already left the house. He had gone out in search of a painter who would give the house a fresh coat of whitewash for the holiday. It was part of the Passover ritual.

Shula awakened her brothers and sisters despite their protests that it was Passover vacation and they had no reason to wake up early. She supervised their washing and dressing and brought them into the kitchen where her mother had breakfast on the table. "Eat and then go out and play," their mother announced, "the painters might be coming. . . ." She turned to Shula. "And you will stay here with me."

"Why?" asked Shula, pretending innocence.

"I need your help."

Shula swallowed her excitement and impatience. After the children had finished eating and had run out to play, she made their beds and helped her mother wash the breakfast dishes.

Her mother finally untied her apron and said, "Now we'll go to the seamstress. She may have time to sew you a new dress."

It was a vain hope. Grazia, a widow of about fifty who had sewn all of Shula's holiday dresses until then, stared in disbelief laced with a tinge of contempt. "You want it by Passover?" she said, repeating

Mrs. Arazi-Cohen's request and pointing to the pile of cut fabric on the floor waiting to be sewn. "At this point I wouldn't even have it ready for *Lag B'Omer*. . . ."

Then, while Shula anxiously held her breath, her mother came to the conclusion: "We'll have to buy a ready-made dress. You need a new one for the holiday."

Years later when Shula recalled the incident, she was amazed by her cunning as she guided her mother past the various dress shops until they reached the one on Jaffa Road. The red dress captured her mother's heart as well. But when they entered the store to inquire about the price, Shula resigned herself; the situation would be hopeless.

The unheard of price, however, was a challenge to Shula's mother. No true Jerusalemite worthy of the title would miss an opportunity to bargain. In the end, after more than an hour of discussion, after Shula had tried on the dress twice while her mother pointed out all its major and minor flaws, after they had twice left the store in a huff, each time "for the last time," everything ended well.

On their way home Shula's mother made her promise. "Swear you won't tell anyone what we really paid. Your father will be furious. . . ."

Shula promised.

Meir Arazi-Cohen was already at home when they returned. He had not succeeded in finding a painter who was free on such short notice. He did, however, manage to complete all their holiday shopping at the Mahane Yehuda market. The contents of two oversized baskets were piled on the table: vegetables, meat, fish, chicken, everything they would need. Shula and her mother immediately began to store the food in the icebox and pantry. When Shula expressed her surprise at the amount of food her father had bought, her mother answered curtly, "Guests are coming; friends from Beirut."

Her mother did not volunteer further details.

As the days went by, the mysterious guests from Beirut became the focal point of the family's interest. Maurice Batash, who now visited them daily, said they would need two guest rooms, and it was decided that all the children, save for the youngest, who slept in their parents' bedroom, would be sent to sleep at the homes of neighbors and relatives. Shula was the only one who was not displaced from her bed. Maurice undertook to meet the guests at the railroad station and escort them to the house on Alfandari Street.

Years later Shula was amazed that she had been so naïve and had not figured out what was going on. There had been so many obvious clues: the sudden and unexplained wealth that filled the house; the mysterious guests from Beirut, "old friends" of their father who lived in a city he had never once visited. More than anything else she should have been alerted to her parents' new attitude toward her. Her father, who until now had stubbornly insisted on treating her like a child, suddenly took an uncharacteristic interest in her hairstyle and (she almost laughed at his awkwardness and the old-fashioned phraseology of his question) even asked her if it weren't time for her to start "painting her eyes." Her mother absolutely went out of her way to prevent Shula from doing any of the more difficult holiday housework. At the same time she kept Shula close by her the entire time, offering up bits of kitchen wisdom and practical advice suitable to a young woman about to start her own household. It seemed that in the eyes of her parents Shula had turned into a young woman overnight.

But this was not the only change in their behavior. There was something else, something quite elusive and indefinable. Only later did Shula realize that it may have been guilt. Her parents were unusually warm and affectionate toward her, but at the same time seemed to be concealing something from her.

The guests from Beirut arrived late in the afternoon on the eve of Passover. A dusty taxi entered Alfandari Street and Naomi, who had been posted as lookout, gleefully called: "They're here! They're here!"

All the children spilled into the street shouting at the top of their lungs, but Shula's mother would not allow her to run after them. "You'll stay here by the door, with me," she insisted.

She watched Maurice Batash alight from the taxi, followed by a short, balding man who looked about her father's age. Meir Arazi-Cohen, dressed in his dark holiday suit and new silk tie, had gone out to the street to meet them, and Shula was surprised when Maurice introduced the guest to her father. "What kind of 'old friend' is that?" she wondered to herself.

A thin woman, slightly taller and older than the man, followed them out of the cab. She looked stern, even condescending, as she stared at the unpaved street and the herd of screaming children surrounding her. Shula immediately classified her as an "old-maid type, most probably a teacher." There were a few sour-faced, unpleasant women like her at school, and all the students detested them.

The children carried the suitcases into the house and the guests followed. Maurice introduced them to Shula and her mother.

"Mademoiselle Marie Kishak; Monsieur Joseph Kishak."

Joseph Kishak took Shula's hand, but his small, beady eyes darted wildly in all directions to avoid looking at her. Mademoiselle Marie, on the other hand, examined her closely, like a schoolteacher passing judgment on a rebellious and unruly student.

They proceeded to the living room where they were offered cold drinks. The guests distributed their gifts—a carton of fine Egyptian cigarettes for Meir Cohen and a bottle of Greek rose water for his wife. The conversation was forced. Meir Cohen politely inquired about their journey. Marie replied (Shula quickly discovered that Marie always answered for both of them, even if the questions were directed at her brother) that they had encountered no difficulties in the eight-hour journey. No, there had been no trouble at the border crossing at Ra's an Naqurah, although they had been delayed while the passports of some Christian pilgrims visiting the Holy Land for Easter had been checked. Mrs. Cohen inquired if the guests would like to freshen up a bit before being served a light lunch. It was Mademoiselle Marie again who replied that they had had a bite to eat in a coffeehouse in the city prior to their arrival, preferring not to inconvenience their hosts with preparing a special meal when the house had already been made ready for the Passover *seder*. If they would be permitted, however, to wash away the dust from the journey and rest a bit they would be very grateful. . . .

It was the last Passover that Shula celebrated in her parents' home. For years afterward she nurtured a concealed resentment toward Joseph Kishak and his sister for inhibiting the family's holiday spirit with their presence. Reason, however, forced her to admit to herself that they had not, in actuality, done anything to justify her resentment.

Joseph—reticent, silent, and undemanding—was politeness personified. He never forgot to thank them for even the smallest favors. Marie, too, was gracious and polite, although she looked stern and severe even when she was trying to be pleasant. It was their presence itself which was disturbing. They seemed critical and judgmental of their hosts. Shula was more conscious of this than anyone else. Marie was constantly examining and evaluating her. This was especially true when her mother would serve some dish and proclaim, "Shula made this." Then Marie's eyes would search Shula's face for verification while she daintily put a morsel in her mouth and rolled it around her tongue for what seemed an eternity before pronouncing her verdict to the expectant crowd: "It's truly excellent." On several occasions she surprised Shula by suddenly addressing her in French, as though she were trying to test the girl's expertise in the language. At other times she questioned her on housekeeping and the laws of *kashrut*.

Joseph did not ask any questions, but he also made Shula feel uncomfortable. He would sit in the large armchair in the corner of the living room, her father's chair, his head hunched between his shoulders, not saying a word, not moving, following her every move with his small, beady eyes.

Once or twice during the holiday week, Shula found herself alone with Maurice Batash. She tried questioning him about the visitors. But all he told her was that Joseph Kishak-Cohen was a wealthy merchant, the owner of a large shop in the commercial center of Beirut, that he had the money to put her father "back on his feet," and that it would be worth their while to be kind to him.

She did her best. With a twinge of remorse she canceled her plans to hike to Abu Ghosh with Maccabi Hatzair, the Zionist youth movement. She also backed out of the trip to the outskirts of the Sanhedriya quarter to pick flowers with her girl friends. Both of these were part of the holiday tradition of Jerusalem youth. She did not even complete the homework her teachers had assigned for the holiday recess. She devoted all her time to the guests. She took them on a sightseeing tour of the Hebrew University campus on Mount Scopus with its breathtaking view of the Holy City. Although they were always the epitome of politeness, the guests did not seem to be interested in the landscape, and Shula felt their impatience to return home. Their excursion to the Old City, however, was more successful, but only because Joseph Kishak was delighted to have the opportunity to pray at the Wailing Wall. He was even more religious than her father. Marie, on the other hand, walked around the Old City with a look of disgust on her face. Any contact with passersby seemed quite repugnant to her. They both obviously preferred to sit at home, leisurely nibbling sunflower seeds and talking with her parents and Maurice Batash.

The holiday came to an end. The guests would be leaving the following day and her brothers and sisters would be back home. In the morning she would have to supervise their washing and dressing while trying to put her briefcase in order. But the house would once more be filled with laughter and crying and singing. She was so relieved at this prospect that she happily accepted the guests' invitation to join them for afternoon tea on the veranda of the King David Hotel. It was the latest fashion of the Jerusalem rich and Shula would be the first of all her friends to have tea at the lush hotel overlooking the walls of the Old City.

It was cool on the veranda and Joseph, in a display of chivalry, offered his jacket to Shula. Even Marie was being exceptionally pleasant and no longer had the countenance and bearing of a schoolmistress. They spoke of Beirut. Marie was quite generous in her praise and Shula imagined Beirut to be an elegant city of captivating beauty, full of life and culture, unlike provincial and dull Jerusalem.

"Would you like to live in Beirut?" Marie asked.

Shula chose her words carefully.

"Buenos Aires is also a metropolis," she said, "but I didn't like it at all. It was too big. But Beirut . . . Beirut sounds nice. Yes, I would be willing . . ."

She thought she saw Joseph and Marie exchange meaningful glances. He stood up suddenly, excused himself, and disappeared. When he returned a few minutes later his sister asked him curtly, "Did you send them?"

He replied, "Yes. Special delivery. They're already on their way."

Suddenly, and without quite understanding why, she was frightened. When they returned home, it all began to make sense. Her parents and Maurice Batash were waiting at the door. As soon as the taxi stopped, Maurice Batash rushed toward Joseph Kishak, embraced him, shook his hand, and shouted, "Congratulations, *Mazel tov!*" Then her father embraced the Lebanese merchant and her mother kissed his sister on the cheek. They were all repeating, "*Mazel tov, mazel tov!* It will be a good match."

Shula was choked with tears as she ran into the house, crying to herself, "No! No!" A large bouquet of flowers, one she had noticed at the florist shop next to the King David Hotel, was standing in the center of the dining room table.

Her mother followed her, urging her to stay. Shula turned to her, tears streaming down her face. There was so much she wanted to say, to shriek, but all she could manage was: "Why? Why?" She turned and ran to her room, locking the door behind her.

She heard her mother knock gently at the door. Then she heard her sister asking to be let into the room. She did not answer her either. She buried her head in the pillow and cried.

That whole night only one thought feverishly filled her head: "They betrayed me!" Everyone, beginning with her parents and ending with that charming Maurice Batash, had led her astray. *They had sold her.* She could not bear the humiliation and pain.

All the humiliation and pain, however, did not incite even the most fleeting feelings of rebellion. She wondered why it never even occurred to her that she could oppose her parents' wishes.

The only answer she could come up with was: "My father needed me. My marriage to Joseph Kishak put an end to all his worries."

But the real reason had very little to do with logic, opportunism, or obligation; it lay in herself, in the way she had been raised, in the way her character had been formed.

From the time she was old enough to understand, she knew that the day would come when she would be married. Emissaries would arrive at her father's house, there would be discussions and negotiations, and in the end she would be presented to the man who had been chosen to be her husband. That was the way it was done. That was how her mother had married her father. That was how all the neighborhood girls had been married. If she ever thought about marriage, she hoped that the man her parents would choose would be young and handsome and kind and rich. Sometimes she would set her hopes on one of the neighborhood boys, but even then her dream was that her *father* would choose him. She never doubted her father's absolute right to select her husband.

Her engagement to Joseph Kishak-Cohen was painful because she was emotionally unready for marriage. She was only sixteen. Although she had the body of a mature woman, she was still an adolescent, more child than woman. Her repulsion to marriage was fortified by the humiliating thought that her parents were eager to "be rid of her," as well as by the underhanded and deceitful way in which the matter had been handled.

The repugnance she felt for Joseph Kishak-Cohen, her mature, balding fiancé with darting, inquisitive eyes, was the least serious aspect of all that now troubled her and was the first thing she was able to overcome.

By the early hours of the morning, after the long, sleepless, tear-filled night, she lay on her bed and began to assess the prospects of her marriage to a man who was neither young nor handsome, but who was rich and apparently kindhearted. What kind of life would she have with him in his large and strange city? Her curiosity, a characteristic of youth, was aroused. The picture in her mind was not very clear. It was shadowed in the fog of her uncertainty.

She finally fell asleep.

The Gilded Cage

2 The following day Marie and Joseph Kishak-Cohen returned to Beirut. Before their departure the engagement agreement was carefully worked out with the active participation of Maurice Batash. The prospective bridegroom not only relinquished his right to a dowry, he even agreed to provide Meir Arazi-Cohen with a generous loan. Shula remained locked in her room throughout the negotiations. However, when Naomi was sent to call her to the living room to bid the guests good-bye, she quickly informed Shula of all the details.

She went out to the guests. A sleepless, tear-filled night had deepened her pallor, and she looked doleful and fragile. Joseph later confessed that he fell helplessly in love with her at that moment. He beamed with joy. Marie kissed both her cheeks and whispered that a wonderful life awaited her in Beirut. Then her mother and father and Naomi approached them to wish them the best of luck. When Maurice Batash came to congratulate the couple, Shula turned her face from him and whispered bitterly, "*You* arranged it all!"

The guests departed. News of the engagement spread rapidly and soon a procession of neighbors, well-wishers, and relatives began to wend its way to the house. Shula felt a sharp change in people's attitudes. No longer was she the little girl not to be taken seriously. She was the fiancée of a wealthy man, and it could be worthwhile to be on her better side. Once she heard two women whispering behind her back as she was leaving the grocery store: "She saved her family with that engagement. . . ."

It was understood that she would not return to school after the Passover holiday. This was another clear indication of the change that had taken place. Her teachers and principal came to congratulate her and wish her well: "We'll all miss you—especially in the choir and in the dramatics club. We're going to have to change the entire program now."

A few days after Passover Shula's engagement was no longer uppermost in people's minds. Troubles with the Arabs had erupted in Jaffa. Nine Jews who had gone to the port city on business were murdered by an angry Arab mob. Many others were injured. The riots continued into the next day, when another seven Jews were killed. This time the rioting took place in the ethnically mixed neighborhoods between Jaffa and Tel Aviv. Houses were burned and looted and a great exodus began. Synagogues and schools in Tel Aviv teemed with seven thousand Jewish refugees from the Jaffa area. Arab political parties sent representatives to Nablus, where they voted to establish a High Arab Council under the patronage of the Jerusalem *mufti*, Haj Amin-el Husseini. They also decided on tactics—sabotage and a general strike until the British mandatory government agreed to renounce the Balfour Declaration, prohibit Jewish immigration, and outlaw the sale of land to Jews.

The riots, which later came to be known as the "Troubles of 36-39" or the "Arab Uprising," spread through the entire country. Jewish fields and orchards were ravaged and burned. Terror increased in the towns. In Jerusalem two Jews were killed in the Old City on their way to pray at the Wailing Wall. Shots were sprayed into a crowd at the Edison Cinema and three people were killed. A children's nursery on the south side of the city near Hebron Road was set on fire.

Fear was rampant. In the evenings people remained at home, cloistered behind tightly drawn shutters; only the footsteps of the hastily organized Haganah patrols could be heard in the streets. Peo-

ple were cautious during daylight hours as well. Entire neighborhoods became too dangerous for Jews to enter. Interurban roads
became the next target of the terrorist gangs. Not a day passed without its count of black-bordered obituary notices in the Jewish press.
Trade was paralyzed. Rumors of approaching bankruptcy spread
wildly through the near-empty marketplaces. No one knew what the
future held.

It may be that the tension and concern that characterized life in
Jerusalem in 1936 made it easier for Shula to accept the idea that
she would soon be leaving the city of her youth for a strange city in
another land.

She left Jerusalem toward the end of July.

Because of the dangers of the trip, as well as for economic reasons, she was accompanied only by her parents and her two youngest
siblings. They traveled to Haifa in a column of buses and from there
they joined an armed convoy of taxis that was escorted by British
soldiers to the border crossing at Ra's an Naqurah. From there they
were on their own.

They arrived in Wadi Abu-Jamil, the street that constituted the
Jewish quarter of Beirut, and were greeted warmly, if with somewhat
more than ordinary curiosity.

The Kishak-Cohens were one of the community's most prominent
families. Mrs. Kishak-Cohen was the scion of a long line of learned
and renowned rabbis who had served in the rabbinates of Aleppo,
Qamishliye, and other Syrian cities. The Kishaks had been successful textile merchants for generations. Joseph and his older brother,
Chaim, had inherited a large shop in the Suk Sursuk, the Sursuk
market, behind the Place de la Bourge, and had enlarged and ex-
panded their trade. Their word was "as good as money" among the
various merchants in the marketplace as well as in the great banks on
Hamra Street. They also contributed generously to the synagogue
and charitable institutions. The only flaw the inveterate gossips could
find with this otherwise perfect family was their poor fortune in
marriage. Marie, the eldest daughter, was a bitter old maid and Joseph, at the age of thirty-six, had still not found the woman of his
dreams. Only Chaim, two years Joseph's senior, had married and
was already the father of two. When Joseph and Marie went to
Jerusalem to celebrate Passover, the rumor in Wadi Abu-Jamil was:
"They went to find a bride." By the time they returned to Beirut, the

news had already reached Wadi Abu-Jamil: "He found himself a flower, a sixteen-year-old girl. . . ." As the taxi from Haifa stopped in front of the apartment building where the Kishak-Cohen family lived, Joseph came out to greet them. All the neighbors gathered curiously around to get a glimpse of the bride. When the crowd dispersed, they all agreed: "She was definitely worth waiting for."

Indeed, she was something to stare at. Not beautiful—there was too much character in her face to be considered classically beautiful —handsome was a more apt description. She was taller than average, with long legs and a good figure, a mature figure though she was only sixteen, with broad shoulders, a narrow waist, and a proud bosom; a figure on which clothes looked good. And in spite of her fatigue after the long journey, she carried herself erect and moved with long, easy, flowing strides. But her most distinguished feature was her eyes, deeply set and steel-blue. Their unusual color had given cause to much bantering in her childhood—and at the time they had made her feel miserable, for children tend to recoil from the exceptional. Now, however, she had already discovered the effect of her bold stare upon boys: suddenly they would become embarrassed and speechless.

Nine days remained until the wedding on August 2, and Shula spent the time becoming acquainted with the city that was to be her new home. She liked what she saw.

It was not, however, the cosmopolitan capital Marie had described in Jerusalem. In 1936 Beirut was no larger than Jerusalem. It had a population of about 150,000 people of diverse ethnic and religious background, and like Jerusalem it was a city of independent and separate neighborhoods. The Moslems lived crowded together in the old Basta quarter with its winding alleyways and side streets near the port. The Armenian quarter, A-Nahar, was in the north, near the Beirut River. The Christians lived in the Al-Ashrafiyah quarter on the slopes of the mountains that closed Beirut off from the east, and the Jews lived in Wadi Abu-Jamil, a short walk from Hamra Street.

Hamra Street was the commercial center of the city. Here were the banks and trading houses and grand hotels, and two of the city's monumental landmarks—the Saraya, the old Turkish fortress, surrounded by a spacious plaza and now serving as police headquarters, and Martyr's Square, a monument to pioneers of Arab nationalism who were publicly hanged by the Turks at the end of the nineteenth century. Martyr's Square was sometimes referred to as "Cannon Square" for the ancient cannons standing at its four corners. More often, though, it was called "Loafer's Square" because of the hundreds of people who idly wandered about and listlessly lounged in its outdoor cafés.

The Suk Sursuk lay beyond Loafer's Square. A stranger could walk the length of Hamra Street and easily miss the entryway—an ornate gate that could readily be mistaken for the entrance to a private courtyard. But once past the gate the heartbeat of the city's business world could be seen and heard. At the beginning of a long, narrow street was the jewelers' market, a row of small shops with large copper scales in their windows for weighing gold. Interlaced among these shops were the *sarafin*, the money changers. Here, pressed between glass, one could see samples of currency from all over the world, along with up-to-date exchange rates scribbled in chalk on blackboards.

Past the jewelers' market the street broadened into a small plaza —the fruit and vegetable market. Slightly farther on lay the inexpensive haberdashery market frequented by *fellahin* (peasants) on days they came to sell their produce. At the far end of the street was the textile market, where all the larger traders in cloth, clothing, curtains, and bedding were congregated. There were no display windows here. Instead, in front of each shop there was a tall pole decorated with strips of materials of various textures and hues from which prospective clients could choose. In the neighboring alleyway quilts and mattresses were sewn to order. When a breeze blew, tufts of quilting floated through the air like cotton candy and the multicolored strips would set in motion like thousands of waving flags and banners, giving the street a festive, carnivallike atmosphere.

The market, like all of Beirut, was multiethnic. Sh'ite Moslems from the south and Maronite Christians from the mountain regions controlled the produce markets while Sunnite Moslems handled the haberdashery shops. Jews and Armenians were friendly competitors in the jewelers' market, and Jews and Maronites shared the textile trade. The only major group absent from this ethnic potpourri was the Druze.

Since each of the religious groups celebrated its Sabbath on a different day, the Suk Sursuk was relatively quiet on Fridays, Saturdays, and Sundays. During the rest of the week, however, a deafening roar emanated from the narrow street. Vendors loudly hawked their wares, attempting to lure passersby into their shops with words, and even by bodily force. Porters, their baskets brimming over, shouted and shoved at anything or anyone in their way. Pack-laden donkeys neighed as *fellahin* loudly prodded them through the crush of shoppers. Peddlers poured cold *sus* (a licorice drink) and *tamarhindi* (a drink made from dates) from oversized brass urns strapped to their shoulders as the glasses and copper trays in their hands clinked metallically. The rich smell of Turkish coffee—no business deal could begin or end without sharing a cup of this strong brew—was predominant throughout.

Shula was familiar with the atmosphere; it was not unlike the alleyways and markets in the Old City of Jerusalem. She felt quite at home with the pealing of church bells and the ululating tones of the muezzin calling the Moslem faithful to worship.

But there was a difference. Unlike Jerusalem, which was predominantly gray as a result of the uniform stone facings of its buildings, Beirut was colorful, warm, and alive. The shimmering blue sea was all around, and the mountains, capped with the lush greens of cypress and pine and flecked with the brown-thatched roofs of the villas on its slopes, added rich color and contrast to the view.

The city, too, was lush and verdant, with garden courtyards enclosed by walls covered with the cascading purple foliage of bougainvillaea.

The major differences between Beirut and Jerusalem, however, were in the atmosphere and the way of life. Beirut was the seat of the French administration in Syria and Lebanon, and the French left their mark on the city—in its architecture, in the street cafés, in the musical French language heard everywhere, in the elegant shop windows, and in the multitude of nightclubs frequented by the troops stationed in Damascus or in the Druze hills. This cosmopolitan commingling of East and West fascinated Shula from the very first moment she set foot in Beirut and served to soften the sting of bitterness and resentment still inside her.

Although it was not the accepted social custom for a bride to live in the home of her fiancé, Shula and her parents were guests of the Kishak-Cohens. They had a four-room flat that took up half a floor on the fourth story of an apartment house. The other flat on the floor was occupied by Chaim Kishak and his family. She hardly ever saw

Joseph. He woke up very early each morning, long before the rest of the family, and rushed off to the Magen Avraham Synagogue, the largest in Wadi Abu-Jamil, for the *minyan*, the quorum of ten men necessary for prayers. After morning prayers he went directly to his shop in the Suk Sursuk and did not return home until dark. Almost immediately after dinner he went to bed.

Despite the cosmopolitan sophistication of Beirut the Jewish quarter remained a bastion of conservative Eastern mores. A woman's place was in the home. Even the family food shopping was left to the men. Every few days Joseph would go the market near his shop and an Arab boy would bring the produce home in a large wicker basket strapped to his forehead and shoulders with a rope. The women of the house remained at home. Only if there was an urgent need for some particular item which was not in the house would a woman rush down to one of the small groceries on the ghetto street. Even then she would hurry back home as though attempting to restore the honor she had betrayed by leaving her house. Sometimes a vendor would drive by selling fruits or vegetables from a wagon. Here the bargaining over prices would be carried on from behind balcony windows. The vendor would carry the purchase up to the apartment and would wait at the door while the woman of the house removed the fruits and vegetables from the scales and returned with the money. It was unheard of for a strange man to enter a home when the master was not present.

Except for their brief encounters with these vendors or with the local shopowners, the women of the Wadi Abu-Jamil quarter were entirely cut off from the world around them. If they ever went visiting, it was to gossip at the homes of their friends, most often close relatives who lived in the ghetto. The entire Jewish community was like a snail enclosed in its own shell, and the women even more so than the men.

Although she was actively absorbed in discovering Beirut, Shula was not able to avoid the presence of the two women of the house, Joseph's mother and sister. She could not help but notice the coolness with which her future mother-in-law and Marie treated her. The momentary affection Marie had exhibited before leaving Jerusalem had disappeared. Here in Beirut she was condescending and disdainful. Her mother acted much the same. Shula was not surprsed. She knew, even in Jerusalem, that a new wife was on the bottom rung of the family ladder, that the woman who ruled the house was the mother of the groom. She was prepared for this and interpreted her mother-in-law's patronizing attitude as an attempt to put her in her place from the very start.

Shula took advantage of any pretext she could find to be out of the house. She spent a great deal of time touring Beirut. Her parents served as chaperons, for a well-brought-up young woman would never be seen alone in a public place.

Time passed quickly and her wedding day soon arrived.

Although the ceremony itself was not to take place until the evening, by noon Shula had already been decked out in the white wedding gown Grazia, the seamstress from Mekor Baruch, had made for her. Her mother took her proudly by the hand and led her to the large dining room. There she was greeted with the admiring clicking of tongues of female neighbors and relatives. A few minutes later, when all the expected compliments had been paid, their attention was drawn to the refreshments which had been served to accompany their gossip. Shula was brought back to her room. No one took any notice of her. Every once in a while a late arrival would enter the room, recite the traditional blessings of congratulation, and hurry off to join the others at the dining room table. Then Shula would be alone once again.

Shula told herself over and over again that this was supposed to be the most important day of her life. But she felt nothing that even bordered on excitement. She felt bored and lonely. When the twelve-year-old daughter of one of the guests came into the room to look at the bride, Shula was overjoyed. She spent the last two hours before her marriage playing dominoes with a twelve-year-old girl whose name she did not even know. . . .

At six o'clock in the evening she was brought to the Magen Avraham Synagogue in a gay procession of singing and dancing women. The groom and his guests, most of whom were merchants at the Suk Sursuk, were already there.

She was marched to Joseph's side under the wedding canopy by her mother and mother-in-law. He did not even look at her. Rabbi Bochbut, the elderly rabbi of Beirut, began to mumble the ancient Aramaic words of the marriage contract. She understood none of it. She stared at his wrinkled forehead. Her mind was a blank. She thought of Shmuel, the Mekor Baruch shoemaker who was also old and wrinkled. Suddenly she felt terribly sad. She had an overwhelming urge to return to her neighborhood in Jerusalem and to be a little girl again. . . .

It was unbearably hot. Her dress clung to her body and seemed to be choking her. Her new shoes were pinching her feet. She lost all contact with her surroundings. It was as though she was hearing the rabbi's words from far off. Her only thought was: "Let it all be over soon. . . ." She let them lead her mechanically around the bridegroom the traditional seven times, feeling nothing but the tightness of her new shoes. Her mother whispered to her to lift the bridal veil and she did. She was told to lower it and she did.

Finally Joseph broke the glass goblet with his foot and the ceremony was officially over.

But the party was far from over. Everyone moved to the hall next door where the tables were laden with food and drink. They sat Shula in the chair of honor in a far corner and everyone came up to shake hands and congratulate the couple. Then they all rushed to the crowded tables like a flock of birds zooming in on an unguarded sack of seeds.

The feast lasted for three hours. Joseph had been carried off by his friends and Shula was left alone. The heat was more oppressive than before. Her feet ached even more now, but worst of all, her stomach grumbled from hunger. She had not had anything to eat since morning. It did not occur to anyone to bring her even a morsel from the lavish spread of stuffed pigeons, baked fish, Oriental delicacies, and cakes that not only testified to the great joy of the occasion but also to the wealth and status of the Kishak-Cohens.

From time to time Marie would bring over some strangers, distant cousins and uncles and aunts, to meet the bride. "Meet my successful acquisition," she would say as she introduced Shula. Shula's resentment toward her new sister-in-law increased.

Her mother also came by several times, with tears of joy streaming from her eyes. But not her father. She saw how he allowed himself to be pushed aside several times, as though he was not part of the celebration. He seemed sad. When he finally did come up to her she wanted to say, "Daddy, we're both feeling the same thing." But Marie was standing nearby and she did not dare.

The last guests finally left and she could now go home and take off her new shoes and change into a more comfortable dress. She was surrounded by an entourage of women—her mother, her mother-in-law, her sister-in-law—and they were all expecting her to say that this was the happiest day of her life. She did not know what to say.

She felt terribly grateful when Joseph suggested that they escape from the suffocating heat by going to one of the seaside cafés.

Sometime during the evening she began to realize the significance of this night, the night she would become a woman. Suddenly she felt a strong desire to remain among all these people in the well-lit café. But she had no choice. Everyone was yawning visibly. Finally, at midnight, Joseph's mother announced: "It's midnight. Let's go."

When they were alone in her room, the room where they were to spend their wedding night, Joseph held her by the shoulders—he still did not dare to embrace her—and looked straight into her eyes for the very first time. Then he whispered softly: "Shula, you'll be my queen. . . ."

She looked at him inquisitively, thinking to herself: "What will he look like in his underwear?" But he was more sensitive than she had given him credit for. He left the room and returned wearing his pajamas. He turned off the light.

When she awoke the following morning Shula knew she had crossed the border into adulthood.

Even years later, after time had worked its cures and filtered out the more unpleasant memories, Shula still recalled the early years of her married life unfavorably. She was lonely. Her parents returned to Jerusalem ten days after the wedding and she no longer had further pretext to be out of the house. Her mother-in-law and Marie made it their business to "put her in her place." She went into periods of deep depression and spent long hours comparing herself to Cinderella. But unlike Cinderella she was neither abused nor maltreated and was never burdened with difficult chores. Her lot was worse. They treated her like an ignorant, irresponsible child. Her mother-in-law ruled the kitchen. If Shula offered to help or if she volunteered to cook one of the dishes she had learned from her mother, her mother-in-law would stare at her, incredulous that Shula could put a pot to fire without burning it. "There's no need," was all she would say. She would not even allow Shula to prepare the Turkish coffee that was served to their guests.

Visitors compounded her depression. During the day there were only women guests. The older ones were friends of her mother-in-law and the younger ones came to see Marie. She found neither group interesting. They spent the entire day gossiping about their neighbors in Wadi Abu-Jamil—people whom Shula did not know. It was apparent that she was of no interest to them either. Male visitors came only on the Sabbath, when Joseph's friends from the Suk Sursuk would visit with their wives. Conversations invariably centered on business matters—the price of Indian muslin or the difficulties of importing Bulgarian lace. The women gossiped endlessly.

In an attempt to relieve her boredom Shula returned to the world of books. At the end of the street there was a small stationery shop that sold cheap French novels. On one of the rare occasions when Shula had to leave the house—the man who sharpened knives was on the street and Marie was out and her mother-in-law did not like to walk up and down the four flights of stairs—she sneaked into the store and bought two books. The magic was gone, though. She could no longer get herself to believe in love which conquered all. When Marie caught her with her nose in one of the books, she made a face and sputtered that women whose homes were dear to them did not waste time on such nonsense.

They would not allow her to be a housewife and they would not allow her to sit by idly dreaming. Only from her mother-in-law's inquisitive glances and Marie's indiscreet questions did she realize: they were waiting for her to be pregnant.

By the time she discovered her condition she felt such great bitterness toward her mother-in-law and Marie that, knowing how pleased they would be to hear her news, she kept her secret from them. The little creature growing in her belly was all in the world she could call her own. She refused to share it with anyone, and especially not with them.

She bore a similar but less serious grudge against Joseph. He seemed to be a good husband. She was sure that he loved her. When they were alone in their room, away from the prying ears of his family, he would shower her with words of love.

But he did not treat Shula as an adult with her own needs and desires. His marriage had not altered his way of life or his way of thinking. He still awoke at dawn, went to the synagogue to pray, and from there went straight to work. In the evening he returned home, to his mother's house. He found nothing odd in the fact that his mother ran the house and cooked and served him as she had before his marriage. At dinner when he spoke about his experiences during the day, he spoke to his mother and sister. They were familiar with the business and knew all his acquaintances. Shula did not. And she was so young. Only when they were alone in their bedroom did she have a place in his life.

Shula realized very quickly that he would recognize her as an individual only if they were out of his mother's house, but she did not have the nerve to discuss it with him. He was visibly unhappy if Shula expressed any criticism of Marie, even in the most veiled and subtle ways.

She escaped boredom and confinement by writing long and frequent letters to her sister Naomi. She wrote of Beirut and only superficially touched on her own life. "Everything is gray, as if the city had been painted in anger," she wrote some months after arriving in Beirut, and she also described the street vendors who felt in their bones the approaching northern wind and would close down their stalls moments before the first gusts would blow. . . .

She told Joseph she was pregnant only after she could no longer conceal her daily attacks of nausea and dizziness. He was so happy she regretted not having told him earlier. Her status in the household did indeed change, but not for the better. Her mother-in-law and Marie had a new excuse to exclude her from work of any kind. They treated her like a fragile object that had to be guarded and preserved. They still regarded her with disdain; they were interested only in what she was carrying in her belly. Her humiliation grew.

There were, however, advantages to her pregnancy: Joseph was eager to keep her happy and after she complained about being imprisoned at home, he started taking her to a seaside café on Sundays. It was only natural that Marie should accompany them, but one Saturday night, alone in their room, Shula whispered, "Perhaps we can go out by ourselves tomorrow, just the two of us?" He agreed. The outings did not last very long, for soon the winter winds began to blow. Even though Shula enjoyed walking down the empty promenade and watching the stormy sea burst on the shore, Joseph was concerned: "You could catch a cold and it might harm the baby. . . ."

He was certain that it would be a son but was the only one in the family who was not openly disappointed at the birth of a daughter and who did not see it as further proof of Shula's general ineptness.

He was quite proud and accepted the congratulations and the bantering of his friends at the market in good humor.

He was very attached to his daughter, whom they called Yaffa. He hired a nursemaid to care for her during the day, and when she awoke at night crying, he was the first at her side.

The babbling little baby wrapped in pink became the center of Shula's world. She tried to keep the baby to herself, but with little success. Her mother-in-law and, even worse, her sister-in-law were constantly interfering. "What does Marie know about babies?" Shula would whisper bitterly to her husband when they were alone in their room. "She never had any children!"

Joseph, annoyed and confused by the divisiveness in his home, tried to make peace. "Let Shula be," he would say when she was not around. "She may be young but she helped to raise eleven brothers and sisters."

Then his mother would look hurt and he would quickly apologize.

It was Shula who refused to make peace. With her position fortified by her new maternal status she was courageous enough to ask Joseph for a home of their own. Joseph would not hear of it.

When she became pregnant again in the autumn of 1938, she wrote to her sister: "I barely had time to finish a pack of cigarettes before I became nauseous again. . . ." She did not conceal her pregnancy from Joseph this time. He was elated.

"This time it will definitely be a boy," he murmured as he stroked her still-flat stomach.

She took immediate advantage of the situation: "If it is a boy, can we move to our own apartment?"

He would promise her anything, provided that she give him a son.

And she did. They called him Abraham Albert for Joseph's late father. Three months after the boy was born, Joseph kept his word: he rented an apartment three buildings away from his mother's house, next door to the Magen Avraham Synagogue. It was a spacious apartment that covered the entire fourth floor. He apologetically explained to his mother and sister that their apartment was getting too small for the two children and for the "others to come. . . ."

Shula could now make another wish come true. Her mother could not be with her at either of the births. None of her family could come for the *brith*, the traditional circumcision ceremony. But as soon as Shula was established in her new flat, she wrote and invited her sister to come and stay with her. Naomi arrived in midsummer.

The next ten months were the happiest Shula had known during her entire married life. She had a nurse to care for the two children. A neighbor, Nazira, who lived on the first floor of their building, helped her with all the heavy housework and would baby-sit in the evenings. But she was no longer depressed at having so much free time. Her sister Naomi was with her.

Naomi was full of news. During her last year at school her father capitulated and allowed her to join the Haganah underground. Shula never tired of listening to stories about life in war-torn Jerusalem, underground army training, secret meetings, and coded operations. As she listened to her sister's words, she could not help thinking jealously, "There's only one year's difference between us, but what a difference! Her life is full of action and excitement and I lead the life of a Beirut matron, a merchant's wife, a mother, a baby machine. . . ."

When she told her sister what she was feeling, Naomi replied: "Who says you have to be a baby machine? Two children are more than enough." On hearing this, Shula realized just how great the gap between them was. Such a thought would never occur to her.

"What can I do?" she asked timidly. "*He* wants a lot of children. . . ."

Joseph rented a villa in the vacation town of Behamdon in the mountains, and the whole family moved there for the summer. He joined them on Fridays, when business was slack, spent the Sabbath, and returned to Beirut on Saturday night.

When they returned to Beirut in the autumn of 1939, life settled into a routine. During the week Shula and Naomi explored the streets of Beirut. Sometimes they gave the nurse a day off and each took one of the babies in a carriage. They would sit at one of the boardwalk cafés, or in Cannon Square, or they would go to the Suk Sursuk, where a delighted Joseph would stop working to play with the children and proudly show them off to all his colleagues. On the Sabbath they would all go to synagogue. Following services they would go to Joseph's mother's house for lunch. There was a "cease-fire" between Shula and her mother-in-law and Marie, a rather unfriendly one; when Shula brought her first son into the world, they were forced to recognize her independence. Saturday afternoons were reserved for social gatherings or receiving guests. On Saturday nights they would go to the movies or a café. Since they were strictly kosher, they never frequented restaurants. On Sunday afternoons they would take trips outside the city.

Life in Beirut in the autumn of 1939 was untouched by World War II. There were a few military parades and processions, a few French nationals had been drafted, but nothing more. The "dormant war" was very far away. By the summer of 1940, when the Germans were taking Paris, the situation changed. Beirut was in a panic. If France fell, what would happen to the empire?

Shula's mother arrived from Jerusalem. Everyone there was concerned that if the Germans conquered all of France, Nazi regimes would be installed in Syria and Lebanon and the Jews would be subject to persecutions. In any case the border would definitely be sealed. She had come to take Naomi home while she could.

She tried to convince Shula and Joseph to take advantage of the open border while there was time and come to live in Palestine under the protection of the British army. Joseph looked at her incredulously and said, "Leave Beirut? The Germans are far away. What would I do in Jerusalem?"

Naomi and her mother left and Shula's life was empty once again.

In the spring of 1941 Shula's second son, Meir, was born. Two years later her second daughter, Arlette, came into the world.

In the period between the two births the Allied Forces invaded Lebanon. The government loyal to Vichy was overturned and General Catroux, a staunch supporter of de Gaulle, was appointed high commissioner. The real power, however, lay in the hands of the British. The British army camped in Saraya and took over the major hotels in the mountain retreats. The New Zealand Engineering Corps laid a railroad along the shore from Haifa to Beirut. Then the British forced the Free French government to grant independence to Syria and Lebanon. The relations between these two yet unborn nations were already sharply strained. The leaders of the Syrian nationalist movement, who viewed Lebanon as an integral part of Greater Syria, declared that they would never recognize an independent Lebanon. More fuel was added to the flames when the French tried to intervene in the first elections for president in favor of their candidate, Emile Eddé. The British supported his rival, Camille Chamoun. In the end, however, a "compromise candidate," Bishara al-Khuri was elected. Chamoun joined forces with him on the under-standing that he would become the next president.

In 1943 Lebanon became an independent nation. A year later it joined the Arab League.

The only effect these great political upheavals had on Shula's life was that postal lines between Beirut and Jerusalem had been re-opened. In 1944, after the birth of Isaac, her fifth child, Shula wrote to her sister: "You asked if a marriage can wither and die. I really don't know. My marriage never really blossomed. . . . He goes off to work and I have babies. . . ."

She was twenty-four years old at the time.

The Man
from the Border

3 On Friday morning, November 28, 1947, President Bishara al-Khuri called a meeting of his advisers. It was not an official meeting—nothing official was ever conducted on either the Moslem or Christian day of rest—although the prime minister, Riad as-Sulh; the ministers of interior and defense; high-ranking army and police officers; representatives of military intelligence and the General Security Service, which was part of the Ministry of Interior, were all present. There was only one item on the agenda: the measures to be taken when the United Nations Security Council would vote the next day on the partition of Palestine and the creation of a Jewish state.

The president, dignified, handsome, and graying at the temples, waved a massive typewritten document before them.

"I absolutely agree with the conclusions outlined in this report. We must prevent violence at all cost; but there must be no armed confrontation between the army and the masses. If they want to demonstrate for the Palestinian cause, let them. We won't interfere. But if they decide to carry out riots in Wadi Abu-Jamil, we will not allow it. It would ruin our image."

In his inaugural address four years earlier Bishara al-Khuri had vowed to "turn Lebanon into the Switzerland of the Middle East." He had made good on his promise. Lebanon was the only country in the area that was not primarily desert. This, combined with its mountainous landscape and gracious French life-style, had turned the country into the vacation playground of the Middle East. It boasted the freest banking system in the world—some claimed it even bordered on the anarchistic—and was fast becoming the Banker of the Middle East. The vaults on Hamra Street brimmed with the wealth of oil-rich sheikhs from the Persian Gulf, successful merchants and businessmen, and statesmen, politicians, and corrupt government officials fearful of being swept from power. The identities of owners of numbered bank accounts were guarded more fanatically than any religious law.

It was an accepted fact that this economic prosperity was entirely dependent on the stability of the regime, and this was not easy to preserve. For although Lebanon was now a state, there was not yet a Lebanese nation.

The largest group was the Maronite Christians but they numbered only half a million, or 35 percent of the population. In southern Lebanon, on the border with Palestine, lived the Shi'ite Moslems, who had isolated themselves for years and were suspicious of anyone and everyone who was not a member of their closed sect. In the north, around Tripoli, there were mostly Sunnite Moslems, who had emotional and familial connections with Syria. In the eastern part of the country there was a mixture of Druze, Moslems, and Christians. In the cities, particularly in Beirut, there were also Armenians, Greek Orthodox, and Greek Catholics—each group living in closed, segregated quarters and fanatically preserving its independence.

This system was not open to change. The parliamentary elections would always reflect the 1932 census—the only one ever taken in Lebanon. The ninety-nine seats of the Lebanese parliament were divided ethnically in the following manner: thirty to the Maronites, twenty to the Sunnis, nineteen to the Shi'ites, eleven to the Greek Orthodox, six to the Greek Catholics, six to the Druze and seven to all the others. Every four years there were free elections—by Middle East standards—with each candidate elected by voters of his own ethnic group for one of the seats designated for that ethnic group alone. Therefore, the loyalty of the elected members of parliament was to their religious and ethnic communities and not to the state.

The delicate ethnic balance was still preserved but with much difficulty. The various communities were divided into power groups, and beneath the ostensibly calm surface there were suspicion and hostility that could explode at the slightest provocation.

Now there was danger to the south. The twelve-year struggle over Palestine had unleashed unprecedented nationalistic feelings among the Arabs. The partition plan had brought the situation to a climax. No one could tell how the tide would turn in Lebanon.

The president repeated his words: "Demonstrations—yes. Riots—no. We're going to put Wadi Abu-Jamil under protective custody. Nothing too obvious though, because that could be provocative. Just a few gendarmes at both entrances to the street, with an army unit on call close by—should they be needed."

Prime Minister Riad as-Sulh added: "We've already received intelligence to the effect that Damascus will try to agitate the masses in Beirut. It isn't clear yet if our brothers across the border will be satisfied with demonstrations against the Jews, or whether they have other plans. Therefore, it is of utmost importance that we avoid any massive street rioting."

"Do you think the vote will go in favor of the Jews?" asked the minister of the interior.

As-Sulh sighed: "To my regret, yes. Malik [Foreign Minister Charles Malik] reports from New York that there is no possibility of preventing it. The Jews did a very good job of enlisting support."

"What will happen then? Will we go to war?"

The president interrupted: "Let's hope that it will not come to that. In any case, now is not the time to discuss it. Our primary concern at the moment is to avoid any outbreak of hostilities in Beirut. Gentlemen, this meeting is hereby adjourned."

The appearance of armed gendarmes on their street did not escape the watchful eyes of the inhabitants of Wadi Abu-Jamil. Along with the U.N. vote, which was to take place the following evening, the soldiers provided the major topic of discussion among the Friday night worshipers at the Magen Avraham Synagogue.

Up in her apartment overlooking the synagogue's courtyard, Shula was flushed with excitement as she followed the news on the radio. She felt very deeply involved, not only because her family in Jerusalem would be in the midst of whatever might result from the

U.N. vote, but also because she sensed that this was a great moment in the history of her people.

Her involvement with the Zionist cause had begun some three years earlier, soon after the birth of Isaac. Bored and lonely, she had been sitting at her window, following the activities in the synagogue courtyard. A meeting of Young Maccabi was taking place there; a group of ten to twelve-year-olds was sitting around their leader, a youth a few years older than they who had spent a year in Eretz Israel. He was teaching them a Hebrew song and could not recall the words. But Shula did. "I'll be right back," she called out to her children's nurse and ran down to the courtyard.

"I know all the words of the song," she said, blushing in embarrassment. Spontaneously she recited the words and sang the song. Then patiently she taught it to them.

That was the beginning. Soon she became a permanent fixture in the movement's activities. She searched her memory for the songs and games she had learned in her own youth group and in school. She told them stories about life in Jerusalem and how the holidays were celebrated in the Holy City. And as she remembered, her memories took on a value she had never attributed to them before. She became an ardent, active Zionist.

Shula was a naturally gifted teacher. Her youth group became popular and the secretary of the community, the advocate Albert Iliya, came to thank her for her devotion. Joseph, however, displayed neither pleasure nor displeasure at his wife's activities. Shula wrote in one of her letters to Naomi: "Anything that has no direct relationship with his prayers, his business, or his family does not exist for him."

Even on this Friday night he did not behave differently. After services he went directly home, opened the door with the traditional Sabbath greeting, *Shabbat shalom*, and called everyone to the table. Only after they had finished their Sabbath meal, recited the after-dinner grace, and sent the children off to their rooms did he say, "They're expecting demonstrations the day after tomorrow. I don't want the children to leave the house."

It was a very suspenseful Sabbath for the Jews of Wadi Abu-Jamil. An armored car joined the four gendarmes at the entrance to the street, and the Jews saw this as a bad sign. Many planned to spend the entire night listening to the U.N. vote on the radio. Shula was among them; her husband was not. He went to bed early, as usual, while Shula stayed glued to the radio the entire night. Even after the voting was over, she could not fall asleep. She kept turning the dial to foreign stations, hungry to hear any and every reaction and interpretation of the historic event.

Early the next morning when Joseph stepped out of his room (they had slept in separate rooms since moving into their own apartment), he found her in the kitchen putting a pot of coffee on the stove.

"Thirty-three for, thirteen against!" she cried joyously, pleased at the opportunity to share her excitement with someone. "There's a Jewish state! They danced all night in the streets of Jerusalem. . . ."

He mumbled something incomprehensible and stared at her in surprise. After drinking the coffee she served him—he was used to making his own coffee in the morning—he took his prayer shawl and went to the door.

He stood there for a moment, then said, "I'm coming home after the morning service. It doesn't pay to open the shop today." As if trying to console himself, he added, "Anyhow, today is Sunday. . . ."

As was expected, mobs of enraged Arabs took to the streets in protest of the U.N. vote. Also as expected, they did not enter the Jewish ghetto of Wadi Abu-Jamil. The gendarmes deterred them. But no guards had been placed in the Suk Sursuk and several Jewish shops had been broken into and looted. Even so, it was a "controlled outburst" and no one was injured. Later that afternoon representatives of the Falanges, the paramilitary organization established by the nationalistic elements within the Maronite community, appeared in the offices of the Jewish community. They said, "Don't be afraid. We won't allow them to harm you. Our *mutran* is praying for the Jewish state."

Mutran Mubarak, the head of the Maronite church, did not hide his feelings. He knew that the establishment of another non-Arab state in the Middle East would strengthen the Maronites' position.

The tide of unrest began to settle.

As days and weeks passed, the unrest returned. Fighting had broken out in Palestine and from what Shula could judge from the press, Radio Beirut, and even from the "Voice of Jerusalem," which was still under British control, the situation was not going well for the Jews. Once again she was concerned about her family, but even more, she was anxious about the newborn Jewish state. Shula was surprised at the extent to which the fate of the Jewish state was important and precious to her.

War was becoming more and more a certainty. The heads of the Arab states met in Shtora, a small mountain resort near the Syrian border. Soon after their historic meeting the newspapers announced the recruitment of volunteers from all the Arab states for the "Arab Liberation Army" which would invade Israel and complete the noble work begun by the Palestinians. Recruiting offices were opened throughout Lebanon and not a week passed without a parade of volunteers marching through Beirut. The newspapers spoke of a volunteer army of thousands which was to be armed by the Arab states from their own military arsenals. As in 1936–39, southern Lebanon again became a base for attacks against Israel.

Shula was embittered by the news. "There are so many of them," she thought to herself, "and so few of us. . . . I wish I could help."

But she was a woman, the mother of five children, with a sixth on the way. She had a house and family to care for. What could she do?

A few days later Shula was standing in her husband's shop waiting for him to notice her. She had come about a new closet. Alongside her, near the shop's entrance, three peddlers were also awaiting the merchant's attention.

The Kishak establishment dealt primarily in wholesale trade, although the brothers were never known to turn a retail customer away. Most of their sales were to peddlers who traveled from village to village. These men carried their goods on their backs, together with a yard-long iron rod which was their trademark. They conducted their business on credit and mutual trust—between peddler and client on one hand and between wholesaler and peddler on the other. Many of the peddlers' connections with the Kishak-Cohen family dated back to the days when Joseph's father was still alive. Most of them came from southern Lebanon.

Shula absentmindedly listened to the peddlers' chatter. One of them told of his good fortune at having stumbled upon a "big wedding" in Kafr Hadsa. A big wedding was what every peddler dreamed of. It meant a dowry of dresses, linens, tablecloths, napkins, and sometimes even curtains.

When the conversation turned to the war with Israel, Shula began to pay more careful attention. One of them said that there were ten volunteers from his village who were currently training and would soon join the fighting across the border. Another bragged that he had seen with his own eyes the commander of the Arab Liberation Army, Fawzi Kaukji, recruiting new volunteers in the village of Tibnin. The third, not to be outdone, boasted that he had also seen the commander, in the village of Bint Jubail.

Bint Jubail, he continued, was soon to be an important military base of operations. Arms from Iraq had been delivered there in great numbers the week before and Syrian officers were offering large sums of money to people who would smuggle the weapons across the border. They were saying that Bint Jubail would soon become a permanent base. . . .

Shula listened attentively, her heart pounding. She did not know whether what she had just heard was important or even true. She knew only one thing: the information must get to Israel!

When Joseph came over to her, she led him into the back of the shop and told him what she had overheard.

"The information has to be passed on to Israel," she declared firmly.

At first he argued. How could she be certain that what she had heard was true? "You know how their imaginations work. And even if it is true, how important can it be?" His main objection, however, had nothing to do with his argument: a woman, he felt, should not be involved in such matters.

When he finally yielded, it was because she was a woman. He was reminded of a proverb he had once heard: "When a woman is stubborn about little things, it is best to give in before she gets involved in bigger things." "Especially," he added to himself, "when the woman in question is pregnant." Actually he had never been able to refuse Shula anything. Even though they had been married for eleven years, he was still amazed that a shortsighted, slight, and balding man such as himself had found such a beautiful young woman—a woman who made him young again and who elevated him in the eyes of his friends and acquaintances. And she was not only young and beautiful; she was a good wife and a good housekeeper. She had not made a cuckold of him and she had given him many children. He had never been able to stop her from doing anything once she had set her mind to it—and he knew it. Even so, he preferred to think that the decision to go along with her was his and that he was acting like an understanding and benevolent father humoring the capricious whim of a spoiled child.

He called one of the peddlers to him.

"This is Abdul Salam Hanoon from Adeisa village," he said, introducing the man to his wife. "His village is right on the border. . . ."

He then turned to Hanoon, addressing him by his more familiar name: "Abu-Yihyeh, my wife has family in Jerusalem. I would like you to help her . . ."

The man immediately agreed. If he helped *hawaja* Kishak, *hawaja* Kishak might see fit to raise his credit. . . .

"*Tahat omrak*, at your command," he replied.

". . . by passing a letter across the border for her, so that it will reach Jerusalem quickly."

"This very night. It's only a few minutes' walk from my village to the Jewish colony of Misgav 'Am. I give you my word, madame, your letter will be delivered this very evening."

She sat at her husband's desk and composed the letter. She was not sure to whom she should address it. She finally wrote:

"My name is Shulamit Cohen. I am a Jewess living in Beirut. I want to help. You can get information about me from my parents, the Cohen family of 10 Alfandari Street, Jerusalem. I want to relay the following information that I have overheard. . . ." She proceeded to outline all that she had heard in Joseph's shop, and closed: "If you should want to contact me, I live in Wadi Abu-Jamil in the building next to the synagogue." She wrote the note impulsively, without the slightest understanding of her own motivation. Years later, she was honest enough to admit that the excitement she had experienced while writing the letter seemed to block out and even compensate for all the years of boredom she had suffered until then. She was thrilled with his new feeling and she wanted to hold onto it.

By the time Hanoon had completed his business with her husband, she had finished the letter, put it in an envelope, and sealed it.

"Give it to the Jews in Misgav 'Am. They will send it to Jerusalem. My family's address is inside. Look, don't lose it."

"Don't worry, madame," he said, smiling. "More than just letters have passed from my village to the Jews. . . ."

Each day during the week that followed, Shula found a different pretext to visit her husband's shop. Joseph knew why she kept coming but he said nothing. He had allowed himself to assist her in establishing contact with Israel by convincing himself it was a passing caprice; now he had no alternative but to wait for the whim to pass.

A week later the peddler from Adeisa returned to Beirut. "I did as you asked," he reported to her. "The letter was in Misgav 'Am that very same night. I swear to you on the life of my father. . . ."

Now the waiting began. Shula stopped visiting the shop. She never left the house and spent entire days sitting at the window looking out over the empty synagogue courtyard. The youth-group activities had ceased with the outbreak of tension. She had nothing to do but wait.

Three weeks passed. She timed a visit to Joseph's shop to the day the peddler from Adeisa was due to be there. She flooded him with questions about the fate of her letter. Again he swore to her that he personally had delivered the letter to Misgav 'Am. "I don't know the man's name. We call him Abu-Ziki. He is their mukhtar, or something like that."

She did not know whether to believe him or not, although he swore on the lives of his old father and children that he was telling the truth. Even if he had delivered the letter, perhaps they did not believe what she had written? Perhaps the information was unimportant. She tried to prepare herself for the unhappy possibility that her letter would not be answered at all. The prospect made her miserable.

The answer arrived five weeks after she had sent the letter. It was one of those angry, gray, rainy evenings in Beirut. The children had already gone off to sleep, followed shortly by Joseph. Shula was alone in the kitchen. The unborn child she was carrying twisted and turned inside her. What would it be this time? A son or a daughter? Most likely a son, judging by the force of its kicks. . . .

The ten o'clock news on the radio had just ended, but she knew she would not be able to fall asleep. When the spasms passed she stood up, took a bag of lentils, and laid them on the table to be sorted.

There was a faint knock at the door.

She was frightened. Who could it be at such a late hour? She told herself that it was only one of the neighbors coming to borrow a pot or a cup of sugar. She knew, however, that her relationships with her neighbors would not permit so late a visit unless something serious had happened. As far as she knew, no one in the building was ill. Her mother-in-law had looked in the best of health when they had lunch with her there on Saturday. . . . Perhaps it was her sister-in-law, Chaim's wife?

She looked through the peephole and saw a strange man. He was about fifty, wore a European suit that was wet from the rain, and had an Arab *kaffiyeh* on his head.

She checked to make sure the chain was in place, opened the door a crack, and said, "Yes?"

"I'm looking for Shula Cohen," he said in Arabic.

"I'm Shula Cohen. What do you want?"

"I've brought you regards from your family in Jerusalem."

She opened the door in excitement: "*Tfadel*, please come in."

As she led him into the living room, her fear returned. He might be a detective. Her letter might have fallen into the wrong hands. In order to gain time she showed him to an easy chair and said, "I'll prepare some tea. It is very cold out."

He cut her off with a wave of his hand. "Later."

She stood before him not knowing what to say. He may have felt her uneasiness, because he began to speak immediately.

"My name is Mussa and I have a letter for you from the people you wrote to." He opened his jacket. She saw that the lining of his jacket was sewn in a very coarse stitch. He ripped it open and after searching around the inside lining removed a piece of paper. Shula took it from him and unfolded it. It was a letter written in Hebrew.

Mussa offered her a cigarette. She distractedly accepted and continued poring over the letter. He lit her cigarette and she inhaled deeply.

The letter said:

"The man who brought you this letter is one of ours. You can trust him completely. He will give you some very important information." She did not recognize the signature.

She reread the note again and returned it to Mussa. He shook his head. "No," he said. "It's for you, though it might be better if you destroy it."

Then she realized he was not a Lebanese secret service agent. If he were, he would never suggest that she destroy "evidence" that could later be used against her. She reached for the box of matches on the table. They both sat silently as the piece of paper went up in flames.

When the note had been reduced to ashes, Mussa removed a passport picture from the lining of his jacket. It was a photograph of a man approximately forty years old with light, thinning hair. She had never seen him before. She looked questioningly at the man sitting across from her.

"His name is Winkler," Mussa said. "He is very important to our friends. He reached Haifa on a ship called the *Transylvania*, but the British wouldn't allow him to disembark. I don't know why. Maybe his papers weren't in order. The ship is leaving Haifa tonight. It might have even left already. It should arrive in Beirut sometime tomorrow morning. In the evening it will sail for Constanta. It's very important that Winkler disembark in Beirut. It will be necessary to keep him hidden until I can manage to smuggle him across the border. . . .

"I would be very happy to have some tea now," he said, and she rushed to the kitchen.

She listened to the beating of her heart as she waited for the water to boil. She was filled with both excitement and fear, but the excitement was predominant. Suddenly she realized that she was wearing the same flannel housecoat she had worn all day. She felt a twinge of regret that Mussa had seen her like that, but she changed her mind: the shapeless material concealed her round belly. She was afraid they might not want to continue working with her if they knew she was pregnant. She slipped into the bathroom to comb her hair and put on some makeup. Then she entered the living room carrying a tray with the tea, two cups, and a plate of cookies. She was afraid that her hands would shake while she poured but they were steady and firm.

"Will you be able to carry out the mission?" Mussa asked when Shula was seated. "The ship will be in Beirut for about six hours. All you have to do is get him off the ship and hide him. I'll take over from there."

"I'll do my best," she said honestly. "What will happen if I don't succeed?"

He shrugged his shoulders. "We might have another chance in Piraeus. I'm not sure. We might be able to get him off in Constanta, maybe not. I don't know. *They* say that it's of the utmost importance that he be returned to Israel immediately."

She wanted to ask who *they* were but controlled herself. She understood instinctively that one simply does not ask questions in these matters.

Mussa stood up. "Will you have another cup of tea?" she offered.

"No, thank you," he replied. "I must go now."

When she accompanied him to the door, she asked, "How will I get in touch with you tomorrow?"

"You won't. I'll be in touch with you."

After shutting the door behind him and replacing the chain on the hook, she leaned with her back against the door for a few minutes, her eyes closed, waiting for her heart to stop its thunderous beating. She returned to the living room, sat on the chair that still retained the warmth of the departed visitor, and looked closely at the passport photo he had left behind. The face was unrevealing. She knew nothing about him except that his name was Winkler and that at this very moment he was standing on the deck of that ship. "No, it's raining and cold," she corrected herself. "He must be in his cabin, standing by the porthole and looking at the lights of Haifa disappearing into the distance.

"We'll get you back. . . ." she said, surprised at hearing herself speak.

Subconsciously she felt that someone was in the room with her. She turned and saw Joseph standing there half-asleep in his slippers and pajamas. He stood at the entrance of the room staring at her.

"They brought you an answer?" he asked sadly.

She ignored the question. "I'm glad you're up," she said. "I need your advice."

He sat down like a condemned man, his head hunched between his shoulders, his eyes shut tight. But he listened attentively to every word she said. For some reason she did not tell him the whole truth. She did not say much about Mussa, and was also quite reticent to reveal much about the mission itself: "A Jew deported by the British has to be saved. He'll arrive in Beirut tomorrow on board the *Transylvania*." On a momentary impulse she added a note of romance: "If we aren't successful, he'll be sent back to Romania. If that happens it will be very bad for him."

Joseph remained seated with his eyes closed for a few moments after Shula had finished speaking. Then he opened his eyes and said cryptically, "Saving a Jew is a great duty."

She waited a moment, saw that he had finished speaking, and then asked impatiently, "But how should we go about it?"

"I think we should consult Abu-Jacques. He would know."

It was a good idea but she was annoyed that she had not thought of it herself. "I'll go to him immediately," she said.

Everyone in Wadi Abu-Jamil knew who Abu-Jacques was—although most people had no idea that his real name was Halfon Tharab. He was about fifty-five years old and ran a barely profitable stall in the Suk Sursuk. In the Jewish ghetto, where status was determined by family genealogy, knowledge of the Torah, and wealth, he appeared to be on the bottom rung of the social ladder. But Abu-Jacques was blessed with a boldness which allowed him to disregard his inferior social status as well as the impatient looks thrown his way when he forced himself on people who were not desirous of his company. He would attend the meetings of the synagogue committee and voice all his complaints even though he was not a member. When a family was in need, he would go from stall to stall at the market and solicit with such exigency that people could not refuse him. He was accepted by everyone, albeit unwillingly by many.

He made his presence felt in other areas as well. When the Vichy government was in power, he was one of the very few in Wadi Abu-Jamil who did not conceal his admiration for General de Gaulle. Nor did he hesitate to argue—both too loudly for their tastes and too forcefully for their nerves—with the rich and conservative landlords of the ghetto who advised him to be more prudent. There were rumors that he had had military training with the Free French underground and that he kept a revolver hidden at home. No one had ever actually seen the gun, but the story was enough to shroud Abu-Jacques in a cloud of mystery which he made no effort to dispel. If anyone in Wadi Abu-Jamil was in need of aid in matters on the margin of the law—getting a residence permit for a relative smuggled in from Syria, retrieving a package that had been "lost" in customs, or receiving payment on an overdue debt by means of threats—Abu-Jacques knew whom to ask.

He lived a few houses down the street from Shula. When he heard her voice, he opened the door immediately. In a matter of minutes he was fully dressed and was stepping in the puddles alongside her on their way to her house.

"We have to smuggle a Jew back to Israel," she whispered while they were walking.

He asked, "Does your husband know?" When she nodded affirmatively, he said no more. He was pleased.

Later, in her apartment, in Joseph's presence, Shula told him everything, beginning with the letter she had smuggled with the "Arab who lived near the border" and ending with the reply she had received that evening. She mentioned no names—neither Abu-Yihyeh's nor Mussa's. Abu-Jacques listened patiently without interrupting. When she had finished, he sat silently, wrapped in thought, staring at the small photograph of the stranger known as Winkler.

Finally he said, "We'll get him out, but we won't be able to do it without the Baltagi brothers. . . ."

Once again she was angry for not having thought of the Baltagi brothers herself.

"All of Beirut" knew about the Baltagi brothers. They were the lords and masters of the docks. No one could say exactly when it started, but ever since the modern port was constructed at the end of the last century, the Baltagis had handled all the loading and unloading. On the docks they were all-powerful. Nothing in the port of Beirut occurred without their active approval and participation.

Shula stole a glance at Joseph. He nodded silently in agreement. Abu-Jacques murmured, as if to himself, "We'll have to establish contact with them." He stood up, looking as though he had just made a crucial decision. "Wait here for me, I'll be back in an hour."

After he left, Joseph stood up and went to his room. He did not say it in so many words, but his entire demeanor announced: "I have nothing to do with all this."

"So be it," Shula said to herself.

At two o'clock in the morning Abu-Jacques returned, wet and blue from the cold. Shula brought him into the kitchen. The kettle was already boiling and she brewed him a cup of hot, steaming tea. As he sat grasping the warm cup and blowing on the vaporous liquid, he said, "Everything has been arranged. Tomorrow I'll be taken to see the Baltagis."

They agreed to meet the following morning at a café near the port.

She was sure she would be unable to fall asleep. She baked a cake.

Then she tried reading, but she was too agitated. She was not tired. She felt the excitement flowing through her veins.

Joseph woke up, as usual, at 4:30 A.M. On his way to the bathroom he stepped into the kitchen and looked at her reproachfully. "You did not get any sleep last night," he chided her.

She did not answer.

"What will come of all this?" he continued to scold her. Then he added tenderly, "It can't go on like this. You'll ruin your health. . . ."

She looked straight into his eyes. How could she explain all she was feeling without hurting him?

"You're good to me," she began hesitantly. "But all these years that we've been married, what have I meant to you? You haven't included me in anything. I never belonged. Nothing. . . . Today, in this matter, I am something . . . I'm doing something important. . . . Don't you understand?"

She waited for an answer, but none came. He went to the bathroom and she heard the water splashing in the sink. He left the bathroom and still said nothing. He dressed, took his prayer shawl and phylacteries, and went to the door. There he turned quietly, faced Shula, and said, "Shula, I'll be eating at my mother's today. . . ." and left the house.

This was his way of telling her that she was free to do as she pleased.

At eight o'clock, after serving breakfast to her five children and sending the three older ones off to school, she left the two babies with Nazira, the neighbor on the first floor, and went to the café. She was wearing her best clothes, a reflection of her high spirits. Even though she had not slept the entire night, she felt alert. She stopped at the window of a perfumery to inspect her reflection. She was pleased to see that she could still conceal her pregnancy. Her eyes were drawn to one of the items in the window, a perfume bottle with a narcissus-shaped lid. It was French and looked very expensive. She promised herself that if the operation was successful she would buy it as a reward.

She saw Abu-Jacques long before she entered the large café. It was early and he was the only customer. As she approached the table, before she even sat down, he called out happily, "Everything's okay. They've agreed.

"There are also a few problems," he added. "The ship was delayed in Haifa because of the storm. It won't reach Beirut until tonight. It will be in Beirut for only two or three hours. That means that they'll have to hurry. But there's also an advantage. The boat will anchor after dark. . . ."

Shula lit a cigarette and he continued.

"At first they considered getting him off the ship as a member of the crew. But now that they're anchoring so late, the crew probably won't be given shore leave. So they'll get him off as a stevedore. They'll provide him with workclothes, everything. . . ."

He also lit a cigarette, inhaled deeply, and continued speaking. His voice became more hesitant now: "They want eight hundred pounds . . . in advance. They'll get him out of the port; the rest is up to us."

"Didn't they want to know who he is?"

"They didn't ask a thing. To them he's just another piece of merchandise. Oh yes, they want his picture . . . to avoid mistakes."

"That's reasonable," Shula agreed. "But they'll have to destroy the picture when they're finished. Do you think we can trust them?"

He was hurt at her lack of confidence in his judgment: "The Baltagis' word is money."

"All right, we'll go to my husband."

On the way he told her he had managed to find a hiding place for Winkler in the cellar workshop of the local tombstone carver.

"No detective would stick his nose in there," said Abu-Jacques.

When Shula told her husband about the arrangements Abu-Jacques had made with the Baltagis, he took out a handful of bills from his bulging billfold. "Will this be enough?"

"More than enough," she answered. They were all hundred-pound notes.

"I hope it all works out," he said, dismissing her. He did not want to know any of the details.

Abu-Jacques took the money and the passport photo and went to see the Baltagi brothers. Shula went to the hairdresser. "A man feels secure when he has money in his pocket," she thought to herself, "and a woman when she has her hair done."

They met again two hours later. Abu-Jacques reported: "They took the money. They'll have him out of the port by eight o'clock."

"The question is," he said, "how long will we have to hide the man? When will the smuggler come?"

"He'll come on time," she replied curtly. "You just worry about getting him to the hiding place."

She was rather surprised at her own impatience. She refused to admit it but she was annoyed with Abu-Jacques's attempt to share in the details. She did not want any partners. Aides and accomplices yes, but this was *her* mission. It had been assigned to her, and she was responsible for making it work. She alone.

The Baltagis had no trouble locating Winkler among the few passengers on board. He had been informed in Haifa that an attempt would be made to get him off the ship in Beirut, and when a young Arab approached him with his passport photo in hand, Winkler turned himself over without hesitation.

He was led to one of the ship's stores where he found himself among a half-dozen stevedores. Within a few moments Winkler had put on the workclothes that the Arab had given him. He attached a porter's cushion to his shoulder and lifted two heavy suitcases. He joined the line of porters descending the ship and no one ever thought to stop him.

At eight o'clock Abu-Jacques was at the gate. A small van drove by and the driver hissed, "Here's your man." The silhouette of a man in soiled workclothes could be seen jumping down the back of the van and looking around suspiciously. Abu-Jacques approached and whispered, "Are you Winkler?"

The man nodded. Abu-Jacques signaled to a car parked at the curb. It drove up unobtrusively alongside of them. Abu-Jacques pushed Winkler in and jumped in after him.

By the time they reached Wadi Abu-Jamil, Winkler had already changed into his own clothes. It was raining again and the streets were deserted. No one saw them enter the tombstone carver's workshop.

A few moments later Abu-Jacques knocked on Shula's door. Her husband and children had already gone to bed.

"Everything's okay," he said. "I left him in the cellar. I'm now going to bring him some food. Do you want to meet him?"

She hesitated for a moment. For the past twenty-four hours all her thoughts had revolved around a stranger about whom, save for a blurred passport photo, she had not even the flimsiest information. Finally she answered, "No. It's best that he knows nothing about me." She was flattered by the look of admiration that filled Abu-Jacques's eyes.

"Have you heard anything from your smuggling friend?" he asked. When he saw her impatient and annoyed look, he quickly added, "It's not important. I'll get back to Winkler. If you need me for anything, you can find me there."

When she was alone, she again began thinking about the light-haired, balding man who answered to the name of Winkler. Who is he? Why is it so important to get him back to Israel? The next question flashed instantly into her mind: what will happen if he doesn't make it? What if something goes wrong and he gets caught? Impatience was beginning to gnaw away at her. Where is Mussa?

He arrived at nine.

She opened the door and could not hold back her excitement. She whispered, "He's here! We did it!"

He looked over her shoulder as though expecting to see Winkler there. She quickly added, "No, not here. He's well hidden." She took him to the living room and told him the whole story in a single breath. "He's with Abu-Jacques. Did we do all right?"

"You did very well," he said, smiling broadly. "Even a professional couldn't have done better."

"I'll make you some coffee," she said, trying to repay his compliment. He stopped her.

"No. I have to make some arrangements. I want to get him out of Beirut tonight. I'll bring him to my house in El-Hiam. I'll be back in an hour with a car. I don't want to be seen coming to your apartment. Could you ask Abu-Jacques to wait for me in front of the synagogue in one hour?"

A few minutes after he left, just as she was putting on her raincoat, the doorbell rang. It was Abu-Jacques.

"What's the story?" he asked with concern. "It's getting late and my wife doesn't know where I am. She's probably getting worried and will start asking around at the neighbors."

"Another hour. He'll be here in an hour. Can you wait that long?"

"An hour? Okay, but no longer. Will you be bringing him?"

"He'll come by car. He'll stop in front of the synagogue. He'll be wearing a brown suit—" She hesitated for a moment. "His name is Mussa."

The minutes trickled by slowly. Every few moments she would look at her watch, hoping to hear a car stopping, but the sounds of the street did not penetrate the closed windows of her fourth-floor apartment. Every so often she would go to the window, but it was dark and rainy and she was not able to see a thing.

Abu-Jacques came again shortly before eleven. "It's all over. Mussa came and took Winkler. Let's hope it ends just as well."

He looked frozen and she offered him something to drink. "Something hot, or perhaps you'd prefer a glass of cognac?"

His eyes lit up. "Yes, but only if you have one, too. A toast to our success. We might invite Mr. Kishak to join us. After all, he paid the expenses."

"No, let him sleep," she answered.

The following days were filled with anxiety. She was eager to know if Winkler had reached Israel safely, but she was not sure that Mussa would return. He might never come back at all. He could disappear from her life just as suddenly as he had entered. The Winkler affair might just be an isolated incident.

In the mornings, nauseous and dizzy from her pregnancy, she would tell herself that it would be best if Mussa did not come back. But as the house emptied and the day wore on, boredom and indolence would set in and she would begin to pray for his return.

Mussa returned on Wednesday.

"I came to tell you that Winkler arrived safely in Metulla. I'm sure you're pleased. He asked me to thank all of you who helped him."

He waited while she brought him a cup of tea and sat down.

"Actually I came for another reason. The people in Israel want to know if you're willing to continue working for them. If you are, they want to meet you. In Israel, of course. I'll take you across the border. . . ."

"When?" she asked breathlessly.

"As soon as possible."

She did not know what to say. Noticing her reluctance, he said, "You don't have to answer immediately. I'll come back tomorrow. If your answer is positive, fill out this questionnaire." He left a yellow envelope on the table.

She opened it as soon as he left. It contained twenty questions dealing primarily with her family background. She sat down and filled in the answers immediately.

She felt cramped at home. She dressed without knowing where she would go. Her feet led her to the Suk Sursuk. First she went to Abu-Jacques's stall. When he was free, she whispered, "He made it. Everything's okay." He responded by holding up two fingers in a victory sign. Then she went to her husband's shop. Joseph was surprised to see her.

"I wanted you to know that Winkler crossed the border safely," she said. For the first time a look of excitement crossed his face. He offered her a chair and sent the errand boy to bring coffee.

She did not want to spoil his good mood, but the news was churning inside of her. "Joseph," she said, "we have to talk. Will you be home for lunch?"

"Is it about this same business?" he asked suspiciously. He continued without waiting for an answer. "In that case it's better that we wait until the evening, after the children are asleep."

She did not go straight home after leaving the shop. She roamed the streets mulling over the things she would tell her husband, trying to imagine how he would respond. She was oblivious to her surroundings until she passed the perfumery shop. The bottle with the narcissus-shaped lid was still in the window. She went in and bought it.

That evening after the children had gone to sleep, Shula and Joseph sat facing each other. They looked relaxed, as though their decision had already been made.

"Mussa was here this morning," she said. "*They* want me to come and meet them. Mussa will take me across the border."

She waited for his reply, but he just sat there and stared. She was his wife of many years, the mother of his children. Yet she was still a stranger to him. What was driving her? The image of a songbird in a gilded cage flashed before his eyes. If he opened the cage, she might fly away forever. If he kept it locked, she might never sing again.

"Have you answered him yet?" he asked curtly.

"Yes. I told him I would do it."

After a moment of silence he moaned, "Let God be with you. . . ."

When she left the room, he was still hunched over in his chair staring blankly into space.

She headed straight for her closet, wondering which of her dresses would best conceal her pregnancy.

Crossing the Rubicon

 While preparing for her trip Shula's primary concern was that she disrupt her family's routine as little as possible.

When Mussa inquired about a convenient time for the journey, she responded automatically, "It doesn't really matter, as long as I am home by Wednesday—to have enough time to prepare the *Shabbat.*"

The Sabbath, lighting candles and blessing the wine on Friday night; synagogue services on Saturday morning followed by lunch at her mother-in-law's. These had all become such ritual, it never crossed her mind that she could break the pattern.

Mussa said: "Well, in that case, we'll leave on Monday."

Her husband made a second attempt to dissuade her from this new mission but relented when he realized the extent of her determination.

"Just take care of yourself," he said feebly. "Remember your condition."

She could hardly forget her physical state. When Mussa had informed her that they would be crossing the border on foot, she had begun to worry. She carefully selected a pair of sensible flat shoes and a comfortable woolen dress. After a few moments of indecision, she also decided on a wide jacket that would conceal her pregnancy.

In the morning, while preparing her children for school, she told them, "I'm going to Aleih for a few days; the doctor says I need some rest. Nazira will take care of you while I'm away. Be good children and don't give her a hard time. I'll be home before the end of the week."

They received the news naturally. Yaffa, who was eleven, was old enough to understand the significance of her mother's expanding belly. And Albert and Meir had been warned so often of late not to upset their mother that they instinctively understood that this would be a period when she might behave strangely.

Nazira arrived and began doing the dishes. Shula took her two youngest children to the synagogue nursery school.

She met Mussa in front of the Alhambra Cinema on Hamra Street. He was wearing the brown European suit he usually wore but not the conspicuous *hata* and *aqal*, the traditional peasant headwear. He was quite inconspicuous and their meeting aroused no interest from passersby.

They entered a taxi and Mussa instructed the driver to take them up the mountain. When they reached a café at the crossroads, he asked the driver to stop and they got out. Only after the taxi disappeared did he take Shula by the arm and lead her to an American car parked in front of the café. The driver and another man sitting beside him did not turn around and Mussa did not introduce them.

At four o'clock in the afternoon they reached El-Hiam, a small Shi'ite village in the southeast, near the border.

It was one of the coldest days of the year and the room to which Shula was shown was unbearably cold. She turned to the fireplace in the far corner, but saw that it was unlit.

Mussa noticed her disappointment. "It doesn't pay to light it. By the time the room warms it will be time to leave. I'll get a heater."

"When do we leave?" she asked.

"At sundown. There's Metulla."

She went to the window. Dusk was setting in, but she could still see a cultivated valley at the foot of a mountain dotted with small houses with red-thatched roofs.

"That's Metulla," Mussa repeated. "That's where you'll be sleeping tonight."

Metulla, the northernmost settlement in Israel, is located in a finger-shaped stretch of land that juts out from the Upper Galilee to the foot of Mount Hermon. When the Jewish settlers purchased the land from Druze landowners in 1896, the entire Middle East was unified under the Ottoman Empire. There were no boundaries or frontiers, and the fields of Metulla spread wide and deep into the valley. Following World War I, the French and the British divided the Ottoman Empire between them. An arbitrary border was established at the foot of the hill. The houses and their inhabitants were in Metulla, the fields in Lebanon. No one admonished the farmers of Metulla who crossed the border each morning to cultivate their fields.

During the riots of 1936–39, when southern Lebanon became a base of operations and refuge for Arab terrorists in the Galilee, the British sealed the border with a barbed-wire fence reinforced with concrete pillboxes and built a patrol road along the length of the frontier. The farmers of Metulla, however, continued to cultivate their land and worked side by side with the *fellahin* from El-Hiam, Kleà and Merj'uyun. Neighborly relations developed and were expressed by a sharing of visits and family celebrations—and also by a mutually rewarding smuggling of goods and illegal Jewish immigrants across the border.

"Will someone be waiting there for us?" she asked.

"Yes, they know you're coming. Don't worry."

He went out of the room. Now she could look around.

The large room was furnished with a row of easy chairs and small copper tables. A coarse rug covered the floor. Framed portraits of moustached, middle-aged, authoritative men, all bearing a strong resemblance to Mussa, hung on the walls. She remembered what she had heard about him and his family. He was the head of one of the largest Shi'ite clans in southern Lebanon, a man with close connections in government, a man of wealth and influence. She thought to herself, "Could he be doing all this for greed alone?"

Then she dozed off. At nine o'clock she was awakened by the sound of approaching footsteps. Two women entered, one carrying a lit oil lantern and the other a towel and a washbasin filled with hot, steamy water. Mussa followed, carrying a pair of men's heavy rubber boots.

"Wash," he said pointing to the basin. "But make sure to dry yourself well. There's a sharp wind blowing. Put these boots on over your shoes. It isn't raining but the fields are very muddy."

"We're going now?" she asked.

"In a little while. We're waiting for the army patrol to return from the border." He smiled and continued, "They'll be back early to-night. My cousin is having a party and their commander is invited. . . ."

Dogs barked at them as they made their way through the village. In a very short time the village was behind them and they were approaching the valley. A shadow suddenly appeared on a stone wall. Shula recoiled in fear as though the shadow had mysteriously sprung from the earth. Mussa showed no sign of surprise.

"Is everything all right?" he asked.

A stranger mumbled something and then began walking behind them.

They were moving slowly. Despite the darkness Mussa walked with assurance. Shula tripped over rocks and sand mounds. After about a quarter of an hour they stopped to rest. Shula was finding it difficult to breathe. She looked back but she could not estimate the distance they had traveled. A heavy fog had covered the valley and the village was completely hidden from view. Shula was amazed at her guide's ability to orient himself under these conditions. She could not even see the trail at her feet.

Twice more they stopped to rest. When they stopped for the third time, Mussa said, "We're here. We'll have to wait until my man finds the Jewish guards. They might open fire."

A few minutes later she heard footsteps. Mussa and his friend helped her through an opening in the barbed-wire fence.

After they had walked a few steps, she felt the ground harden. Asphalt. She saw two figures bundled up in heavy coats with rifles slung over their shoulders.

One of them said, *"Shalom."*

They had made it. They were in Metulla.

The small houses to either side were mostly dark. They approached a well lit house much larger than the others. The sign on the front door said, The Cedars Hotel.

Three men and a woman were waiting for them in the lobby. They shook Mussa's hand. He nodded in her direction and said, "Here she is."

"Welcome," one of the men said simply in Hebrew.

He then introduced himself as Grisha, as though his first name alone should suffice. Grisha, a member of Kibbutz Kefar Gil'adi near Metulla, was well known throughout the north of Israel. He represented the mysterious "Immigration Authority" which handled all the so-called "illegal" immigration of Jewish refugees who had survived the Holocaust or who were escaping persecution in Arab lands. Whenever a group of "illegal" immigrants reached the northern border, it was Grisha who officially greeted them and who, before the British authorities could discover them or begin searching for them, had them quickly dispersed among the northern Jewish settlements.

The others introduced themselves with the same informality. There was Reznick, the Haganah commander of Metulla, and Mr. and Mrs. Belski, the owners of the hotel.

Mrs. Belski disappeared for a moment and returned carrying a tray of hot tea and an impressive plate of thick meat sandwiches. Shula could not eat. She had still not caught her breath. The walk had been too much for her and she was very excited. But even though she had no idea what lay in store, she knew that having crossed the border, her life would never again be the same.

Mussa did not stay very long. After a brief discussion about the explosive situation between the Jews and Arabs in Palestine he got up to leave. He turned to Shula. "I'll come for you tomorrow evening."

Reznick interrupted: "No, tomorrow she has to go to Haifa. Come back the day after tomorrow."

Mussa looked at Shula inquisitively. She merely shrugged her shoulders without saying a word.

He left.

When they were alone, Grisha said, "Our people in Haifa want to talk to you about intelligence matters. We here have to speak to you about helping Jews cross the border. But you must be tired. It will be better if we wait until you return from Haifa."

She could only vaguely recall the trip to Haifa. She rode in a Jeep that followed a small van carrying about a half-dozen armed young men wearing wide-brimmed Australian hats. Even though the Jeep was closed, a cold wind seeped through the cracks, chilling her to the bone. She tried consoling herself by thinking about the men sitting in the unprotected open van ahead, but it did not work. She felt sorry for them, but she still felt frozen and wretched. The rolling of the jeep did not help either. The driver seemed to make a point of going over every little bump and pothole in the road.

They finally arrived at a tree-lined street filled with one-story houses in Qiryat Haiyyim, a workers' neighborhood in the Haifa Bay area. She was given a few moments to stretch her legs and was then taken into the house. The room was furnished with a desk and chairs and maps on the wall. A short, bespectacled man sat behind the desk. He was about forty years old, had a high forehead, and was graying at the temples.

"Shalom," he said to her. "My name is Tschervinski. I would first like to thank you in Winkler's name for everything you did for him."

She was tired and cold after the three-hour journey, but the mention of Winkler brought her back to life.

Tschervinski began to interrogate her. The letter she had sent with the aid of the peddler from Adeisa was stretched before him. He wanted to know where she had obtained the information.

She answered him impatiently. When he asked the next question, she understood his train of thought: "A woman like you, without any background in the underground, the wife of a rich Lebanese merchant, the mother of five small children . . . why are you getting involved?"

She had been asking herself the same question ever since she had begun this journey, and subconsciously, even before—ever since she had handed the letter over to the peddler from Adeisa. But now, when the question was actually put to her, the words came out naturally: "I want to help. . . . I'm a Jew and this is my country too."

She did not now if her answer had satisfied him, but his questions took another turn. He asked her about her husband's family, her house in Beirut, her friends who came to visit them at home, whether they had any connections with people in government, if they knew any officers in the army or the police.

She was forced to admit that no one in her family had any connections of these kinds. A sudden wave of self-confidence made her want to reply, "But they can be arranged," but she restrained herself.

He mentioned the peddler again. How much could she rely on his loyalty?

She shrugged her shoulders. "He owes my husband a great deal of money. He would do anything for money. . . ."

"Try to renew your contact with him. Don't use him again as a messenger, but try to get information from him."

"What are you interested in knowing?"

"Everything. Terrorist training camps, arms shipments, the names of commanders, the numbers of troops, et cetera. If you can get any information about the Lebanese army, that would also help, especially if Lebanon joins forces with the other Arab countries after May fifteenth."

"Do you think that will happen?"

"We're almost positive." When he saw her turn pale, he added, "The Lebanese army doesn't bother us too much, but it had better bother you. If Lebanon should join the war, you'd be considered a traitor. Do you you understand what that means?"

She had never thought about that. She shook her head.

"Are you still willing to help?"

"Yes," she said decisively.

"All right. Pass on the information through Mussa. You can trust him completely. We'll arrange a post office box for you in Beirut."

She was still not familiar with the professional jargon and she imagined that the post office box would be located in the main post-office in Beirut, with two keys, one for her and one for Mussa. "When you have any information, get in touch with him. How's your financial situation? Should we pay you a salary?"

She answered without hesitation, "No. My husband gives me everything I need."

"Expenses?"

She wavered a moment, remembering the eight hundred pounds she needed to smuggle Winkler off the ship.

"If you should run into expenses," Tschervinski said, "send us a bill with Mussa and we'll reimburse you. Would you be able to handle large sums of money?"

"I'll manage," she said with assurance.

"There's another thing. Jews. As the war goes on, the Jews of Syria and Iraq will be in a precarious position. Perhaps the Lebanese Jews, too. There'll be many refugees. They will have to be smuggled into Israel. Would you be willing to handle this?"

She nodded in assent.

"Good. You'll hear more about this in Metulla. Grisha will tell you everything you have to know. I guess we're finished." Then, as an afterthought, he added, "Congratulations on joining us. Let's hope that it all works out for the best."

A troubled look came over her face. He encouraged her to speak her mind.

"My family in Jeruslaem," she said. "Could I find out how they are?"

"We'll find out," Tschervinski promised. "If they're in need of anything, we'll help them. But for the present, it's better that they know nothing of your connection with us."

His answer satisfied her.

She spent the night in Qiryat Haiyyim. She slept on a narrow field bed in the small room next to Tschervinski's office. She was so tired she fell asleep immediately despite the unfamiliar and uncomfortable surroundings.

The following day she was returned to Metulla in the same round-about way she had come. She spoke with Grisha and Reznick for a long time in a room put at their disposal by the Cedars Hotel. They discussed the smuggling of Jewish refugees from Syria and Iraq. Mussa was to be the key man in all their future plans.

"When you have a group ready to go, contact Mussa," Grisha said. "He'll make all the necessary arrangements. We'll cover all the expenses, of course. But have the refugees cover as much as they can. They have to learn that freedom doesn't come cheap."

Mussa arrived that evening. After she put on the heavy rubber boots and covered herself with the black woolen scarf, they left.

She spent the night in his house in El-Hiam. On Thursday morning she sat in the back of Mussa's car with the other two women of the house. She was wearing an embroidered black peasant dress over her clothing and a tight shawl that concealed her light hair.

They were not stopped on the road and arrived in Beirut at noon.

War

5 On the surface everything at the Kishak household returned to normal. Once more Shula was a model housewife, caring for the apartment, cooking the meals, preparing the children for school—but with increased help from Nazira. She visited the family physician weekly and was pleased to hear that her pregnancy was progressing satisfactorily. Her husband never mentioned the three days she had spent away from home.

Behind this routine front Shula began to build up her "network."

The first person she recruited was Halfon Tharab—Abu-Jacques. The night she returned from Israel he had been so eager to hear every detail of her journey that she could barely resist telling him everything. But she had developed a new sense of caution and she refrained from revealing all the specifics. She told him only about her meeting in Metulla with Grisha.

"They want us to help them smuggle Jews to Israel," she told him.

"That's all?" Abu-Jacques asked, looking disappointed.

"That's a great deal," she responded sternly. "Jews will be coming from Syria and maybe even from Iraq. Someone will have to take care of them."

Without saying it directly, and without even being certain, she hinted that they would be part of a larger network working in Iraq and Syria to smuggle Jews across the border. Her words reassured Abu-Jacques. Being part of a large secret network was much more important than taking care of a few refugees.

She noticed that he had unconsciously accepted her leadership. When he suggested recruiting new people, he presented the idea in the form of a question. When she replied, "Not now, maybe later," he accepted her decision without protest.

A few days after her return, she went looking for Abu-Yihyeh at the Suk Sursuk. It was his day to be at the market and she planned her route in such a way that she just "happened" to meet him at the entrance, far away from her husband's shop.

"Madame Kishak," he called out gaily, bowing subserviently in her direction. She stared at him angrily.

"*Ya* Abu-Yihyeh," she said severely. "I received a letter from my family. The note I sent with you never even reached them."

"I swear to you on my children that I handed the note over personally. Maybe Abu-Ziki lost it. Who knows? I'm willing to take a new letter to him. Even tonight!"

"There's no need," she said, dismissing him with the wave of a hand. "What I want from you," she said defiantly and impulsively, "is information."

He was quiet for a moment and she thought she had made a mistake. Desperately she added, "I'm willing to pay."

The greedy smile on his face assured her that intuition had not failed her. For the right price he would do anything.

For the next few weeks they met at the market. He told her everything he had heard in his village and in the surrounding villages in the area where he traded. He provided her with information about the terrorist bands being recruited and trained in the villages, the amounts and kinds of weapons at their disposal, and the places from which they infiltrated across the border. She was very careful to keep their meetings as far away as possible from her husband's shop and she paid him personally for the information he provided. When *hawaja* Joseph graciously extended his credit, he knew to whom to be grateful.

Passing information across the border remained the exclusive role of Mussa, and he smuggled Shula's long and detailed letters on several occasions. The Jewish refugees from Syria, however, now became Shula's major concern.

Jewish refugees from Syria began streaming into Beirut at the end of January, after the great synagogue in Qamishliye was burned to the ground and Jewish stores in Aleppo were looted.

The first families arrived with nothing. The poor, having nothing to lose, are always the first willing to take the risk of starting a new life. These families were accommodated in the synagogue until they could find inexpensive living quarters and until the head of the family could find some sort of employment. The Jews of Wadi Abu-Jamil collected spare furniture and bedding for the newcomers and solicited monetary contributions from the shopkeepers at the Suk Sursuk. That Abu-Jacques was one of the first to be active in aiding these refugees caused no surprise. He had always been involved in philanthropic work.

The greater the number of refugees who arrived, the greater the concern that spread through Wadi Abu-Jamil. The small Jewish community of Beirut, which numbered only five thousand souls, could not easily absorb large numbers of newcomers. It was becoming increasingly difficult to find warehouses and cellars that could be turned into suitable living quarters. It was also becoming increasingly difficult to find employment for the refugees, most of whom had been shopkeepers and had almost no marketable skills. To make matters even worse, the refugees were all "illegal" aliens in Beirut and the policemen in the small station just off the Jewish street had already begun to notice their presence. Not a day passed without one of the refugees being asked to show his identity papers.

Until now there had been no major incidents. The police accepted explanations that papers had been forgotten at home and, more often than not, a small baksheesh helped to convince them. But what would happen if news of the illegal refugees ever reached the authorities? The Arab-Israeli war had already created tension between the Jewish and Moslem traders in the Suk Sursuk. If the fact that they were sheltering "illegal" refugees ever became known, it would drastically increase the tension.

Shula was part of the small group of people who helped the refugees. Most of her activity centered on the raising of funds. Every time a new group of refugees arrived, Shula would be at the market collecting for them. Her status as the wife of one of the most respected and prominent merchants, as well as her protruding belly, made it very difficult for anyone to refuse her. They would very often tell her their fears as they handed over their money: "How much longer can the situation go on like this? There are *tens of thousands* of Jews in Syria. We can't support them all!"

It was these openly expressed fears which gave her the pretext to go to the head of the Jewish community, Dr. Yitshak Attia.

Dr. Attia, a renowned physician of about sixty, had important patients and friends in all of Beirut's religious and ethnic communities. Shula knew he was a Zionist of long standing. She had not forgotten the enthusiastic compliments he had showered on her for her work with Maccabi Hatzair. But like most of the other Zionists living in Beirut, he looked upon Israel as a refuge for others—the remnants of the European Holocaust or persecuted brothers from Syria and Iraq. He could not imagine ever abandoning his beloved Beirut. She decided to be frank with him.

"The merchants are frightened," she said to him. "They're worried that the authorities will learn about the large numbers of illegal immigrants concentrated in Wadi Abu-Jamil. Our abilities to care for them physically are being drastically strained. There are already over sixty families with us—over five hundred souls. The refugee children already amount to more than a quarter of all the students studying in our school."

"I'm aware of this," the gray-haired physician replied patiently. "But what can we do about it? We can't refuse to help our brothers in distress."

"Correct, but we can move them on to Israel. Then they won't be concentrated here in such numbers."

He thought for a moment, digesting her words. "How will they get there?" he asked.

"I'm sure it can be arranged . . . if you could only persuade them to go. It would be to everyone's benefit."

Later she added, "It will be expensive. But it will be cheaper in the long run than having to support them here."

She left him pondering what she had said. She was sure that although she had revealed nothing, he would understand her implications. Two days later Albert Iliya, the community secretary, stopped her in the street. "Mrs. Kishak, if you should have some spare time, would you be kind enough to come to see me in my office?"

She went to see him that afternoon. He made sure the door was closed before he said, "There are three families among the refugees who are willing to continue on. Dr. Attia asked me to inform you of this. There are twenty-seven of them."

From then on both Dr. Attia and Albert Iliya shared her secret.

She needed a few days to make the arrangements. She informed Mussa and he in turn checked with Metulla to make certain about border guard arrangements. Only when all this had been done could they decide when the transfer would be made. He returned three days later with the following news: "It will be all right for next Monday."

Now they had to prepare the refugees. These families had arrived in Lebanon penniless, and now the few worldly possessions that they did have could not be taken on the trip across the border. Mussa was obstinate on this point: He said, "They're going to have to go on foot. My men will carry the children on their shoulders, but they won't carry pillows and blankets."

She was still not ready to identify herself to the refugees. She asked Abu-Jacques to speak to them, to try to persuade them to leave their possessions behind. He returned absolutely exhausted from the effort.

"The poor devils," he complained as he fell into a chair. "You wouldn't believe the way they cling to the most worthless junk! There's one old woman who refuses to give up her old wrought-iron Sabbath pot. She claims she inherited it from her grandmother and won't be able to cook a Sabbath meal in any other. She'd rather give up going to the Holy Land than give up her old pot. What do we do with her?"

On Monday morning while they were waiting for Mussa to arrive, Abu-Jacques suddenly appeared at her door.

"There's trouble."

She took him into the living room and waited to hear what he had to say.

"The Mazliach family has changed its mind."

"Because of the pot?"

"No, I already gave in on the pot. He claims that he heard that his brother's family has decided to follow him to Beirut and should be arriving soon. He wants to wait for them. The truth is, I think, that he found work and he wants to stay here."

"Does he have an apartment?"

"How could he have an apartment? The Wadi is overcrowded. He plans to stay where he is."

"And when more refugees come, where will we put them? Explain that to Mazliach. Tell him if he isn't out of here we'll have no place to put his brother when he comes. You can also tell him that if he doesn't have proper papers he could cause trouble for everybody."

"You tell him. My tongue is worn out from all the unsuccessful pleading."

When the truck that the villagers from El-Hiam used to take their produce to market arrived, the stubborn Syrian refugee finally agreed to make the trip. Mazliach stood up and ordered the members of his family onto the truck. All three families crowded in. Empty vegetable crates were piled high to conceal them from view.

"We'll reach El-Hiam by evening and they'll be in Metulla by midnight," Mussa promised Shula.

"I want some sort of verification that they arrived safely," Shula blurted out. She immediately regretted her words. Mussa had been deeply insulted.

"You'll get it," he said curtly as he entered his car.

Three days later he returned with a printed invoice from the Cedars Hotel, Metulla. The message scribbled in pencil said: "27 brothers were received. Grisha." Shula apologized to Mussa on the spot, but he continued to bear a grudge and remained cool and distant for a long time afterward.

When Shula entered the more advanced stages of her pregnancy, her work virtually came to a halt. She barely left the house, but the network she had created continued operating. Abu-Jacques received the refugees, found them temporary housing and the bare essentials they would need to live, evaluated their characters, and tried to persuade them to continue on to Israel. When he found a family willing to go, he would immediately report it to Shula, who would pass the information on to Mussa. Mussa continued his weekly visits. Sometimes he would come alone, and at other times he would bring one of his two sons, Mahmud and Fathi, who assisted him in the smuggling operations. All of the missions had been successful and the number of signed receipts from Grisha verifying the arrival of the refugees continued to accumulate. Despite the fact that Shula constantly hinted to Mussa that she was no longer interested in receiving the notes, he stubbornly continued to present her with them after each successful mission, as if to remind her that she had doubted him.

The tide of war repeatedly changed course during the following months. March was the worst. The embryonic Jewish state suffered setbacks and defeats. Convoys were ambushed, settlements attacked, cities bombed. The headlines in the Beirut newspapers were jubilant with victory and the Moslems began treating the Jews with condescension and contempt.

The tide turned in the Jews' favor in April. The Arab Liberation Army led by Fawzi al-Kaukji suffered a bad defeat at Mishmar Ha'emek. The forces led by Abdul el-Kader Husseini were routed in a battle on the road to Jerusalem and he was killed in the skirmish. Although the Beirut papers mentioned nothing of these defeats, rumors spread quickly through the city. The condescension and contempt quickly changed into open tension and hostility.

On April 20, Tiberias was taken by the Haganah forces; three days later Haifa was in the hands of the Jews. It was impossible to conceal these victories. Beirut swelled with tens of thousands of Arab refugees from Haifa, all of whom were still in a state of shock at the cruel vicissitudes of fate.

Even though they knew there would be difficult times ahead, the Jews of Beirut silently prayed special prayers of thanksgiving for the great miracle that had occurred to their brethren in Israel.

Shula gave birth in the beginning of May. It was a girl and Shula named her Carmela in honor of the Jewish victory in Haifa, which is located near Mount Carmel. Her in-laws were filled with concern when they heard the name and pleaded with Joseph to change her mind. Shula, however, was obstinate.

"Her name is Carmela and that's that!"

Joseph had no choice but to give in.

The April victories of the Jewish forces changed the attitude of the Arab leaders. If they had previously hoped that the "Zionist bands" could be annihilated by volunteer troops, they soon realized that they would be forced to send in their regular armies. From his office in Damascus, Iraqi general Ismail Sawafat, commander-in-chief of the Arab forces in Palestine, admitted: "The Jews of Israel are stronger than we assumed. They're well organized and are receiving outside aid. They have their own small-arms factories and are better trained and disciplined than their Arab counterparts."

The Arab League made its decision at the end of April. On May 15, the day that would mark the end of the British mandate, the regular armies of the Arab states would invade Israel. Even Lebanese President Bishara al-Khuri supported the decision. Although the Lebanese army was small, with only two brigades and a few auxiliary units, he had no choice but to join his "sister Arab states" in their holy war against the new state of Israel. He still believed it would be a fast and simple war. After all, how long could the Jewish forces, armed only with light weapons, withstand the combined forces of the regular armies of five Arab states supported by artillery, armor, and air forces?

On May 12, the commanders of the Arab armies met to formulate their war plans, to establish their goals, and to divide the area into war sectors.

The Lebanese army's task was to be relatively simple: they would concentrate all their forces on the eastern section of the border—the western side of the border was almost entirely under Arab control—and would then attack in an easterly direction toward the finger-shaped section of the Galilee that jutted out toward Mount Hermon.

The Lebanese army opened its offensive on the night of May 15 and succeeded in a manner that seemed to verify the president's optimism. The arab villages of Malkiya and Kadesh were "conquered" and the road to the "finger" was opened. But the Lebanese advance never came into being. Small mobile Jewish units opened attack on the Lebanese rear, raiding the Lebanese supply lines and bombing connective bridges. When the actual attack began, it was a Jewish counterattack, which uprooted the Lebanese forces from Malkiya and Kadesh and pushed them back across the border.

From this point on the Lebanese army gave up all intention of further attack. It concentrated on defending its own positions on the Lebanese side of the border and on providing logistic assistance to the Arab Liberation Army of Fawzi al-Kaukji, which was fortified in a large "pocket" in the Galilee around Nazareth.

On July 9, however, the newly established Israel Defense Forces succeeded in capturing Nazareth and routing the forces under al-Kaukji's command. The campaign was called Operation Dekel. Once again, tens of thousands of Arab refugees sought shelter on the Lebanese side of the border.

During Operation Hiram at the end of October the remainder of the Arab Liberation Army was entirely wiped out and the entire Galilee fell into Jewish hands. By the time the operation was completed, the Israeli forces had reached the former international boundary. On the eastern sector, the Israel Defense Forces crossed the border into Lebanon and captured fourteen Lebanese villages including Adeisa.

A third wave of Arab refugees streamed into Beirut.

During the months of the active war Shula's network halted all immigrant crossings.

Mussa still crossed the border carrying Shula's letters whenever possible. The last letter had been sent on May 2, a few days after Carmela's birth. Upon his return he brought Shula a present—a knitted baby outfit he had purchased in Metulla's only shop.

In the summer of 1948, Beirut was not a particularly pleasant place to live—especially for Jews. Over 140,000 Arab refugees took shelter in Lebanon. They had come in three great waves and more than half of them filtered into Beirut. The few who were well off and had succeeded in escaping with some of their wealth fought for the few apartments still available, causing real estate prices to soar. The others concentrated in public buildings until they were transferred to army camps abandoned by the French years before in the south of the city. Shantytowns sprang up on the outskirts of these camps and the Arab refugees living there became progressively more bitter as the chances of their returning home steadily diminished.

Employment opportunities were scarce. The United Nations Relief Works Agency had not yet been established and hunger and want were rampant. The refugees served as a constant source of agitation and incitement. There was always someone instigating them to riot. Carrying banners and screeching at the top of their lungs, they would break out of their camps and invade the city. One of the first targets of their attack was, of course, the Jews. "Their brothers murdered our brothers in Palestine. They plundered our homes. And here they are living off the fat of Arab land!" This would be the battle cry of any one of the various demagogues who converted the first empty wooden crate he saw into a speaker's podium. The angry crowd would cry out in unison: "Death to the Jews!" It never came to that, however, because of the gendarmes the president had ordered to protect the Suk Sursuk and Wadi Abu-Jamil. But the Jews lived in constant fear. Joseph would often come home in the middle of the day with a worried look on his face and announce, "We were ordered to close all the shops and lock ourselves at home. They expect a demonstration. Are the children home?"

The president of the republic was concerned that angry mobs of Arab refugees might attack the Jews. Aware of the refugees' potential danger and anxious that they might upset the fragile ethnic balance of Lebanon—since the vast majority of those arriving were Moslems—he established a special intelligence unit. He attached it to the office of the chief of staff, making it the "property" of the Christians. It became their responsibility to infiltrate the camps, to provide information about life there, and to forewarn the authorities of any signs of rioting. A young army major, George Anton, was appointed to head the unit and his men performed so thoroughly and admirably that the president personally expressed his satisfaction. Nevertheless, al-Khuri was frightened.

Beirut lost the gay, sophisticated atmosphere of a French resort town. Angry-looking Galilee *fellahin* in black *sharwal* work trousers lined the streets, and peasant women nursing their infants could be seen on every corner. The streets were overcrowded and there was much poverty and bitterness.

Among all this confusion, the influx of Jewish refugees from Syria and Iraq was hardly noticed. But in Wadi Abu-Jamil there was deep concern.

One day Albert Iliya met Shula on her way to the grocer. He complained: "When will it all end? This month there have been more than one hundred of them. . . . There are policemen at the station who are making a steady income by stopping the illegals and asking for their identity cards. It can't go on much longer, and they keep coming. . . ."

She was not unaware of the situation. Abu-Jacques, who was still conscientiously working with the refugees, would report to her about each new group that arrived. His reports verified her suspicion that this was not a spontaneous movement. Some of the refugees from Aleppo told of a mysterious man named Eliahu who would contact anyone who expressed even the slightest interest in going to Israel. It was he who made the connection between them and the Arabs who smuggled them across the border to Lebanon.

"If only I had a connection with Israel," she thought, "I might be able to set up contact with this Eliahu."

But there was none. Ever since the Lebanese army had entered the war, the entire south had been taken over by the military, and neither Mussa nor Abu-Yihyeh could reach Beirut.

They both arrived, however, at the beginning of September.

Abu-Yihyeh came first. One day Joseph returned home for lunch —it had become his custom since the tension had mounted, to go home, assure himself that his family was safe, and then, depending upon the atmosphere in the market that particular day, decide whether or not to return to work. "Abu-Yihyeh was in today," he casually announced. "He's in terrible straits because of the situation, but I've extended his credit. Maybe the other peddlers will be returning soon, too. He's coming back tomorrow to pick up the goods he ordered."

The next day she waited for him at the entrance to the market.

He moaned about the disastrous effects the war had had on his business.

"The peasants have stopped buying," he said, "and people are afraid to set foot outside their villages these days. All the heroes who were trounced by the Jews are lying in ambush on the roads, stealing and plundering from any innocent who happens along."

"The end will come soon," she tried to console him. "The war is over—"

He looked at her in wonder. "What do you mean? Has the Lebanese army returned to its bases? Not at all. On the contrary. They're digging in and fortifying their positions. Just a week ago a new artillery unit arrived and set up base. The supply and weapons lines are still flowing to al-Kaukji in Sasa. They're still angry about having lost Nazareth and they're screaming and blaming each other. But rumors have it that they're planning a new offensive in the near future."

She began questioning him for more details about the new company and the specific kinds of cannon that it brought with it. He quickly realized that this was no longer a social conversation but a business meeting. With financial rewards in mind he provided her with as much information as he could. He was not able to give her the exact names of the guns but he knew that they were French-made and he could give her a rather precise picture of their positions and number. He also knew that the unit was headed by an officer with the rank of lieutenant colonel. It sounds like a battalion, she thought to herself. She regretted that she had no way of passing all this information over to Israel.

The following day, as if by magic, Mussa knocked at her door.

He looked thinner than she had remembered, but he immediately reassured her: "No, nothing happened in El-Hiam; all the major battles took place farther to the south and west." Metulla was safe as far as he could tell. There had been some exchanges of fire and the Lebanese army had bombed the village a bit at first, but all the forces moved out to the front lines near the Malkiya-Kadesh area and Metulla had been forgotten.

"Do you think you could get there?"

He looked very serious. "Only if it was something extremely important. You know, people are being hanged these days just on suspicion of treason."

"It's important," she said decisively.

He waited while she prepared her report. When she handed it to him, she added: "Ask them if we should start sending refugees. Tell them there are several hundred in Beirut and the situation is getting very bad."

A few days later when Mussa returned, he remarked on the ease with which he had crossed the border. "It's like the good old days," he said confidently. "The army is dug in everywhere, but they're more concerned about what may be coming *from* Israel than in preventing infiltration *into* Israel. I don't think it should be too much of a problem to smuggle over a small group of refugees. . . . But," he continued, "Grisha said to hold off for the time being. He didn't say why."

The reason became clear enough the following month when Operation Hiram began.

This operation, which brought the Israeli army to the banks of the Litani River in Lebanon, put a halt to all of Shula's intelligence activities. Her agent, Abu-Yihyeh, was now in Israeli-occupied territory. Since the Arab Liberation Army had suffered total defeat, the regular Lebanese forces quickly withdrew from the border areas and the war between Israel and Lebanon virtually came to an end.

It became easier, however, to smuggle the illegal Jewish refugees into Israel. Mussa smuggled the first group across the border in November and from then on small groups of one or two families would make the trip every week. This, however, did not relieve the pressure in Wadi Abu-Jamil; the influx of new illegal refugees far surpassed those leaving for Israel.

After the long period of inactivity which had been forced upon her, Shula began her work with renewed enthusiasm. She would go from shop to shop in the market, openly and aggressively demanding money for the refugees.

"Monsieur Algasi," she would say, "I want you to give me two hundred and fifty pounds to aid the refugees."

Most of the merchants met her demands, usually adding a complaint or two.

Everyone in the ghetto knew that her activities were not limited to collecting money. One could hardly avoid noticing the large vegetable truck from El-Hiam which stopped at the entrance to the Wadi, took on its refugee passengers, and then disappeared from the city. It did not take long for the neighbors to make the connection between the truck and the Arab peasant in his *kaffiyeh* and *aqal* who frequented the Kishak apartment.

Joseph stubbornly ignored the gossip about his wife. His mother and sister, however, absorbed every word. When the two complained to him that people were "talking about Shula" and begged him to talk some sense into her, he stood by his wife and defended her actions.

"It's God's commandment that we should help our fellow Jews," he replied.

"It may cost you a very high price," his mother warned. "And why does it have to be Shula? She's the mother of six young children!"

"Someone has to do it," he intoned, "and Shula is the one. The sages used to say, 'Where there are no men, you be the man.'"

He did his best to appear proud of Shula's activities, but beneath the surface he was very frightened.

On December 27, 1948, a larger group than Shula had ever dared to send set out for Israel: seven families, fifty-six souls, forty of them young children.

When she told Mussa about the group, he was visibly agitated.

"It won't work," he said. "It's the middle of winter, the fields are filled with mud, and snow could fall any day now. Do you know what could happen to forty children? We'll have to carry them on our shoulders. I don't have enough men...."

But Shula remained obstinate. The police in the neighboring police station knew that there was a concentration of illegal refugees in Wadi Abu-Jamil. The information might soon be passed on to their superiors. If the refugees should be discovered, they would be tried and deported to Syria, where they would suffer the worst of fates. It was imperative that they be smuggled out of Beirut.

"Do you know what it means? A baby carried by a stranger, in the cold, in the middle of the night. . . . He could burst out crying at the very moment we pass an army post. . . ."

They sat down, staring at each other helplessly.

"You know what?" Mussa said. "If we drugged them before we left—I could give them some tea mixed with a little opium. . . ."

Shula's maternal instinct was aroused.

"Not opium," she said. "I'll find something else."

She asked the advice of her family physician. She did not tell him the entire story; she merely said she wanted something harmless yet potent enough to put a baby or small child safely to sleep for several hours with no chance of his waking up. The doctor cast an inquisitive glance in her direction, shrugged, and wrote her a prescription.

"Half a teaspoon of this in a cup of tea will put a child to sleep for a minimum of three hours."

Later she discovered that he had given her a prescription for nothing less than opium.

When snow began to fall on the evening of December 26, she had already made her decision. She said to her husband, "Tomorrow I am leaving with the refugees for El-Hiam. I want to make sure everything goes all right. This is the largest group I've ever sent."

Actually she had already decided that she was going to cross the border with them. She had not explained the reason why even to herself. On the surface it was as if the snow had prompted her decision. She knew that her presence would not change a thing either way. But still . . .

Joseph asked her in a muted voice: "Only to El-Hiam?" She wondered whether he could read her thoughts.

"Only to El-Hiam," she replied. This was the first time in her married life that she had deliberately lied to her husband. But her conscience did not bother her.

Mussa recruited two large trucks for the mission. He suggested that she join him in his car but she insisted on riding in one of the trucks with the refugees. As usual, there were long-drawn-out arguments about the number of bundles that the families would be permitted to take with them; and as usual they sneaked on as many extra packages as they could.

"You're going to have to leave them all behind when we start our journey on foot," she warned the heads of the three families that were with her in the truck. But for the moment the bundles of pillows and blankets softened the bumps along the rough roads.

The snow continued falling and the trucks proceeded at a snail's pace. It was freezing cold and the children soon tired of the long and arduous trip. Some of them asked for food and others wanted to relieve themselves. All of them started whining.

It was already dark when they arrived.

The truck stopped on the outskirts of the village, next to a wooden hut used for storing sacks of fertilizer.

There was a single oil lamp inside and after Mussa lit it, he went out to look for some twigs for a fire. The hut immediately filled with smoke and some of the children began to cough and cry. Others fell asleep in their mothers' arms.

"We'll stay here until nine," Mussa said. "If you brought any food with you, now is the time to eat it. I'm going for water so we can make some tea. Try to rest. You have a long road ahead of you."

"How long will we have to walk?" asked a young woman who on the road had mentioned to Shula that she was the mother of three.

"Six or seven kilometers."

"The children won't be able to make it," she complained.

"You'll have to carry them on your shoulders," Mussa said. "My

men will help. The most important thing to remember is that there
has to be absolute silence. No talking will be allowed. We'll have to
move quickly. As long as I walk, you follow me no matter how tired
you are. When I signal to stop, stand still and don't move an inch.
And if we have to run, you better run as fast as your legs will carry
you."

"This is madness," the young woman said. "We're not soldiers. Albert." She turned to her husband. "I want to go back to Beirut."

Others began moaning in agreement. Shula knew that this was the
critical moment.

"No one is going back to Beirut!" she commanded. "Just remember, if you're caught and tried, you may all be deported to Syria.
You could also cause a lot of trouble for all the people who helped
you escape. Don't be afraid," she said with a new appeasing tone in
her voice. "Other people have safely made this trip before you.
You'll make it, too. Tomorrow you'll look back on your fears and
laugh."

She felt the effect her words had on the frightened refugees and
their complaints were silenced. Only the young woman who had
started the little mutiny remained firm.

"It's easy for you to speak. You're sending us out into the cold
and snow and danger, while you'll be home sleeping in your warm
bed in Beirut."

If Shula had any doubts about the wisdom of her decision to cross
the border with them, they disappeared at that moment.

"I'm not going back to Beirut," she announced. "I'm crossing the
border with you."

The young woman stared at her in silence.

A short while later the water began to boil in the five-gallon can
that had been placed on the bonfire. With a sigh of relief Shula
ordered the fire extinguished. Soon the commotion died down. After
having finished their tea and whatever food they had brought with
them from Beirut, they remembered Mussa's advice and began resting for the trek ahead. In the smoky, scattered light of the oil lamp
she saw them banding together into family groups in different corners of the hut. Some of the women unfolded their bundles and
spread blankets and sheets for already-sleeping children. Some of the
men hunched over their packs whispering to each other. They were

all tired and worried. One of the women began to nurse a baby and a four-year-old boy watched spellbound.

Shula's heart quickened at the sight of them. They reminded her of newsreels she had seen after the war, of desperate European refugees wandering all over Europe, their entire lives packed in bundles containing all that remained of homelands which no longer existed, of dear ones, most of whom had been exterminated, entire pasts packed in coarse blankets, their future vague and unknown. She was suddenly filled with regret. "Who are you, Shula Cohen," she asked herself, "to uproot these wretched and unfortunate people from the little refuge they have found and drag them across snowy fields and dangerous borders in the middle of a dark, cold night? In God's name, what kind of person are you?"

Mussa returned from the village at nine. He came with his eldest son, Fathi, and ten strong men in military attire, their heads and faces covered with dark woolen scarves so that only their eyes could be seen. They came with canvas slings—the kind that the peasant women use to carry their children on their backs while they work the fields.

"The Bint Jubail patrol passed," he said, handing Shula a pair of heavy rubber boots. "They won't bother us anymore this evening. We can start moving."

The bonfire was rekindled and a new pot of tea was set on the fire. Shula put a few drops of opium in the cups of all the younger children who were to be carried. They fell into a deep sleep. It was more than an hour, however, before the adults were ready to move. Mussa grumbled incessantly. "They're waiting for us there; they won't know why we're late."

A moment later: "Hurry up, hurry up, we have to get back while it's still dark."

Finally, after all the sleeping children were strapped on the backs of the adults and all the bundles had been packed, they were ready to go.

Mussa opened the door and left. Fathi, a young man of about twenty-five; motioned to the Jamily family to follow him. One of Mussa's men, carrying a child, accompanied them. After waiting about three minutes he sent out another group, which was also accompanied by one of the villagers. It was now the turn of the Saadon family—nine children, their parents, and a pair of grandparents who insisted on staying together. A short argument ensued. Fathi was quick to relent. "Okay, you can all go together. Madame Cohen, go with them. You'll be able to help them."

When they stepped outside, they were hit by a harsh, cold wind. Shula pulled her jacket tightly around her and covered her face with her woolen scarf. It was a moonless night but the brightness of the snow illuminated the darkness. Some lights from the village shone on her left. She turned to the right and followed in the footsteps of Mussa's man, who was carrying a small child on his back. She recalled Fathi's words and slowed down, letting the Saadon family precede her as she counted them. There were only twelve. She was gripped by a sudden fear. There were supposed to be thirteen! Before she could call out to their guide she remembered that the little girl strapped to his back was the thirteenth member of the family.

Mussa waited for them at the foot of the hill. In the distance they could see the dim lights of Metulla. While they were still waiting for the others to arrive, he said to her, "Do you see those lights to the right? That's Kleà. Between Kleà and Metulla there is another single light, slightly dimmer than the rest. That's the army post, right on the border. That's where we're going to have to be the most careful."

Everyone had arrived. Despite his repeated pleading that they maintain absolute silence, the women raised their voices, calling after children who began whining. Mussa passed Shula, angrily grumbling under his breath, "Never again. This is the last time I take a group of this size. It's impossible to control them."

Finally they all stood in line. Shula found herself in the middle, between eight or nine women, some of them very old, and eighteen children. Mussa and Shula counted and recounted until they were sure that everyone was present and there had been no mistakes.

"Eighteen children," he said. "Watch them carefully. Make sure they stay together."

Twelve of the older children marched behind with the men who were carrying the bundles.

They began to move. Soon they were off the road and walking in a field that had been ploughed before the winter rains. The earth was crumbly and absorbent beneath the snow. Their feet sank deep into the cold, soggy earth and Shula was grateful for the rubber boots Mussa had given her. The others were wearing boots or high shoes, but some of them, particularly the women, were wearing ordinary shoes that kept falling off in the mud. When this happened they had to wait until the shoes were retrieved. One of the women carrying a baby in her arms could not find her shoe in the dark. In desperation, she removed her other shoe and went on barefoot.

As they continued tramping through the mud Shula began to envy her. The mud and slush clung to her boots, doubling their weight. Every movement drained her of strength. After the first kilometer she was afraid she would not be able to go on.

The women plodded on, breathing heavily. The children tired quickly. They began whining and Mussa came running, spewing rebukes. But he had no choice. He had to order a rest.

There was no place to sit in the cold, snow-covered field, so they stood. A child began to groan, "Mommy, I'm cold," and the other children followed suit.

They started walking again.

From then on they took a break every half kilometer, but these frequent pauses did not help them regain their dwindling strength.

They approached the army post. Mussa stopped in front of a row of low bushes and called for a lengthy rest. He went to each group, admonishing them in a sharp whisper: "In the name of Allah, absolute silence from here on." In utter desperation he mumbled under his breath, "Allah is punishing me for all my sins. . . ."

Shula knew that they had now reached the most dangerous part of the journey. She realized that if she was going to worry, now was a good time. But she was too exhausted; she did not even have the strength to be afraid. There was in her shocked and numbed consciousness room for only one thought: "Eighteen . . . there have to be eighteen children." Every time they tarried she would nervously count the little shadows, silently praying to herself: "Dear God, don't let any of them be missing."

All of a sudden she heard a motor close by in the darkness. She could distinguish the shadow of an open Jeep with four figures sitting inside. Her heart sood still. "It's the army," she said to herself in desperation. "We've been caught."

She looked around her in terror, like an animal caught in a trap. She did not have the strength to flee. And then she realized that there was no place to hide.

One of the women next to her began to scream. The man Mussa

had assigned to their group stood up tall in his army uniform and whispered, "Shhh, quiet! It's all right. They're our men."

When she calmed down she could see Mussa's shadow moving away from the Jeep.

"It's okay," he said as he approached her. "The army post is quiet. They haven't sent out any listening posts. We can pass safely."

They continued walking. This last bit of excitement had exhausted all her energy. Her legs would not carry her. When they took their next rest, she fell to the ground. She felt the cold snow beneath her. She feared that when word came to go on she would not have the strength to rise.

Their next rest, however, was at the foot of the entrance to Metulla. She heard the sound of footsteps approaching on an asphalt road and a voice calling out in Hebrew, "Welcome to the homeland."

After they had all passed through the fence and had made their way to the Cedars Hotel, she recognized the man who had greeted them: Grisha.

He recognized her, too.

"It's you?" he cried out happily. "What luck! We've just received a message that they want to speak to you in Tel Aviv."

They let her rest for two hours. Then, still half-asleep and clutching a thermos of coffee spiced with cognac, she crawled into the back seat of a car. She took one sip of the coffee and fell fast asleep.

When she awoke the next morning the car was making its way through the streets of Tel Aviv in the direction of Jaffa. It stopped in front of a green two-story house with balconies jutting out on all sides.

Code Name
The Pearl

6 She hadn't imagined that Intelligence headquarters would look like this. The green house had once belonged to a rich Jaffa Arab who had left some of his possessions behind. Expensive, heavy, carved furniture stood side by side with improvised army tables made of unpainted boards sitting on wobbly legs and covered coarse army blankets. A lush Persian carpet covered the living room floor, but the long corridor was bare. There were no doors that mysteriously opened and closed at the pressing of a secret button, no special passwords for entry, and the only sentry in sight was the single guard at the gate.

She was led to a second-floor room where two men sat at an ordinary office desk. A very ornate closet with four doors, a legacy of the former tenant no doubt, and a metal filing cabinet were the only other furniture in the room. An expensive crystal chandelier crowned the room, but the tile floor was bare. There was a large map of the Middle East on the wall to her left and a curtainless window to her right.

One of the men sitting at the desk rose and shook hands. "I'm Benjamin," he said, pointing to an empty chair in front of him.

He was in his thirties, very tall—he towered over her by at least a head—and thin but well built. He had a hungry, almost cruel look which robbed him of being what was conventionally considered handsome. The balding, red-headed man with freckles sitting to his right did not bother to rise or introduce himself. Once or twice during the conversation Benjamin referred to him as "Gingi" and this is how he remained in her memory.

"We wanted to meet you," Benjamin said as she sat down, "and congratulate you on the good work you've been doing." He did not wait for her to nod her head in recognition of his compliment, and continued: "Of course, all the good work you've done is still a bit amateurish. We have bigger plans for you."

He began questioning her. Just as in her first interrogation in Qiryat Haiyyim, the questions dealt with her life in Beirut, her current acquaintances and connections, and the potential ones she could establish with people in government and the military.

While questioning her he gave her a penetrating look and asked, "Do you understand the great change that has taken place since you first started working with us? There is a state of war between Israel and Lebanon now and if you should be caught, you could receive the death sentence. Is that clear? If something should happen, we wouldn't be able to help you and would most likely deny your very existence."

He waited, but she did not reply. "And you're still willing to work with us?"

She answered in the affirmative and he smiled with pleasure.

"I see here," he said, reading from a paper, "that you refused to accept a salary. Would you like to change your mind?" She shook her head in refusal. "All right. Were you reimbursed for your expenses? Good, it will be the same in the future. You can continue sending us your bills through Shukry Mussa."

He went on: "He will continue to be your contact. We trust him implicitly. His family has worked with us for years. However, we want you to stop sending us open reports. There is always the possibility that he or one of his men will be caught. We'll provide you with invisible ink and a security code which will ensure both of us that the letters we receive from each other are authentic."

He then briefed her about the latest developments in the war.

"Did you people in Beirut receive the latest details about our Egyptian offensive?" He continued even though she had nodded her head: "We caught them by surprise. If the British and Americans hadn't interfered, we could have reached the Suez Canal and thrown them out of Sinai completely. Even now we're convinced that they're beaten and will have to give up fighting. King Abdullah of Jordan wants out as well, but he's in an awkward position as long as Iraqi troops are on his territory to the north. The situation is similar on the northern front as well. Lebanon isn't particularly interested in continuing the war, but they can't make any moves without the Syrians. We're under the impression that moves for a cease-fire will begin in a few weeks. But it's Syria and Iraq that hold the cards. In Beirut you're in a good position to hear what's going on in Syria. We want you to establish contact with people in positions to know what is happening in Damascus. Do you think you could help us?"

Her imagination took flight and her heart beat rapidly in excitement throughout his brief monologue. But when he asked her a direct question, she became flustered and had to admit that she did not have even the slightest idea where to start or to whom to turn.

"Gingi will provide you with a few tips," Benjamin said. "You can, however, work according to your own initiative and sources. Just be careful. What we're asking from you is very important, but don't take any unnecessary risks. Always remember what could happen to you if you are caught."

"If I am in danger," she said thoughtfully, "my children will also be in danger. I would like them to be taken out of Lebanon, at least the older ones."

"Would you like them brought here to Israel? To your family?"

"No, not to my family. I would like them enrolled in a good agricultural school. I want to be sure that they'll receive an education no matter what happens to me."

"No problem. When you're ready to send them, I'll take personal charge of putting them in one of our best schools."

After she finished speaking with Benjamin, Gingi led her to the next room, his office, which contained the same strange combination of lavish and military furniture. This time, however, they sat in large, overstuffed red armchairs around a comfortable coffee table in the corner. Gingi lectured her for about an hour on the political situation in Lebanon, the fragile ethnic and religious balance, and the various interethnic rivalries. Shula had been generally aware of the situation in Lebanon, but not to the detailed extent that she now heard.

"When you look for accomplices and connections, be wary of the Sunni Moslems. The Shi'ites are more cooperative. The fact is we've been working with them for years. They're a minority in the Middle East and for the most part are persecuted in the various Moslem states. They constitute a majority in only one Moslem country, Iran, which isn't even an Arab state. So they tend not to identify with any of the Arab regimes. The Sunnis, on the other hand, identify most strongly with the Arab nationalist movements. Even those who don't support unification with Syria would still like to see Lebanon as an integral part of the Arab Middle East. Of course, you can always find someone among them who is willing to be bought, but in general it's best to be wary of them.

"There's also a problem with the Maronite Christians. For the most part they're sympathetic to our cause. Their dream is to have a Christian Lebanon and their greatest fear is a Moslem takeover. As far as they're concerned, Israel is a non-Moslem state in the Middle East that could one day come to their aid. But not all the Maronites are the same. Pay careful attention. The church authorities are okay. Their *mutran* testified in our favor before the U.N. inquiry and most of them follow his orders. The Falanges support us and, to a slightly lesser extent, so do Camille Chamoun's National Liberals. The Maronites in the north, on the other hand—possibly because they're a Christian minority surrounded by a Sunni majority—are less interested in isolating themselves from the Arab majority. They view themselves as Arab Christians, and in order to demonstrate their national loyalties, they very often take an even more extreme position than their Moslem counterparts. Who, for instance, was the most severe opponent of the cease-fire in July? None other than your President Bishara al-Khuri. It doesn't matter that the Lebanese army didn't lift a finger, even after the cease-fire. The most important thing was that al-Khuri could prove that he wasn't any less of a nationalist than Abdullah in Jordan, or King Farouk in Egypt, or Shukri al-Kuwatli in Syria.

"So you have to be very careful when you come in contact with the Maronites. Particularly with people from al-Khuri's clan or from Frangié's clan, or with anyone from the north."

She asked some questions and he answered her carefully and patiently. He then went to the wall closet and took out a bottle of a milky liquid and a jar containing what looked like talcum powder.

"This is invisible ink," he said, lifting the bottle. "You write with it just like with any ordinary ink. You can use fountain pen or the end of a match. After the ink dries, it completely disappears from sight. But if you spread some of this powder on the page, the writing comes back into view, but only for a short time. After an hour or two it disappears again.

"In order not to arouse the suspicion of the police, if they should catch one of our emissaries carrying a blank piece of paper, you have to disguise your writing. After you've written your report, wait for the ink to dry and then write something in regular ink between the lines. You don't have to write anything special, but something that won't arouse suspicion in case your man gets caught. If you're using Mussa, you can write that you want him to bring you two lambs for the holiday, or something like that."

She nodded her head to indicate that she understood and he continued speaking like a teacher pleased to have found himself an apt and willing pupil. "But what would happen if your man is captured, the police discover the invisible ink, and then write a provocative letter in order to catch you; or they send us a letter in invisible ink in order to make us think that you wrote it? How can you—and how can we for that matter—verify the authenticity of the letters we receive?"

He waited expectantly for a response. So did she.

"Well," he said, "for this purpose we prepared a special code. It's very simple. You begin the open letter, the one written in ordinary ink, with a specific letter of the alphabet. The open letter you'll receive from us in response will begin with the next letter in the alphabet. Your response to us will begin with the next letter in the alphabet, and so on. You'll have to wrack your brains a little sometimes to come up with a word with the appropriate letter of the alphabet, but it can be done. You will always have to remember the letter of the alphabet that you used before. If the emissary brings you our response and it doesn't begin with the appropriate letter of the alphabet, you'll know that our letter, or maybe even your letter, fell into the hands of the police. Then you have to rely on your own judgment concerning what to do. If possible, get out of Beirut as soon as you can. Do you have any questions?"

She did not. Even so, he repeated his instructions. "I wish we had more time to teach you some serious codes. There's no possibility of your staying here another day or two, is there?"

"No. That would be absolutely impossible."

"Well, then there's nothing we can do. It's obvious that you have to keep the invisible ink and the code a complete secret from everyone, including Mussa. Actually, especially from Mussa."

By noon she could no longer keep her eyes open.

"We're finished," he announced. "The only thing left to do is to give you a code name. Actually that has very little to do with you. It'll be used primarily for our internal reports. But it will be your name for us. How does 'Pearl' suit you?"

"Pearl?" she said, running the word over her tongue as if to test the sound of it. She liked it.

"Fine. I'll order something for you to eat and then I'll get a car to take you back to Metulla. Mussa will be there tonight to take you across the border."

Once again she slept for most of the trip. She even slept for a few hours in the Cedars Hotel while waiting for Mussa. They reached Mussa's house after midnight and his wife got up to give her something to eat. Shula apologized and asked to go straight to bed. If they had let her, she would have fallen asleep there in the chair.

She was still tired the next morning when one of Mussa's daughters knocked on the door and brought in a basin of hot water.

Washed and dressed, she followed the scent of the food cooking in the large kitchen where Mussa sat drinking a cup of steaming liquid from a ceramic cup.

"Good morning," he called, pointing to an empty chair next to him.

His wife turned from the stove and brought Shula a cup of strong dark tea in a small glass.

"We'll be leaving immediately," he said. He added with a satisfied smile, "This time we'll be driving with a friend of mine. Don't be frightened when you see that he's a police officer. He's all right. He's quite well known around here as a ladies' man and no one will be surprised to see a strange woman from Beirut in his car. It'll save you the bother of dressing like a peasant."

The police officer, a middle-aged, heavyset man, arrived and introduced himself. He opened the front door of the car for Shula to sit next to him, and Mussa sat in the back. For the remainder of the trip, however, he ignored Shula completely and spoke only to Mussa. Their conversation made it clear that they were relatives. They discussed the upcoming marriage of a distant cousin and labored over some protracted land dispute between El-Hiam and one of the neighboring villages to the north, Abel a-Saki.

Shula gradually stopped listening and became lost in her own thoughts. She wondered how she would explain her unexpected two-night absence to her husband. She decided to tell him the truth. He would be angry. . . . "Let him be angry," she thought to herself. This sudden indifference to her husband's expected reactions frightened her. "What's happened to me?" she thought in surprise.

She realized that a year had passed since she had crossed the border the first time. She remembered how cold and frightened she had been. And now, a year later, she was wandering across borders, smuggling people, meeting with the heads of intelligence, and riding in the car of a Lebanese police officer who was probably corrupt. . . . She, too, would probably be in a position to buy her way with politicians and army officers in the not too distant future. . . .

She shuddered in fear mingled with pleasure and excitement. She knew one thing for sure: her new career had given meaning to her life. She would never agree to relinquish it and to go back to her old routine as housewife and mother.

A few days after her return to Beirut, Benjamin's predictions came true: Egypt agreed to cease-fire negotiations on the Sinai front. Egyptian and Israeli delegates met at the "Roses" Hotel on the Island of Rhodes. The American statesman Dr. Ralph Bunche acted in the role of U.N. mediator. A month later, on February 24, 1949, a cease-fire agreement was signed between Israel and Egypt.

As was to be expected, Lebanon was the *second* Arab nation to come to terms with Israel. In mid-March cease-fire negotiations between Israel and Lebanon began in the customs house at the border crossing station at Ra's an Naqurah. The negotiations were difficult not because of any terms the Lebanese had presented, but rather because the Israelis refused to relinquish the fourteen Lebanese villages they had conquered in Operation Hiram unless Syria returned Mishmar Hayarden—the only village west of the Jordan River they had managed to conquer. However, when the Israelis realized they could not use Lebanon as a means to pressure Syria, they reconsidered, and on March 23, 1949, the Israel-Lebanon cease-fire agreement was signed at Ra's an Naqurah.

Ten days later Jordan signed a cease-fire agreement with Israel just after the Iraqi army units stationed in Samaria were sent home; and Dr. Ralph Bunche announced that even Syria, the most extreme of the Arab States, had agreed to open negotiations with Israel.

The signing of the Israel-Lebanon cease-fire agreement did much to reduce the tension in Beirut. The Palestinian refugees were beginning to adjust to the idea that the return to their homes would be delayed for an indefinite period. The more enterprising among them, mostly Christians, increased their efforts to start a new life within the framework of the Lebanese economy, many of them with great success. Others became progressively more desperate, but for the time being it was a desperation born of helplessness.

In the spring of 1949, a military coup, headed by Colonel Husni az-Za'im, took place in Damascus, creating a steadily increasing number of Jewish refugees in Beirut. Mussa and his men from El-Hiam could handle neither the numbers of illegals nor the rate at which they had to be smuggled across the border. On more than one occasion when Shula informed him a new group was ready to cross, he gave the evasive reply: "Not this week." He generally would not give reasons for his refusal and Shula never knew if he was involved in more important matters—although they never spoke of it, she knew he performed other services for Israeli intelligence—or if the conditions on the border were not particularly favorable that week.

Once she blurted out in anger: "If that's the case, I'll just have to find another way to smuggle them across the border."

He was not offended and replied, "It would be good for you to develop other channels. It's not a good idea to keep all your eggs in one basket."

This was how Chaim Molcho joined their network.

Molcho was Abu-Jacques's friend. He worked in a Beirut book shop and was the father of nine children. In the days of the Vichy regime he was among the first to join the Gaullist underground and it was he who had convinced Abu-Jacques to join their ranks. After the Allied victory the Free French government awarded him a medal and his picture was published in the newspapers. Since then he had enjoyed good relations with the Maronites in general, and especially

with the officers of the Falanges, whom he had met in the underground. Abu-Jacques had often urged Shula to include Molcho in
their work but she had always fended him off. The fewer who knew
about their activities, she insisted, the better. But now she had to
relent.

Molcho set out for the south where he recruited two of his underground friends, Maurice Hajaj and Selim Tanus. They were both
Christians and professional smugglers. They had "bought" their own
customs and police officers with a share of their profits. Unlike
Mussa neither had any connection with Israeli intelligence. Therefore, all "financial arrangements" were made directly with Shula. It
was she who agreed upon their fee; 175 Lebanese pounds for smuggling an adult and 75 Lebanese pounds for a child. Shula also paid
them directly—after they brought a personal note from Grisha verifying the number of brothers who had arrived safely in the homeland. She had to rely more and more on loans from her husband, and
although she always reimbursed him, he was finding the entire business a source of constant aggravation.

Shula actually preferred to "work" with the two smugglers, whom
she looked upon as "her own." They had been recruited by her and
their allegiance was to her alone. Mussa, on the other hand, had an
independent connection with the Israeli authorities.

Mussa, however, still enjoyed his special status within her organization. He was the sole courier for her intelligence reports, which
were not very frequent of late. Even more than that, though, he was
a friend and guide with whom she could discuss her problems and to
whom she could turn for advice.

One of the problems which concerned her during the summer and
autumn of 1949 was obtaining documents for the illegal Syrian refugees. There were more than one hundred of them hidden in Wadi
Abu-Jamil at any given time, and the chances that they might be
caught by the police were steadily increasing. Baksheesh still held its
powers of persuasion among the local police force in the Wadi, but
there was always the possibility that one of the refugees would be
picked up by a policeman outside of the ghetto, or that he would not
have sufficient money to pay, or that by some strange quirk of fate
which was hardly likely he would encounter a policeman who was
honest. If this was the case and the illegal refugee broke down under
investigation, the whole community would be put in danger and the

entire smuggling network might be exposed. If it were only possible to supply these illegal refugees with documents of their own!

Shula asked Mussa's advice.

"There are places in this world," he replied, "where it is possible to buy children. In Beirut, if you have enough money, you can buy parents."

She quickly adapted to his manner of speaking.

"There's money. Enough to buy very rich parents. But where does one purchase parents?"

"Beirut isn't my territory," he said. "But it always pays to buy from the one who comes to investigate."

"You mean from the chief of the police station in the Wadi?"

"Check it out. Although he won't handle the documents himself, he'll know where you can get them, and if he serves as your middleman, you'll be able to breathe easily."

On October 4, 1949, a bomb exploded in the courtyard of the Alliance School next to the Magen Avraham Synagogue in Wadi Abu-Jamil and three people were killed.

The panic that spread through the Wadi caused many parents to withdraw their children from the Jewish school and enroll them in Christian schools outside the confines of the Jewish ghetto. Shula also fell prey to the increasing panic. She enrolled Yaffa, her oldest daughter, in the French school for girls, and Bertie and Meir, her two oldest sons, in the Catholic school attached to Saint Joseph's Monastery. For weeks following the explosion, she would get up early enough to take her children to school. When calm returned to the Wadi, she allowed them to travel by themselves. The incident also afforded her the opportunity to lay the groundwork for plans she had for her children: she began discussing with her husband and his friends the possibilities of sending their children out of Lebanon. She did not reveal that she had any specific goal in mind. She would merely say, "What kind of future can they look forward to here? The country is becoming more and more Levantine; by the time they're grown Lebanon will be just like Syria and Iraq. Where will they study? What will they do?"

At first Joseph was not particularly eager to hear these outbursts. His mother and sister were even more adamant. But although Shula did not insist upon the immediate emigration of her children, she never allowed the subject to be forgotten. Whenever Joseph would return home from the *suk* angry over a minor argument he had with one of his neighbors, or after having been insulted because of his religion by an irritated customer, Shula would immediately challenge him: "And here is where you want to raise your children?"

The subject of the illegal Jewish refugees from Syria gave her no respite. After an extremely active period during which all three of her smugglers were taking groups across the border two or three times a week, the entire operation came to a standstill. Mussa explained: "The garrison in Bint Jubail has been replaced. New men are like a new broom—They sweep strongly. Give them a little time to settle."

It took almost the entire winter for the garrison to settle and for the traffic of refugees across the border to be resumed.

Spring returned.

While making her preparations for Passover, Shula took advantage of the holiday spirit and stepped up her fund-raising activities among the Jewish merchants in the *suk*, prepared two groups of refugees for the journey south, one group with Mussa the other with Maurice Hajaj, attended an end-of-semester parents' meeting at her older daughter's school, and nursed her husband, who had fallen ill. Through all this, however, the reminder Mussa had brought her from the Israeli side of the border kept gnawing at her: "Our friends are inquiring about the other subject they spoke to you about."

Impatience seethed inside her. She resented her family and housework; they were millstones around her neck. Even so, she never wanted to be entirely free of this burden. She found herself relying more and more on Nazira's assistance with the housework and the children.

Something else was disturbing her as well: she was beginning to lose some of her self-confidence. Everything was going too well. She was having premonitions that her luck would change for the worse. She told herself: it can't go on like this. Something bad is going to happen.

Then one evening a week after Passover Chaim Molcho burst into her house pale and frightened. It was ten o'clock at night and everyone else in the house had already gone to bed.

"There's trouble!" he exclaimed, standing at the door. "The Assyrian guide who works for Hajaj, was caught."

Seeing her color change, he quickly added, "They made it across safely. He was caught on his way back."

She was relieved. If that was the case, it was Hajaj's problem. He was responsible for his own men. Molcho continued nervously, "You don't understand! He had a letter for you in his hand when he was caught."

"What kind of a letter?"

"How do I know? Hajaj called me. He doesn't know either. He hasn't been able to see his man yet. But he knows that your name appears on the letter. It could be one of the regular "receipts" that Grisha is always sending you, or he might have added something important this time. At any rate, Hajaj is positive that your name is mentioned in the letter."

Her mind began to work furiously. She thought she heard her husband's footsteps, but his pajama-clad, sleepy-eyed figure did not appear in the doorway. "Just let him sleep!" she thought to herself. She admonished Molcho firmly: "Calm down! Let's think this over rationally. What else did Hajaj tell you?"

"That it was the work of informers. He thinks the Palestinian Office in Beirut was behind it. The soldiers that set up the ambush weren't from the garrison of Bint Jubail. They came from Beirut. The Assyrian was also brought to Beirut for questioning. Hajaj is afraid that he'll open his mouth. He called to tell me that they might be coming for us any time."

"Just a minute, what does the Assyrian know? Does he know you? He doesn't know me, I'm sure of that."

"Yes, he's seen me a couple of times. When I brought a group to the south. And I'm sure he's heard of you. Hajaj and I have spoken about you in front of him."

"But you always referred to me as *Um-Ibrahim*, right? You never used my full name I hope. . . . So the Assyrian knows about you and Hajaj. We don't have to worry about Hajaj; he'll find the right people to get him out of this mess. The question is, will they get to you or not."

Her tranquil voice calmed Molcho. He was sitting opposite her.

"If they come for you, it'll either be tonight or at the latest tomorrow morning," she continued, trying to suppress the fear rising inside her and to think rationally and logically. "It's a pity we don't have enough time to smuggle you across the border. It wouldn't be possible to get your entire family out at such short notice. So if they come for you, what could they possibly have against you? Probably nothing. Try to deny everything. If you have no other choice, admit to having smuggled a few Jews across the border. Say that they're relatives of yours from Syria and that you had to help them. Just don't panic. At worst you can get a few months in prison for smuggling Jews, if we can't get you freed before the trial."

Molcho calmed down and left, but Shula could not sleep.

The next morning, a young army officer accompanied by two gendarmes arrived at Shula's house. The children had already left for school. Joseph was at the shop and she was at home alone with Carmela.

"Madame Cohen-Kishak?" the officer asked politely at the door. "I've been ordered to bring you to the *Sûreté Générale* for questioning. Can you come with us immediately?"

She did not ask the reason for their sudden presence in her house.

"Come in," she said, turning to the officer and motioning him to enter. "It will take a few minutes for me to dress and ask the neighbor to watch my baby. Would you like a cup of coffee?"

He answered, "No, thank you," and sat on the sofa. The two gendarmes remained standing. She asked permission to dress and locked herself in the bathroom where she quickly emptied the invisible ink into the sink. She dressed quickly but carefully, put on her makeup, did her hair, and then one of the soldiers accompanied her downstairs to Nazira's apartment on the first floor.

"Could you come up to watch Carmela until I return? I've been asked to go down to police headquarters. . . ." She knew that Nazira would repeat every word she said to Joseph. "Actually I may be there a long time. Could you also cook dinner for my family?"

Nazira adopted Shula's cool, businesslike tone. "It will be all right. Don't worry. Come back soon."

A crowd of curious spectators stood around the black Peugeot bearing the familiar police license plates that was parked in front of Shula's building. When Shula sat down next to one of the soldiers in the back seat, a faint murmur went through the crowd. Shula knew: in a few minutes the entire Wadi would be buzzing with the news of her arrest.

The Man
from the Sûreté

From the very first Shula had known that she might someday be arrested. But the thought did not frighten or plague her. She knew that it could happen, but she never believed it would. Now it had.

She thought about everything Molcho had said the night before, particularly about her name being mentioned in the letter that had been found with the guide. It was impossible, she decided: Grisha was too experienced to do anything so irresponsible. But, what if? She made her decision: she would deny everything. If her name really did appear on the letter, they would not believe her; but it would be her word against what some unknown person on the other side of the border allegedly wrote. A good lawyer could tear that "evidence" to shreds. . . .

A good lawyer. . . . It was eleven o'clock. Within half an hour the news of her arrest would reach the *suk* and Joseph would rush to a lawyer. More probably, however, he would be very concerned, but he would not do anything but wait until noon, the hour he usually closed the shop. He would then go to his mother and sister or one of his acquaintances for advice, and finally, in the late afternoon or more likely evening, he would come to the conclusion that he would have to bring his shame out into the open and he would go to speak to Albert Iliya. Therefore, there was no possibility that Shula would have a lawyer before the following morning. She was filled with impatience with her husband. She was fond of him and admired some of his qualities, but at that moment she would have preferred that he were made of stronger stuff.

She turned her attention to the young officer sitting beside her.

"Would you happen to know why they're interested in seeing me at the *Sûreté?*" she asked, trying to give her voice a nonchalant tone.

He looked at her, smiling. "Really, madame, don't tell me that you don't know. Your accomplice has admitted everything."

"My accomplice?" she said incredulously.

"Yes. The old Jew. What's his name?"

Molcho? Broken already? She couldn't believe it.

At the *Sûreté* they led her down seemingly endless corridors until they reached the office of the secret police on the second floor.

An attractive man of about thirty-five was sitting behind a large desk. He had intelligent brown eyes, brown hair, and a thin moustache. He was wearing a brown suit and a matching silk shirt and tie, probably Italian. A scrupulous dresser, she thought, but it was his face that disturbed her. She was certain that she knew him, that they had met before, but she could not remember where. A wooden plaque stood on his desk with his name written in Arabic and French: Major George Anton. His name did not mean anything to her.

Her thoughts, however, turned to the man sitting in front of the desk: Chaim Molcho. The collar of his striped shirt was wrinkled, his tie was loose, and his thin white hair fell over his forehead. From the vanquished look on his face she knew immediately: he had confessed.

An old sergeant with two rows of decorations on his police uniform stood behind Molcho.

The lieutenant who had led her into the room saluted and left, shutting the door behind him. The man sitting behind the desk rose and politely pointed to an empty chair.

"Madame," he said graciously, "I am George Anton. Please be seated."

He sat down again: "Do you know this man sitting here?"

Without looking in Molcho's direction she responded:

"Certainly. He's one of my neighbors and acquaintances."

Anton motioned to the sergeant, who opened a side door. An unshaven man about forty years old, with a moustache, wearing brown woolen breeches and a vest, entered the room. She guessed his identity: the Assyrian guide.

"And do you know this man?" Anton inquired.

"I've never seen him before in my life," she replied immediately.

"Well, we arrested him crossing into Lebanon from Israel with a letter allegedly addressed to you, madame."

He threw a wrinkled piece of paper on the desk and moved it in her direction. "Here, read it. It's written in Hebrew."

A quick glance at the paper was enough for her. It was one of Grisha's "receipts." It also said: "1500 British pounds to cover the last bill will be delivered in the usual manner. Good luck." Nothing else. Her name did not appear on the letter.

"I don't know how to read Hebrew," she mumbled.

"Madame!" he raised his voice, "we are well aware of the fact that you were born in Jerusalem."

"I can only read block letters like the ones in the prayer book."

He gave a sign and the sergeant removed Molcho and the guide from his office.

When they were alone in the room, he smiled at her. It was a friendly smile and not the sarcastic grin of a hunter watching an animal squirm in a trap. He said, "I knew we would meet again, ever since the first time I saw you."

"Ever since you saw me?" she repeated in astonishment.

"You don't remember me? At the last parents' meeting at the Saint Joseph School. I sat right behind you."

He laughed pleasurably at the surprised expression on her face.

"Yes, my son Phillip studies with your son Albert. My daughter Annette is in the same class as your daughter Yaffa. They're even friends. It's a strange world isn't it?"

"Your face looked familiar," she said softly, trying to adjust herself to the friendly atmosphere he was creating, "but I couldn't recall from where." She continued as if she were talking to herself, "It's so strange that we should meet here, at the headquarters of the secret police. . . ."

"Why, I was sure that we would meet here," he said in a more serious but gentle and relaxed tone. "Don't you understand, Madame Cohen? We've heard a great deal about you."

She was suddenly gripped with fear. Yet an inner voice convinced her that this man did not intend to do her any harm. She did not have enough time to analyze her intuition fully.

He continued, "Look, Madame Cohen. We caught the Assyrian with that letter and he led us to Molcho who points to you as his leader. What do you have to say?"

There was no doubt. Molcho had confessed. She began to think furiously. All that so-called charisma, a war hero, a man with experience in the French underground. . . . But she couldn't permit herself the luxury of languishing in her disappointment. "I have to get out of this," she said to herself. "I have to lie."

"Call in Molcho," she said, sounding somewhat outraged, "and I will prove to you that I have nothing to do with this entire affair."

He pressed a button on his desk. The side door opened immediately and the sergeant appeared. "Bring the Jew in," Anton ordered.

When Molcho was brought before her, she looked straight at him and cried, "Are you crazy? What kind of business are you trying to get me involved in?"

He avoided her angry glance. Anton interceded gruffly. "Madame Cohen denies everything you have said. What do you have to say for yourself now?"

Molcho turned to face Shula. "Didn't I bring letters from Israel in the past? Didn't we smuggle Jews to Israel together?"

"You're out of your mind. You never brought me any letters." She turned to the major. "*Monsieur le Commandant*, could I have a few words with you in private?"

When Molcho was removed, she said in an embarrassed tone, "Look, monsieur, I don't know exactly how to put this. . . . Molcho is an old Jew. He has nine children to take care of and he recently lost his job. My husband is a wealthy man. We wanted to help him, but without embarrassing him into taking charity. So every week when my husband went to the *suk* to do the Sabbath shopping, he bought for the Molcho family as well. That's how Molcho began coming to my home. But one day when the two of us were alone in the house, he got a bit fresh. He started behaving in the way a man should not behave toward a married woman. I threw him out of the house. Perhaps this is his way to get revenge. . . ."

She was sure that Anton did not believe a word she had said. Yet he did not refute her.

"We'll have to investigate everything you've said. You may go home now. I'll want to see you again. Don't leave Beirut."

She turned to move, but he stopped her. "Wait. Don't go alone. I'll send someone with you." He ordered his driver to take Madame Cohen home.

The news of the arrest of Shula Kishak-Cohen and Chaim Molcho spread through the Wadi like lightning. The news of Shula's being released and returned home in the chauffeured car of a high-ranking police officer spread with the same speed. Joseph, who was at his mother's as Shula had guessed he would be, immediately came running.

"Are you all right?" he called out at the door. "Did they do anything to you?"

She had never seen him so upset. Only after her repeated assurances that she was all right and no harm had come to her did he regain sufficient composure to ask about Molcho.

"He's being detained," she answered curtly. "He'll probably be brought to trial."

"We have to help his family then," he answered. He was frightened again. "Do you see? Maybe you'll stop now? Think of your children."

She had already decided to halt the network's smuggling activities for the time being, until everything cleared up. She waited for Mussa to come. She wanted to send a report to Israel about Molcho's arrest and explain her decision to put a temporary halt to the smuggling. She continually reminded herself that this cessation of activities was merely temporary. She was not willing even to consider the possibility of ever again living the life of a bored Beirut housewife.

But Mussa stopped coming. It was as though he knew what had taken place and feared that her house was under surveillance.

Two afternoons a week she would report to Major Anton's office for interrogation.

She returned home from the first investigation surprised and confused. Anton received her politely and repeated the same questions
he had asked previously. She realized he was not even listening to
her answers. He rang for the sergeant and ordered coffee and when it
arrived, the coffee was brought not to his large desk but to a small
coffee table in the corner where they sat in two facing armchairs. He
continued to treat her with the utmost courtesy, but it appeared that
the investigation had been concluded. They talked about everyday
matters and he tried to steer the conversation to their "common
interest," their children. Their conversation was so free and relaxed
that Shula had entirely forgotten where she was and the circumstances that had brought her there.

Until she rose to leave. He said to her, "I'll want to see you again
on Thursday. You remember my warning not to leave Beirut?"

She was filled with ominous fear: During the ride home—he again
sent her home in his official car—as well as for the next few days
until their following appointment, she kept reviewing their conversation over in her mind. She could not come up with any clear or
logical picture. "He's playing cat and mouse with me," she thought
to herself.

As the day of their meeting approached, she became more and
more nervous. On Thursday morning she awoke with a severe headache and took sedatives all day. But as the hour of their meeting
approached, she put on her best dress and made herself up carefully.

The third investigation was exactly like the second, a quarter hour
of the same questions and answers and then a relaxed conversation
over a cup of coffee. When she felt sufficiently comfortable to dismiss
her fears, she found Anton a pleasant and entertaining conversationalist and she made every effort to be the same. She would match each of
his witty remarks with an appropriate comment or proverb of her
own. But she could never totally free herself of the questions: What
does he want from me? Where is all this leading?

One day her children told her they were called to the principal's
office where they had been questioned by a strange man. He had
asked about their home life, the people who came to visit their
mother, and the things their mother did. She was more angry than
frightened. During her next "investigation" she taunted Anton. "I
didn't know you adopted communist methods, turning children
against their own mother."

He apologized. "I wasn't the one who ordered it. It was my assistant. I didn't like the idea, but I had to go along so I wouldn't be accused of showing any partiality toward you. I'm sorry. It won't happen again."

Convinced by his honesty, she began to reappraise the relationship that had been developing between them, looking for hidden meanings behind his words. She reached the conclusion that the investigation was merely a pretext. But she still could not decide: was he interested in her as a woman or in her connections with Israel?

Her self-confidence returned. She found an excuse to go to her husband's shop and stopped off at Abu-Jacques's stall on the way.

"I want you to go to El-Hiam and make contact with Shukry Mussa. Tell him I think we can renew our border crossings. If he agrees, we'll begin at once."

"What about Molcho? And what about you? Aren't you under investigation?"

"Yes. Therefore, we'll have to be very careful. Tell Mussa that for the time being he isn't to come to my house. You'll be my contact with him. And we'll temporarily stop working with Tanus and Hajaj."

The illegal border crossings were resumed at a very slow pace, one or two families a week. Mussa's truck no longer came to the Wadi. Instead, the refugees were taken by taxi to one of the dirt roads east of Beirut near the airport where a truck would be waiting. The truck continued in an eastward direction toward Syria before turning south on a small road that later was to become famous as one of the supply lines for the Palestinian terrorists in "Fatahland." The road wound between mountains and passed near the villages of Abel a-Saki and El-Hiam before it reached the border.

Meanwhile her twice-weekly meetings with George Anton continued, but she no longer felt any fear. It was certain that the officer from the secret police wanted something from her, but she grew increasingly more confident that he meant her no harm.

She was shocked, therefore, when he told her, "I'm obliged to bring your case before the military court."

"But why?" The words came out unexpectedly. "You only have Molcho's word against mine."

He was silent for a moment and then said, "That's the very reason. My influence is strong enough in the military court to ensure that you'll be tried only on the basis of that evidence. Many other things can influence the civilian courts."

It took her a minute or two to understand: he was trying to help her. This was the first time he openly implied his readiness to assist her. But why?

She asked about Molcho.

"He'll be tried along with you."

"He's putting pressure on the community to hire a lawyer."

"Yes, I know. You'll also need a lawyer. But perhaps it would be better if you wait. When you find out who'll be sitting on the bench, you'll be able to choose a lawyer more wisely."

"How will I find out?"

"I'll let you know."

She was grateful. Every judge had a circle of friends and "generous followers" among the community of lawyers, and advance knowledge of the judge sitting on the bench at one's trial was considered halfway to an acquittal.

However, after a few more meetings Anton announced, "We've decided not to bring your case to trial."

"You couldn't find anything against me. I told you!"

"I didn't say that. I decided not to bring charges against you."

He rang the bell for coffee, which was a sign for them to move to the small table in the corner where they could sit next to each other without his large desk separating them. He turned to her and said, "Look, Madame Cohen. I've been interrogating you for more than three months and now we are finished. But I feel that a continuation of our relationship would be beneficial. I am willing to help you even though I imagine that you have connections with Israel."

As hard as she tried, she could not keep her face from turning pale. She lost her breath. "It's a trap," she said to herself. In her confusion she paid no attention to his opening words. All her thoughts focused on the latter part of his statement.

"What do you mean?" she stammered. "You said yourself that my case has been closed because you can't prove I had any connections with Israel. Maybe Molcho does. Why don't you ask him?"

He stared at her for a long time and said sadly, "It will take time before you begin to trust me. But I'm sure it will come."

She stood up and collected her purse. When she was at the door he said, "I no longer have any pretext to force you to come, but I would be very happy if we could continue to meet."

She stood silently for a moment with her hand on the door. Then she said quietly, "So would I."

She told no one of the decision not to bring her case to court. She felt more guilty about this than about agreeing to continue seeing George Anton. She suppressed her feelings of guilt, however, by telling herself that it was for Chaim Molcho's sake that she continued to visit the *Sûreté* office twice weekly.

Two weeks later Anton told Shula the name of the judge who would preside at Molcho's and the Assyrian guide's trial, and gave her a list of lawyers from whom it would be worthwhile choosing.

A week later he said, "I spoke with the judge. It will be impossible to give him less than a year."

He saw the disappointment on her face and quickly added, "It's not so terrible. By the time the trial begins, he'll already have been in for five months. He'll get a third off for good behavior. He'll be left with only two or three months."

She wanted to thank him, but he would not let her. "Wait. There's still another problem. The day he's released from prison he has to be taken out of the country. The Palestinians know that he worked for Israel and they're beginning to organize. If he stays here, they'll murder him. Will you be able to arrange his departure?"

An alarm bell went off inside her, but this time it rang rather softly. In a sudden decision she decided to ignore it and rely instead on her woman's intuition.

"I'll try," she said, avoiding all the denials that were on the tip of her tongue, "but his family has to be consulted. He'd never agree to go without them."

That very evening she met with Molcho's wife and eldest son and explained: "Before I speak with him, I have to know if you're willing to go to Israel. You have to be sure of one thing. You won't be able to stay in Lebanon."

It was not very difficult to convince them. When she met with Molcho—George Anton obtained special permission for her to visit him in prison—he also readily agreed. Anton was waiting for her in his car outside and when informed that Molcho and his family had agreed, he said, "Good. Then the trial will take place tomorrow." It was as though he had delayed the trial until this complication had been cleared up.

Molcho did receive a year's sentence. (The Assyrian guide received two years). A little more than two months later, on the eve of the Jewish New Year, he was released, and without even returning home he was driven in a police vehicle directly to the border post at Ra's an Naqurah. He had the privilege of being the first Jew to cross the border there since the state of Israel had been established.

That same evening the rest of the Molcho family crossed the border. It was a "luxurious crossing." Mussa's truck picked them up in front of their house in Wadi Abu-Jamil, with all of their possessions, and drove directly to the border fence at Metulla. The fence was opened and the truck drove through and down the main street of Metulla. There the family and all their household belongings were transferred to another truck which drove to Haifa where Chaim Molcho was awaiting them. The Lebanese truck returned to El-Hiam, the border fence was sealed, and the Lebanese garrison, which had been detained in Bint Jubail by military order the entire evening, was ordered to continue its regular night patrols.

Chaim Molcho's trial and particularly the verdict, which George Anton had predicted in advance, convinced Shula of the extent of his power and influence.

He constantly occupied her thoughts. She relived each visit over and over in her mind, pondering everything he had said in search of a clue that might explain the meaning of his attitude toward her. Her feminine pride told her he was attracted to her as a woman and was courting her favors. But there was nothing in his overt behavior which would indicate this. He was polite and formal and would address her only as "Madame Cohen." She would sometimes ask herself if this feeling that he desired her was not merely an echo of a secret wish that came from within herself. Her self-confidence was on the rise. She was sure that he would continue to protect her as he had in the Molcho affair. Reassured by these feelings, she immediately resumed operations with Maurice Hajaj and Selim Tanus.

During the last two months of the summer of 1950 more than four hundred Syrian Jewish refugees were smuggled into Israel. For the first time some members of the Beirut Jewish community chose to join them. They were mostly young people who were tired of living as a minority when there was a dynamic sovereign Jewish state across the border. The emigration of these youths caused an uproar in the community and many people spoke against "that woman who incited the youth to rebel and who will only bring trouble on all of our heads." But there were others who praised Shula's activities.

As a result of Molcho's release and passage to Israel and the two-day Jewish New Year, which coincided with the Sabbath, Shula did not see George Anton for more than a week. When Monday, one of their regular meeting days at his office, arrived, Shula was surprised at her excitement. She had allowed herself to think that he was the one who initiated, or even forced, their meetings. She was often annoyed with the way she had to adapt her schedule, or even lie, in order to justify her frequent absences from home. For some reason she had not revealed to her family the fact that she was still seeing the Sûreté officer. Now that Molcho had been tried and released, she no longer had any pretext to continue their meetings. Joseph never interfered with her activities and he was always at the shop when she would report to the Sûreté. But the older children, Yaffa and Bertie, were aware of her frequent absences, and despite the fact that they had learned that "mother has important things to do," this did not prevent them from complaining and asking awkward questions.

Therefore, Shula expected that she would be relieved that there had been a break in their weekly meetings. She discovered, however, that she missed them, and this discovery confused and upset her.

He pretended not to notice her embarrassment. He took her hands in both of his, led her to the armchair in the corner, and rang for coffee.

"Have a healthy and happy New Year," he greeted her with the traditional New Year's blessing. "How was your holiday?"

She was annoyed at the banality of his question.

"Just like all the other holidays. I spent it in the kitchen," she complained. "I can't even begin to count the number of meals I served during the last few days."

"Is that a rebellious tone I hear?" he noted with a grin. "I've been led to think that Jewish women make marvelous wives. Some of my father's friends married Jewish women and they still bless the day they made their choice."

"Good for them. I . . . I sometimes find being a housewife a burden. Don't misunderstand me, I appreciate my husband and love my children and am proud of my home. But being trapped behind four walls can be very depressing."

"Please don't tell me that you have no other areas of interest."

The words were said with such emphasis that she looked at him, expecting him to continue. When she saw that he had finished speaking, she said sharply, "I thought we agreed that I wasn't involved in those areas of interest. If you don't think so, why do you continue seeing me?"

He looked at her for a moment or two in silence before saying, "Because in addition to the fact that you're a beautiful and attractive woman, I'm sure you're working for Israel."

This open declaration, as opposed to the veiled hints he had used so many times before, frightened her. She was quick to protest, but his raised hand put an end to the familiar denials that had been on the tip of her tongue.

"Please, I'm not accusing you. On the contrary, I believe that connections with Israel might be beneficial. But," he continued with a smile, "don't ever repeat what I've just said. I would deny it. We have no other choice but to conceal our true thoughts."

She was completely confused. She knew he was trying to tell her something, but she needed more time to interpret his words rationally. She prefered to take refuge in her femininity.

"Would you also deny saying that I'm a beautiful woman?" she asked provocatively.

"Never. But I would deny telling you that the Syrians have a file on you."

She stared at him in shock. He continued speaking with a calm, forced indifference. "We maintain good relations with the Syrians. We sometimes exchange information. Not too long ago they requested some information about you. Why, only this week I sent them my reply: that we were unable to find any incriminating or suspicious information about you."

She returned his stare and mumbled, "I'm very grateful. How can I thank you?"

"By agreeing to have a cup of coffee with me."

"By all means, but we're drinking coffee."

"No, not here. Tomorrow evening I have to be in Zahle—some unimportant matter that shouldn't take more than a few minutes. I have to meet a certain man. I would be very pleased if you would agree to accompany me."

She feigned reluctance.

"We'll only have dinner and return to Beirut immediately," he pleaded. "You'll be home by ten. Please."

She agreed.

By the time she arrived home Joseph was already there.

"Mussa was here again asking for you," he said in a reproachful tone.

"The father or the son?" she asked. Mussa's eldest son, Mahmud, had begun to play a more active role in his father's activities.

"The father," was Joseph's reply. "He said he would be back later."

"Thank you. By the way, tomorrow I have to go to the mountains. A meeting has been arranged for me with the head of the Syrian smuggling ring. I'll be back late. It's important," she added in an apologetic tone.

"Of course," he taunted ironically. "Your whole life is spent doing important deeds. . . ."

She felt the bitterness in his voice. "He feels neglected," she told herself. "I'll have to pay more attention to him. But not now . . ." Now she wanted to be alone and think about her trip to Zahle.

Joseph had already gone to bed, and the children were in their rooms by the time Mussa arrived. He had only come to bring one of the "receipts" for "brethren who arrived safely" as well as money with which to reimburse her husband. She counted the money, which was in British five-pound notes, served tea, and asked casually, "Does the name George Anton mean anything to you?"

He sat up straight in his chair. "What do you have to do with him?"

"He's the detective who was in charge of Molcho's case. He also interrogated me."

"He's no detective, he's from intelligence, *Le Deuxième Bureau.*" The last three words, said in French, sounded very awkward coming from him.

She was surprised. "But he has an office in the *Sûreté.*"

"It's only a cover. He's from military intelligence, although I hear that his primary concern is internal security."

"What kind of a man is he?"

He considered for a moment. "I've never met him. I've only heard about him. They say he's a rising star in the intelligence service. Very sharp, but surprisingly decent and fair. He's close to the president, but he maintains good relations with Camille Chamoun as well, which shows you how sharp he is . . . and young. He will probably go far. Why do you ask?"

She shrugged her shoulders. "It's interesting. . . ."

They left Beirut at four o'clock in the afternoon.

The heat of the day was beginning to subside. As they began ascending the mountain road that led to Damascus, she could feel a slight chill on her bare arms. She reached back for her light suit jacket and placed it casually over her shoulders.

He quickly looked over in her direction.

"Are you cold?"

"No. Just a little chilly. It's refreshing after being in Beirut the whole summer."

He drove along in silence, his eyes fixed on the road. The silence made her feel uncomfortable. He left her alone with her thoughts, which she tried to avoid by concentrating on the passing scenery.

"It's pretty here," she said blandly. He answered without taking his eyes off the road.

"Yes, but it's even nicer in the spring. Then the poppy fields are in bloom. You know that this is the land of hashish. Everyone who lives in the mountain region up to Baalbek, or even further north, makes his living by growing hashish. And they make a very good living."

"And what do your police do about it?" she teased. She wanted to begin a light conversation so she could escape her thoughts. But an unintentional critical tone crept into her voice.

"Absolutely nothing," he admitted honestly. "Hashish brings Lebanon over forty million sterling a year and thousands of Lebanese make their living from it. But what's probably more important, you can find some of the most important people in the country among the growers. You'd be surprised to hear how many of the best families in Lebanon owe their wealth to hashish."

"Yes, but it is against the law."

He shrugged his shoulders.

"The law exists so that we can live with it. The hashish doesn't do us any harm. There must be something about our race. For hundreds, maybe even thousands of years we've grown hashish without ever becoming habituated to it. Not like the Egyptians . . . but that's their problem."

"And opium? People don't get addicted to opium here?"

"Opium is something else. But we don't produce opium in Lebanon. We get it from Turkey and export it from here. It's true that the same people who deal with hashish also smuggle opium."

"Then why don't you take any action against them because of the opium?"

He smiled, as if to himself. "It's not easy, because they're the ones who control the hashish market. It's big business, an entire industry with trademarks and the works. Every one of the hashish gangs has its own private army, and all the farmers here in the mountains are their allies. It's interesting. All the various gangs compete with each other, they even fight each other, but the moment they smell the police they all unite as one. Just like your men Hajaj and Tanus."

Shula was immediately put on her guard.

"What Tanus?" she said sharply.

He chuckled quietly.

"The one you paid thirty-five hundred pounds last week."

She was shocked into silence. She quickly regained her composure and hoped her sarcasm would conceal her discomfort and confusion. "You speak with the assurance of a man who may have received a kickback."

He drove the car to the side of the road and slowly came to a stop. Only then did he turn to Shula.

"I want you to know that I'm not interested in his money," he said softly, "just as I don't want him to play any part in what I hope will be between us."

She tried to meet his glance, but quickly lowered her eyes.

"How do your children feel to be back in school?" she said, changing the subject.

He answered immediately but unwillingly.

"It's not a problem, Madame Cohen," he said coolly. "They're good students, although not as good as your children. . . ."

They didn't go to Zahle. He stopped the car in front of one of the best restaurants on the main street of the resort town of Behmadon.

She had heard of the restaurant during the summers she had spent in the town, but had never eaten there.

"We'll eat here," he announced.

"And what about Zahle?"

"I'll call and cancel my meeting."

"Why?"

"Because I want to talk to you and I want you to trust me. And trust can only come when two people sit down and look in each other's eyes, and not when they're on the road."

Shula was filled with excitement when they entered the half-empty restaurant. It's time for his confession, she told herself, pleased and anxious. For weeks she had known that it would come, but now that the moment had arrived, she was not sure how she would react.

He concentrated on ordering their meal. Despite her protests he ordered an entire dinner of assorted Oriental salads, fish, and chicken stuffed with almonds and pistachio nuts. They picked at their food with apparent indifference. They hardly spoke. He seemed lost in his thoughts and she appeared impatient. Somewhere at the back of her head the thought that this was the first time she was eating nonkosher gnawed at her. She told herself that it was un-important, yet, unconsciously, she skipped the chicken, nibbling only the stuffing.

Only when the coffee and dessert arrived was he ready to speak his mind.

"Look," he said cautiously, trying not to frighten her. "We're both involved in the same business. The difference is you have more nerve and I have more experience. The two of us together could make a perfect couple."

She turned his words over in her mind angrily. He was being ambiguous again! What was he really trying to say? Was he trying to get her into bed or use her to establish contact with Israel? Perhaps he was still trying to set a trap for her?

She remained silent. He sighed audibly.

"I see that you still don't trust me. All right, finish your coffee and we'll go. I'll show you to what lengths I'm willing to go in order to establish our relationship on a basis of trust. I'm going to take you to the place where the Lebanese army's new central ammunition ar-senals are going to be built."

She was relieved and disappointed, and then she thought to her-self, "They're never going to believe this in Israel . . ."

They drove off the main road and after riding for half an hour on a winding, narrow dirt road, he stopped the car. "This is the place," he said.

"Here? But there's nothing here at all."

"True. But there will be. And you know this before a lot of our top officers. The tender is going to be announced next week."

They rode most of the way back to Beirut in silence. When she saw the lights of Beirut, Shula said, "With your knowledge and what you call my 'nerve' we could really be a perfect couple. But the people who should be hearing your information would probably be interested in hearing it from its source. Don't you think it would be worth your while to meet them yourself?"

He smiled at her. "I see you're convinced. I'm pleased. But no. In principle I'm willing, but it's still too early. At the moment I'm only interested in meeting with you."

He stopped the car a short distance from Wadi Abu-Jamil. When Shula turned to get out of the car, he suddenly leaned over and kissed her on the cheek.

"After all," he laughed embarrassedly, "we are the perfect couple."

She spent a long time writing the report she would send to Israel via Shukry Mussa. But just as she finished, the expressions on Benjamin's and Gingi's faces flashed into her mind. They'd be astonished by her success and would say, "An achievement like this was worth waiting for. . . ."

Then she made her decision: she wanted to hear them say it with her own ears. She deserved it.

She tore her report to pieces and burnt it until it was reduced to a pile of ashes.

Then she wrote, "There have been some very important developments which demand a direct report."

Meeting in Istanbul

8 Shula was surprised when the car from Metulla stopped in front of the "Green House." It was almost two years since her last visit, but nothing had changed. Only a sentry box had been added at the narrow entrance of the heavy stone wall that surrounded the building. The neighborhood, however, had changed completely. In the winter of 1948 Jaffa was a conquered city, almost entirely devoid of civilians and with barbed-wire fences surrounding structures requisitioned for military units. Now the entire area was populated. She counted scores of new stores, simple in appearance, with signs in at least half a dozen languages. Wash was hanging out to dry from every balcony and the streets were filled with children. The town was teeming with life.

The people looked poor. The men were dressed in workclothes or in the remnants of military uniforms; the women wheeled baby carriages down the street or rushed about obviously pregnant. An outdoor market had been set up about one hundred yards from the house. She could hear the peddlers screaming out their wares: vegetables, fruits, secondhand clothes. Jaffa had been transformed into a city of new immigrants with a population of about fifty thousand: survivors of death camps with numbers tattooed on their arms, people who had been collected from refugee camps that had sprung up throughout Europe after the war, tens of thousands of Bulgarian Jews who, upon hearing the news of the establishment of the Jewish state, emigrated *en masse* to Israel, and thousands of Romanian Jews who were part of the large-scale wave of immigration that inundated Israel during its first years of existence. Living alongside them were about five thousand Arabs who had not abandoned their city when it surrendered to the Jewish forces.

New procedures had been set up in the "Green House." The casual atmosphere was lost. Now, after giving her name to the sentry, Shula had to wait on the paved path until a woman soldier in a starched skirt appeared and motioned her to follow. A wooden counter had been added to the front room where another woman soldier sat and recorded Shula's name and her time of arrival in a thick black notebook. The first soldier led Shula to Benjamin's office. It was still at the end of the corridor on the second floor.

She glanced quickly around the room. The elegant wooden closet had been replaced by a metal filing cabinet with a prominent lock, and curtains had been hung over the window. Benjamin rushed toward her and embraced her warmly.

"It's good to see you," he said sincerely. "We were very worried about you a few months ago. . . . Come, sit down." He led her to a straight-backed chair and stood in front of her. "I spoke with Molcho after he arrived. He wasn't able to explain how you managed to free yourself from the whole business without being tried. But he knows that he was let off easily because of you. The same with his passage to Israel. I must tell you, when the U.N. observers told us to be at Ra's an Naqurah to pick up a Jew whom the Lebanese authorities were deporting, we were quite surprised. Tell me, how did you arrange it all?"

His warm greeting confused her a bit.

"How is Molcho?" she asked.

"He's all right. He lives in Tel Aviv. His son is working for a publishing company. Everything is all right. I can arrange a meeting if you like."

She did not reply, but began instead to tell her story. She started with her first meeting with George Anton and ended with the trip to

Zahle and the side trip to Behmadon. When she finished speaking he was pensive.

"Yes, this is a very interesting development. Not the information so much, but the man himself. He has a lot of possibilities. Why do you think he helped you? Is he attracted to you?"

She felt herself blush behind the ears but tried to maintain a note of cool, professional indifference in her tone. "I don't think he's the kind of man who would let that influence his decisions. I believe he's interested in establishing contact with you. Possibly for money or for political considerations. He once hinted at possible common interests between Israel and Lebanon. Perhaps he was referring only to Israel and the Maronites. He's a Maronite Christian himself."

"I understood that. Look, Shula, I would like you to meet the man who's replaced Gingi. He'll be your new contact man. But he's out of town today. Can you stay until tomorrow? It's very important that you speak with him."

The following day Benjamin introduced her to Shimshoni. He was about forty years old, short, slightly plump, and balding. Had it not been for his icy-cold blue-gray eyes, he would have looked like an ordinary shopkeeper.

While seated in his office, Gingi's old room, Shula repeated her story about George Anton. Shimshoni asked her to repeat everything Anton had said during their conversation. She was surprised that she could remember every word he ever said to her—both during the short interrogation period and during their leisurely conversations over coffee.

"Yes," he finally said. "There's no doubt that he can be of great use. Did he ever tell you why he's not willing to meet with us?"

Shula repeated what Anton had told her at their last meeting.

"Keep working on him," Shimshoni advised. "We're very interested in him."

Then he changed the subject to immigration.

"How did you solve the problem of getting false identity cards for the refugees?" he asked.

"We buy them from the police chief in the ghetto," she replied. "You receive the bills."

"Who handles the transactions? You?"

"No. Molcho used to do it and now Abu-Jacques does. But it's not working out. There aren't enough identity cards. But since we began buying them they've almost completely stopped checking in the Wadi. On the other hand, the police chief can also get a fairly clear picture of the number of refugees by the number of identity cards we buy."

"And you don't have any direct contact with him?" he asked.

She was terribly annoyed with his habit of ignoring what she was saying.

"No," she said curtly.

"Good. Keep it that way. We might have to ask you to gradually dissociate yourself from the whole refugee business."

She wanted to protest, but he interrupted.

"It's only a possibility, and if this should be the case, it won't happen for a while yet. I only want you to keep it in mind. Don't get your name too involved with the immigration business. The more you can use other people to handle it the better. Do you have a telephone at home?"

The suddenness with which he changed the subject startled her. She mumbled a confused reply and he recorded her number.

"Now, listen, we'll open a post office box for you in Beirut. Do you know Shlomo Adut's pharmacy near the Saraya?"

She nodded.

"He'll be your post office box. When we want to send you some information without using Mussa, we'll use the pharmacy. They'll call you and tell you that the prescription you ordered is ready and you can come down for it. The message will be on the reverse side of the label. It'll be written in invisible ink. Have you been taught how to use it?"

Shula informed him that she had gotten rid of her ink and the decoding powder when the police came to arrest her.

"You did the right thing. We'll give you some more before you leave. You'll use the post office box to send us messages as well. Write your message on the back of a doctor's prescription. Do you have a passport?"

This sudden switch annoyed her again. "Yes, but I think it may have expired."

"Renew it. That's the first thing you have to do when you get back to Beirut."

"Why?"

"You never know when you might need a passport. Now, I want you to memorize the following telephone number. Don't write it down. Learn it by heart."

He recited a six-digit number. "It's a number in Istanbul. The man who will answer there is called Epstein. He'll be your second contact man, besides me. If you should ever have to leave Beirut in a hurry, fly to Istanbul and get in touch with him. He'll help you. We'll try to arrange a meeting between you in the near future. Will it be a problem for you to fly to Istanbul? Will you be able to find some reasonable excuse?"

She said that her husband imported Turkish lace and she could always say she was going there to represent him.

"Excellent. Now the most important thing you have before you is George Anton. We want him. Do the best you can to get him."

On the ride to Metulla she kept reviewing her conversation with Shimshoni. She thought about the man himself. His icy-cold eyes repulsed her, but she could not help admiring the power he commanded behind his seemingly unimpressive appearance. He's probably much more important than Gingi, she thought to herself. The fact that he would now be her direct superior raised her self-image in her own eyes. It was as though she had been given a higher rank.

For the next few weeks Shula made a conscious effort to return her house to its normal routine. She devoted her afternoons to her children. On several occasions she took the younger ones to the café overlooking the sea, near the Raucha Stone. She paid more attention to her older children, Yaffa, Bertie, and Meir. She helped them with their homework and listened to their stories about school. She also told them about her childhood in Jerusalem. She made a special effort to make them like Israel and they gradually began to think of it as the place where they would someday make their home.

She continued to see George Anton. They stopped meeting in his office. It was his idea and she willingly agreed. Once or twice a week he would pick her up on a street corner and they would ride to a café on the mountain road from Beirut to Damascus or sit on the promenade in the southwest part of the city.

Since kissing her on the cheek he had made no further physical advances. Their relationship, however, was very comfortable and relaxed. They spoke a great deal about their children. Shula told him about her husband and his family, particularly her relations with her mother-in-law and sister-in-law. He never mentioned his wife. They even openly discussed Shula's activities. He knew when a new group of refugees was to be sent to Israel.

Only once did he supply her with information she thought worthy of passing to Israel, but it was not sufficiently important or urgent to use the post office box. It was a detailed account of personnel changes in the Lebanese chief-of-staff's office. At their next meeting he cautiously asked whether his information had reached the proper people.

She replied in the affirmative but took advantage of the opening. "But why does this information have to go through me? You can pass it on directly yourself."

He smiled. "Do you think that would be more lucrative?"

"Anything dealing with remuneration," she answered, "would most definitely have to be worked out directly with them."

He avoided the issue. "Not yet. We'll see."

One day at the end of October the telephone in her house rang.

"Madame Cohen?" an unknown voice asked in French, "this is the Adut Pharmacy."

Her heart began to pound.

"Yes."

"I wanted to inform you that the prescription you ordered is ready."

"Thank you. I'll come by during the day to pick it up."

The delicate-featured, white-haired pharmacist served her himself. When she mentioned her name he put a dark brown medicine bottle on the counter and said with a face devoid of expression, "That will be three pounds. Do you know how to use the medicine? One teaspoonful three times a day. It's written on the label."

She returned home, locked herself in the bathroom, and placed the bottle in water. The label came off effortlessly. She waited for it to dry, spread some of the decoding powder on the reverse side, and a few minutes later yellowish handwritten letters appeared. She read the note quickly:

"Be in Istanbul next Tuesday. Call the number you have."

When she told Joseph she had to go to Istanbul for a day or two, he immediately understood. A look of displeasure crossed his face but he did not object.

It was the first time she had ever been in an airplane. She flew in a

Middle East Airlines DC3 and was very nervous. The three-hour flight was quite pleasant. She conversed with the man sitting next to her, a heavyset American who was with the American University in Beirut who bought her a whiskey and soda. By the time they arrived at the musty and small airport in Istanbul, she felt like a seasoned traveler.

Shula collected her small suitcase. She changed some money, stopped at a public telephone booth, and began dialing.

"This is Shula Cohen," she said in French after hearing a man's voice at the other end of the line.

"Ah, *Geveret* Cohen," was the Hebrew reply. "I'm so glad you could make it. Please wait for me in the airport coffee shop. I'll be there in less than an hour."

Epstein was a chubby man of about fifty with a pleasant voice and constant smile on his spectacled face. In the half-empty coffee shop he was able to pick her out quite easily among the thin, sharp-faced Turks.

"Madame Cohen," he said in French, "I'm so happy to see you." As soon as he sat down he started speaking Hebrew. "How was the flight? How did Istanbul look to you from the air?"

"I'm certain I was not instructed to come to Istanbul to answer questions of this sort," Shula answered with a touch of sarcasm.

He was not offended by her curt reply. "Actually, you were," he answered self-confidently. "The very purpose of your trip was to test the effectiveness of the contact between us. I guess the connections were effective. Oh yes, there's something else: our friends in Israel would be pleased if you could speed up the establishment of contact with your friend. They want you to bring him here, to Istanbul. This is why it was so important to test our lines of communication. When he's ready to come, let us know. Then you'll receive instructions as to when to come."

"And that's all?" she asked angrily.

"Actually yes. Unless you would like to come to my office. You should know where it is in any case."

"And if I wouldn't, could I go straight home?"

"Of course. We'll only have to check on the schedule for the next flight to Beirut. I'll be right back."

When he returned he said, "There's a flight at five. That's another three hours. If you like, we can go to the city, have lunch, and return in time for your flight." They drove to a seafood restaurant on the lower level of the Galata Bridge. Although it was cloudy, it was neither cold nor raining. They ate on the wooden balcony about three feet above the water, observing the heavy traffic on the Golden Horn. There were fishing boats, ferries, an occasional freighter sailing down the strait. The hills of Istanbul, adorned with minarets, seemed to frame this tranquil scene and Shula was captivated by its beauty. Epstein chattered away incessantly and Shula was charmed by his anecdotes. When he said they had better be getting back to the airport, she regretted not having elected to postpone her flight to the following day.

"But I'll be back," she consoled herself, realizing that she might be returning to Istanbul in the company of George Anton.

A week after she returned from Istanbul Shukry Mussa appeared at her house. This time he had not come to pick up a group of refugees or to bring her a letter from Israel. He claimed to be in Beirut visiting his two nephews who were studying at the American University. While talking with his nephews he had come up with an idea that might be of interest to Shula—opening a nightclub in Beirut.

"My nephew found an old café for sale. It's in an excellent location but it is old and run-down and can be bought cheaply. With another modest investment it could also be renovated."

She stared at him in surprise. "But what do I have to do with this? My husband imports textiles; he's not involved in nightclubs."

"You don't understand. A nightclub like this, if it's successful and attracts the right kind of clients, could become an important source for gathering information. A man all decked out to have a good time, with a few drinks under his belt and a beautiful and charming hostess properly trained to entertain him, would reveal all his secrets. My nephew is willing to go to Germany to bring the right kind of hostesses. . . ."

She began to understand and almost laughed out loud. "You mean that Israel should pay for establishing a nightclub in Beirut?" She thought of Shimshoni's face as he read the suggestion in an intelligence report. Once again she had to suppress her laughter.

"Why not?" he protested. "If it's properly run, the investment could be returned in no time and even be a profitable business. Look at the advantages. Anyone can enter a nightclub without arousing the slightest suspicion. It's an ideal meeting place, not to mention the possibilities of making contacts and gathering intelligence. Everybody does it."

"Who's everybody?"

"Syrian intelligence runs several nightclubs and so do the Iraqis and the Egyptians. Even British intelligence has a café. The Russians don't. They run a library."

"The next thing you'll be saying is that we'll have to buy a daily newspaper because the Syrians have one." The idea didn't seem so bad to her, despite the ironic twist to her words. "About how much would the whole thing cost?"

He was encouraged. "About two hundred thousand Lebanese pounds. That would include the rental, renovation, importing the hostesses, and the necessary equipment. It wouldn't include the initial period until the nightclub got on its feet. Here, we figured out all the costs. A quarter of a million should cover everything."

"You know that I can't decide on these things myself. I'll have to pass the plan over to Israel."

"I know. But if you recommend it there's a better chance of the idea being approved."

It suddenly became clear to her. He had already mentioned his suggestion to his own sources in Israel and they obviously had not been overly enthused. He wanted to enlist Shula's aid to revive the idea. "He has big ideas, this Mussa," she said to herself. A quarter-million-pound nightclub and a job for his nephew as manager—not a small prize for so loyal an employee as Mussa.

She did not want to provoke him:

"All right. I'll suggest it to Israel and we'll see."

About a month later, while she was sitting with George in a small restaurant overlooking the sea, he suddenly said without warning, "Do you remember asking me if I would be willing to meet your people? Well, I'm ready."

She stared at him in surprise. "Why? What happened?" she heard herself whispering.

He grinned. "You're a funny woman. For months you've been

pestering me to establish contact with your people, and when I finally agree, you start asking questions."

Only later when she thought about their conversation did she realize that he had never answered her question.

"I'll need a few days to arrange everything," she said.

"That's all right. You know what our Moslem friends say: haste is the work of the devil."

"Will you be able to travel abroad if you have to?"

It was a rhetorical question. He had left Lebanon on business on several occasions during the past few months, although he never openly admitted it.

He answered briefly. "Yes, of course. There's no problem." He immediately returned the conversation to the subject they had been discussing before he had interrupted her.

Shula visited the Adut Pharmacy that very same afternoon.

A week later, on the date written on the reverse side of the prescription label, they took off for Istanbul. They arrived at Beirut Airport separately and only "recognized" each other when they had boarded the plane.

"Ah, Madame Cohen, are you going to Istanbul, too?"

They shook hands like two acquaintances who just happened to meet. They did not sit near each other during the three-hour flight. They "chanced" to meet again while waiting for their luggage at the Istanbul air terminal.

"May I drop you off in the city?" he asked politely. I have a car coming to pick me up. Come have a cup of coffee with me while we're waiting."

"Thank you. I just have to make a call."

Epstein answered immediately, but he sounded surprised to hear her voice.

"It's you? Today?"

"Yes. What's the matter?"

"Something's happened. I was expecting you tomorrow. . . . Is *he* with you?"

"Yes, of course."

"Okay. No problem. I'll tell you what. Go to town, but don't travel together. Wait for me at the Palace Hotel. By the time you arrive I'll have rooms for you. We'll meet in the hotel."

The Palace Hotel was at that time the most luxurious hotel in Istanbul. It was an impressive six-story building off Taksim Square. Shula arrived first. George arrived a short while later and stood directly behind her at the registration desk. They were registered consecutively in the guest book. Epstein isn't going to be too pleased, she thought to herself.

She took the elevator to her room, unpacked and wondered what to do next. She went out on the balcony. There was slight drizzle and the air was bitingly cold. Heavy black clouds loomed over the roofs of the city. The balcony overlooked a steep hill which descended to the shores of the Golden Horn. It was so dark and gloomy she could barely distinguish between the dull gray masses of sky and water. The smoke from the chimneys on the houses crowded together on the hill brought an unfamiliar but surprisingly pleasant sharp odor of burning coal to her nostrils. There was sadness in the view as well as in the air. She shivered in the cold and returned to her heated room.

A little while later she went down to the dining room. She stopped off at the registration desk to inquire about postal rates and quickly glanced at the open guest book. George Anton's name was last to appear. He was staying in room 217.

He was not in the dining room. She ate alone and with little appetite. She returned to her room, wrote brief messages on the postcards she found in the desk drawer, and went to the receptionist to buy stamps. She had still not found George.

Epstein arrived at four. He phoned from the registration desk, identified himself, and said that he had the letter of recommendation he had promised her. Could he come up to her room?

He did not wait for a response, hung up the phone and two minutes later knocked on her door.

"There's been an unpleasant complication," he said right after closing the door behind him. "The people who were supposed to meet you here can't make it. They want you to meet them in Rome. Can it be arranged?" He waited for her reaction.

"That depends on *him*."

"Can you ask him to come here? He's in room two seventeen."

She wanted to say, "I know," but stopped herself. She dialed his room and when he picked up the receiver, she said, "George, could you come here for a moment? Something's happened. I'm in room—"

"Four twenty-two," he interrupted. "I've already checked. I'm on my way."

When he arrived, Epstein repeated the story. "I'm very sorry," he finished, "there's been an unfortunate misunderstanding."

Anton did not conceal his displeasure. "I hope it's only a misunderstanding," he said angrily.

Epstein laughed nervously. He stood up very quickly. "All right, I'm going now to arrange the tickets. You'll be flying Alitalia tomorrow morning at nine. You're free for the rest of the evening. If you decide to leave the hotel, please don't go together. There are too many Lebanese merchants wandering about Istanbul."

Epstein left. They stood staring at each other awkwardly. Shula tried to break the silence and forced herself to smile. "How will we spend the evening? It's too cold to go out. Maybe there's something here in the hotel? A nightclub? An orchestra? Do you feel like dancing?"

He looked into her eyes for a long time.

"Shula, I've been thinking about our first real evening together for a long time now. Just the two of us alone. Actually, it was because I hoped we would have an evening like this together that I agreed to come. But I wasn't thinking of a nightclub or an orchestra."

She was blushing. "What will we do then?"

"First we'll go down to the restaurant and have a hot cup of English tea and if there's an orchestra, we'll listen to it and talk. I don't care if we're seen. If it's someone we know, we can say that we met by accident. Anyone who doesn't know us will think we're a married couple killing a cold rainy evening in Istanbul. Then we'll have dinner and talk some more and then—we'll see."

She preferred to ignore his last words.

"Shall we go?" she asked.

Anyone in the hotel who might have noticed them would have immediately assumed they were married. They were free and relaxed with each other and conversed comfortably. They praised the beauty of Istanbul and expressed their disappointment at having reached the city in such bad weather. The rain had covered the sidewalks with mud puddles that were as dull and gray as the smoke coming from the ever-present chimneys. Shula said that she would have liked to visit the great bazaar. George mentioned that he was sorry to have missed the Topkapi Museum. They both agreed that Istanbul must be beautiful in the spring.

They were the only ones aware of their repressed tension . . . the tension of expectation.

They ate in the large, half-empty dining room. Even though she was not hungry, Shula spent a long time looking over the menu and deciding what to eat. She scanned the names of the dishes written in Turkish and French and finally decided to order the funniest entry on the list: *Imam Bayildi*, "The Imam Fainted." When it was finally served it turned out to be a slightly fancier version of an eggplant dish she remembered from her mother's kitchen. George ordered swordfish steak grilled on skewers with tomatoes, onion, and bay leaf. They drank wine with their meal and for dessert they had a "nightingale's nest," a honeycake filled with pistachio nuts. They completed their meal with hot, sweet tea.

They ate slowly, as though they were enjoying every morsel; in fact, they were trying to postpone the inevitable end of their meal.

By the time they had finished, there was no one left in the dining room save the waiters standing in a row waiting for them to leave. George ordered two cognacs.

Finally they had no further pretext to remain and they went out to the lobby. George went up to the mist-covered glass door and looked out into the street.

"It's pouring," he said over his back. "Do you want to take a walk in the rain?"

"Who has the strength to move?" she sighed.

They walked to the elevator in silence. They did not exchange one word while the elevator climbed to the fourth floor, nor while they walked down the long, carpeted hall to her room.

They stood in front of her room. George took the key from her hand and opened the door. When she crossed the threshold and turned to him, he embraced her.

"Have you forgotten?" he whispered, his breath heavy on her face. "Everyone has to think we're a happily married couple. . . ."

She heard the door lock shut.

Her attempts to analyze her feelings the next morning met with no success. By the time she was dressed, Epstein had arrived and had come up to her room.

"Good morning," he said, his eyes darting about the room. "Did you enjoy yourselves last night? Did you go out?"

She told him that the weather had been so bad that they had decided to spend a quiet evening in the hotel.

"He isn't annoyed at the misunderstanding that occurred?" he worriedly asked. "He doesn't have any regrets? No? That's good. We wouldn't want to lose him. Are you packed? Good, then I suggest we go down to the breakfast room. We don't want to leave him alone too much. . . . Before we go, remember, in Rome you'll be staying at the Quirinal Hotel. Rooms have already been reserved for both of you. When you arrive, call this number." He handed her a slip of paper with a telephone number typed on it. "Tell them your name and that the package has arrived. They'll set up a meeting place. After you bring him to the meeting, your job will be done. You can go home to Beirut or, if you want, you can spend a few days vacationing in Rome. Actually," he added with an apologetic tone, "your job's already done, but our people think that it would be better for you to accompany him to Rome. They think your presence will ensure his arrival. I hope the trip to Rome won't spoil your plans?"

"No, it's all right."

"Then call him and tell him to meet us in the breakfast room."

There was no answer and they found him in the breakfast room sipping coffee, ready to go. Shula was grateful once more, this time, however, for Epstein's presence. They ate in silence, stealing furtive glances but avoiding looking directly into each other's eyes. Epstein chatted away incessantly.

Finally he had to leave to settle the bill and order taxis for them. While they were waiting on the sidewalk in front of the hotel, the doorman's umbrella shielding them from the downpour, he turned to her and on a momentary impulse said, "I don't know how you feel about what's happened. I only want you to know I don't regret it. I love you."

Rome was a bitter disappointment. It was rainy and cold and the view through the mist-covered windows of the taxi was one of poverty. The streets were poorly lit and the houses looked in need of a fresh coat of paint. The black political slogans which embellished practically every building added to the grimness. It was evident that Italy was still in the grips of a postwar economic depression. When they reached the center of the city, there were more signs of life, however. People were walking about; there were more stores, and more light.

Their hotel was quite luxurious. There were uniformed doormen, and smartly dressed workers scurried about the glass and chrome lobby. The few guests were elegantly dressed. The women dripped with jewels and furs.

Once again rooms had been reserved for them on separate floors. When they separated, George said, "Shall we meet in the lobby in half an hour?"

She nodded in agreement.

Once in her room, she asked for an outside line and called the number Epstein had given her. A man's voice answered: *"Pronto!"* and she answered in French: *"Ici Madame Cohen."*

"Mrs. Cohen?" the voice replied hesitantly, "do you speak English?"

"Also Hebrew."

"Wonderful," the voice answered in Hebrew. "We've been waiting for you. Is everything all right?"

"Yes. We're at the Quirinal."

"Good. We'll be there immediately."

The two men who knocked on her door a quarter of an hour later were younger than she had expected. They were tall and about thirty. One was blond and muscular, the other dark and slight, with a thin moustache. They were both wearing well-tailored suits and soft suede moccasins that were the latest fashion. The blond introduced himself as Bar-Lev, the darker one's name was Abraham Malchi.

"Where is he?" asked the one called Malchi.

"I'm supposed to meet him in the lobby in five minutes. We should be going."

"Just a minute," he said. "Look, as soon as you introduce him to us, we'll be taking him from the hotel. He has to meet someone to discuss matters that no one else should know about. You're not insulted, are you?"

She was, but replied, "It's all right."

"It's nothing personal, you understand, but it's better this way."

"Of course."

"Now, tell us something about him. Why has he agreed to work with us? Is he doing it for money or is he just frustrated or angry with his superiors?"

She tried to suppress the resentment welling up inside her.

"I don't know for sure. I think he may be interested in money, but that's not the only reason. I think he views Israel as a potential ally for the Maronite Christians. He might even have been sent on the orders of one of his superiors."

The one called Abraham Malchi lit an American cigarette and inhaled audibly. "If you're right, that will make everything easier. Shall we go?"

George was waiting for her. A look of disappointment crossed his face when he saw her walking in the company of two strange men. It remained there even after the introductions were over. They sat down in armchairs around a low table. A waiter wearing a red jacket approached at once.

"No," Malchi replied in Italian, "we're leaving." When the waiter disappeared, he continued in English, "Mr. Anton, there's someone here in Rome who is eager to meet you. There are many things we have to discuss. We'll be going immediately."

George looked at Shula inquisitively.

"I won't be going," she answered briefly. "I have a headache."

The displeasure on his face deepened, but he did not say a word.

During the evening Shula wrapped herself in her raincoat and took a short walk near the hotel. It began to rain and the streets were soon filled with puddles. The mud splattered her stockings. Men cast admiring glances in her direction and a few of them began calling out to her. She went back to the hotel.

At about midnight she called his room, but there was no answer. She made a decision and dialed the reception desk in the lobby.

"Could you reserve a seat for me on tomorrow's flight to Beirut?"

The following morning before taking the hotel bus to the airport she wavered for a moment. Should she call him? She decided to leave a short note: "I'm returning home. We'll meet in Beirut." She left it with the reception clerk.

She spent her last half hour on Italian soil in the airport souvenir shop buying little gifts for her children.

The Prince of Thieves

9 Two weeks passed before George called.

They were two weeks of moral castigation for Shula. She could still feel the bitterness of the humiliation she had suffered at the hands of those two "dandies" in Rome who so obviously did not want her tagging along. Even so she realized that the world of espionage had it own laws and rules of behavior and that she could not expect them to be altered in consideration of her feelings. Yet at the same time she was glad that it had ended that way. Now that she was home with her family, she realized that she did not want to lose them. She was not willing to give up her children and was also rather surprised to discover that her husband was very dear to her, just as he was. With all her being she looked forward to the day she would see George again, but she feared their meeting as well.

When she recognized George's voice on the phone, she was filled with both happiness and fear.

"I want to see you," he said with a heavy voice. "Could you meet me for lunch?"

He was already seated at a corner table at "their" restaurant on Amir Bashir Street when she arrived. He looked at her as she entered but did not smile. He was not looking well. He had gotten thinner and his eyes were clouded with worry.

"You can congratulate me," he smiled joylessly. "I've been promoted."

"*Mabruk,*" she congratulated him with the traditional Arabic blessing. "Does it make you happy?"

He shrugged. "It was expected. But it means I'm no longer affiliated with the *Sûreté*. I've been returned to intelligence. Here's my new number in case you want to contact me."

She sat back in silence. He, too, was quiet. After a prolonged pause he asked, "Shall we order?"

They carried on an evasive and fragmented conversation while eating. Their words hovered in the air without any connection. When he finished his meal, he put his knife and fork down and said, "When I found your note I was furious at you for leaving without seeing me. But I was secretly pleased that you weren't there."

She wanted to cry. "Well then, I'm glad I left. . . ."

His fingers absentmindedly played with the edge of the tablecloth. She sat and waited.

"Look," he said. "What happened between us in Istanbul was not just a fling for me. I can't give you up. But I can't give up my family or my work either. Can you understand that?"

She looked at him through her tears and nodded.

He clasped her hand on the table.

"We'll always be together," he said, "won't we?"

They became friends. There was a wonderful understanding between them. She never discussed his wife with him. He also stopped asking about her husband. Yet they would discuss their children freely, comparing their grades and advising each other. Shula would sometimes think, "Why we're just like a family. . . ." There were a few limitations, however: she never asked him about his work, even about the duration and success of his meeting in Rome. She also kept her own activities secret from him, although she never hesitated to ask his advice or help. She knew they both were working for a common cause, but when he passed information on to Israel, it did not go through her. She assumed that he had a post office box of his own and the thought that she had unknown competition in her "own territory" displeased her. But she never asked questions.

The winter of 1950–51 was a difficult one. Frequent avalanches cut off the mountain roads and sometimes even the Damascus–Beirut highway. Very few refugees managed to arrive from Syria. This break permitted Shula and her men to empty the Wadi of most of the refugees who had gathered there. Toward the end of the winter, however, a few families who had bribed their way across the border arrived and Shula learned from them that things would be different as soon as the mountain roads were open. She was told that a new, energetic Israeli agent had reached Damascus and this, coupled with the frequent political instability were potential factors favorable to a massive Jewish emigration from Syria. The Sunnite dictator az-Za'im had been overthrown and executed by a military coup at the end of 1949. The succeeding government was not particularly stable either. Colonel Sami al-Hinnawi, az-Za'im's successor, had himself been overthrown, and even though the government under the presidency of Hashim al-Atasi remained intact, the behind-the-scenes ruler was Colonel Adib Shishakli, who was already showing signs of wanting to rule openly. Shula was informed that groups larger than any preceding them—about 150 persons in number—were being organized in Damascus and Aleppo and were waiting for the mountain roads to be cleared.

She consulted with Abu-Jacques. He was not very optimistic either. "There are already people in the Wadi claiming that it's because of us that the Syrian Jews are coming to Beirut in the first place. Such large groups can only turn the community openly against us."

"I agree," she sighed, "but we both know that I have no say in the matter. They're simply coming."

"Then we'll have to smuggle them out faster."

"But how? Both Mussa and Hajaj are complaining that the situation on the border is getting tighter and tighter. A lot of Palestinians are concentrating in the south and many of them are connected with Syrian intelligence. They can't be bought like the customs officers at Bint Jubail. The smuggling of such large groups is simply impossible."

"Then we'll just have to make contact with someone bigger. But it would have to be someone *really* big."

"Yes, but who?"

"If we could only get Abu-Sa'id. . . . But no, he's really out of our reach. You probably couldn't even get to see him. . . ."

Even if she hadn't for several years been associating with characters outside the law, it would have been impossible for Shula not to have heard of Abu-Sa'id. He was a legend in Beirut. A familiar figure, he was trim and elegant, always dressed in a white suit which he reportedly changed two or three times a day, and always with a fresh red carnation in his lapel and a red tarboosh worn at a jaunty angle over his right brow. His blue Buick was known all over the city, and was treated with great deference. When his bodyguard, who sat next to the chauffeur signaled to a policeman, the latter would stop even trams to make way for the car and its majestic owner.

The police were not the only ones to try to win his favor; politicians, statesmen, and foreign diplomats also sought his company and approval. It was said that he was a "minister without ministry."

His power and influence were undoubtedly greater than those of many a real minister. The fact that he had begun life as a poor fisherman added to the legend. In strongly feudalistic Lebanon, despite its economic anarchy and pseudo-Western ways, almost anyone could become rich, but only a select few could break the rigid social barriers and become accepted by the "better families."

The base of Abu-Sa'id's empire was the Olympia Casino, one of Beirut's largest; two smaller gambling houses in the mountains; and partnerships in some of the most famous of Beirut's nightclubs and hotels.

Using the elegant front of these legal enterprises, Abu-Sa'id was also willing to become involved in any venture, provided that the profits were high. He smuggled opium from Turkey, processed it and exported it to France. He smuggled gold to India. He smuggled pearls in oil cans from the emirates on the Persian Gulf. He was active in Lebanon's largest export, hashish, which his agents bought in the fields by the acre, then processed, packed, and exported by sea and camel caravan to Egypt, the largest hashish market in the world. Under the guise of importing entertainers for his nightclubs, his men supplied prostitutes to the larger Lebanese brothels and blonde concubines to the harems of desert sheikhs. In keeping with his persistent reach for power, wealth, and influence at any cost, he also bought and sold weapons and state secrets to and from *any* country. He had a network of informers who kept him in touch with everything that happened in Beirut. What he could not obtain by extortion he could purchase with bribes. He was omniscient—but with one single limitation: his power was restricted to the Christian sector of Lebanon. "In the Moslem sectors," he admitted openly, "I am a Samson sheared of his locks." The Moslem population had their own Samsons.

Many considered Abu-Sa'id a "gang baron" or an arch-criminal, albeit one with considerable stature and vision. But in Lebanon, where the hashish smugglers commanded armies larger than the entire police force and the "better families" maintained more soldiers than the Lebanese army itself, one's vision and stature transformed quantity into quality. Size was a source of admiration and respect in Lebanon and Abu-Sa'id was a giant.

He also had style.

In his luxurious office on the third floor of the Olympia Casino a table was always laid for twelve, even if Abu-Sa'id dined alone—"in case there are guests." He lived with his wife and only son, Sa'id, (he later had two daughters) in a mansion in Msetbeh, one of the wealthier Christian neighborhoods at the top of the mountain in eastern Beirut. Before long people came to refer to his house as "the Castle." There was no one in Beirut who was above accepting an invitation to "the Castle" or boasting about it afterward. A large garden surrounded the house and an old, half-deaf gardener made sure that Abu-Sa'id had a constant supply of fresh red carnations (white carnations reminded him of funerals) for his lapel. His house and office were always filled with flowers and he would spend much of his free time in the garden inspecting the plants with a skilled eye while his bodyguards stood about at a discreet distance.

Abu-Sa'id was known for his generosity. Over half a dozen charitable organizations in Beirut permanently enjoyed his support and women collecting for worthwhile causes knew they would receive generous donations from Abu-Sa'id. He supported the families of men who were killed in his service as well as of those who had died natural deaths. Even gamblers suffering from a bout of bad luck would sometimes enjoy his charitable side. More than once, while observing the proceedings in the casino from his private balcony between the second and third floors, he would send one of the men always surrounding him to the main roulette wheel. The man would whisper something in the croupier's ear and a particular player's luck would suddenly change for the better. With other players Abu-Sa'id would extend credit that was entirely unjustified by their weak financial situation. But always he kept accounts of his generosity and goodwill. Abu-Sa'id enjoyed having people beholden to him, and only he knew when he would call upon them to repay him for his favors.

In Wadi Abu-Jamil admiration for Abu-Sa'id was mingled with the feeling that "he's almost one of our own." Abu-Sa'id had married a young Jewess. Intermarriages between Christian men and Jewish women were not a rare phenomenon, but in most cases ties between the woman and her family were severed. Um-Sa'id, however, maintained a good relationship with her family even after she moved to Msetbeh. It was reputed to have been true love which brought her to leave the Wadi to marry a man more than twenty years her senior. It was also rumored that his love for her was just as great. Abu-Sa'id, it was said, had known no other woman since his marriage. "He treats her like a queen," said the gossips in the Wadi. "Anything her heart desires . . . and no matter how busy he is, he's always home for lunch. . . ."

This was the man who could solve Shula's problems and about whom Abu-Jacques declared, "He's out of our reach. You probably couldn't even get to see him."

For years Shula had been one of the preferred clients of Madame Narvoni, the seamstress for the wealthier families of the Wadi. Twice yearly, at the changing of the seasons, Rosh Hashanah and Passover, Madame Narvoni reserved four days for the preparation of Shula's wardrobe for the coming months.

In the spring of 1951, when Madame Narvoni arrived with a stack of the latest Paris fashion magazines tucked under her arm, Shula said to her, "Could you possibly give me two additional days this year?"

"I'm terribly sorry, I'm completely booked. Perhaps after the holiday."

"Couldn't you postpone your other client until then?"

"What do you mean, Madame Cohen? How can I postpone Um-Sa'id?"

This was how Shula was to make her way into "the Castle" in Msetbeh. While serving tea and assisting Madame Narvoni, Shula kept up a lively conversation. Madame Narvoni was an efficient and reliable source of gossip about the richer families in the Wadi. She knew all about Madame Cohen's "extracurricular" activities and would keep Shula informed of the other women's reactions—not all of them favorable—to her work. Shula continued to steer the conversation to Um-Sa'id.

"Have you been sewing for her for a long time?"

"A long time? I made her first dress when she was a young girl in the Wadi."

"Are you friends?"

"Of course! Other than her family, I'm the only person from the Wadi who visits her home. She invited me over right after the wedding. She said, 'Madame Narvoni, you made me my first dress and you will be the one to sew me my last.' That's exactly what she said. It's so silly. She's so much younger . . ."

"An interesting woman. I would like to meet her. Do you think you could arrange it?"

The older woman was immediately suspicious.

"Is it in regard to your 'other activities'? Look, Madame Cohen, you're a good woman and you're performing a great charity; but I don't want to become involved. You have a husband and a family to look after you. I'm all alone."

For the next three days Madame Narvoni worked in Shula's house and Shula did not miss an opportunity to bring up the subject of Um-Sa'id. Finally, Madame Narvoni said, "I'll tell you what. I'll be going to Um-Sa'id's house in two weeks to bring her Passover *matzo*. I do it every year. Did you know that she doesn't eat bread on Passover and she fasts on Yom Kippur? If you want, you can come with me. I'll introduce you as a friend. I can't promise more."

Shula paid for the cab that drove her, Madame Narvoni, and the two boxes of *matzo* from the only Jewish bakery in Beirut to the mansion in Msetbeh. Luxurious and expensive homes were the rule in that exclusive neighborhood, but Abu-Sa'id's home stood out from all the others. It was a stone mansion surrounded by a high stone wall with a heavy iron gate that opened into a magnificent garden. The house stood in the middle of the garden. While walking on the tiled path that passed a goldfish pond and rows and rows of fragrant flowers in full bloom, Shula could only marvel at this elegant style of life so different from her own. She wondered if the lives inside were as beautiful as their surroundings.

A servant wearing cloth shoes led them to two immense armchairs facing the back window and silently climbed the steps to the second floor to inform the mistress of the house of their arrival.

Um-Sa'id, a plump woman of thirty, more charming than beautiful, warmly embraced Madame Narvoni and shook Shula's hand.

"I've heard of you," she said briefly. After thanking Madame Narvoni for the *matzo*, she rang a bell on the table. A maid wearing a black uniform and white apron served tea and pastry. They discussed the approaching holiday and mentioned the annual Passover fund which was being arranged to provide the poorer families, particularly the refugees from Syria, with all the necessities for the holiday. Um-Sa'id offered a generous donation. Shula was quick to take advantage of the opening.

"I see you haven't forgotten our customs," she said. "We have more needy families this year than ever before and their numbers are constantly increasing. These are hard times for the Jews of Syria and Iraq and they are fleeing those countries in great numbers. A number of my friends and I are helping them."

"Yes, I know," said Um-Sa'id warmly, waiting for Shula to continue. Shula was encouraged.

"Until now we have managed on our own. But it's becoming increasingly more difficult. Do you think your husband would be willing to help us? I don't mean with money," she quickly added. "And we'll pay for any service he would be willing to provide. I'm sure he could advise us. People say he knows everything and everyone. I would like very much to meet him."

Um-Sa'id was hesitant.

"I don't know whether he'd be willing to help you or not. You know what? I'll ask him. Call me tomorrow morning."

Shula waited impatiently for the morning. Her tension had kept her awake all night. She was not sure what she would ask of Abu-Sa'id, even if he did agree to see her. She only felt, and her intuition grew stronger after visiting his house, that if they should reach some understanding, a whole new world would open up to her.

She could barely restrain herself until ten o'clock, when she eagerly dialed the number.

Her fear that she may have called too early disappeared when she heard Um-Sa'id's voice.

"Madame Cohen? It's good to hear your voice. I was afraid you might have forgotten. What? Too early? What are you talking about? I have a child . . . I've been awake for hours. Listen, my husband is willing to meet with you. He'll send his car for you at four."

Nazira was called to prepare lunch and Shula ran to the hairdresser.

At exactly four o'clock the blue Buick stopped in front of the Magen Avraham Synagogue. The chauffeur blew the horn several times and children gathered around. As Shula hurried down the steps, she thought that soon the gossips of Wadi Abu-Jamil would have another juicy topic for discussion.

The car parked in front of the Olympia Casino, a wide, three-story building in a narrow street off the beach next to the Olympia Hotel, a towering skyscraper. Wide stairs led to the entrance of the casino.

A man in a gray striped suit approached. "Madame Cohen, please follow me."

The restaurant and nightclub on the first floor were empty at this early hour. The workers were putting the plush red velvet chairs onto the tables and busily sweeping the red carpets with heavy-bristled brooms. A freshly painted staircase led to the gambling hall on the second floor and here, too, the color red predominated in the upholstery and rugs. Crystal chandeliers hung over the roulette and card tables. There was already a crowd of early gamblers. They continued to the third floor.

The man accompanying her knocked gently and opened the door for her. She found herself in a large room. A quick glance at the enormous rug was enough to convince her that it was a real Persian carpet from Kashan. The room was furnished in expensive good taste. The colors were subdued and there was no gaudy display of gold and chrome. The room did not contain a desk. A low mahogany coffee table surrounded by four leather chairs stood in the corner.

Her eyes focused on the man in the immaculate white suit with the red carnation in his lapel. Abu-Sa'id was fifty-three years old. He was of medium height and slight physique, but his masterfully tailored suit and superb posture made him appear much taller. Without his tarboosh his partial baldness was exposed. What remained of his hair was closely cropped and graying.

"Madame," he said softly in French as he bowed to kiss her hand, "I have been waiting to meet you for the past two years."

He led her to one of the leather chairs.

"Have you eaten?" Abu-Sa'id asked. He did not wait for an answer. She did not realize that he had rung until a servant suddenly appeared at the door.

"Prepare a table," Abu-Sa'id ordered.

The man disappeared without a sound.

Abu-Sa'id turned to her.

"I spoke with your wife . . ." she said hesitantly.

"Now speak with me," he interrupted, and as if to put her at ease after the apparent sharpness of his words, he added, "I know about everything you have done up until now. You have good men. Mussa as well as Hajaj and Tanus are reliable and honest. What do you want from me?"

She was ready with her answer.

"I want to smuggle more people than they're capable of handling. And I want," she said, flattering him, "to work with people who are acceptable to you."

He considered her words for a moment. "Madame," he said, "the road you want to take runs in two directions. I can help you, but how can you help me in return?"

"What can I offer you besides money?"

"I don't know yet. But you must realize that you will have to pay. Not money. Whatever you could pay me would be less than what I spend in one month on my orchids."

His disdain angered her. Her attempt to build herself up in his eyes caused her to commit a tactical error. "I'm expecting over two hundred people in the next few weeks. Could you handle a group of that size?"

She immediately realized her mistake. A spark of anger glared in his eyes.

"Madame," he replied haughtily, "I've bought pearls before they were removed from the sea. I've sold arms that I didn't have in my possession to a client entirely unknown to me. Now shall we eat?"

He led her to the adjacent room. It was dominated by an immense round table about two yards in circumference, surrounded by twelve straight-backed antique chairs. A few smaller tables and chairs were spread around the room. The large table was decked with at least forty dishes heaped with delicacies: *hummus* and *tahina* and several other salads including *tabbouleh*, a must on every Beirut table; patties made from meats; vegetables of every imaginable kind in a wide variety of sauces; and a choice of fishes and fowls stuffed, roasted, and sautéed in pomegranate juice. With the skilled eye of an experienced hostess, Shula estimated that there was enough on that table to feed at least forty people.

"*Tfadli*, please," Abu-Sa'id said, waving his hand over the feast. "Whatever you wish." There was still a slight coolness in his tone.

"But this is a banquet," she said in feigned astonishment. He merely shrugged his shoulders, but she knew he was appeased.

The waiter rushed toward them and filled her plate with whatever she indicated—a piece of fish, some *taboulleh*, and eggplant salad—and brought it to the smaller table Abu-Sa'id had pointed to. After they were seated, the waiter returned and placed a plate of grated raw carrots before Abu-Sa'id. He noticed her surprised look and said:

"How else can I maintain my figure?"

"Then who is all this food for?"

"For whoever may wish to see me. People may leave my establishment with empty pockets, but never with empty stomachs."

She was not hungry. She picked at her food indifferently and when he noticed that she was about to move the plate away, he asked, "Would you like something to drink? Something cold perhaps? I myself drink only cocoa during the day. Shall I order something for you?" He gave instructions to the waiter and after the latter left the room, he said, "So be it. Shall we return to the matter you came to discuss? Two hundred people. It should not be too difficult. When they arrive, get in touch with me and I'll tell you what to do. The price will be one hundred fifty pounds per adult, fifty per child, to be paid after they have arrived safely at their destination. Do you agree? I have only one condition: there is to be no middleman between us. I don't want contact with anyone but you. Is that understood?"

She nodded, slightly intoxicated by her success. Not only was Abu-Sa'id willing to cooperate with her, but he was willing to do it for less than she was paying her other smugglers.

"I'll relay your conditions to the proper places," she said in a businesslike manner. "And I'll contact you as soon as I receive an answer."

"And how will you relay the information?" he asked.

"I have an address in France," she said cautiously, but he laughed out loud.

"Ya Um-Ibrahim," he scolded her. "Everyone knows old Mussa is your courier and he doesn't carry your letters to France."

She made no reply. After a moment a servant arrived with an ice bucket, a bottle of Antiquari Scotch, a siphon of soda, and glasses.

"It's already after six," he announced. "May I offer you some?"

"Just a drop."

They sat and talked. He told her about the renovations that had just been completed in the casino and mentioned the gala opening he was planning for the following week.

"I'll send invitations for you and your husband. Will you come?"

She agreed. She added that neither she nor her husband had ever been in a gambling casino. Looking interested, she asked, "Is it a profitable business? After all, everything here is based on luck."

He examined her closely to ascertain whether she was serious or not.

"I never learned how to read or write," he announced suddenly, "but I'm very good at arithmetic. Roulette has a mathematics of its own. Half of the numbers are black yet more than eighty percent of the players lose anyway. When they lose, I win."

His frankness startled her. "Why is he telling me he can't read or write? It's not the kind of thing people boast of."

Somewhat reluctantly, she said, "I have to go now. I have a family."

"I know all about your family," he said magnanimously, "but for the future, let it be clear: you'll always know when you'll be coming to me, but only I will know when you'll be leaving."

A shudder passed through her body, the same shudder of fear and excitement that always surged through her in the face of danger. "Underneath that smooth exterior, he's as terrifying as a shark," she told herself.

He rose to accompany her to the door.

"Then we have agreed," he said. "You and your husband will be my guests at the gala opening of the club. You'll enjoy it. There will be a lot of interesting people here."

He sent her home in his car. She thought about the phenomenon called Abu-Sa'id all the way back to Wadi Abu-Jamil. She was sure that for some reason he liked her, and she was equally certain that he had reserved a place for her in his future plans. But why he was drawing her into his plans and his exact purpose was still unknown to her. It frightened and excited her. She felt as though she was standing on the threshold of a dark room, and that danger lurked in the shadows.

She knew that once across that threshold, she would find herself in a strange and unknown world, unlike any she had ever known.

High Stakes

10 The following week Abu-Sa'id's famous blue Buick appeared in Wadi Abu-Jamil a second time—to deliver to Joseph Kishak-Cohen and his wife a gold-embossed invitation to the gala reopening of the Olympia Casino. It was then that Shula discovered a new, unfamiliar trait in her husband: the modest textile merchant from the Suk Sursuk was actually rather conceited and vain. The invitation, along with the blue Buick that parked in front of his house, proved a connection between the legendary Abu-Sa'id and himself and this put him a few rungs above his cronies in the market. He became their major subject of conversation and envy. And he reveled in his newfound status. He pretended, of course, that only the by-products of the connection were of interest to him. "You wouldn't believe it," he said to his wife, "when I went into my bank this morning, the manager invited me into his office. He told me he decided to extend my credit, and he hinted that he would be most grateful if I somehow mentioned him favorably to Abu-Sa'id. . . ."

In the same breath he asked Shula if her evening gown would be suitable for so plush an event as the reopening of the Olympia. He would not rest until she promised to buy a new gown.

When George heard about her meeting with Abu-Sa'id, he was somewhat less enthusiastic.

"I hear you have connections in high society."

She asked where he had obtained his information.

"It doesn't matter. I understand your motivations. Abu-Sa'id can help you a great deal. But he can also be very dangerous. Dealing with him is like holding on to a lion's tail."

"How?" She feigned innocence. "He strikes me as being a perfect gentleman."

"Perhaps. But be careful. I wouldn't want to see you get entangled in his world. No man is an angel, but, there's a difference. . . ."

She was pleased by his concern but refused to believe there was any foundation to his fears.

The gala event was unsurpassable in splendor. All the men wore tuxedos—Shula easily picked out a number of politicians whose faces she recognized from newspapers—and the women were draped in elegant gowns and jewels. Abu-Sa'id, dressed in a white tuxedo with the perennial red carnation in his lapel, was one of the few men not accompanied by his wife. Shula later learned that he completely disconnected his business from his personal life. His wife had never been in the casino, nor had she ever attended a business meeting or any other event connected with her husband's work. If Abu-Sa'id had to meet with business associates at "the Castle" in Msetbeh, Um-Sa'id always found some pretext to remain in the family wing on the second floor.

Abu-Sa'id greeted Shula and Joseph at the entrance to the restaurant. Guests stood around tables and waiters scurried back and forth carrying trays laden with plates and ice buckets filled with bottles of champagne. Several striking blondes wandered from table to table smiling at guests who had arrived alone. They were fresh off the plane from Germany and Sweden. At least two of them would be on their way to join the harems of wealthy sheikhs in the Persian Gulf emirates the following morning and Abu-Sa'id's bank account would swell even more with procuring fees.

"Stay with me," he said at the door. The words were intended for

Shula alone. "Everyone is busy having a good time and I have to stand here and be bored."

She was not sure if he was serious, but she remained at his side nevertheless. Joseph, a trifle perplexed, stood there, too

Guests continued to arrive and Abu-Sa'id exchanged greetings and courtesies with each of them. Some of them he introduced to Shula and her husband.

Abu-Sa'id warmly embraced the chief of the Lebanese customs service, who arrived with his wife.

"*Ahlan ve-Sahlan, Ya* Abu-Umsen. Make yourself at home. But," he continued with a mischievious smile, "if you find a single bottle here that passed through customs, I'll give you a thousand pounds in gold."

The customs official laughed raucously. "I won't even bother to check. I'm sure you're right. I'm willing to bet you don't even have a license to operate a casino."

A short while later Joseph left them and went to the gambling hall on the second floor.

Shula and Abu-Sa'id wandered among the guests. She could sense the surprised looks being cast in her direction and could hear people whisper behind her back as she went by. She felt uncomfortable and on several occasions suggested to him that she join her husband.

"Why? Don't you enjoy being with me?"

"It's not that. I'm only surprised. There are so many beautiful women here tonight. Who knows what you may be missing?"

He stared into the crowded room as though he were looking for confirmation of her words.

"When the moon shines in all its splendor, the stars are invisible," he said chivalrously. "Besides, it will be good for you to be seen in my company."

Long after midnight Abu-Sa'id signaled that the party was over. He stood next to the roulette table. When everyone was silent, he called out, "As Allah is my witness, this was a grand evening! And I thank you all for honoring me with your presence. But," he added provocatively, "if there's anyone here who won at roulette, let him raise his hand and I'll fire the croupier here and now."

Everyone laughed and began to disperse and head for the door.

Shula went to find her husband. Joseph was flushed from the excitement of the game. He had won a few hundred pounds and was already thinking about what he would tell his friends at the market the following morning.

"It was really a great evening," he said contentedly.

A few days after the opening, Abu-Sa'id sent his blue Buick for Shula.

"Nothing's happened," he quickly reassured her as she entered his office. "I missed you."

"You can have your pick of the most beautiful women in Beirut," she said, "and instead you choose me, the mother of six children."

He replied in a serious tone, "None of the others has your qualities. But don't misunderstand me. I'm happily married and I'll never do anything to compromise either my wife's or your honor."

They had a relaxed conversation. Abu-Sa'id casually remarked that according to his agent in Damascus, the Jewish community in Aleppo had shrunk considerably and that the Damascus authorities had closed many Jewish shops, causing great concern among the Jews. He gave no further details. It was as though he wanted her to reach her own conclusion that there would be a new wave of refugees in the near future, this time from Damascus. She soon discovered that this was his style with her in all matters. She could not decide whether he was motivated by caution or if he was merely playing with her to test her intelligence and perception.

She included his information in a report she sent to Israel with Shukry Mussa.

The great exodus from Damascus, however, did not take place just yet. Only a trickle of refugees filtered through, and their numbers were not large enough to justify turning to Abu-Sa'id. The Mussa family and her two other smugglers were able to handle them comfortably. Nevertheless, Abu-Sa'id kept sending his car for her.

The frequent appearance of the blue Buick in Wadi Abu-Jamil caused a new wave of tongue wagging. The more malicious gossips claimed that Shula had become an incorrigible gambler. She wasn't at all disturbed. The more she thought about it, the more she realized it was to her benefit. It was far safer for people to believe she was an addicted gambler than to have them inquiring into the true nature of her relationship with Abu-Sa'id. Her family did not agree. Her mother-in-law and sisters-in-law were quick to relate all the rumors to Joseph and a new feeling of tension filled the house.

Late one afternoon as she arrived at the casino, Abu-Sa'id greeted her: "I'm glad you're so well dressed. I want you to stay awhile. Something interesting may develop."

He was wearing a pink rather than the usual red carnation. He removed it from his lapel and gave it to her, saying, "Look, even my carnation has paled in your presence."

They were brought cocoa and she joined him on his private balcony overlooking the casino. It was early and the gambling hall was only half-full. There were about half a dozen players at the roulette wheel and about the same at the *chemin de fer* table. A four-handed poker game was in progress at a small table in the corner. One of the players was a houseman.

Jamil, Abu-Sa'id's right-hand man, approached them. He leaned over to whisper in Abu-Sa'id's ear, but the latter moved away, forcing Jamil to speak loud enough for Shula to hear.

"He lost another fifty thousand."

"That's all right. Give him another twenty-five."

They went to the restaurant. Some of the musicians had already arrived and were tuning their instruments, even though the orchestra did not begin to play until seven. Hostesses were lounging on the stage conversing with the musicians. There were a few clients sitting at the bar.

A beautiful, raven-haired woman of about thirty approached. She was tall and svelte in her low-cut black gown. Shula had met her on a previous visit. She was an Italian ex-show girl named Renata.

"Your man was here," she whispered to Abu-Sa'id. "I tried to amuse him, but," she added with a shrug of her shoulders, "the second floor attracted him more than I did. He's there now."

"Yes, I know. It's all right." He took a folded fifty-pound note from his jacket pocket and put it in her hand.

Shula was by now familiar with his style. Even seemingly impulsive acts were meticulously planned in order to create a particular image. Before leaving his office to make rounds of the casino and restaurant, he would fill his pockets with carefully folded bills of different denominations. He would place ten-pound notes in his left vest pocket, twenty-pound notes in the right, and fifty-pound notes in his jacket pocket. If for whatever reason he wanted to reward one of his workers, all he had to do was put his hand in one of his pockets and pull out a bill that "just happened to be tucked away there." The employees were already familiar with his habits. Abu-Sa'id told Shula that Renata avoided coming up to him until he had a glass of champagne in his left hand, thus assuring herself of a twenty or possibly even a fifty-pound note. He enjoyed telling Shula the story. It was obvious that he admired Renata's cleverness.

Jamil approached as they went up to the second floor. "He's playing high and he keeps on losing," he said out loud, no longer trying to conceal his message from Shula.

"Give him another twenty-five."

A half hour passed and Jamil knocked on the door of Abu-Sa'id office. "He's lost again. Should I give him more?"

"No, bring him here to me."

Shula understood that this was the "interesting development" he had promised. She had already learned that he had the power to "influence" the roulette wheel. But when he had hinted about his power to adjust the game, he had indicated that he would do so only to prevent a client from "drowning," and even then he would do so only on rare occasions. He had said at the time, "Rich men can afford to lose once in a while, and it's better for beggars to lose once and never come back. I'm not interested in either."

"Then who are you interested in?"

"In those people who have more status than money," he said cryptically.

"Now," she told herself, "I'll get to see someone he's interested in."

The man Jamil brought into the office was about fifty. He was wearing a European suit and had an air of authority about him. Abu-Sa'id stood up and embraced him warmly.

"How's the weather in the Gulf?" he asked, and Shula understood that he was speaking for her benefit. Abu-Sa'id made no attempt to introduce them.

The man seemed impatient.

"Ya Abu-Sa'id, did you invite me to discuss the weather?"

"May Allah forgive me. I wanted to see your face, Ya sheikh. Please sit down and have something to drink. The sea is calm and my ship sails smoothly." When he felt good Abu-Sa'id always spiced his conversation with nautical expressions to remind other people, as well as himself, of his humble origins.

"Ya Abu-Sa'id. Let's get to the point. May I continue playing?"

"Ah, but the roulette wheel must be oiled with cash."

The man rose in anger but Abu-Sa'id stopped him.

"It's all right. I was only joking. Jamil, give the sheikh another fifty thousand."

After the sheikh left, Shula forgot one of her self-imposed rules and asked Abu-Sa'id a direct question. "Who was that?" she inquired curiously.

He hesitated for a moment before answering. "At home he wears a uniform."

Despite the gossip in the Wadi she continued to visit the casino frequently. Once Abu-Sa'id sent his car and requested that she come on an urgent matter. When she arrived, he asked her to read aloud a letter in English that had just arrived. It was from a German agent who supplied blonde entertainers to the Middle East. "You know I can't read or write," he said to her almost as if in apology.

She wanted to ask: "And who read your correspondence to you before you met me?" But she changed her mind and said nothing. She realized that Abu-Sa'id, despite his great wealth and power and his happy home life, was a very lonely man. It might have been because he completely isolated his wife from the casino and his business dealings. But she was still at a loss to understand why he had chosen her to fill the void in his life.

Despite her great self-confidence it appeared that Shula could not see herself as others did. She was truly an exceptional woman, especially when seen against the background of Beirut in the early fifties. At that time any woman who did not stay within the confines of her home, happily raising her children, was considered wanton or even a prostitute. Certainly no one could call Shula Cohen wanton. She was the wife of a wealthy and respected merchant, the mother of six children, and she maintained a beautiful home. She was attractive and stylish and a witty and clever conversationalist. Yet, she dared to question prevalent social norms and behave in a manner that no ordinary respectable woman would. Yet only in the eyes of so unusual a man as Abu-Sa'id would Shula be the object of admiration and respect.

He demonstrated his admiration by inviting Shula and her husband to participate in the other side of his life; he asked them to attend an intimate party at "the Castle" in Msetbeh. Each and every guest at the party could have been included in the Lebanese *Who's Who*: statesmen, bankers, high government officials, and members of the diplomatic community. When he introduced Shula to Camille Chamoun, he said, "On my word, sir, this woman is very close to my heart." The tall, thin, elegant, gray-haired man, who everyone knew was to be the next president of Lebanon, leaned over and kissed Shula's hand. He said:

"Any woman worthy of your respect, my brother, will always be the object of my esteem."

Later that night, after the blue Buick had brought them home, Joseph declared proudly, "Camille Chamoun, no less! Who would have dreamed that we would ever shake his hand let alone spend an evening with him?"

She did not scoff at him this time. She had similar feelings herself. It was as if she was standing on the threshold of a dark room that suddenly turned out to be a lavish palace drenched in light.

On July 20, 1951, a bulletin on the radio announced that Jordan's King Abdullah had been assassinated by a Palestinian terrorist on his way to pray at the al-Aqsa Mosque in Jerusalem. That same day Mussa brought her an unexpected message from Israel. While waiting for the decoding powder to react with the invisible ink, she mused that the message was probably related to the assassination. But when the letters began to appear, an entirely different and more personal message stood before her unbelieving eyes:

"Your father died last night of a heart attack. Our sincere condolences."

There was no signature.

"Mussa," she said with sudden urgency, "can you get me through tonight?"

"On such short notice? Yes, but only if we leave immediately."

Only after she ran for Nazira and was half through packing a small bag did she remember to ask, "When did you receive the message?"

"Two nights ago when I was in Metulla. But I didn't get back until last night."

"Then I won't make it in time for the funeral," she told herself. There was no point in going.

But she observed all the traditional Jewish mourning customs and did not leave her house for seven days. Nazira did all the housework while Shula silently sat on the living room rug trying to recall her father's image. Members of the family arranged to take turns sitting with her and friends and neighbors made condolence calls. Joseph came home early each day and gathered a prayer quorum from among the neighbors for the afternoon and evening prayers. Most of the time, however, Shula sat alone.

She was surprised at the warm memories she had of her father. The bitterness she had felt toward him during the early years of her marriage had disappeared and was long forgotten. She wanted only to remember the pleasant times she had spent in his company, and all the presents and the elation that filled their house on his trips home from South America.

"He was a good man," she said softly to her eldest son, Bertie, who sat beside her one afternoon after school. "He always tried to make people happy. You remind me of him," she said affectionately, patting his head.

Her father's death and the memories of her childhood in Jerusalem reinforced her decision to send her children to Israel. When the seven days of mourning were over, she informed Joseph of her decision.

Once more Joseph refused to listen. Two weeks after Shula's father's death, Joseph's mother passed away. After his seven-day mourning period he was more open to her suggestion. Shula understood why: until then he had been afraid of his mother's reaction. Now, after her death, he was the head of the family.

She continued to press him on the matter. When they discussed it at a family meeting, Marie bitterly challenged Shula. "Sending young boys to a foreign country? Who ever heard of such a thing! One might think you were trying to get rid of your children."

Shula denied it emphatically. She claimed that Israel could hardly be considered a foreign country. Her entire family was there and they would watch over the children. She repeated all her usual arguments. But when she was alone, Shula asked herself if there might be some truth to her sister-in-law's accusation. She admitted to herself that she might indeed be subconsciously preparing for the day when she would have to urge the people in Wadi Abu-Jamil to send their children to Israel; she might be shielding herself against their challenge: "And what about your children?"

Joseph finally agreed to send twelve-year-old Bertie and eleven-year-old Meir to Israel. The decision was kept secret from the children lest they imprudently boast to their schoolmates of the wonderful and exciting adventure awaiting them. But Shula indirectly prepared them for the trip. She told them about the exciting life of kibbutz children, of setting up camps and night marches and games. Most of the stories were spun from her imagination, but the children were completely captivated by them. After the children went to bed, Shula and Joseph argued about how to send them to Israel. Joseph could not understand why they should be subjected to crossing a dangerous border in the middle of the night. "Why don't you fly with them to Istanbul or Nicosia and then to Israel? They're only children. Why should they be exposed to unnecessary danger?"

Over and over she reiterated that there was no danger. Hadn't she herself crossed the border on several occasions?

"Then," Joseph replied firmly, "what about the discomfort! On a plane they could take all the baggage they need and they won't arrive in Israel like gypsies."

"They'll get to Israel with all the suitcases you buy for them . . . and in comfort, too. You have nothing to worry about."

True to her word, she called Selim Tanus. It was the first time the aging smuggler had set foot in her house. Her husband was also present for the meeting.

"Selim *effendi*," she said, "I want to put my two children in your charge. I want you to take them across the border to Kefar Gil'adi. My old mother in Jerusalem has never seen them. She is alone now and she wishes to be with them before she is taken from this world."

"It is upon me and on my head, *Ya* Um-Ibrahim," Selim swore, touching his forehead with his fingers and placing his palm on his lips and then his chest.

"And I want it to be a special crossing," she continued, "just the two of them, without any refugees. I know that transporting two people is not worth your while; I will, therefore, pay your men as if there were ten."

"Allah forbid it!" the old man cried. "I would never take money for your children, *Ya* Um-Ibrahim, they will be my guests! My oldest son will carry them across the border in his arms!"

"He alone will not be sufficient. There will be many suitcases."

"Have no fear. They will cross with everything they own as if they were being transported in a royal chaise."

She looked at Joseph. It seemed that his fears had been placated. But after Selim left and a date was set for the following week, Joseph looked at her hostilely. "You know, sometimes I think Marie is right. Your 'activities' are more important to you than your own children."

Nevertheless, he devoted himself entirely to preparing his sons for their departure.

He bought four sturdy leather suitcases. On Vigan Street he bought them summer and winter wardrobes as well as several outfits that would fit them the following year.

As though in passing he mentioned to the owner, an acquaintance from the synagogue, "We're sending them to school in Switzerland."

"In that case you must buy them skis. We just received some beautiful equipment from Austria."

Joseph stumbled over his words and finally bought the ski equipment, along with a pair of tennis rackets, skates, and a football for Bertie. He wanted to buy him a bicycle, too, and reminded Shula, "I promised him one for his Bar Mitzvah." Shula restrained him from buying the bicycle only by promising him that she would find a way to have one sent directly to Israel. She quickly changed the subject. She knew how deeply hurt her husband was at the prospect that he would not be present when his eldest son was called to read from the Torah for the first time and, according to Jewish law, become a man.

They revealed their plans to the boys the night before the trip. As expected, they were exuberant and felt cheated at not being able to run out to the street and shout the news of their adventure to all their friends in the neighborhood.

The following morning Shula took them to Tanus's home by taxi. At the last moment Joseph decided against going with them.

They parted at dusk. Selim Tanus's eldest son took Bertie's hand and another member of the family gently took Meir's. Silently they disappeared into the darkness, followed by two of Selim's men driving pack donkeys laden with luggage.

She could barely hold back her tears. Tanus whispered, "Don't be frightened. If they get tired on the way my sons will carry them." He motioned to her to enter his house.

She remained with the Tanuses but refused to go to bed until his sons returned. At 2 A.M. she was informed: "Everything went well. Grisha sends his regards. And your sons—they're men. They showed no fear and they walked proudly."

A few days later Shukry Mussa brought a longer than usual message from Shimshoni:

"The children arrived safely. They are well. We brought them to your family in Jerusalem for the summer vacation. After the holidays they'll be enrolled in Nitzanim Children's Village, near Ashdod. It's the best educational institution we have for their age group. We'll continue to watch over them and make sure they have everything they need. Best wishes."

Two enthusiastic letters written in Albert's and Meir's childish handwritings were enclosed.

Uncharacteristically, she hurried to Joseph's shop. Joseph was somewhat encouraged. Since his sons had left, he had been bitter and angry and had wandered restlessly through the house as though he were searching for something he could not find. Now he read and reread his sons' letters, as he would for many nights to come.

Shula threw herself into her work with unbridled enthusiasm. On more than one occasion she realized she was not living a double life, but was actually simultaneously living in three or four separate worlds. Sooner or later she knew she was bound to fall. But she would never allow herself to dwell on depressing thoughts.

She devoted her days to caring for her family. She spent more time on the house than ever before. She went out of her way to prepare Joseph his favorite dishes and made a special effort, only partially successful, to make peace with his brother and sister. On the Sabbath she had open house both for the family and Joseph's friends. Perhaps out of a subconscious need for consolation, she spent more time with her children and indulged them.

At the same time she continued to supervise the smuggling of Syrian refugees to Israel, although she increasingly withdrew from direct involvement and delegated greater authority to Abu-Jacques.

Mussa continued to visit her home regularly to deliver and to receive messages. She reported to Israel regularly, communicating all the information and "gossip" she collected at the casino, as well as any news George did not find sufficiently important or urgent to include in his own reports.

She saw George at least once a week. Their relationship had stabilized and continued to be both comforting and satisfying. They shared a rare honesty which permitted them to discuss any subject freely, and she was no longer filled with feverish excitement each time they met. When she realized that their relationship had begun to follow a routine, it pleased her. It was a much-needed escape from the pressures and uncertainties that filled the other areas of her life. When George had to leave Beirut for any extended period of time, she found that she missed him terribly.

Then there was Abu-Sa'id. Within a very short time she had become his confidante. Once she was convinced that he had no desire to become her lover, she felt free to express her growing affection for him. She was captivated by his personality and charm. But she had no illusions or doubts about his character. When he went after something he wanted, he could be absolutely merciless. She sometimes mused what her own fate would be if one day he decided she was standing in his way. Yet cruelty was not a fundamental part of his character. He preferred to achieve his goals through charm and manipulation. They spent many hours together—she visited his office twice and thrice weekly and often accompanied him on his inspections of the casino—and she found herself in a strange and fascinating world whose existence she had not even dreamed of a few months before.

She was present for the last act of the "interesting development" whose commencement she had witnessed two months previously. One evening while sitting and sipping Antiquari with Abu-Sa'id in his office, Jamil brought in the sheikh from the Persian Gulf emirate.

The man was evidently confused and frightened and there was not even a hint of the aggressive individual she remembered from their previous meeting.

"*Ya* Abu-Sa'id, it seems that I owe you a few pounds."

Abu-Sa'id waved his hand in the air as if to indicate the unimportance of the matter. "If I can't trust you, then who can I trust? Sit down and have something to drink."

The man complied and Abu-Sa'id poured him a drink. The sheikh disregarded the three traditional refusals which etiquette demands and downed the entire drink in a single gulp.

"How can I pay my debt?" he demanded. "You know very well I don't have the means to reimburse you."

"*Ya* sheikh, I'm not interested in taking anything from you. I would much rather give you something."

The sheikh looked at him in surprise.

"That's right. I want to give you something," Abu-Sa'id said sweetly. "I want to provide you with a service. We both are aware of how important it is for you to know what is happening with your neighbors to the north. I also know that your government has allotted half a million dollars in order to obtain that information. Am I right?"

He paused to see the effect his remarks had on the sheikh. The sheikh sat silently, an enraged look coming over his face.

"So what will happen?" Abu-Sa'id calmly continued. "You'll send half a dozen secret agents across the border. Half of them will probably take your money and disappear. The others might get caught, and if they do, they'll sing at their trials. And you'll be left with renewed tension on the borders. On the off chance that you do get any information for your half-million, it will be partial, fragmented, and unreliable. I'll provide you with all the information you need, and my sources are tried and tested. And my fee is only three hundred thousand dollars, including your debt."

"But all I owe you is two hundred and fifty thousand Lebanese pounds!" shouted the sheikh. "You're asking for more than ten times that!"

"Don't I have to make a profit, too?" laughed Abu-Sa'id.

The man continued to protest. "This is outrageous. You're taking advantage of my situation."

A smile spread over Abu-Sa'id's face, as if the wolf were beginning to shed the lamb's clothing. "I'd like to remind you that you are in no situation to bargain." His voice was as cold as ice. His eyes shone like daggers. "You have no other choice. But"—his voice assumed a tone of conciliation—"what I'm offering you is a favor. I'm providing you with a necessary service for a cheaper price than you yourself were willing to pay. And in addition I'm also doing you a personal service. Your position is such that if you should present your government with a personal bill for obtaining the information they want, they'd pay it without asking any questions. On the contrary, they'll probably reward you for doing it so inexpensively. . . ."

After a few more drinks, the sheikh slowly began to see the wisdom and efficacy of Abu-Sa'id's words. They began to discuss the dates of payment and the way in which the sheikh would present the matter to his superiors.

When the man left the room, much more encouraged than when he entered, Shula said, "There's still one thing that isn't clear to me: why did you allow me to hear all this?"

Abu-Sa'id smiled. "Because you're going to help me get the information I promised him from your Israeli friends. That's the price they're going to pay for my services."

Once again she was forced to cross the border to Israel. Upon her return, right before Rosh Hashanah, she found all of Wadi Abu-Jamil in an uproar: a massive group of about three hundred refugees from Damascus had come all at once while she had been away. They filled every available corner of the ghetto. It would be necessary to send them on their way as quickly as possible.

Disaster
on the Shore

11 Shula returned from Israel with a heavy heart.

While there she had visited her two sons at the Nitzanim Youth Village. She found them tanned and happy after their three-week stay with their grandmother in Jerusalem. The boys had met all their uncles and aunts for the first time and had just arrived at Nitzanim to prepare for the new school year. Their dreams of a summer camp atmosphere had come true. They had arrived before school officially opened and the school counselors had been able to devote all their time to the few students, mostly with no families, who had arrived early. They studied Hebrew for two hours a day and spent the remainder of their time on the playing fields or at the beach.

Now that she had seen the boys, she missed them more than ever. But she decided against revealing her feelings to Joseph. Instead she became involved with the new group of Syrian refugees that had just arrived.

But as had happened so often before, a change of garrison took place and the border was once again sealed. Both Shukry Mussa and her other two smugglers refused to take any refugees across the border for the time being. Worried by the overcrowding in the Wadi and pressed by the community leaders, Shula decided to hold Abu-Sa'id to their old bargain. He was not overly enthusiastic, but said, "Three hundred all at once? And the border is closed? There's only one alternative—we'll have to send them by sea. Do you know where Fisherman's Wharf is? It's not far from the Raucha Rock. Go there and look for Abu-Amar's restaurant. Talk to him—"

"But you promised—" she interrupted.

"Talk to him," Abu-Sa'id repeated sternly. "It will be the same as talking to me."

Later that afternoon she summoned Abu-Jacques. Without disclosing her reasons she instructed him to find out all he could about Abu-Amar. By evening he came to report:

"It wasn't difficult; everybody on the wharf seems to know him. He's a well-to-do fisherman, owns several fishing boats and a boatyard, and the restaurant, too. He's not educated, but he's not stupid either. He's built everything he has with his own hands. And they say that he's very honest. Whenever there's a disagreement between the fishermen or the smugglers, they go to him to settle the dispute. They say he's on good terms with the police, too."

She wore her best clothes and even went to the hairdresser before taking a taxi to Fisherman's Wharf. When she arrived, she felt a bit conspicuous in her elegant dress and meticulous hairdo.

It was a beautiful afternoon, one of those balmy autumn days that are found only in the eastern Mediterranean. The sun was bright but not burning; a northern breeze was blowing, but gently; the sea was as smooth as a mirror. The tables and chairs from the restaurant had been placed outdoors and several sailors were lazily playing backgammon in the sun. They raised their eyes in her direction and followed her movements with undisguised curiosity. She was the only woman in the area.

A waiter motioned for her to follow him. They walked passed the backgammon tables to the back of the restaurant where she could see a small shack surrounded by a wooden fence with vines growing on it.

Abu-Amar was sitting in front of the shack beneath a grape arbor that would provide shade in summer but which was now bare of leaves. Without rising from his chair he motioned to her to sit.

Shula examined him carefully. His hair was gray, but not his moustache. He had huge shoulders and a wide expanse of chest, emphasized by the blue turtleneck sweater he wore. The sleeves were rolled up, exposing strong, hairy arms as thick as a man's legs.

"Do you know who I am?" she asked.

"Of course," he nodded. "You're Um-Ibrahim."

"And you know why I've come?"

"Yes, I was told. Three hundred, is it? No problem. I have a large fishing boat that can take on twenty-five, even thirty if they don't have too much luggage. If we start out after dark, we could be in Nahariya before daybreak. The important thing is that your people be ready for us there. We don't want any incidents, and we'll need help getting the people to shore."

"That'll be arranged. But how many trips can you make a week?"

He raised his brow. "I could make a trip every night, but that won't do. My boat has to come back with fish or questions will be asked. Let's say one trip a week."

"That means ten or twelve weeks. That's no good. I have to get them out of Beirut much faster."

He thought for a minute. After a while, he said, "There might be a way. There's a ship loading cargo for Famagusta in the port. I know the captain. I could persuade him to sail immediately. He could take on a hundred people at one go." Then, seeing her eyes light up with enthusiasm, he added, "But you must understand that this will cost more than the price agreed upon. . . ."

"Of course. That's all right. I'll need a few days to make arrangements on the other side," she said. "How soon after that can the ship leave?"

"Within one day. You'll send your people down to one of the bays down the coast in small groups. We'll have rowboats waiting for them. They'll have to come light, with no heavy baggage. When do you think you'll have your reply?"

She hesitated for a moment. "Three days at the most."

"Good. Let's hope the sea stays calm. Remember, when we decide to move, we'll have to move quickly."

"Don't worry. We'll be ready."

The affirmative reply from Israel came within two days, but getting the refugees ready proved more difficult than she had anticipated. There were refugees who refused to travel on the Jewish New Year. Abu-Jacques tried his best to persuade them, but with no success. Shula was then forced to turn to the elderly rabbi of the Damascus synagogue, whose authority was recognized by the Syrian refugees. Only after his pronouncement that the commandment to return to the land of Israel overrides the desecration of the holiday was a group of 107 refugees assembled. They were to start out for Israel immediately after the holiday prayers.

There were other problems as well. The refugees had to be transported from the Wadi to the seashore by taxi. It was not easy to find Jewish taxidrivers who would agree to work on the holiday, even for so humanitarian a mission. In the end even this complication was solved.

Shula waited impatiently at home. Joseph's brother, Chaim, his family, and, of course, Marie, came for dinner. Shula was grateful that she had to spend most of the evening in the kitchen cooking. At dinner no one insisted that she participate in the conversation, which revolved around business and the state of affairs in the Suk Sursuk.

Around midnight, after the guests had left and the children had gone to sleep, Abu-Jacques arrived to inform her that all had gone well.

Two days later a message verifying the refugees' safe arrival reached her door.

The second group of ninety-seven left the night after Yom Kippur.

In the meanwhile her feeling of foreboding returned to agonize her. George Anton gave her an explicit warning:

"The Syrians know all about you. They captured a Kurdish guide who confessed to helping smuggle a large group of Jews to Beirut. Yesterday we received a very rude communique from Damascus. They demand that we carry out a public action against the refugees. I suggest you get them out of the city as quickly as possible."

Shula immediately contacted Abu-Sa'id and informed him that she would be willing to pay any additional expenses so long as it would expedite the departure of the last of the refugees from Beirut. The ship was ordered by cable to return from Cyprus empty.

On the eve of the Sukkoth holiday all the remaining refugees were assembled and ready for the last voyage. Also present were a half-dozen local youths who had decided to emigrate to Israel.

With no warning southerly winds began to blow and the sea became rough. When Shula contacted Abu-Amar to confirm the departure time, he pointed to the high waves breaking on the shore.

"How can you send boats out in such a sea?" he said. "You Jews have a holiday tomorrow. You better pray for the sea to calm down."

The next day Shula kept her ear pressed to the window, listening for the wind. She thought the gale had subsided a bit, but in the afternoon when she took a taxi to the port, the tidings were not good.

She returned to the pier early the next morning.

"It's in the hands of Allah," Abu-Amar said stoically. "If the wind is gentle, your people come aboard. If not, the ship sails without them."

The wind subsided in the early afternoon and the sea was calm.

"Tonight," Abu-Amar declared.

Shula found herself a lookout point—a café overlooking the shore from the Corniche, Boulevard Charles de Gaulle. She watched as the first taxi approached the shore. A group of people carrying bundles alighted and began descending the steep incline to the water's edge. The taxi turned around and immediately sped off in the direction of town. The second taxi was not long in arriving.

By the light of the full moon Shula was able to discern the shadow of a rowboat leaving the bay and heading in the direction of the dark freighter anchored about three hundred yards from shore. The Petite Suisse café was crowded and, like Shula, many of the people were looking out over the shore. If any of them had noticed the shadow of a rowboat slowly making its way towards the freighter, he did not find it worth mentioning.

An hour slowly went by. She counted the arrival of eight taxis, watched them empty of their human cargo and return to town. Four trips were made from the bay to the freighter. From the time it took for each boat to make the round trip, Shula concluded that Abu-Amar had recruited only two rowboats for the mission. This meant there would be a long night ahead and she cursed him under her breath.

Suddenly the shrill sound of whistles pierced the noise of the busy café. She saw shadows racing from the southern end of the shore, the beams from their flashlights dancing in the air. She thought she heard a shot.

The foreboding that had been gnawing at her for weeks made her quickly realize: the police! Fear paralyzed her body but her mind was surprisingly clear. Without a moment's hesitation she rose from her seat and rushed outside to the promenade. The ninth taxi filled with refugees braked in front of her.

"Get back to the Wadi immediately! Tell them to stop everything." Her voice had such a tone of urgency to it that the driver automatically slammed the door, turned around, and sped off without paying any attention to the oncoming traffic.

Shula rushed back into the café, grabbed the purse she had left on the table, and ran to a public phone. She dialed a number and was relieved to hear Abu-Jacques on the other end of the line.

"Abu-Jacques," she cried in a choked voice. "Stop everything! The police are here!"

When she left the café she hesitated, trying to decide whether she should run down to the shore or leave the scene as quickly as possible. The need to know exactly what had happened overcame her concern for her own welfare. She began to walk down the stone path leading to the beach. As she emerged from behind a rock she could see an empty rowboat floating in the water, its prow stuck in the sand. Farther off she spotted the other rowboat speeding toward the freighter. Someone shouted for the boat to return to shore, but it raced out to sea with the smacking clatter of oars. The moonbeams' reflection in the water had a blinding effect and soon she could no longer see the boat.

She watched the blurred mass of bodies that hovered over the empty rowboat. There were about twenty men in uniform. Some of them carried flashlights in their hands and others rifles. They completely surrounded a smaller group of people wearing civilian clothes. The men in uniform were screaming and pushing the others with their rifle butts. Some cried out in fear as a short policeman with glasses gestured at them menacingly.

Shula squealed. Some heads turned in her direction and it was only then that she realized that she was at least as visible as those she was observing. She turned and fled.

"Stop! Hey, you there, stop!" someone shouted after her.

She kept running.

By the time she reached the promenade, she was out of breath. Just then two police vans pulled up with a screeching of brakes and uniformed policemen poured out in all directions. For some reason they took no notice of her. She returned to the café.

"Could you order a cab for me?" she calmly asked one of the waiters.

"I'm very sorry, madame, it may take awhile. Something's happened on the beach and the police have closed the road."

"What happened?" she asked innocently, while secretly praying that her choked, breathless voice did not give her away.

The waiter shrugged. "Maybe smugglers?"

She sat down and waited at a table facing the road. A few minutes later a long queue of people made their way up from the shore. A police officer carrying a revolver led the procession, followed by armed policemen. Then a group of civilians came into view. She quickly counted about a dozen of them. She assumed the barefoot man among them was one of Abu-Amar's men. The others were the illegal immigrants and she also recognized four young men from the Wadi among them. A group of armed policemen brought up the rear.

They were loaded into one of the empty police vans and disappeared. Quiet returned to Raucha Beach.

Shula phoned Abu-Jacques again, but there was no answer. She tried calling Dr. Attia at home. Before even identifying herself she blurted out, "Do you know what happened?"

His reply was cautious: "Yes, we've heard."

"How are you?"

"Everything here is fine."

"Do you know where Abu-Jacques is?"

"I think he's gone to make arrangements for some friends who have come to visit."

She was somewhat relieved. The refugees were being hidden. Now there was only the matter of the twelve or so who had been caught by the police. And the others who had made it to the ship? She peered out toward the sea, but the freighter was no longer in sight. After straining her eyes she was able to make out a large shadow sailing off in the distance. What would happen if they sent the coast guard after it? She struck the thought from her mind. "We'll cross that bridge when we come to it." Now she had to concentrate on those being held by the police and to figure out how they had been informed of the operation. She had no doubt that this was the work of informers.

But who could have informed the police? The Syrians? The Palestinians? Could it have been someone from the Wadi?

She put her speculations aside momentarily and thought of how she could free the refugees before they were interrogated and official reports were submitted. Perhaps a little well-placed bribery would put an end to the entire matter.

But she did not know to whom to turn or whom to pay. If only she could call George! But she wouldn't think of contacting him at home, not for all the money in the world. And besides, hadn't he hinted at their last meeting that he would be away from Beirut for a few days?

There was only one person who might be able to help her. She quickly dialed the Olympia Casino.

"Abu-Sa'id," she said when she recognized his voice at the other end of the line, "Something's happened. I must see you."

"Where are you speaking from? Are you at home?"

"No, I'm at a café near the beach on Le Boulevard Charles de Gaulle. La Petite Suisse. Near Chtila Street."

"Wait there. I'll send my car for you immediately."

It was 1 A.M. by the time she sat down in his office. He handed her a glass of straight whiskey.

"Drink," he consoled her. "It'll quiet your nerves. You said that one of Abu-Amar's men was caught? Let's hope he had enough brains to pretend to be a refugee! The commanding officer was short and wore glasses? I don't know who that could be. Wait, we'll check!"

He dialed a number, asked a few questions, and then dialed another number. Finally he told her: "They know nothing about it at police headquarters. The Manara station knows nothing about the operation either. That isn't good. It means that it could only have been from the Kuraytem station or one from a Palestinian refugee camp."

"Why is that so bad?" she asked without thinking.

"Because they are controlled by the Moslems. I have no influence in either of these places."

Her heart sank. "What are we going to do?" she asked in desperation.

"You go home. I'll try to make a few more calls. Be here tomorrow at noon. We'll see what we can do then."

She spent the whole night tossing and turning, reliving the incident on the beach. She was now thoroughly convinced that someone had informed on them. She was equally sure that the police knew all about her!

She left Carmela with Nazira and was out of the house as soon as her children were off to school. She bought a copy of *L'Orient le Jour,* and quickly skimmed through it. There was no mention of last night's incident. This gave her some hope. If the event had not been reported, it could still be kept quiet.

Later at the casino Abu-Sa'id crushed whatever lingering hopes she may have harbored.

"It's just as I thought," he said. "It was the work of informers and the arrests were made from Kuraytem. Captain Hasan Nasrallah was the arresting officer. Our luck, would have it that he's Druze and I have no way of getting to him."

He was silent and pensive. She waited for him to speak.

"There's no other way," he finally said. "The only person who can help you now is Baidon. That's his territory."

Her heart froze when she heard the name.

Darwish Baidon was no less infamous in Beirut than Abu-Sa'id. Actually they functioned in similar roles. Abu-Sa'id was the undisputed lord in the Christian sector and Baidon in the Moslem. Baidon was active in the same kind of enterprises as Abu-Sa'id: gambling, smuggling, procuring "entertainers" for the Middle East, and espionage. But while Abu-Sa'id was referred to as the "Prince of Thieves" Baidon was thought of as a gang leader and nothing more. It was said in Beirut that while Abu-Sa'id generously supported orphans and widows, Baidon lent them money at exorbitant interest.

"You . . . couldn't you talk with him?" she stammered.

"I probably could," he said after a prolonged silence, "and he'd most likely agree to help, but his price would be more than I'm willing to pay. I made a rule many years ago that I would never have any dealings with him. I'm sorry. . . ."

Shula wrung her hands in despair.

"Those people have to be released," she cried.

"Look, my advice to you is to stay out of it. There are bound to be slipups. They're unavoidable. But even if your people remain in jail, it's better than doing business with Baidon."

She refused to accept his advice. When he saw that he could not persuade her, he finally said, "If you're going to be stubborn, I'll give you the name of the man who can set up a meeting with Baidon. It's your Shukry Mussa." When he saw the shocked look on her face, he added, "His clan's representative in parliament is a good friend of the speaker of the house, a Shi'ite from the south, who happens to be Baidon's patron."

When she arrived home in the afternoon, the news of the refugees' arrest had already leaked out and the Wadi was in an uproar. The lawyer whom the community leaders had sent to the Kuraytem station was not permitted to see the prisoners since the "investigation is still being conducted."

"There's a lot of talk against you," Abu-Jacques informed her. "Anyone who even hinted that you were endangering the lives of the Jews in Wadi Abu-Jamil is now shouting, 'We knew this would happen!' "

"It doesn't matter," she cut him off impatiently. "Can you bring Mussa here?"

Mussa arrived the following day. He already knew what had happened. He even knew that the Greek freighter had safely reached Nahariya and that thirty refugees had disembarked. The ship had sailed on.

Mussa's face turned serious with concern when he heard Shula's demand.

"He's not a good man," he mumbled.

"But don't you understand? I must see him. He's the only one who can put an end to the affair. Otherwise there'll be a public trial and then everything will come out."

Only after hearing this was he willing to try to establish contact with Baidon's men.

A few hours later he returned with a young man whom he introduced as his nephew Nabil, a student at the American University.

"Baidon will see you tomorrow afternoon in his office. But," he added with a note of concern, "I don't want you going there alone. Nabil will go with you."

After the two of them left the house, Shula began to think of the task before her. She recalled everything she had ever heard about Baidon and she was petrified. She was so frightened that when Joseph returned home from work she could not restrain herself from telling him everything.

He listened without interrupting. When she finished speaking, he simply asked, "Then why are you going?"

"Because we have to get the refugees out of jail. They've already been there for three days."

"Let the community hire a lawyer for them. Why do you have to do everything?"

"Because if we don't put a stop to the whole business," she explained patiently, "there'll be a trial. I'll be involved anyway."

He thought about what she had said.

"Shula," he said finally, "you know my opinion. Why don't you take the risk of being tried and get yourself out of this whole business once and for all? But I know you won't listen to me. What can I say? Only this—people who do God's work are not harmed."

Her tension increased the following morning. At eleven o'clock she phoned Abu-Sa'id at the casino.

"I only wanted to inform you that I have an appointment with Baidon this afternoon at four in his office."

"Are you going alone?"

"No. One of the Mussas is coming with me. I wanted you to know, just in case . . ."

"I understand. Let's hope it works out."

She was still uneasy. She phoned George Anton's office and was relieved when she was asked to wait on the line.

"Monsieur Anton," she cried with joy when she heard his familiar voice, "*ici* Madame Cohen. I wasn't sure you were back in Beirut. Can you hear me?"

"Yes," he answered tersely.

"I called because I have a meeting at four with Darwish Baidon. Can you hear me?"

"Yes. I hear, but I'm not pleased. Are you sure it's the right thing to do?"

"Yes. I'm positive. I called because I wanted you to know . . ." She wanted to add: "Where to find me."

"I'm glad you did. Call me immediately after you see him."

At four o'clock, accompanied by Nabil Mussa, who was trying his best to conceal his anxiety, she arrived at a large office building on Hamra Street. Baidon's offices were on the fourth floor. The sign on the glass door read: "Baidon Brothers, Import–Export."

The man who greeted them was about thirty-five years old, wore a moustache, and had the air of chief clerk. Two secretaries sat in the room but neither raised her eyes from her typewriter.

"Madame Cohen?" he said. "The *effendi* is expecting you." He pointed to a closed door. When Nabil started to follow her, the man stopped him.

"Madame Cohen will enter alone," he said sternly, as if expecting trouble.

Shula made a desperate motion to Nabil not to object.

When the clerk opened the door, she could not believe her eyes. Before her was a mountain of a man sitting in an armchair whose armrests had been removed to enable it to contain his bulk. She estimated his weight at a minimum of four hundred pounds. Everything about him was swollen out of proportion and unnatural: his shoulders, the layers of fat rippling down his protruding belly, his bald head and puffed up eyes. His enormous legs were spread apart. A heavily made-up blonde in a short, strapless evening dress sat on one knee feeding him large pieces of halvah from a huge bowl. A bottle of whiskey sat on a footstool near his other knee.

He did not bother to stand when Shula entered the room.

"So you've finally come," he said with his mouth full of halvah. "I've been waiting for you for years. Sit."

She remained standing.

"You know why I'm here," she said curtly. "Perhaps you'll tell that little toy of yours to leave?"

"Don't pay any attention to her. She understands only German anyway. But perhaps you'd rather we speak this evening? Then we can be alone."

"I came on business and I do business only during the day."

"Even with Abu-Sa'id?" His fleshy·mouth widened into a malicious grin. She ignored his lewd suggestion.

"I meet Abu-Sa'id in the evenings only when I'm with my husband."

He snorted disdainfully. "Your husband must be a very small man since no one can see him."

Her fears exploded within her. She was terror-struck.

"Then let's talk business. What do you want?" He was obviously enjoying her distress.

"You know. It's about the people who were caught on the beach.

They committed no crime. All they wanted to do was take a little sightseeing trip—"

He snorted contemptuously. "Let's stop playing games, Madame Cohen. We both know very well why they were on the beach. So do the police. They say that Abu-Sa'id *effendi* doesn't abandon his friends, but it appears that your friends are not so important to him. Never mind. I'll take care of your people. You want to get them to Israel? They'll get to Israel."

He suddenly patted the blonde's buttocks and she jumped off his knee, half-amused, half-annoyed. He leaned with all his weight toward the table, rang a copper bell, and sat back in the chair, panting and gasping from the great effort.

The chief clerk who had led her into the room stuck his head in the door.

"Run to the police," Baidon ordered, "and tell them to give the Jews something to eat and drink and to let them wash. And tell them to give them some mattresses, too."

With the same wave of his hand with which he dismissed his errand boy he motioned for the blonde to leave the room. He looked at Shula and smiled.

"They say that a deal isn't a deal unless an advance is paid. That was my down payment; now let's make our deal."

"They're so unfortunate," she stammered. "You're the only one who can help them. I came for your advice. . . ."

"Have you ever been to a restaurant where you can pay your bill with advice? You came to offer me a price. Never mind. I'll set the price. A thousand pounds per head."

"They're not the sons of sheikhs!" she cried. "They're poor unfortunate people who have nothing—"

He silenced her. "I'm not here to bargain with you. You Jews, you're a very strange people. The whole year you steal from each other, but if anything happens to one of you, you sell your mother's wedding ring to save him. One thousand per head."

"I don't have that kind of money, nor can I promise you that amount. If you get a thousand per head, that will be your price from now on. For a thousand, let them stay in jail."

"Then how much are you willing to pay?"

"I can offer you one hundred and twenty."

Baidon burst out laughing. Saliva mixed with bits of halvah oozed from his lips. "Do I look like a beggar to you? Look, the pleasure of seeing you has cost me many years of patience. Now that you're here, I'm still willing to pay. For you—five hundred."

"Don't haggle with the Angel of Death when he comes for you," she recited a well-known proverb. "And don't try to take money from the empty pockets of the poor."

"Good. I see you're intelligent as well as obstinate." Baidon sneered scornfully. "Meet me tonight at the opera and we'll decide on the price."

When Beirutis spoke of the opera, they meant the Roxy Theater at the Place de Canon, where imported revues were presented. Shula thought quickly. No decent woman would want to be seen at the "opera," but it was a public place filled with people. She would not be exposed to too much danger there.

She agreed. "How will I find you?"

"Your friend Abu-Sa'id," he snorted, "has a private box there. But I own the place. Don't worry, you'll see me."

"I'm the mother of six," she said as she stood. "Don't put my honor on the line."

Baidon's man was waiting for her when she arrived at the Roxy Theater. He led her to the reserved boxes and knocked on one of the doors. It was an ordinary theater box, but all the seats had been removed and replaced with two armchairs, one of which resembled the armless chair she had seen in Baidon's office earlier that day. Darwish Baidon was seated in it. At his feet stood a stool with a bottle of whiskey and an enormous bowl of halvah. A single orchid in a cellophane-wrapped carton had been placed on the other chair.

Without facing her he said, "You're late. But the smell of your perfume has already appeased my anger. Sit."

"Thank you for the corsage. You really are a special kind of man. You have two faces."

"Only two?" he laughed. "Anyone who says a man has only two faces doesn't know how to count. The flower? It's nothing. Baidon can supply everything. The only thing I don't have control over is the weather. But with a single phone call I can change the weather forecast that will be printed in tomorrow's papers. . . ." The laughter welling up in his throat developed into a cough that shook his huge body and threatened to choke him.

A group of svelte dancers, purported to have just arrived from Paris, were doing a vigorous cancan on the stage. At the end of the performance Baidon said, "Let's go."

"You're not interested in the girls?" she said, frightened again.

"I imported them. I've already seen the show three times. Let's go."

She saw no way to refuse and followed. His car, a custom-made Chrysler with an immense door built especially for him, was parked at the entrance in front of a "No Parking" sign.

The driver turned on the motor without waiting for instructions and they were soon traveling up the mountain on the Beirut–Damascus highway. Baidon motioned to the driver to stop at a roadside café.

"Go and drink some coffee," he ordered brusquely. "If I need you, I'll blow the horn."

They were alone. His heavy breathing was the only sound that broke the tense silence.

Shula began to feel more and more uncomfortable. "I brought the money," she said in an attempt to establish a businesslike atmosphere. "One hundred seventy-five pounds per head. I can't offer any more."

He did not respond. He bent over and pressed a button on the back of the driver's seat, which dropped into a small bar with liquor and some glasses.

"When I left the house, my daughter wasn't feeling very well," Shula lied. "I don't want to be late. Let's finish our business."

While pouring a glass of whiskey, he turned to her and said:

"A man brings flowers to his lover, or a diamond ring to his fiancée. I, madame, present you with twelve Jews. They're already in Wadi Abu-Jamil. They were released while you were sitting with me in the Roxy."

She stopped breathing for a moment.

"I-I owe you more than money," she stammered.

"That's true," he said in an icy tone. "You can burn a written contract, but not a debt of gratitude." He offered her a glass of whiskey, but she refused it with a shake of her head. He drew nearer.

"I'm willing to give you even more," he continued in a choked voice. "I'm ready to give you everything. A mansion on the mountain, money, and all my men will be at your service."

She broke out in a cold sweat. "What do you want?" she asked.

"First of all, that you stop being afraid. Second, that you promise not to tell a soul—no, that won't be necessary, I know you won't. I can't ask you to share my bed. I'm fat, very fat, and sick. I can't—doctor's orders," he quickly added. He hesitated a moment and then went on. "I want . . . to watch you make love. Don't worry, I'll bring you someone clean, who won't talk. And I won't do a thing. I'll sit back and watch. Then I'll go."

As sophisticated as she thought she was in the ways of the world, she had never experienced anything like this before. She was filled with fear—and disgust. His heavy breath so close to her in the darkness, the smell of alcohol and sweat and perfume nauseated her. She pulled herself back, away from him, without thinking, until she could feel the door handle against her skin. She stealthily took the handle in her hand.

"You were right. I won't tell a soul," she said. With an attempt to sound aggressive and sure of herself she added, "I'm going now, and don't try to stop me. Several people know where I was tonight and with whom. They'll be worried if I don't contact them immediately."

She pressed the door handle and escaped into the cool night air. He made no attempt to stop her. As she ran into the café, she heard the horn blow.

The following day she sent Shurky Mussa's nephew to Baidon's office with a sealed envelope containing 2100 Lebanese pounds. Nabil Mussa informed her that Baidon's clerk took the envelope without a word.

A few days later, Shula Kishak-Cohen was ordered to appear at the Kuraytem police station. She was informed by letter to see the investigating officer, First Inspector Hamdi Shakiu.

A fair-haired, fair-skinned man of about thirty, dressed in civilian clothes, he met her at the reception desk and brought her to his office on the second floor. He treated her courteously, but his words were frightening nevertheless.

"I have been ordered to investigate the incident of last Monday at Raucha Beach. Does that mean anything to you?"

"Vaguely," she answered with forced indifference. "I was there, sitting at a café on the promenade. I heard some noise and the waiter told me the police had captured some smugglers. That's all I know."

"I must warn you, madame, that this is an official investigation and you are obliged to tell the truth. What you have just said is not the truth. I have in my possession a sworn statement from a reliable source that positively identified you at the scene of the crime."

She tried to think rationally. No one could have seen her on the beach. On the rock, perhaps? Was there enough light from the full moon to permit a positive identification from twenty or thirty yards? It was possible.

She answered cautiously, "It's possible that I stepped out to get a closer look, out of curiosity. But I didn't go any farther than the stone path. I wasn't even near the beach."

"Permit me, madame," he was still polite, but aggressive, "you know very well what was taking place on the beach. There was an organized attempt to smuggle Jews out of the country illegally. And we have testimony that clearly points to you as the leader of this smuggling network."

She was overcome with fear but could still think clearly. She knew for a fact that the refugees had not informed on her. During the three days they had spent in jail, they were treated roughly and humiliated, but they had not been interrogated. Only their names had been recorded, along with the charge of attempting to leave the country illegally. They had been released on bail. What kind of testimony could the police have? It had to be an informer. . . .

"I want to see that testimony," she said forcefully.

"You know very well that I am not permitted to show it to you."

"Then I have nothing to say."

"May I inform you, madame, that that is not very wise. Something much more serious occurred on the beach that night. When the police arrived, someone fired a shot in the direction of the law. The bullet knicked the sleeve of Captain Nasrallah, the commander of the operation, and it was a miracle that he wasn't injured. The man who fired the shot was seen escaping in the rowboat that managed to sail out to sea to a ship that was apparently waiting for it. It doesn't matter. We know who it was and we'll find him. But it turns this incident into a very serious matter, indeed, an attempt to murder a police officer in the course of his duty. According to the law, everyone involved in the incident is responsible. Including you."

She interrupted: "I want to consult with my attorney."

"It's your right. But what I wanted to say before you interrupted me was that it is you who will determine whether we accuse you of attempted murder or not by the amount of cooperation you show."

"I don't know a thing. I've never held a gun in my life. I wasn't on the beach. I was waiting for a friend at the Petite Suisse café. The waiters are sure to recognize me. When I heard all that commotion on the beach, I went out to look, out of curiosity. That's all. I have no connection with what happened there."

"Are you willing to state that as official testimony?"

She suspected that he was laying a trap. "No. With such serious charges being made against me, I want to consult my lawyer before I say anything. Am I being charged with anything?"

"Not yet. This is merely an investigation."

"Am I under arrest?"

"Of course not."

"Then I want to leave. I am not willing to speak with you without consulting my lawyer first."

"You're free to leave, madame. We will call you in for further investigation in the near future. In the meantime consult with your attorney and do not try to leave Beirut. In the eyes of the law an attempt to escape is an admission of guilt."

The Hot Summer

12 For Shula and her family, as well as for all the residents of Wadi Abu-Jamil, the weeks that followed were filled with fear and tension.

The lawyer Joseph had engaged to represent his wife was of little assistance when he accompanied Shula to the Kuraytem station. He was a Christian who had represented Joseph in several civil cases connected with his business; Shula had the impression that his presence only antagonized the young Moslem investigating officer.

When the session was over and Shula, on her attorney's counsel, refused to sign a statement, the investigator announced that she was being freed in her own custody. Nevertheless, Shula left the police station disappointed and depressed.

In her depressed state Shula decided to seek Abu-Sa'id's counsel. Suddenly, however, it became impossible to reach him. Every time she phoned the casino, she was informed that "he had just left." When she called his home in the afternoon, his bodyguard rudely told her, "Monsieur and madame are resting and cannot be disturbed."

George stood by her, as strong as a rock, but he was forced to admit that there was very little he could do to help, since the investigation was being carried out by the Kuraytem station. Even the security services were not informed of the operation until the arrests had already been made.

"This means that someone from the outside was behind it all," George reasoned, "but it doesn't sound like it could have been the Syrians; the tip-off might have come from the Palestinians." He paused. "Still, we can't dismiss the possibility that the informer lives in Wadi Abu-Jamil. Someone with a grudge against you might have contacted the police."

Shula refused to accept this possibility, even after George provided her with all the information he could gather on the Kuraytem police commander, Captain Hasan Nasrallah.

"Nasrallah is a Druze," George said, "and very ambitious. We have no knowledge of any connections he may have with the Palestinians. It's more logical to assume that some information came into the captain's hands and he simply decided to exploit it to further his own career."

"He's a liar!" Shula burst out in anger. "He testified that he saw me on the beach when I wasn't there at all! Even if he had seen me, it would have been at such a distance that he could never have made a positive identification. Yet he even knew me by name."

"That just proves that it was the work of an informer," George continued patiently. "The informer told Nasrallah you had organized the operation, and when he saw a woman in the area he assumed it had to be you—and rightly so, I might add."

"What should I do?"

"The first thing you have to do is change lawyers," George advised. "You should have known that you don't send a Christian lawyer, particularly a commercial one, to a police station in the Moslem section."

"He's my husband's attorney, and in all the confusion—"

"The confusion has passed. Now you have to act more prudently. Get yourself a good Moslem attorney, preferably one who knows how to pull strings. The problem is not getting you acquitted; we want to make sure your case never even gets to court. Once you've hired an attorney, instruct him to drag out the affair for as long as possible under any pretext he can come up with. Then if after all his efforts the case is brought to court, have him play up the fact that

Nasrallah is terribly nearsighted. I got to see his personal service file; he had to use influence to pass the physical."

Shula continued to resist George's suggestion that someone from the Wadi had informed on her. Nevertheless, she began to feel she was under surveillance and developed symptoms of paranoia. She was convinced that her telephone was being tapped, despite George's insistence that his office was directly responsible for such matters and that her name was not on his list. She cautioned him to refrain from calling her at home. She would go to the drugstore on the corner whenever she needed to use the phone. When she had an appointment in town, she never took the first cab at the station, preferring to stop a taxi on the street. She tried to make herself as inconspicuous as possible.

Throughout the winter of 1951–52, Shula was preoccupied with the police investigation and her upcoming trial. Joseph, meanwhile, was becoming more and more depressed as the date of Bertie's Bar Mitzvah approached. He tried to hide his feelings from Shula, but with little success. She could read his thoughts from the hopeful way he asked, every evening after work, if there was any mail from Israel. Often he locked himself in the boys' old room, mumbling to himself as he strained to read the titles of the books on the shelves with his nearsighted eyes. One Saturday morning he came home from synagogue, his eyes red and swollen from crying, and only then did Shula realize that one of the neighborhood boys had been called to the Torah for the first time.

One evening soon afterward when she turned from her work in the kitchen, she found him in the living room reciting the Torah portion that Bertie was to read for his Bar Mitzvah. Shula was very moved. He had been such a patient and faithful husband through the years, despite his feigned indifference. His one dream in the world was to celebrate his sons' introduction to manhood publicly, according to Jewish law; but because of her, even this was denied him.

A sense of regret filled her. She sat next to him, gently taking his hand in hers, and whispered, "Don't worry, Joseph, Bertie will have a beautiful Bar Mitzvah, in Jerusalem."

Joseph burst into tears and Shula placed her hand on his head and cradled him like a baby at her breast, repeating softly, "It's all right, Joseph. He's happy. He's better off there."

Never before in the long years of their marriage had she felt so close to him. He sobbed like a child as she led him to his bedroom and comforted him.

When the first spring winds arrived, Shula felt as if she had awakened from a long winter's hibernation. She began to visit the casino regularly once again, to Abu-Sa'id's apparent delight. He went out of his way to please her, as if trying to revive their old friendship and make amends for his neglect.

One evening when she joined him for an inspection tour of the casino, they stopped off at a table where a man of about fifty was sitting alone and eating. The man stood when he saw them approaching. He looked familiar, and when Abu-Sa'id introduced him, she remembered that she had seen him several times in Saraya Square when she was being investigated at police headquarters by George Anton.

"This is a dear friend of mine," Abu-Sa'id said, pointing to Shula. "Any request she makes should be treated as if it came straight from me."

The man bowed in her direction. "Your wish is my command."

"It would be worth her while to meet others of our friends," Abu-Sa'id cryptically told the man as they continued their walk.

Shula knew that this "chance encounter" with the detective had been planned in advance and wondered why. But she completely forgot the incident until one evening Abu-Sa'id phoned to invite her to the casino.

"You won't be sorry if you come tonight," he ventured.

When she arrived, it was Jamil who met her at the door, apologizing for Abu-Sa'id. "There's a meeting going on in the *effendi's* office. He asked that you wait in the restaurant." Shula's surprise disappeared the moment she saw the police detective waiting for her. She understood that Abu-Sa'id preferred not to be directly involved in whatever he had arranged.

"There's a man here I think you should meet," the detective said, motioning toward someone standing to the side. The stranger was introduced as Monsieur Mahmud Hoj of the Ministry of the Interior.

Shula still had no idea why Abu-Sa'id had set up the meeting. Out of the corner of her eye she could see him observing the scene from his private balcony. The detective noticed him, too, and, excusing himself, rushed off to join Abu-Sa'id, leaving Shula and Hoj alone in the restaurant.

Hoj broke the silence. "I understand that I am in a position to help you," he said. "If so, I'm at your service. Generally I'm in my office every day until three, but if you need me I can stay longer, since I imagine it's difficult for you to get out during the day. In any case it's more convenient for me to see you after all the workers have left, when we'll be able to speak without interruption."

She wasn't sure exactly what service this Hoj could provide until he asked, "Do you know where to find me? I'm in the registration office at the Ministry of the Interior."

Everything was clear to her now. This introduction was Abu-Sa'id's reconciliation gift.

Afterward, when she joined Abu-Sa'id for a stroll around the casino, he whispered, "Did you make a deal with him?"

She replied that Hoj had invited her to his office.

"That's fine," said Abu-Sa'id. "He'll be able to supply you with whatever identity cards and passports you need. Don't be timid with him. Call him whenever you think he can help, but don't go into detail on the phone. And if he demands too much money, let me know."

Shula's first chance to put Hoj's services to use came two weeks later, when a wealthy family arrived from Damascus, not by the traditional illegal route, but by bribing their way across the Lebanese border.

Abu-Jacques presented their case to Shula. "They have money, but they don't want to emigrate to Israel. They say they have relatives in France."

"Then why should we even get involved?" she questioned.

"Because they were given my name in Damascus," Abu-Jacques sighed, "and if they're caught, they might talk. For our own sakes we'd better get rid of them before they have a chance to endanger the other refugees."

Shula remembered Mahmud Hoj's offer of assistance.

"I hope they're willing to pay the price," she said.

Shula made an appointment to see Mahmud Hoj in his office that afternoon at four. When she arrived, Hoj was the only one left in the building. The guard led her to the office and opened the door, smiling conspiratorially.

"I have a father and four children," she told Hoj without further explanation. "They want to leave, but they don't have the necessary documents."

"At your service," he smiled. "A *laissez-passer* will cost you five hundred pounds, a Lebanese passport, one thousand five hundred. Which do you prefer?"

"The passports, but I only have half that amount."

"I won't quibble over price with a friend of Abu-Sa'id *effendi.*"

The following day she returned with passport photos and the necessary information, and Mahmud Hoj produced the passports immediately. After presenting them to her and counting the money he advised, "It's best if they don't show the passports around Beirut. When they decide to leave, send them to the Trans-Mediterranean Airlines booth at the airport. There they'll find a clerk named Fahed Hamouda; I'll write down his name for you. Have them say that I sent them. Fahed will see to their tickets and arrange for their visas. They'll have to pay him a commission, of course, but it will be well worth their while. He'll make sure that no one inspects their passports any more than is absolutely necessary."

Shula learned later that Fahed Hamouda and Mahmud Hoj had established a very profitable relationship. Fahed would send "clients" to Hoj, who would in turn recommend Hamouda's services once the visas or passports had been obtained. Each man received a handsome commission for providing clients to the other. The detective from the *Sûreté* enjoyed a similar arrangement with Hoj. Shula wondered whether Abu-Sa'id also received a cut for his participation, but decided he didn't; Abu-Sa'id's commission was gratitude. Beirut was full of people who owed something to Abu-Sa'id.

At the end of April, 1952, Shula's trial began. The eleven refugees were accused of attempting to leave Lebanon illegally. The name of the twelfth, Abu-Amar's man, had mysteriously disappeared from the list of defendants, and no mention of him was ever made in any of the pretrial testimony. Shula was charged with helping in their attempted escape.

The attorney chosen from the list George Anton had provided proved his worth right away by arranging to have any mention of the shooting incident removed from the indictment. This seriously reduced the severity of the charge against Shula, so that her case was now to be tried in a lower court.

The new lawyer was optimistic. "The maximum sentence that the magistrate's court has the power to declare is a year," he informed her. "I imagine you'll only have to pay a fine, since it's your first offense."

But after consulting with George, Shula was unwilling to take even the slightest risk.

"The best thing is to postpone the trial as long as you can," George cautioned. "The more time between the date of the trial and the date of the crime, the better your chances of a lighter sentence. In the meantime, Captain Nasrallah might be transferred or promoted, and without his testimony they don't have a case against you."

He found out that the judge at her trial was to be a Shi'ite Moslem.

"Set the Mussa family into action," he advised her. "They don't have to push too hard. They only have to get a postponement, and if they must, let them pay your way out of a speedy trial. It will be best for everyone concerned."

Shula knew the outcome even before she and the other eleven defendants faced the judge. After he read the charges against them and recorded the "not guilty" plea of each of the defendants, the judge placed his glasses on the lectern and motioned for the attorneys to approach the bench.

"I see that we have a long list of witnesses," he began. "It's obvious that the two days set aside for this trial will never suffice. So if you have no objections, I would prefer to postpone the trial to a later date, when it would fit into the court's schedule."

There were no objections, and the trial was postponed to the twelfth of June.

Just as the magistrate announced the new date, a sudden wave of nausea swept over Shula. Her face grew pale and she broke out in a cold sweat. The judge was the first to notice. Sounding concerned, he asked, "Are you all right, Madame Cohen? Do you feel ill? Please be seated. Clerk, a glass of water for Madame Cohen!"

Shula sipped the cold water, regaining her composure, and assured the judge that she felt better. But as she left the court she had to lean on her attorney's arm. Her nausea returned, but this time she could identify it.

Shula Kishak-Cohen was pregnant.

The initial annoyance she felt when she discovered the cause of her condition quickly faded. Her family doctor examined her and announced with a broad smile, "Everything is fine, and why shouldn't it be? You're a superb baby-making machine." By then Shula had no misgivings. She was truly happy. Her pleasure was reinforced by Joseph's reaction to the news. Her husband was ecstatic. Treating her with the same indulgence he had shown during her first pregnancy, he forbade her to exert herself doing housework and scolded the children for not helping enough. Joseph often came home early from the market, bringing her little presents, to take her out to a café on the Corniche. He even rented a summer home for the family in Behmadon. He greeted his wife's amused protests with a firm declaration: "You need fresh air, and it will be good for the baby."

The attention Joseph lavished on his wife began to annoy his eldest daughter. Yaffa, now fourteen and a half, had developed into a tall, attractive, pleasant, yet introverted young woman. She had always been the apple of her father's eye, and now, Shula thought, she was jealous.

Yaffa had entered that precarious stage between childhood and adulthood and had begun to awaken, albeit unconsciously, to an awareness of her womanhood. She spent most of her time daydreaming or reading romantic novels, learning all about love from books. Her strict convent school education, however, taught her that sex was forbidden, a sin. The sudden revelation that her parents had committed such a sin hit Yaffa like a slap in the face. She was disgusted by the thought.

Her feelings made her ill-humored and spiteful, and since she couldn't discuss them freely, she began to rebel.

"None of my friends in school ever have to help around the house!" she challenged Shula. "If you can't work, why don't we hire a maid like everybody else? Daddy earns enough to afford one."

Once she blurted out, "I wish I were a boy. Then I could get out of here just like Bertie and Meir."

Yaffa had spoken without thinking, but Shula saw in her outburst a possible solution to an awkward problem that was becoming increasingly intolerable.

"Would you like to join them?" she asked cautiously.

Yaffa was in a particularly foul mood that day. "Would I like to? I'm dying to leave this house!"

Shula had a talk with Joseph. Her husband was astonished.

"Send a young girl away from home? She'll soon be old enough to be married! Who'll watch over her? Who'll marry her off when the time comes?"

"Exactly!" Shula had carefully thought out her arguments in advance. "Can you think of even one young man in the Wadi you would like to see as your son-in-law? Yaffa's getting older, Joseph. In a little while we won't be able to stop her from dating. Do you want her to fall in love with a Christian? Or a Moslem?"

He continued to protest, but she had touched a sensitive spot and he began to weaken. "Where can she go? Are there special girls' schools in Israel? Maybe we should send her to study in Switzerland?"

"And who'll take care of her there?" Shula argued. "In Israel she has family at least."

He relented, agreeing that it might not be bad to send Yaffa to live with one of Shula's married brothers and sisters.

"Or even better, with my mother," Shula prompted, continuing his train of thought. "My mother's not young anymore, but Yaffa is old enough to take care of herself. And Jerusalem is a large city with very fine schools."

But Joseph voiced another objection: he would not permit Yaffa to cross the Israeli border on foot. "I almost died when you sent off Bertie and Meir," he said. "You can't expect a young girl to climb hazardous mountain trails in the middle of the night, surrounded only by smugglers, with no one to protect her. I'll never agree to it!"

"There'll be no need," Shula promised. "Yaffa will fly to Israel like a queen, in first class."

She wrote to Epstein in Istanbul the following day and sent Shimshoni a note through Shukry Mussa. Without waiting for a reply, she filled out the necessary forms to get Yaffa a passport "to visit relatives in Istanbul."

On June 12 the court heard the witnesses for the prosecution. Shula's lawyer cross-examined each one carefully, focusing all his energy on Hasan Nasrallah. He wanted to cast doubt on the captain's claim to have seen Shula on the beach with the refugees.

"How far were you from the defendant when you claim to have seen her?" the lawyer began.

"She was about twenty yards away," Nasrallah answered.

"Perhaps it was more like forty yards? Or fifty? Think again, Captain. I might have to ask the court to visit the scene of the alleged crime and judge the distance for itself."

Nasrallah angrily admitted that she may have been thirty yards away from him.

"And all of this took place at night," the attorney persisted.

"Yes, but there was a full moon. I had a clear view of the beach."

"Captain Nasrallah," Shula's lawyer shouted, "I am going to prove to this court that not only did you not see the defendant there, you are not even capable of identifying a man you know well from a distance of twenty yards—in daylight! But to return to the accused, Shulamit Kishak-Cohen, why didn't you arrest her then, on the beach?"

Nasrallah claimed that Shula had fled from the scene of the crime, and since his men were occupied with the other defendants on the beach, they could not pursue her.

"Yet in the report you filed that night you mentioned her by name. How could you have known her precise identity if she wasn't even in your hands?"

The police captain was forced to concede that he had been given the name of the accused by "reliable sources," whose identity he could not disclose. The judge ruled that Nasrallah was not obligated to tell the court the identity of these sources.

"We've succeeded in shaking him up a bit," the attorney assured Shula during the break. "We've established the fact that there were indeed informers involved. But that won't be enough."

At the end of Nasrallah's testimony the judge postponed the hearing of the witnesses for the defense until the twenty-fifth of September.

The summer of 1952 was a hot one for the Middle East. An "officers' revolution" in Egypt on July 23 deposed the royal family that had sat on the throne for over 140 years. The removal of the corrupt King Farouk and his replacement by a group of young, idealistic, and patriotic army officers rocked the entire region. Historians later theorized that the officers' revolution was the major factor behind the downfall of the traditional governments that had ruled the Middle East in the shadow of the ex-colonial powers. In any case, the uprising threw the Arab world into a whirlwind of increasingly radical and unstable political regimes that left their mark on the Middle East for many years to come.

The unrest that broke out in Lebanon that summer was not directly related to what had happened in Egypt, despite the almost simultaneous timing of the turmoil in the two Arab countries.

The real reason for the turmoil in Lebanon lay in the simple fact that the government had been in power too long. When he was elected President in 1943, Bishara al-Khuri, aligning himself with the larger, more influential Moslem families—particularly the Sulh clan, whose leaders, Riad and Sami, served alternately as prime minister —represented a national consensus that was broad enough to ensure government stability. His position was so strong that in 1949, after six years of rule, al-Khuri had no trouble convincing a parliamentary majority to amend the constitution to enable his reelection.

But an additional three years under al-Khuri had proved to be more than enough. The thought that they might have to wait twelve years for their own turn at power prompted a group of the president's underlings to create a "coalition of the underdogs."

Camille Chamoun and Pierre Gemayel led the coalition, backed by the Falanges. Support from the Moslem sector came both from the families that had been pushed aside by the Sulh clan and from Kamal Jumblatt, the Druze feudal lord, whose power over five thousand land tenants did not prevent him from heading the socialist party.

Riots broke out in various parts of the country, and when the government tried to suppress them with a firm hand, a very effective general strike was called. Several attempts were made on the president's life, and armed Falanges took to the streets.

The President had but one choice: to call the armed forces into action. Lebanese Chief of Staff General Fuad Chehab refused, however, to follow al-Khuri's orders, insisting that the army was a symbol of Lebanese unity. If the army were to become involved in the present turmoil, he claimed, the soldiers would be forced to choose between their loyalty to their religious or ethnic communities and leaders and their duty to their military commanders. General Chehab feared that in such a situation, the army—and, indeed, Lebanon itself—would collapse.

Bishara al-Khuri resigned, appointing General Chehab as temporary president, in the hope that Chehab would protect his predecessor's personal interests and find a way to stop his detested enemy, Camille Chamoun. The old general, however, called for a general election, and when Chamoun and his coalition emerged as victors, he readily handed over the reins of the government to al-Khuri's old foe.

For the greater part of August, when political turmoil in Lebanon was at its peak, the Kishak-Cohen family escaped the tension at their summer retreat in Behmadon. But unlike most of the Jews of Beirut Shula was not indifferent to the political upheavals plaguing Lebanon. Her preference, like that of the majority, was for Camille Chamoun and his followers. Although the Jews were grateful to the ex-president for his past protection during periods of unrest, they feared his close association with the pan-Arab nationalist movement. While Chamoun paid lip service to the Arab cause, he emphasized his Maronite Christian faith, and his allies, the Falanges, viewed themselves as Maronites first, favoring Lebanon's withdrawal from the Arab League.

Shula's primary interest, however, was not politics, but Yaffa, who soon would be leaving the Kishak-Cohen home.

All signs of the girl's rebelliousness had disappeared once she was promised she could leave for her grandmother's house in Jerusalem at the end of the summer. Realizing that she would soon be separated from her family for a long time, Yaffa was suddenly filled with love for them. She couldn't stop hugging and kissing her younger brother and sisters and continually latched onto her mother. When Joseph would arrive at the summer home for weekends, Yaffa refused to leave his side. The change was so great that as the summer went on Shula began to have second thoughts about their decision; but if Yaffa felt any regrets about the approaching separation, she kept them to herself.

On the twenty-fifth of August the family returned to Wadi Abu-Jamil. The general strike had finally ended and life was returning to normal in the besieged capital, so there was no longer any reason to postpone Yaffa's departure. They spent a few days buying the girl a new wardrobe for her trip. Then the time arrived to take Yaffa to the airport.

Up to the very last minute Shula tried to persuade Joseph to accompany Yaffa to Istanbul. She might have taken the girl herself, but she was unable to leave Beirut because of the upcoming trial. But Joseph resisted the suggestion, afraid that he might break down at the last moment and refuse to let his daughter leave. He reassured Shula as they stood in the airport departure hall that all would go as planned, telling her, "Your man will be waiting for Yaffa in Istanbul, so we have nothing to worry about."

When it was time for their final good-byes, Yaffa fell into her parents' arms, becoming, in the last minutes, a small, frightened child again. She and Joseph clung to each other and wept. Then Shula and Joseph watched their daughter, now a composed, smartly dressed, attractive young woman, walk proudly toward the departure gate and disappear through the turnstile.

The following morning Shula reported to court for her trial.

But after the witnesses for the defense were heard and the defense counsel began his summation, the trial was postponed again, this time to the beginning of October.

When October came, Shula stood in the dock, now very obviously pregnant. The judge announced his verdict: Shula and the other defendants were found guilty and sentenced to forty days' imprisonment. At once the defense counselor sprang to his feet and asked the court to postpone the verdict for Shulamit Kishak-Cohen, in light of her condition. The judge agreed.

In December of 1952 Shula Kishak-Cohen gave birth to a son. Joseph wept with joy at the circumcision ceremony, where he proudly announced to the world the name chosen for his new son: David.

Shula was too weak to attend the festivities. This had been the most difficult of her childbirths and the doctor had forbidden her to leave her bed. Only when the squalling baby was brought to her, screeching in protest for the injustice he had suffered, and the wine-soaked wad of cotton she gave him to suck began to take effect, did she look at her new son and whisper lovingly in Hebrew, "David. Like the King of Israel. Like Prime Minister David Ben Gurion."

She fell asleep with her youngest child in her arms.

Three weeks later an officer from the prison authority came to take Shula Kishak-Cohen to jail.

The Serpent's Spell

13 The decision had been made to send Shula to Judeida Jail.

Judeida was a small town in the mountains, about twenty kilometers northeast of Beirut. What was called a "jail" was not really a prison at all, but rather a large detention center within the town's police station. The officer in charge, a Shi'ite Moslem, was known as Abu-Yusuf.

Old Shukry Mussa had contacted him as soon as he had successfully "persuaded" the judge to approve Judeida Jail as the prison in which Shulamit Kishak-Cohen would serve her term. The persuasion was quite costly, but Joseph met the expense without the slightest hesitation. He entered the amount in a little black book kept hidden in a drawer in his desk in which, through the years, he had recorded a long list of bribes paid out to remove various obstacles from his wife's path. It added up to quite a sizable amount, money he would never see again.

After the judge had agreed to the choice of Judeida, the details were easily arranged. Captain Abu-Yusuf "discovered" that his detention center had no women's division and, since it would be unthinkable to house a woman prisoner within the men's unit, he authorized a special order to transform one of the small residential quarters into a women's prison. Um-Tonius, the elderly widow of a police officer whose job it was to clean the police station, lived in the cottage. She was given an increase in salary for her new role as prison guard, a bonus out of Joseph Kishak-Cohen's pocket.

A painter was brought to Judeida to whitewash the room where Shula would be held, and a truck delivered a new bed and mattress, a crib, a chest of drawers, a table, and some chairs.

Coincidentally, just when Shula's term began, Um-Tonius received some other visitors: her only son arrived from America, bringing his wife and their two-year-old daughter Jeanette. They shared the little house with Um-Tonius and her prisoner. In good weather Um-Tonius could be seen strolling around the grounds, her granddaughter on one arm and David Kishak-Cohen in a wicker basket on the other.

Shula often sat in the small garden in front of the house, daydreaming, reading, or embroidering a blouse for her daughter Arlette. She had promised herself to finish the needlework before her brief prison term ended. She was not allowed to leave the confines of the cottage and garden, but within the area she was free to do as she pleased. She sewed curtains for her room and cooked her own meals, and no restrictions were made on outside visits. Joseph came to see her at least twice a week, bringing the children. Jamil arrived twice on Abu-Sa'id's behalf, carrying enormous bouquets of flowers and a large tin of Dutch cocoa. And, of course, Mussa came.

The first time Mussa arrived he brought letters from Bertie and Meir. The children had been told of the birth of their new brother and sent congratulations to their parents, inquiring about the baby's name. They knew nothing of their mother's imprisonment.

During that visit Mussa informed Shula that the new garrison commander at Merj 'Uyun was settling into a routine, after his initial burst of activity, so the situation at the Israeli border would soon be back to normal. Mussa had invited the officer to his home for a big celebration and had managed to make a friend of him. "I think he can be bought," Mussa suggested, "but only for a very high price. He won't get his hands dirty unless it's worth his while. At any rate he's stopped interfering and our relations with Metulla have been reestablished."

When Abu-Jacques arrived two days later with the news that another two families had arrived from Syria, Shula was happy to tell
him, "You can send them ahead. The border is open again."

George Anton was the only one who didn't visit her in prison.
George hadn't tried to contact her since the end of her trial, and
many a morning Shula would wake up determined to ask Um-Tonius
to take her to the station to phone Beirut, but she always changed
her mind at the last moment.

Her return home after thirty-six days of confinement was the cause
of great celebration. Nazira had prepared a festive meal for the
occasion. The children greeted their mother at the door with a
chorus of cheers, and the house overflowed with flowers. Well-
wishers paid their respects later in the evening: Dr. Attia, Albert
Iliya, Abu-Jacques, and various functionaries from the Wadi
streamed in, each reciting the traditional Jewish prayer of thanks for
the redemption of prisoners. An emissary of Abu-Sa'id stopped by to
invite Mr. and Mrs. Kishak-Cohen to be the guests of the house at
the casino that Saturday night. Only George was missing from the
gala welcome.

Shula suppressed her desire to call George until the following
morning. Under the pretext of shopping for cakes for the Sabbath,
she walked to the coffee shop at the end of Wadi Abu-Jamil and
dialed his office number. Her heart sank when she heard him answer
in a cool, official tone. He asked where she was calling from and
when she replied, he said only, "Wait for me there."

Whatever doubts Shula felt vanished the moment she saw George.
He ran to her, his face glowing with joy, and he could barely keep
from embracing her in public.

"God, am I happy to see you!" he exclaimed, pressing her hand.
"Each day seemed like a year."

"But you were so distant on the phone," she pouted. "You had me
worried."

He led her to a small table in the corner, where he ordered coffee
and cake. Once the waiter had disappeared, he looked at her and
said, "You know you have nothing to fear, but now we simply have
to be more careful than ever."

He told her that since they had last met he had been promoted to a
position of greater authority. "This means," he boasted, "that I get to

see the president often." His tone shifted. "But there are many more people watching me now and checking what I do. You never know who may be listening in on my phone conversations."

Her fears melted under the warmth of his affection, and their relationship was soon back to where it had been before her arrest. With his new rank George had at his disposal a suite at the officers' club on the Avenue Foch. It became their meeting place. The doorman, used to Colonel Anton's clandestine visitors, would lead her to the suite without asking questions.

"And if someone should ask questions," George told her with self-assurance, "I could always justify our meetings by claiming that I was interrogating you. After all, we do have a file on you and the Syrians are constantly asking for more information about you."

Without Shula's awareness her character and personality were undergoing a change, and her relationship with her husband shifted along with it. The textile merchant whose entire life, bound by tradition and convention, centered around his home and business could never understand the drive and enthusiasm motivating his wife to defy all norms. Yet he granted her almost total freedom, an unusual move for a man of his background and position. He defended all her activities, although he didn't understand them, and gave her whatever financial support she needed, but he continued to hope that there was nothing more significant than a belated burst of youthful restlessness spurring her on, and he was confident that it would eventually pass.

For that reason his wife's imprisonment came as a tremendous shock to Joseph. All his hidden fears came to the front and he was forced to accept the possibility that Shula's adventurousness might pose a serious threat to their well-established lives.

Still, he believed she would learn a lesson from her detention and abandon her causes once she was released.

But Shula's involvement only accelerated upon her return from Judeida, and he blamed her confinement for the new, more rebellious Shula.

For Shula the change was more complex and gradual, and looking back at her life years later, she decided that the imprisonment at Judeida had been the real turning point. The Shula who came home from prison was no longer the provincial girl from Jerusalem who had been forced to marry a man twenty years her senior, a man whose wealth and position in the community awed her. She remembered how she had felt the first time she visited Joseph's business in the Suk Sursuk, how impressed she had been by its size and by his international connections. Now she could not help thinking how much bigger her own "business" was. Whenever Joseph came home disappointed by a business deal that had fallen through and sought his wife's comfort, she could barely control her impatience with the scope of his problems. She suppressed an impulse to snap, "You only deal with money; I deal with people's lives!"

Yet Joseph was still the head of the family. She had taken his name, and she was expected to obey his rules. Unconsciously Shula started to rebel.

Her independent spirit began to show in smaller, everyday matters. Ever since he had taken Shula for her first wardrobe after their marriage, Joseph had been involved in all decisions about Shula's choice of clothes. In the early years of their marriage, whenever Madame Narvoni came for her semiannual "four-day visits," she and Shula would pore over the European fashion journals, consulting Joseph for his opinion. Although he expressed his views rarely, Shula would never decide on a style without first obtaining her husband's approval.

But gradually, in deciding upon a suitable dress for crossing the border or the proper outfit for an unexpected trip to Istanbul, Shula stopped consulting her husband. One day, gazing into Shula's closet, Joseph suddenly realized that he was no longer even familiar with his wife's wardrobe.

Still, Shula was dependent on Joseph's money. A strange sort of pride prevented her from taking a steady salary from Israel or making any changes in the financial arrangements by which she and Joseph had always lived. She continued to borrow money from her husband to support her work, reimbursing him only after she had been reimbursed.

Although Joseph had never refused to lend her money, Shula began to realize that she might one day find his funds tied up in a large purchasing order, and that without his support she would have nowhere to turn.

Shula established contact with Zuheir the money changer, stopping by frequently with the British sterling that Shukry Mussa brought from Israel. She preferred the money-changing shop to the bank; all business with Zuheir was conducted over the counter, and there were no official forms to sign. He also ran a money-lending business on the side, which was quite popular for the same reason—secrecy.

Now Shula approached him with a request for an open-credit account that could be used whenever she was in need. Zuheir did not hesitate for a moment.

"Will fifty thousand be sufficient?"

"That's more than enough for the moment," Shula smiled. "What kind of collateral do you need?"

"Collateral? From you? Your word is enough, Um-Ibrahim. Please come to me with *all* your business affairs, and I will be happy to help you."

Zuheir's reply shocked and frightened Shula: *he knew about her.* Yet despite her fear, she was pleased to realize that not once during their entire conversation had he referred to her as "Madame Cohen." Zuheir was not granting her an open-credit account because she was the wife of Joseph Kishak-Cohen, the successful textile merchant, but because she had earned it in her own right, as Um-Ibrahim.

Shula was in her prime. She was thirty-three years old, but neither age nor seven childbirths had left a mark on her appearance. While her figure was full, she wasn't the slightest bit overweight and never had to diet. Whenever she walked down the street, she felt the men stare at her. She was a tall, elegant, and beautifully dressed woman full of self-confidence.

Her new contacts, the secrets she had learned from Abu-Sa'id, the patient counseling she had received from George Anton had opened a new and inviting world of politics, power struggles, intrigues, and counter-intrigues to her. She was fascinated by it all. She was not unaware that this world was fraught with hazards, but she was entranced by its spell. Sometimes she felt like a trapped rabbit who sat transfixed by the serpent as it stared down its prey before the kill. She could not free herself.

One afternoon in George's suite at the officers' club, he told her, "We had another cable about you from the Syrians. Look."

Shula laughed. "You know I can't read Arabic," she reminded him. He put the telegram back in his briefcase.

"I forgot," he said seriously. "But this isn't a laughing matter. Never take the Syrians lightly."

Her reply was condescending. "And even if they find out that I've helped a few Syrian Jews make their way to Israel, so what? The Syrians themselves are interested in getting rid of the Jews; otherwise they wouldn't treat them so harshly."

"I don't think the Syrians really care about your activities on the Lebanese-Israeli border," George said. "They're more interested in exactly how you're smuggling the Jews out of Syria. As far as they're concerned, if you are helping the Jews, you must be bribing people in high places in Damascus. If my suspicion is correct, they won't be satisfied by our reports about you. They'll want to interrogate you themselves, to find out which Syrian officials are collaborating with you. They might even try to kidnap you to Damascus."

"But you know that's utter nonsense! I have no contacts in Damascus whatsoever."

"You know it and I know it, and the people who are helping out behind the scenes in Syria know it. But let's assume that one of them works for Syrian intelligence and is aware of your existence; he might be the one who instigated their renewed interest in you, to divert suspicion from himself. But then he would be the last person to want you investigated. So if he found out about a plan to kidnap you, he might be tempted to find you first and have you killed."

Shula was frightened. "George, you're scaring me!"

"I mean to. You have cause to be frightened and you must be particularly careful!"

Despite her fears Shula continued to be entranced by the serpent's spell and her excitement only grew with her next visit to Abu-Sa'id. As they sat chatting in his private office, Jamil stuck his head through the door to announce that a man outside wanted to speak with Abu-Sa'id. The visitor's name meant nothing to Shula, but Abu-Sa'id seemed anxious to see him.

"Bring him in," Abu-Sa'id ordered. He turned to Shula. "This should be interesting. Watch this man; he'll pretend to be a diplomat, but he's really in charge of all Egyptian espionage activities in Beirut."

The officers' revolution in Egypt the previous summer had served as a powerful source of inspiration for radicals throughout the Arab world. Extremist groups now looked upon Cairo as the symbol of the Arab hope in a new Middle East that would rise above the ruins of its colonized past, represented by the deposed King Farouk. Beirut had become a focal point of the revolutionary spirit, filled as it was with diverse groups of political emigrés who would sit in the city's elegant coffeehouses plotting schemes of revolution and political up-heaval based on every conceivable political ideology. Yet despite the fervor of the radicals, the Middle East, with its history of mutual suspicion and hostility, was as divided as ever. The subversion and sabotage had only increased with the new Egyptian regime.

Jamil showed the visitor into Abu-Sa'id's office. He looked about forty and was dressed with exaggerated elegance. His blue suit had been custom-made, and the matching shirt and tie had obviously been chosen by an expert. However, something in his bearing be-trayed him as the military man that he was.

Abu-Sa'id, departing from his usual custom, introduced Shula to his visitor. He generally enjoyed letting his confused guests stare at Shula inquisitively and relished their obvious discomfort at her pres-ence. Bound by the rules of etiquette, the bewildered visitors would have to refrain from asking to speak with Abu-Sa'id privately.

Shula knew that Abu-Sa'id was not particularly fond of Egyptians. Once when he overheard an Egyptian criticizing the corruption in Beirut, Abu-Sa'id had replied, "For every whore in Beirut you have three blind beggars sleeping in the streets of Cairo. Who says your beggars are any better than my whores?" Abu-Sa'id liked the Syrians even less and was even sharper in his criticism of them. He once told Shula, "Every Syrian would be willing to sell his father for a pit-tance, if he only knew who his father was." The only people he seemed to respect were the former Bedouins who had become the potentates of the petroleum-rich states on the Persian Gulf. "They are the true Arabs," he used to say, but Shula suspected he was more impressed by their wealth than by the purity of their racial origins.

That evening, however, Abu-Sa'id refrained from his usual sar-casm. He greeted his guest politely, served him his prized Antiquari whiskey, and treated him with the utmost respect. Shula listened attentively to their circuitous conversation, with every implication clouded by veiled suggestions and hidden meanings, and forced her-self to try to understand what was being said between the lines.

Abu-Sa'id's guest reminded them of the mutual interests that bound Egypt and Lebanon and spoke of their common enemies: the military regime ruling Damascus, with its dream of a "Greater Syria," and the Hashimite monarchies of Jordan and Iraq—whom he called "nothing more than sniveling lackeys of the British"—who, even after Jordanian King Abdullah's assassination, still dreamed of uniting the Fertile Crescent. Egypt was the only Arab power interested in preserving the current boundaries of the Middle East, he stressed, arguing that every Lebanese patriot should therefore support his country as a strong and influential ally.

"President Chamoun understands this well," he remarked, "but there are many other Lebanese, unfortunately, who have been duped by vile Syrian propaganda. Some of your countrymen even seem to actively support the traitors ruling Baghdad and Amman. Worse still, Beirut has become a haven for exiles from the former Egyptian regime, who have used their wealth and influence to gain control of the Lebanese press. They have poisoned your newspapers with villainous propaganda against my country's able rulers, President Naguib and Colonel Abdel Nasser."

Abu-Sa'id punctuated his guest's remarks with perfunctory murmurs of agreement. Encouraged, the Egyptian revealed the real reason he had come: he wanted to use Abu-Sa'id's organization to scrutinize and limit the activities of the Egyptian emigrés in Beirut. He offered no details of the methods he intended to employ.

Abu-Sa'id replied curtly, "My people might be willing to help you, if it were profitable."

The guest jumped at his chance. "If you're suggesting payment—"

Abu-Sa'id cut him short with a wave of his hand. "I never discuss money in front of a lady."

The Egyptian understood. He remained a few minutes longer, shifting the conversation to inconsequential matters. Then he rose and asked permission to "contact Abu-Sa'id-*effendi* in a few days."

When they were alone again, Shula asked Abu-Sa'id point blank, "Why did you want me to hear all this?"

"Don't you understand?" he grinned. "My Egyptian friend now knows two things: first, that I have a connection with Israel and second, that you and I are closely allied. The first will raise my price if I should decide to work with him. And if I don't, he might try to influence me through you. That will be your bonus from the deal."

Suddenly Abu-Sa'id turned to her and said, "I heard the Israelis are holding secret discussions with Colonel Shishakli."

Shula stared at him in disbelief. Syria was considered to be Israel's most bitter enemy in the Arab world, and Adib Shishakli, as Syrian chief-of-staff, was in effect the ruling power of Israel's northern neighbor. In the spring of 1948, when he was still a captain in the Syrian army, Shishakli had taken leave from his post to join the irregulars who had volunteered to fight the newborn Jewish state. He had served as commander of the Arab forces in the Upper Galilee and was the first Arab officer to suffer a crushing defeat at the hands of the Haganah. Despite their overwhelming numerical advantage, his men had been expelled from Safad, and with them the approximately ten thousand Arab residents of the city. Since then, Shishakli bore a personal grudge against Israel, coupled with his unbridled ambition to revenge his great shame.

"Shishakli?" she stammered. "That's impossible!"

"I assure you that the fact has been carefully verified," he scolded. "Last week Shishakli met with Israel's chief-of-staff, what's his name? General Makleff. The meeting was kept a strict secret. Makleff arrived alone and Shishakli refrained from bringing any of his staff, although he came accompanied with four tanks, just in case." Abu-Sa'id laughed. "Those Syrians! They don't even trust their own mothers! Anyway, Makleff and Shishakli discussed the possibility of a joint Syrian-Israeli effort to exploit the waters of the Jordan River."

The use of the Jordan had remained one of the most hotly disputed points separating the two countries since they signed the cease-fire agreement in the summer of 1949. Israel wanted to use the water to irrigate the Negev desert. However, access to the Jordan, from which the water was to be diverted, ran through a stretch of land that had been declared a demilitarized zone and was within firing range of the Syrian troops stationed on the Golan Heights. The Syrians had declared publicly that any attempt by the Israelis to divert the Jordan's waters would be thwarted.

"What does all this have to do with Lebanon?" Shula asked innocently, hoping Abu-Sa'id would volunteer further information.

"We're in favor of the deal," he answered, sounding pleased. "If a mutual agreement can be reached, allowing Israel and Syria to share the water of the Jordan, the Syrians will buy all their pipelines from us."

"You sell pipes?"

"No, but Shishakli's brother, Salah, will serve as the purchasing agent for Syria, and he's an old client of mine. The next time he's at the Olympia I'll introduce you."

"What will happen if the deal falls through?"

He was unconcerned. "If he can't buy the pipes, Salah will be forced to sell something. He's addicted to my roulette wheel."

When she met with George a few days later, she manuevered the conversation around to the Syrian-Israeli connection she had discussed with Abu-Sa'id.

"Do you believe there could ever be any kind of agreement between Shishakli and the Israelis on the use of Jordan River?" she asked with apparent innocence.

George gave her a surprised look, as if to ask how she knew about the secret talks.

"Shishakli thinks he has the power to do whatever he wants," George replied. "He's hoping to overthrow the President."

"What are his chances?"

George hesitated for a moment. "It's hard to know what to expect with Syria, they've had so many changeovers in government since the military coup in 1949. You can't deal with the Syrians as if they were a unified nation. The Alawites are an isolated, fanatical Moslem sect. The Druze still haven't decided whether they're a religious group or a nation. The Kurds don't see themselves as either Arabs or Syrians; their loyalties are to their tribal leaders, who are in Iraq.

"These minorities alone constitute a third of the Syrian population. But besides them there's the Syria of Aleppo and the Syria of Damascus. These two factions have been at odds since the days of the Ottoman Empire, and they still haven't reconciled. The larger families of Aleppo masterminded the overthrow of Colonel Za'im, while Shishakli came into power with the help of the Damascus clans. We have information that there is already unrest brewing in Aleppo."

He smiled for a moment. "This is a strange coincidence, Shula, but the president himself asked me the very same question only yesterday. As a matter of fact I have a copy of the report I prepared for him." He handed her a folder.

"I know it's written in Arabic," he teased, "but take it anyway. You may know someone who might be interested in reading it."

That evening Shula contacted Nabil, Mussa's nephew, and handed him the typewritten report. "It's urgent," she said.

A few days later she received a confirmation from Israel through the Adut Pharmacy: "We'd like to see more of the same material."

Within a few days George's prediction came true. Syria's ruling military council, headed by Shishakli, declared all political parties illegal except for the Liberation Party and took away all restraints on the power of the presidency. Elections were called in October of 1953 and Shishakli was the only candidate. He was elected president with what appeared to be the overwhelming support of his country.

Syria's illusive peace did not last long, however.

In January, 1954, troops stationed at Aleppo revolted and it soon became apparent that this was more than the usual petty skirmish between the two rival Syrian factions. When additional forces were sent out from Damascus to crush the uprising, the Druze began to revolt in the mountains and demonstrations were staged in the streets of the capital, protesting Shishakli's rule. A carefully planned, united front had risen against the Syrian leader, supported by the citizens of Aleppo, the Druze, and all the political parties that had been declared illegal.

In February Shishakli fled to Switzerland. Abu-Sa'id was thrilled by the news.

"Shishakli probably emptied the Syrian treasury before his escape," he gloated to Shula. "Soon he'll be pulling strings and greasing palms, and Salah will be back in Beirut carrying out his brother's scheme. We'll all be rich!"

When Salah Shishakli arrived, however, Abu-Sa'id's enthusiasm quickly turned to dismay.

"He's broke," a disappointed Abu-Sa'id informed Shula. "I doubt whether I'll ever get to see the credit I advanced him."

With Shishakli out of the way, Syria's party system was restored and the former President, Faisal El-Atasi, was returned to power. But the across-the-board coalition that had succeeded in routing Shishakli was short-lived, and the country was soon thrown into political turmoil once again. An effective political opposition had been born, and some of Syria's top intelligence officers had joined its ranks.

One day George told Shula, with a worried look on his face, "The Syrians have lost their minds entirely. They're bringing Abdul Hamid Saraj back from Paris."

The name meant little to Shula, but George quickly added, "Saraj is the Biblical snake brought to life! He was Shishakli's right-hand man until he began to plot against Shishakli. But instead of executing Saraj as he deserved, Shishakli sent his former protégé to study in Paris. Now he's being recalled to Damascus to take control of Syrian intelligence and strengthen the new government." George sighed. "They don't know him! Saraj will betray them, too. If that snake had his way, they'd no longer pray to Mecca in Damascus, they'd be praying to Moscow."

The Joker

14 1954 was a fateful and historic year for the Middle East. Egyptian President General Muhammed Naguib was overthrown and replaced, after a lengthy behind-the-scenes power struggle, by Colonel Gamal Abdel Nasser.

Colonel Adib Shishakli was also deposed that year, at last, but the choice of a successor to the Syrian president was not as clear-cut. An attempt was made to return a civilian government to power in Damascus, and Shukri al-Kuwatli, a leading Syrian politician who had spent several years in exile in Egypt, was elected. President al-Kuwatli's power was maintained only by a complicated coalition of various small parties but, luckily for the new president, the opposition was divided as well. The precarious situation recalled the political atmosphere of 1949, prior to the first military coup led by Colonel Za'im, when new governments were being established and then dismantled within days, lacking any clear and consistent policy.

The never-ending turmoil in Syria encouraged the Hashimite alliance of Jordan and Iraq to believe that conditions might be ripe for a Union of the Fertile Crescent. As Syria struggled to stay free of the

grip of the Hashimites, Abdul Hamid Saraj used the political confusion to his advantage, increasing his own power. The relatively
unknown intelligence officer, and the man George had called "the
Biblical snake come to life," was now settled in Damascus, where he
had made a secret alliance with the socialist Ba'th party.

Beirut became the major observation point for what was happening in Syria. The city was filled with foreign agents, political exiles,
and representatives of diverse underground Syrian movements, both
real and imaginary, and it seemed that every second Beiruti was
working for one of these foreign elements. Newspapers were incor-
porated overnight for the sole purpose of spreading rumors and mis-
leading bits of information about the opposition.

The Olympia Casino became known as the center for the American CIA, and Abu-Sa'id developed a new tolerance, opening his
doors to a new class of clientele he would never even have permitted
to enter in former days. Abu-Sa'id once turned to Shula as they
watched the bustling activity in the casino from his private observation deck and said, "Everyone here is a double agent trying to sell
counterfeit documents. But as long as I know who they really are
and they continue to lose at the roulette wheel, I couldn't care less."

Shula wriggled through the infested waters of Beirut like a nimble
fish. The flow of immigrants from Syria to Israel was once again
running smoothly. She had strengthened her bargaining position with
her various "contractors" to make each one feel as if he was vital to
her expanding operation without letting him think he was indis-
pensable. She had bought several blank Lebanese passports from
Mahmud Hoj and sent them along to her contacts in Israel at their
request. George would verify whatever information she gathered
from Abu-Sa'id and the news would be relayed to Tel Aviv.

As time went on, her relationship with George deepened and they
reached a complete understanding. There was no longer a need to
discuss their closeness, for it had developed into an integral part of
their lives. But Shula and George had become more than friends;
they had become partners. She looked forward to their weekly meetings at the officers' club because he was the only person in Beirut
with whom she didn't have to pretend, to whom she never had to lie.
Shula knew she could discuss her problems freely with George, and he
would always be there with wise and sincere advice.

She exulted in her great wave of success. Everything seemed to be going perfectly. Shula was riding on an ascending wave that seemed to have no limit, and she never stopped to consider that every wave must eventually break on the shore.

One day Mahmud Hoj casually informed her that Ahsan El Kawassi, the head of internal security affairs in Damascus, had come to Beirut. She filed this bit of information away in her mind and later asked George about the new visitor.

George was dumbfounded. "How did you find out?" he asked suspiciously.

She gave him her source. "If he knows, half of Beirut must know," George said resignedly. "El Kawassi arrived as part of a Syrian delegation working at combining the intelligence efforts of Lebanon and Syria, to counter Israeli intelligence. He met with Farid Shihab, head of the Lebanese security service.

"I was planning to pass the information on to our friends, but since you've asked, you might as well take this." He placed a sealed envelope in Shula's hand. "This is a copy of the protocol of Shihab's meeting with El Kawassi. We start working together in a few days."

The following day Shula boarded a plane to Istanbul with the envelope carefully sewn into the lining of her coat.

Shula carried an oversized coat whenever she flew. She never actually wore it, but would drape it on her arm until she entered the plane and then hang it in the compartment for passengers' coats.

When the plane landed, she would "forget" to retrieve the coat, knowing it would be discovered by the stewardess and brought to the airline counter.

Before approaching the ticket counter, however, she would wait a few minutes, observing the activity there. If anything suspicious caught her eye, she could always leave the coat and make a hasty retreat without it, but so far this had never happened.

She stepped up to the counter. "I forgot my coat on the plane."

The clerk nodded. "Is this it?" he asked, placing the coat before her.

Shula didn't reach for the coat right away. She stared at it absently for a moment or two, hesitating in case secret agents suddenly lunged at her from behind. Should that happen, she had a reply prepared: "No, that's not my coat." The proof would be in the fact that it was obviously several sizes too large for her. Fortunately she had never had to put the plan to use.

Confident now that no one was following her, she took the coat, thanking the clerk, and walked out to the lane of taxis waiting at the entrance to the airport.

The document she handed over to Epstein inspired a terse compliment on the back of the label of the next bottle of medication she ordered from Shlomo Adut's pharmacy. Nevertheless, despite the success of her mission, the newspapers were filled with stories about Israeli spies being captured in Beirut and Damascus.

She asked George about the recent headlines, and he merely grinned.

"Our friends aren't stupid," he said with admiration. "They left us a few small fish to catch—all Palestinians, by the way. The spies who really mattered disappeared just in time."

Shula continued to follow the witch hunts in the Lebanese capital through George's eyes. He confided that the subversive acts on the part of Syria had not stopped, despite the pact of cooperation that had been pledged by the two countries. Syrian intelligence men were still trying to bribe Lebanese officials in key government positions and establish underground cells.

"They've also enlisted the aid of the Egyptians in their efforts against Israel," George said, "and it looks like they're dividing the work between them. The Egyptians are concentrating on the Palestinian refugee camps here. They recruit volunteers for the *fedayeen* and pack them off to Egypt for training. The majority of Palestinians never come back to Beirut; I imagine they're sent to the Gaza Strip or to Jordan. The few that have returned are actively enlisting new recruits.

"This wouldn't bother us at all—we're not overly saddened by any Palestinian who leaves Lebanon—if the Egyptians weren't also arming the refugee camps," he went on. "Their embassy has become one huge arsenal." George paused. "By the way, I have regards for you from an old friend. Darwish Baidon is working for the Syrians now."

The mention of Baidon's name revived all of Shula's forgotten fears. "If that's the case, I'm sure he's told the Syrians all about me," she said quickly.

"Not necessarily. Baidon doesn't do anything for free, and I don't think he'd volunteer any information unless he was being paid. Anyway, the Syrians know all about you. Even El Kawassi was asking around about you. If nothing else, they're aware of your role in getting the Jews across the border, and they're suspicious of your other activities as well."

Despite the increasing danger Shula's self-confidence was absolute. With George Anton's canopy of security spread above her and the protective aura of being Abu-Sa'id's protégée, she lulled herself into complacency, positive that no harm could come to her.

At the end of autumn Shula was finally introduced to Salah Shishakli. Their meeting took place at the Olympia Casino and left Shula quite disappointed. Despite Salah's resemblance to his more famous brother, he seemed to her a weak and spineless man, suffering Abu-Sa'id's sarcasm without any sign of protest.

"Meet the man who didn't know how to sell when he had something to sell," Abu-Sa'id leered. "Now that he has nothing to offer, he's demanding credit."

They chatted with Salah for a minute or so and then continued their stroll through the casino. Two or three days later an acquaintance from the Wadi, a minor official in the Treasury Department named Joseph Mann, approached Shula with the news that his supervisor, Muhammed Awad, had been asking questions about Shula Cohen. Shula had never heard of Awad before and didn't know how to react.

"Awad mentioned he'd heard about you from Salah Shishakli," Mann volunteered. "Does that name mean anything?"

That still didn't explain why this Awad was interested in her. Had this happened years before, when she was more cautious about her involvement, Shula would have avoided Awad at all costs. But now she was more cavalier in her attitude. A friend of Salah Shishakli and a high-ranking official in the Treasury—why not? It might pay to find out exactly what Awad wanted.

She pressed Mann for details about his supervisor and learned that Awad was a Moslem, about fifty-five years old. As Mann described him, he was a rather mysterious character around the Treasury Department.

"I don't know anything more about him," Mann added, "except that he's forever in need of money. He's already borrowed from every worker in the department. I've heard he has thirteen children, but he's still an old lecher. If you ever need to find him, check Madame Bianca's, behind the Majestique Cinema; he's there even during office hours. When he does show up for work, he spends his day roaming around from office to office, and he can never be found at his own desk. If any other worker behaved like that, he would have been fired long ago, but not Awad. Someone is protecting him. To hear him tell it, he's close friends with the most important people in Lebanon."

Mann's portrayal of Awad made Shula more and more curious. She decided to ask George's advice before contacting this mysterious stranger.

But Shula didn't have a chance to learn more about Awad just yet. A few days later her secure little world was dealt a tremendous blow: old Mussa was arrested.

"What happened?" she cried when Nabil called, but he could supply no details.

Shula scoured her house for any incriminating evidence and waited tensely for the police to knock at her door.

A few days passed before she finally learned that Mussa had been imprisoned for one of his secondary business affairs, smuggling gold. He had been caught in a surprise ambush by police officers from Sidon. Someone had obviously informed on him. The customs officer from Merj 'Uyun knew little about the incident and could do nothing to help his friend. Mussa had been placed in solitary confinement in the Sidon jail.

Upset as she was for Mussa, the news put Shula at ease. As long as he was charged with only a "civilian offense," she was sure his influential family could arrange his release fairly quickly. Nevertheless, with Mussa's imprisonment, the flow of refugees across the Israeli border was disrupted. Shula tried to think of alternate routes. Her hopes were raised when she remembered about Awad at the Treasury Department—perhaps that mystery man could help solve her problem.

She arranged to run into Joseph Mann on his way home from work.

"That supervisor of yours, Awad," she said, "is he still asking about me?"

"As a matter of fact, just today he came up with all sorts of questions about you," Mann replied. "I was planning to tell you about it."

"When he asks about me again, answer that I'm willing to meet him."

She suspected that Mann didn't wait for Awad to approach him, but went directly to his supervisor with Shula's offer. The next day he reported that the meeting was set for the following morning.

Awad repulsed Shula at first sight, although there was nothing terribly offensive about his appearance. He was of medium height and looked younger than his age. While he wasn't really ugly, his loudly striped double-breasted suit and the tarboosh that sat on his head at a jaunty angle annoyed Shula. He was quick to smile, spoke glibly, and seemed very charming. Yet somehow she sensed an unpleasant slipperiness about him, the same feeling she got from holding a live fish in her hand.

Mann disappeared after making the introductions. They sat at a small table at the far end of a café, uncrowded at that early hour. Shula had a sudden desire to cut the meeting short.

"You were asking questions about me," she began severely. "Why?"

"Because you have what I need, and I can tell you what you want."

"What is it you need?"

"Money," he said with an unabashed smile.

"And what are you trying to sell?"

"A connection with the Syrians."

Shula was more surprised by his impudence than by his suggestion. Awad hadn't even bothered to look around to make sure no one was listening to their conversation.

"What would I want with the Syrians?" she asked, feigning innocence. "I'm not interested in what you have to offer."

Awad wouldn't give up. "Then tell me what you are interested in and I'll supply it," he shot back. When he saw by her expression that she was about to refuse him, he added hastily, "Don't be so quick to make up your mind. Think it over. I can supply the same services through the Moslems that you're getting now from your Christian friends. They all worship the same almighty dollar."

Now more than ever Shula wanted to get away. "If I think of anything, I'll let you know," she murmured, rising.

But Awad wouldn't let her leave. "I'll prove that I have something to offer," he insisted, taking an envelope from inside his jacket. "Here, take a look at this. I'll come around tomorrow and you can tell me whether you want to work with me or not."

After he had left, she opened the envelope. It contained a type-written document in Arabic.

When Joseph came home for lunch she showed him the paper. "What does this say?" she asked.

He put on his glasses to look at the document, and his face paled. "Where did you get this?" he demanded.

"I found it on the street," she stammered. He didn't believe her.

"This is very serious, Shula. You had better return it to the person who gave it to you and stay away from this sort of thing." He refused to tell her what the document contained.

But Shula's curiosity was piqued. As soon as Joseph set off for the market, she called George.

A serious look came over his face as he skimmed through the Arabic. "How did you get this?" he asked. She told him the entire story.

"What's written here isn't of much use to you," he remarked when she finished, "but it is quite important for me, and for the police as well. It's a list of all the detectives from the Beirut police force who have been assigned to keep an eye on the underground cells the Syrians have been establishing here. At any rate this proves that Awad has access to highly confidential material. I'll have to investigate him myself."

"Do you think I should contact him again?"

"Perhaps. But be extremely careful. He may be setting a trap for you. Don't make any definite arrangements with him until I've found out what I can about him. Then try to get him to be a little more specific about this connection he's offering with the Syrians. Perhaps that will help us figure out what his real intentions are."

She waited for Awad in the coffee shop the following morning.

"How much do you want for yesterday's envelope?"

"Two thousand pounds," he replied without hesitation.

"I'll give you a thousand, even though it isn't really the sort of material that interests me. But at such exorbitant rates I won't be able to do much business with you."

"Give me an idea of the kind of material you want," he said, unperturbed. "We can negotiate the price. But you must bear in mind the cost of living in Beirut today. Why, the amount I've asked isn't even enough to hire a virgin for a night!"

Shula's face reddened with fury. She spoke quietly but firmly. "Take your money and get out of here. Don't ever try to speak to me again or I'll arrange to have you taken care of. What do you think I am, one of your women from Madame Bianca's?"

Shula's rage startled Awad into silence, but only momentarily. Seconds later the most affable smile appeared on his face. "A thousand pardons, madame. I should have known I was dealing with a true lady. I swear on the lives of my thirteen children that I will never again speak that way to you."

Although she was still trembling with anger, she allowed him to make his peace.

"You said something about establishing contact with the Syrians," Shula said, calming down. "Of what use can the Syrians be to me?"

"I don't know," he admitted. "They were the ones who asked me to set up a connection with you."

She was convinced that Salah Shishakli and his men were behind this but, remembering George's warning, she continued to press for more details: which Syrians had spoken to him? How was Awad involved with them?

Awad avoided her questions. "Look," he said, "if you're really interested, I could arrange a meeting; if not, let's forget about the whole thing. But don't ask me to reveal my connections."

She agreed to see the Syrians, stipulating one condition: that she and her new contacts would meet alone.

She was sorry afterward that she hadn't been more specific about the terms of their arrangement, because the following day Awad knocked at her door, and he continued to appear at her house whenever he had anything significant to tell her. It didn't take him long to captivate her children and charm Joseph, and he quickly became a familiar figure around the household. Awad was a crafty con man, adept at sensing each person's weakness and exploiting it to his advantage. He volunteered to help Isaac with his mathematics and played long games of backgammon with Joseph.

On his first visit he brought Shula the instructions for her rendezvous with the Syrians. The meeting was to take place in Behmadon at a large restaurant in the center of town. For some reason Shula assumed that two men would await her. Awad explained they had decided to dress in dark blue suits with white silk scarves, to make sure they would stand out among the influx of skiers staying at the winter resort. She was to wear a green scarf.

George was excited by the news of the proposed meeting, but he had other plans. "You won't show up at Behmadon; we will," he instructed. "That will give us an opportunity to explore which Syrian faction Awad is working with."

By the next time they met, George was able to fill in a few holes about the mysterious Syrians. "We photographed them without their knowledge and they're not from Beirut. But we don't have any files on them and we still haven't a clue about Awad's part in the whole game."

When she saw Awad she apologized for failing to appear at Behmadon, claiming she had been sick. He offered to set up a second appointment for her, but she turned him down.

"Syria isn't my territory," she said curtly, and Awad seemed to accept her refusal with no ill feelings.

He continued to supply her with secret documents from time to time, which she would send on to Israel after George had examined them. The messages were greeted enthusiastically on the other side of the border, winning her more compliments and requests for "further material of the same kind." But the information he conveyed lacked continuity, and it was hard to pin down his source.

"There's no consistency in the material Awad gives you," George complained. "Sometimes I have the impression he just wanders through government offices grabbing at anything in his reach. Yet much of the material is too confidential to be so readily available, and once or twice he's passed on secrets that can only have been kept in a locked safe to which he'd have no access without maximum security clearance."

It was sometimes hard for her not to like him. Awad was a reckless, uninhibited egoist who never seemed to give a thought to his enormous family. Often he would stay away from home for days at a time, roaming from brothel to brothel, from casino to casino, followed by younger and richer adventurers, to whom he was a kind of spiritual leader. When his pockets were full, he was generous to a fault, and when they were empty, he attached himself to his friends' wallets like a leech. Yet he wasn't an evil man. Shula saw him as an overgrown child, devoid of responsibilities, morals, or honor, and he seemed simply unable to judge between right and wrong.

One day he told her that he had spent the previous night in the company of Darwish Baidon and that Baidon had asked to be reconciled with her.

"He wants a slice of the refugee trade," Awad said. Shula was about to refuse when she thought of Mussa. He had been in jail for over two months and his arrest might even have been Baidon's revenge, or at least a means of pressuring her.

"I have no place for Baidon in my smuggling operation," she told Awad, "but there is another matter where he might be of service. An old friend of mine, Shukry Mussa, is in prison in Sidon. I'd be willing to pay Baidon to get him out and have the case closed."

Awad promised to try, but before he could get Baidon to agree, Mussa's cousin, the member of parliament, managed to have him released on bail.

Mussa stopped by to visit Shula even before returning home to El-Hiam. Her heart twisted when she saw him. He had turned into such an old man! He had lost more than twenty-five pounds in solitary confinement, and his head was a halo of white. He had grown a beard in prison and it, too, was completely white. He was stooped over as if he suffered from stomach pains and only his wise old eyes retained their former alertness.

Those same eyes stared incredulously at Shula when she told him of her suspicion that Baidon might have been responsible for his arrest.

"By the prophet's beard, I never thought of that!" Mussa exclaimed. "That would explain why the police at Sidon refused to be bribed. Baidon was paying them more! But why? He's also a Shi'ite."

She was reluctant to tell him the real reason.

"He wants to get in on the smuggling of Jews into Israel," she said.

"Then let him!" he cried. "Otherwise he won't let any of us even near the border."

"We'll have to find someone to establish contact," he sighed. Perhaps my cousin could handle it. But until we reach a truce with Baidon, you'll have to rely on the air route. The border won't be safe for a while."

She tried to cheer him up with the good news she had been saving since his first week in prison.

"I've received approval for your idea of a nightclub," she smiled, "with financial backing. They'll send us a quarter of a million pounds in installments, depending on the speed with which the renovations are carried out. We can get to work right away."

Mussa was obviously pleased.

"Nabil will be thrilled," he said with a grin. "He really has his heart set on that nightclub. He even has a name for it, The Star. Now that he'll have something to occupy his mind, maybe he'll get over his movie mania."

Nabil's mad love for the cinema had been a standing joke between them for a long time. Mussa's nephew was capable of watching three films a day, one after the other. If he liked a movie, he would see it over and over again. He once sat through thirteen showings of *Guadalcanal*.

Early in the summer of 1955 Muhammed Awad finally withdrew the joker from his sleeve.

"Would you be interested in the services of Nagi Aslan?" he threw out one evening.

Shula was astonished, but her reaction was automatic. "You mean Fathi Aslan," she said, "and I think you've lost your mind."

Awad laughed, obviously enjoying her response. "No, not Fathi. Nagi, his eldest and dearest son. The Playboy of Beirut."

She was shocked at his audacity. The Aslan family was one of the largest Moslem clans in Lebanon. Their feudal estates spread throughout vast tracts of land in the north, and they rented to enough tenant farmers to be able to mobilize an entire army. Ever since the founding of the state there had been at least three or four members of the family serving in parliament at a time, and one or more was always in the cabinet. Fathi Aslan was a strong force in Moslem politics and close to the coalition government headed by Sami Sulh, although he had a reputation for sitting on the political fence. His name was always bandied about by the radicals who hatched elaborate schemes to topple the government.

Nagi Aslan was equally famous, but for an entirely different reason. At twenty-seven the handsome youth was, as Awad said, the prime contender for the title of Playboy of Beirut. At a time when many candidates were vying for that distinction, Nagi was perhaps the most talented and intelligent of the bunch.

He had attended the American University of Beirut, earning impressive grades until one day he lost all interest in his studies. His attentions turned to women and he had scores of affairs. But when one of his girl friends, a Christian from one of Beirut's more prominent families, became pregnant, he was shipped off to Europe, where he spent a year in London and another in Paris, to wait for the effects of the unfortunate incident to be forgotten. But the European sojourn did little to cool Nagi down. He became a connoisseur of liquors and developed a fondness for vodka martinis, which he guzzled incessantly from the moment he awoke at noon until sunset, when he would switch to vodka champagne cocktails. Rumor had it that the only time he wasn't drinking was when he was making love, but even that wasn't a hard-and-fast rule.

Still, Nagi had learned one lesson from the fiasco: he no longer seduced women from Lebanon's better families. "Only a fool would play with fire when he could be serviced by Madame Afif," he used to say. Madame Afif ran an exclusive brothel, admitting only the upper echelons of Beirut's society by personal invitation. She supplied the men with thirteen- to fifteen-year-old virgins, charging twenty-five hundred Lebanese pounds for a night. She also maintained a fair supply of "almost virgins," offering the girls for a two-week period after their deflowering for the more modest price of five hundred pounds. After the two weeks they would be reclassified as prostitutes and sold to the more pedestrian brothels, and Madame Afif would announce to her regular clientele that a fresh batch of young girls had arrived.

The truth was that Nagi wasn't one of Madame Afif's regular customers, but he was still given a special place at the top of her invitation list. Young Aslan preferred the more experienced blonde hostesses who worked in the larger Beirut nightclubs. But even in the more elegant clubs the privilege of "the first night" was always reserved for him. Wherever he went, Nagi was surrounded by a group of eager admirers.

More often than not Nagi's evenings would end in a brawl or fistfight, but his father was always willing to pay for whatever damage was caused. Fathi Aslan loved the young man, his only son by his beloved first wife. Even though he could not relax his conservative spirit and values enough to condone Nagi's wanton behavior, he never stopped believing that the Aslan blood would work its magic and Nagi would eventually assume his rightful role as the responsible head of one of the leading families of his country.

And this was the man Awad wanted to recruit for the service of Israel!

"You've lost your mind," Shula repeated incredulously.

"I'm not the crazy one, his father is," Awad explained. "Fathi hopes he can clip Nagi's wings by reducing his allowance. So Nagi is in desperate need of money—and lots of it."

"So are you, I suppose," Shula added sarcastically.

"So am I," Awad admitted without a trace of embarrassment. "But think it over; it could be a profitable investment for you. Can you imagine the kinds of secrets that are served up at Fathi Aslan's table?"

"I suppose they're served so freely that his son can just come and collect them?"

"Nagi has a free hand in his father's house," Awad assured her. "Whatever he doesn't hear or see, he can find out by merely looking into his father's desk. But I'm sure he'll hear more than enough. And who would ever suspect the drunken son of the great Fathi Aslan of being a secret agent for Israel? Not only does Nagi hear about every government decision before it's made public, he knows about all the conspiracies to overthrow the government before they're even organized."

Shula was tempted, but she still had her doubts. "I can't help but find it hard to believe that he would be willing to work against his own father."

"If you don't believe it, then let him tell you with his own mouth. I'll set up a meeting between you. If you like, I can drive you to see him right away."

He spoke with complete confidence, convincing Shula and putting her off guard at the same time. "I'll have to think it over," she replied.

She thought of little else for the next few days, and at last she concluded that such an important decision could be made only by the Israelis themselves.

She flew to Istanbul and took the first connecting plane to Lod.

Shimshoni listened to the story without interrupting, his inquisitive eyes riveted on Shula the entire time.

When he had heard the plan, he encouraged Shula to follow it through. "It doesn't sound like a trap. And if Nagi really is serious, it could be very promising. I think you should go ahead with it."

For the first time since the Winkler affair Shula was afraid she wasn't brave enough for the task at hand. She longed for the simpler days when all she had to do was purchase petty bits of information and smuggle handfuls of Jews across the border, when she was involved with uncomplicated people whose intentions and motivations she understood. She turned to Shimshoni doubtfully and asked, "Wouldn't it be better if you were to deal with Awad yourselves? I could bring him to you."

Shimshoni thought it over. "Yes," he said finally. "Bring him along, but only after you've had your meeting with Nagi. A bird in the hand is worth two in the bush."

Shots in the Night

15 But Shula's "bird in hand" almost flew away.

In fictional spy stories, every detail is worked out in advance, every incident has its own relevance to the development of the plot. The gun waved by the hero or villain in the first chapter is shot at the appropriate moment in a later chapter. The suspense rises gradually and logically until it reaches its ultimate climax in the final pages.

However, things do not fall into place so neatly in reality. The life of a true spy is laden with false suspense and tension, dramas that die without reaching a climax, and frustrations that have nothing to do with the central plot.

Shula was ecstatic when she came home from Tel Aviv after what she considered her greatest achievement yet, the recruitment of Nagi Aslan to the service of Israel. However, she found a newly evasive and elusive Awad awaiting her. She suspected he had reconsidered and concluded that it would be more lucrative for him simply to continue as Nagi's exclusive agent, rather than establish a direct contact for him with the Israelis.

But what disturbed Shula even more was the new crisis that developed in her relationship with Joseph.

Shula returned to an embittered and angry husband. Joseph was unwilling to be placated even when she showed him snapshots of their tanned and smiling sons and told him of their success in school. She also brought good news of Yaffa. Their oldest daughter, now eighteen, had developed into a beautiful young woman. Yaffa had completed her studies and obtained an exemption from military service. Shula thought this would brighten Joseph's mood, since the thought of his daughter's serving in the army had been a constant source of concern for her husband. Yaffa had found a job working in the Jewish Agency in Jerusalem, and she was dating a charming young man from a good family whom she had met at work. Shula stressed the fact that he was Orthodox, hoping this would appease Joseph, and told him that her mother had predicted the two would marry within the year.

But Shula's news made Joseph even more belligerent. His eldest daughter would be married and he would not even be able to attend the ceremony! "It's all your fault!" he shouted. "As if it weren't enough that you've broken up the family, now you're neglecting the house and ignoring the children that we have left. Have you noticed that in the past few months Nazira has done more of the cooking than you have? Isaac spends more time with Muhammed Awad than with his mother! Enough is enough!"

This was the first time Joseph had ever raised his voice to her or given her a direct command. She realized they had come to a crossroads in their relationship, and she chose her path without hesitation.

"I gave you all the children you wanted," she answered through clenched teeth. "I didn't stand in your way. Now don't stand in mine!"

They glared at each other angrily. Joseph saw the challenge in her steel-blue eyes and had no alternative but to relent.

From that day on Shula made an earnest attempt to ease the tension between them by playing the role of the ideal wife. She stayed at home and dedicated herself to housework and caring for young David, her little "Dudik." But their relationship had changed. Joseph's face always wore a bitter, tight-lipped expression and he barely spoke to her.

"So be it," Shula said to herself at last in exasperation. She called

Abu-Sa'id to ask whether he would like her to visit the casino that evening.

"Did you ever have any doubts?" he replied gallantly.

That evening Shula met Major Talal Abudi for the first time. Every bit the military man, the fifty-year-old major maintained his erect posture and disciplined bearing even when leaning over the roulette wheel to place his bet. He was not very lucky at the game, as his dwindling pile of chips proved, and he was obviously becoming increasingly nervous. He glanced politely in Shula's direction when Abu-Sa'id introduced them, but his attention didn't swerve from the ivory ball. After they exchanged a few banal amenities he turned back to the roulette table with noticeable relief.

"He could prove to be a very interesting man," Abu-Sa'id commented in reply to Shula's inquisitive look as they stepped away from the table. "He's with the office of the chief-of-staff, but he has little chance of advancement there. His family supported Bishara al-Khuri in nineteen fifty-two, so the current president is not too fond of them." Abu-Sa'id went on to gloat that the major was already heavily in debt to the casino and would soon have to look around to find something to sell.

Still preoccupied with her problems at home, Shula listened to Abu-Sa'id only halfheartedly. A short time later when Abu-Sa'id mentioned the major again to say that he had been sent to Great Britain for advanced military studies, she could barely remember whom he meant.

The next time she would hear the name of Major Abudi, it would be from Muhammed Awad.

As the year went by, Awad began to play a more important role in Shula's life and his visits to her house became more frequent. He was the only one of her associates for whom Joseph developed a fondness, and Isaac was quite taken by him and appreciated the hours Awad devoted to his lessons. Only Arlette continued to be hostile toward him, and would grimace with obvious displeasure whenever he affectionately pinched her cheeks.

Shula had settled into an ambivalent tolerance of Awad. She was still repulsed by the shameless greed that prompted him to bargain heatedly over the price of every piece of information he brought her. But more than that, each meeting with Awad left her with the feeling that he was revealing only one side of his character. The fact that he kept after her to include Darwish Baidon in her smuggling activities and persisted in defending Baidon disturbed her. On the other hand Awad was so eager to please and so diligent in his attempts to make himself likable that sometimes she wondered whether the resentment she felt toward him wasn't just an extension of the self-righteous disapproval he aroused in her by boasting about all his adulterous liaisons.

In any case Awad had become her most valuable source of information. She showed all the documents he supplied to George, and even he was often surprised and impressed by Awad's knowledge. "This character has access to confidential material that is kept even from me," he admitted.

George had initiated an investigation into Awad's sources, but so far had come back empty-handed. "Awad seems to know everybody in Beirut," he reported, "and his friend Nagi Aslan has obviously opened many doors through his father's position in the government. But that still doesn't explain how Awad gets his hands on such highly classified material—unless, of course, it isn't Nagi at all he's working with, but his father. And I find that hard to imagine."

Shula remained silent. One of the few things she concealed from George, more intuitively than logically, was Awad's proposal to enlist Nagi's help. She had increased her pressure on Awad to fulfill that promise, but he remained evasive, though he continued to justify his exorbitant fees by claiming he had to share the money with Nagi, whose needs were apparently insatiable.

Soon afterward Shula had tangible cause to doubt Awad's sincerity and reliability.

"Does the name Burhan Adham mean anything to you?" George asked one day.

She looked up. "Who is he?"

He hesitated for a moment, seeming reluctant to reveal the man's identity. "He's a Syrian intelligence officer, or at least he was. He headed their intelligence service in Quneitra when Shishakli was in power. As soon as Shishakli was overthrown and Saraj took his place, Adham was dismissed from the army. Today he drives a taxi."

"Why should I know him?"

"Because he seems to be very good friends with your Muhammed Awad. Whenever he's in Beirut they get together for a wild evening at Madame Bianca's."

Shula felt that instinctive wave of disgust go through her at the reference to Awad's debauchery.

"Even if they are close friends, what of it?" she asked.

"Nothing," George responded patiently, "if Adham really is only a taxi driver. But can we be sure? Intelligence officers aren't usually put out to pasture after they've been removed, at least not in Syria, and especially not a man like Burhan Adham. Before he left the army, Adham had reached the rank of captain and was in charge of all the Palestinian terrorist groups operating out of the Golan Heights. If I were Abdul Hamid Saraj and had decided for whatever reason that Adham was no longer reliable, I certainly wouldn't give him free rein to ride all over the country and cross international borders in a taxi."

"What's your conclusion?"

"I suspect that Adham may still be working for Syrian intelligence, and his dismissal may have been only a cover for his current assignment. If that's true, then I'd say his friendship with Muhammed Awad is rather interesting, especially for you. Has Awad ever brought you anything that was supposed to have come directly from the Syrians?"

"He set up that appointment for me with the Syrians in Behmadon," she reminded him.

"Yes. But has he made any other overtures about Syria since then?"

She thought back over the past weeks. "No. He never mentioned Syria again. Every document he ever brought came from Lebanese government offices."

"At any rate we shouldn't eliminate the possibility that Awad is reporting to the Syrians about you and your activities," George cautioned. "He may even be unaware he's doing it. Keep that in mind whenever you're together."

She mentioned Awad's strange friendship with Burhan Adham in her next report to Israel, describing his contacts with the retired Syrian intelligence officer.

Not long afterward, early in 1956, Awad finally gave in to her repeated requests that he arrange for her to meet Nagi Aslan.

They were sitting in Shula's living room, the latest documents he had given her spread out before them on the coffee table, when he announced his change of heart. She and George had already discussed Awad's most recent communiqué, the protocol from the last meeting at the prime minister's office, which dealt with the Jordanian government's intention to build a deep-sea port in the Gulf of Aqaba. The Jordanians wanted to free themselves from their dependence on the port in Beirut, but the Lebanese government was concerned about losing the large portion of its national income that came from Jordanian transit trade. The prime minister and his aides discussed means to delay the construction of the Aqaba port.

Awad was now demanding five thousand pounds for the particulars of that meeting. "This is important material," Shula agreed, "but not for my purposes. It simply isn't worth enough to me to pay such an inflated price. Besides, I've been giving you altogether too much lately for information I don't even need." She was adamant. "It won't work this way. I must meet your source and explain to him once and for all exactly what kind of documents I'm interested in."

"That won't help," Awad replied indifferently. "Nagi supplies whatever material falls into his hands. But if you insist, we can go and visit him."

"When?" she demanded with amazement.

"Now. He's at home. But it will have to be a short visit. We're invited to a party tonight."

They took a cab to the Aslan family's Beirut residence, a luxurious two-story estate. The armed guard recognized Awad immediately and opened the iron gate leading to the garden.

Awad addressed the guard familiarly. "Who's home?"

"Only the young master," said the servant. "The *pasha* is at Parliament this evening."

A maid dressed in black opened the door, and through the entrance they saw Nagi Aslan come down the stairs, wearing the slacks from a tuxedo and a starched white shirt with no tie.

"Getting dressed already?" Awad called out. "This is Madame Cohen. She'd like to speak with you." He turned to Shula. "But please be quick about it. I still have to rush home to change."

"I've heard a great deal about you," Nagi said, shaking her hand. He was taller and even more handsome than photographs in the paper showed him to be, with curly black forelocks that made him resemble the film actor Victor Mature. The cynical smile cast on his lips gave him a lustful and cruel look, and his slightly puffy eyes were those of a much older man, one free of any illusions about life. He glanced at Awad. "Why go to all that trouble? Take one of my father's suits. You've done it before."

Nagi led Shula into the parlor, which was richly furnished with many beautifully upholstered armchairs. A fire blazed in the large hearth. Shula remained standing.

"I wanted to discuss the information Awad has been supplying. It's not exactly what I need," she said.

He waved his hand, dismissing her objections. "You can choose what you like," he yawned. "But the money Awad pays isn't exactly what I'd expected either."

"That might be changed, depending on the material. Do you mean to say that I could select the information I want?"

"Come, I'll show you."

He led her to another wing of the house and opened a door to an office dominated by a massive multidrawer desk. A luxurious carpet covered the floor, and the walls were lined with heavy bookcases filled with volumes in French and English. Scattered around the walls were portraits of leading members of the Aslan clan. A coffee table stood in a corner of the room, flanked by armchairs, and about a meter above the table was a built-in steel safe.

"This is my father's office," Nagi declared, though Shula had already guessed that. He approached the desk and rummaged through some papers and files. "Here he has the protocol of this morning's cabinet meeting. Does that interest you? This is the type of report I get to see every day. But you'd have to do better than the few pennies you throw Awad's way."

"I'm prepared to negotiate a higher fee for really valuable material," Shula said coldly. "But the price is determined by those who receive the information from me. Perhaps it would be better if you dealt with them directly?"

Nagi straightened up and looked directly into her eyes. She felt as if he were mentally undressing her and began to blush. He smiled scornfully.

"No," he answered, "not yet. Awad is my friend. He'll continue to serve as our middleman. But that doesn't mean that we can't also meet from time to time, does it? I mean, so you can explain exactly what sort of information you'd like . . ." His real intentions were quite obvious. Shula squirmed in her place.

Awad suddenly entered the room, saving her the embarrassment of responding to Nagi's lewd suggestion. He had put on a tuxedo and bow tie, and the suit hung loosely from his shoulders.

"Ah, you're here," Awad grinned. "What do you think of the holy of holies?" He pointed to the wall safe. "Doesn't it make your mouth water?" He peered at Nagi. "You're not finished dressing yet? They'll be waiting for us."

"Right away," Nagi replied. "I just want to say *au revoir* to the gracious Madame Cohen. My dear lady, I truly hope this shall not be the last time we meet." He made an exaggerated bow and suavely kissed her hand. "Please forgive me for not accompanying you to the door. Awad will call you a taxi."

She could feel his eyes searing through her as Awad led her out of the room.

Immediately after the encounter with Nagi, Awad brought up the name of Talal Abudi, unaware that Shula already knew about the major. He broached the subject carefully.

"There's a certain man in Beirut who might be of interest to you. He's a high-ranking officer in the army, but his family is not on good terms with Chamoun's people. Ever since Camille Chamoun became president, they've been removed, one by one, from their key positions, and now they're hungry for revenge."

"You must be talking about Talal Abudi," Shula ventured. A look of admiration spread across Awad's face.

"How did you know?"

"I didn't know he was back in Beirut," she stammered, hoping to avoid answering his question.

"Yes. His uncle suffered a heart attack and he was called home from London. I was with Talal when he visited the hospital, and this uncle of his is absolutely mad! You should have heard him curse Chamoun! He was practically foaming at the mouth, even though he can hardly afford to get excited in his condition. I was right there in the room when he ordered Talal to restore the family honor by wiping out the president."

"And what did Talal say?" she murmured. Family feuds were a fairly common phenomenon in Beirut; this one didn't surprise Shula.

"Talal is just as crazy as his uncle," Awad answered. "He may just go along with his uncle's scheme."

She blinked at him, feigning disbelief that spurred him on even more.

"No, this may be serious! Only yesterday Abudi took me to a meeting of conspirators in his family's village. He thinks of me as his closest confidant." He stared off into the distance. "I've offered to help him."

"Who was at that meeting?" Shula asked, becoming more excited.

"A few low-ranking officers who served under Abudi in the past, and a major from the chief-of-staff's office. There were one or two others I didn't know."

She was curious now. "Do you think they're serious?"

"Talal is perfectly serious about the whole thing, but he lacks the necessary funds. You know very well that without money you can't get the wheels rolling. I suggested that he try to recruit support from certain foreign countries."

"What did he say to that?"

"He claims he would even be willing to take money from Israel."

So this was the point of the conversation! Shula knew that Awad had planned his words very carefully and that he had purposely sprung the news on her for dramatic effect. But she pretended the idea didn't appeal to her.

Shula reported the development to Israel. She was reluctant to pass the news on to George as well, and decided not to in the end. Camille Chamoun was considered a good president, especially from Israel's point of view, but if the Israelis felt it necessary to warn him about Abudi, they would find their own way to do so. Anyway she was sure that George kept things from her as well.

A few days later Awad informed her that Talal Abudi had returned to London. She sent word to Israel.

Perhaps as a result of the abundance of information being passed on from Beirut, all suddenly connected with Muhammed Awad, Shula soon received orders that her contacts in Tel Aviv had changed their minds. She was told to send Awad to Istanbul.

He returned a week later, more self-confident than ever, but just as defensive. He informed her that he had met Epstein and afterward had been sent to Tel Aviv, where he agreed to new working conditions. A bank account had been opened in his name in Switzerland.

"From now on," he told Shula in a conciliatory tone, as if trying to apologize for what he saw as her obvious dispensability, "we won't have to argue over money. You'll only have to reimburse me for my expenses. I'll also be relaying material through you until I find a radio operator. They told me they'd provide me with a radio transmitter as soon as I found an operator."

This latest bit of news startled Shula. The reports she had gotten from Tel Aviv made no mention of the radio transmitter or operator, and she assumed this was nothing more than another of Awad's attempts to build himself up in her eyes. The message from Israel did confirm the rest of his story, however, so Shula's fears were allayed. She would continue to supervise him just as before, sending along whatever documents he supplied and guiding him in his choice of material.

From the first months of 1956 on, heated excitement spread like wildfire throughout the Middle East.

The match that lit the flame had been kindled a year earlier when the American Secretary of State, John Foster Dulles, had proposed the establishment of a pro-Western alliance binding the Arab states, the United States, Britain, and Turkey. The purpose of Dulles's Baghdad Pact was to unify the Western alliances against the Eastern Bloc countries, which spread from northern Europe to the Pacific Ocean. But whoever it was that suggested the idea to Dulles was obviously unfamiliar with the deeply rooted hatred that had divided the Arab states since the dawn of their civilization.

The Hashimite monarchies of Iraq and Jordan had accepted the proposal enthusiastically, making it a foregone conclusion that Egypt, Iraq's traditional rival for the role of most powerful Arab nation, would immediately reject the agreement outright. As expected, Gamal Abdel Nasser, the young *rais* of Egypt, declared all-out war against the plan. When Dulles answered the Egyptian leader in kind by canceling American arms deals with Egypt, Nasser secretly signed the "Czechoslovakian Deal," his first arms contract with the Eastern Bloc. Overnight Nasser became the hero of the radical Arab left, the first Arab leader to dare to pluck a feather from the tail of the great American eagle.

The Middle East was split over the issue. Lebanon's Camille Chamoun joined the pro-Western elements of Iraq and Jordan. Saudi Arabia straddled the fence. Egypt voiced its virulent opposition to the West, followed reluctantly by Syria, whose government was increasingly influenced by the Socialist Ba'th Party. A full-fledged war of words broke out over the radio. Quietly, without fanfare, the secret services of both political factions instigated their own witch hunts.

Once again, Beirut found itself the center of subversive activity, as each side bought itself supporters and organized and secretly armed them. Camille Chamoun became one of the prime targets of virulent political attacks from Radio Cairo. He was branded a traitor to the Arab cause and an imperialist lackey, and Cairo openly called for his overthrow.

In February Major Talal Abudi returned to Beirut from London, and was once again given a position in the army's general headquarters. Shortly thereafter Shula was summoned to Tel Aviv.

"We have information," Shimshoni began, coolly scrutinizing Shula's face, "about pressure on the Lebanese government to sign a defense pact against Israel. The Syrians want to station their army in southern Lebanon and launch terrorist raids against us from there, just like their operations from the Golan Heights, Jordan, and the Gaza Strip. Needless to say, we have to prevent them from doing this. How do you think this can be achieved?"

She knew his question was a rhetorical one and waited for him to continue.

"We thought of Major Abudi," Shimshoni went on. "We'd like you to reestablish contact with him.

She understood from his remark that a connection had already been made with the major during his stay in London, and she was secretly proud that all this had come about as a result of her reports.

"Our feeling is that Abudi is ready to cooperate with us," Shimshoni explained. "That will be your assignment: to set up contact with him."

She asked how much she should offer for his services.

"If you manage to bring him that far, to the point of bargaining over fees, stay clear of the financial end and leave the settlement to us. If money ends up as a point of contention, we'll offer a price he won't refuse."

"I may have to work through Muhammed Awad," Shula added reluctantly. "To tell you the truth, I don't trust him at all. He talks too much."

For the first time in all the years she had known him, Shimshoni smiled. It was a cold smile, and it sent a chill through her.

"Set your mind at ease, Shula," he said. "We took plenty of photographs of Awad when he was in Tel Aviv. It will be clear from those pictures exactly where they were taken, so if Awad ever gets out of line, we'll simply send them to whoever we feel would be interested in Awad's activities. In fact, it might not hurt to clarify that point with him."

She wanted to remind Shimshoni that the danger worked both ways, for if Awad was ever arrested he could turn her in as well. But she remained silent.

Upon her return to Beirut Shula had yet another quarrel with Joseph. "Where have you been?" he demanded indignantly.

"You know very well," she said flatly.

"I don't want you to continue with this!" he shouted.

She answered in the same reproachful tone, "I've already told you, Joseph—you can't stop me!"

He rushed off, slamming the door behind him, and wouldn't speak to her for days.

The warlike atmosphere at home completely exhausted her. The political crisis in Beirut kept George very busy, and he was forced to cancel their meetings on several occasions because of out-of-town assignments. When they did manage to see each other, he was so distracted and preoccupied that she had to make an effort to hide her tears of disappointment. Shula began to fear that the never-ending tension would destroy her nerves completely, and she often contemplated simply turning her back on everything and shutting herself in at home with what was left of her family. She knew, however, that she would not be able to tolerate domestic life; she had been under the serpent's spell for too long.

Changes began to occur in the Middle East at an astonishing rate. On July 19, Secretary of State Dulles announced that the United States was no longer willing to finance the construction of Egypt's Aswan Dam. A week later, as if he were following a film scenario, President Nasser nationalized the Suez Canal.

The excitement in the Arab world knew no limits. Nasser's popularity grew by leaps and bounds, surmounting even the considerable religious and ethnic barriers traditionally dividing the Lebanese population. Even the Maronite Christians were willing to follow the charismatic Egyptian ruler, who preached a vision of a united Arab nation, in which there would be freedom and equality for Christians and Moslems alike.

The tension increased daily. The British and French, calling back their emissaries, began to make war cries, and the Soviet Union quickly followed suit with threats of its own. It was obvious that one single spark would be enough to ignite the entire world, and people feared that the flame would be kindled in Israel.

The situation in Israel would have been dangerous even without the drama unfurling over the nationalization of the Suez Canal. The murderous attacks on Israeli citizens by *fedayeen* terrorist bands were multiplying, and Israeli reprisal raids were becoming more and more severe. Many of the return attacks were aimed at the Jordanian front, and some were directed against the Jordanian army, even though it was clear that the terrorist raids were not connected with King Hussein's forces and were, in fact, being carried out against his will and in defiance of his authority. But the Palestinians in Jordan, comprising more than half of the country's population, were rebelling against the king's rule, and many army officers were beginning to defect to the Palestinian cause. It was no secret in Amman that the real ruler of Jordan was Colonel Salah el-Din Mustafa, the Egyptian military attaché in Amman, who masterminded the *fedayeen* attacks on Israel.

The Egyptian embassy became a shadow government in Beirut, too. The military attaché, Captain Hassan Ali Halil, served as Egyptian liaison with the Palestinian refugee camps in the southern end of the city, and hardly a day passed that he didn't organize a massive demonstration of Palestinian refugees in the center of town against the "colonial powers and their lackey, Camille Chamoun." The protests were usually staged on Hamra Street and the Boulevard de France, where the American, French, and British embassies were located, but several times the demonstrations spilled into Wadi Abu-Jamil.

It was an unusually hot and suffocating summer, and the weather only added to the buildup of tension before the storm. At the end of July Adib Shishakli arrived in Beirut from his exile in Switzerland.

Abu-Sa'id told Shula that the former Syrian dictator was back and added with a cynical leer, "The jackals are closing in on the smell of a bloody corpse. The question is, whose corpse will it be?"

Shishakli's appearance in Lebanon infuriated the Syrian regime, which made it very clear to President Chamoun that an offer of political asylum to Syria's "public enemy number one" would not be tolerated.

But as Shula learned from George, Lebanon had refused to be intimidated. "We informed the Syrians that as far as we were concerned, Shishakli was just another tourist in Beirut," he told Shula gleefully. "And as long as he remains just that, we won't lift a finger against him."

"But is he really only an ordinary tourist?"

"Of course not. Shishakli showed up because he senses that things are about to explode, and he hopes to exploit the tense situation and win back his power in Syria. He's already begun to plot his return. He's met with every Syrian exile in Beirut who opposes the current regime, offering huge sums of money in exchange for support, and promising even more. I wouldn't be surprised if Shishakli's being backed by American funds.

"By the way," he added, "you'll be interested to learn that one of the men he approached, and on more than one occasion, was no other than Burhan Adham. Remember our Syrian ex-intelligence officer who became a taxi driver?"

"Awad's buddy," she nodded. "And what about our friend Awad?"

"Nothing. We haven't been able to find any link between Awad and Shishakli. Not yet anyway."

Shula had plenty to occupy her time during those turbulent days. She tried to keep abreast of all that was happening and to predict how the events might be resolved, based on the fragments of information she was privy to. Her visits to Shlomo Adut's pharmacy became more and more frequent, and there were very few days when she didn't have an important message to relay across the border to Israel.

She was so involved in the melee that she barely had time to worry about Shukry Mussa's fate. Her old friend's trial in Sidon was at last drawing to a close. The tense political situation may have prevented his influential friends and relatives from working in his behalf, but it might also have been that the same forces behind his arrest were the ones that were pulling the strings in court. Whatever the reason, Mussa was found guilty and sentenced to four years in prison.

Shula had barely recovered from the shock of the news when she had yet another setback. Muhammed Awad showed up at her house pale and frightened, announcing that Alfred Shawab, a former sergeant in the Lebanese signal corps who had agreed to be his radio operator, had disappeared.

"I'm afraid he might have defected to the Egyptians," Awad suggested hesitantly.

"Why?" she asked sharply. "What makes you think that?"

"He's greedy," said Awad evasively, "and the Egyptians pay more than anyone else."

But under further pressure Awad admitted that his suspicions had a much firmer base. Ever since Shawab had agreed to work with him, he had persistently urged Awad to try to sell their services to Egyptian intelligence as well.

"I wanted to stop him," Awad cried defensively. "I shouted at him that only the lowest kind of animal without any conscience could work for two masters at the same time. But I'm afraid he wasn't convinced. He claimed that if we were ever caught, the fact that we were serving the *rais* Nasser would protect us from being punished for working for the Israelis." Awad looked at her fearfully. "Now he's disappeared, and I'm certain he's joined the Egyptians."

Something about Awad's story failed to ring true, so Shula questioned him further. She learned that this wasn't mere conjecture on his part, and that he knew for a fact where Shawab had gone. Shawab's lover, one of the whores at Madame Bianca's, had also run off, after confiding her plan to go to Cairo to some of her closest friends—Awad's Greek lover Erica among them. Erica had immediately relayed the news to Awad.

Shula was really worried now.

"How much does he know?" she asked quickly. Awad claimed he had given Shawab very little information. "I told him, of course, that I'm working for Israel," he admitted. "But I didn't mention anything about you, I swear. He knows absolutely nothing about your existence."

With Awad's tendency to boast and build himself up at other people's expense, Shula was ready to believe him. It would be just like Awad to present himself as Israel's exclusive agent in Beirut, rather than acknowledge that he was working under someone else— particularly a woman.

She immediately sent out a terse warning to Tel Aviv: "Awad is too hot to handle at the moment." The Israelis broke off all direct contacts with Awad at once.

A few days later Shula learned that Awad had one outstanding characteristic that overpowered even his egotism—an inability to tell the truth, even when a sharp sword was hovering over his head.

Her older children were still at school and little Dudik was playing with Nazira in the synagogue courtyard when the doorbell rang un- expectedly. Shula opened it to find two elegantly dressed young strangers. One of them announced simply, "We're from the Muha- barat, Egyptian intelligence, and we'd like to have a word with you."

Her heart skipped a beat. Her first impulse was to slam the door in their faces and lock it, but it was too late. One of the agents had already lodged his foot in the door. There was nowhere to escape. Shula opened the door and let them in.

"We know all about you," the young man went on, while his partner remained silent, "and we want to make you an offer to work with us."

Awad's radio operator! It must have been Shawab who told the Egyptians about her! She restrained the feeling of suffocation that rose in her throat and tried to compose herself enough to think logically. Even if Shawab had tipped them off, what did he actually know about her? What could he prove? Nothing. At most he could repeat the stories he'd heard from Awad.

"Are you mad?" she spit out angrily. "Do you think you can just break into a private home like this and attack a decent woman, the mother of seven children?" She was carried away by the force of her feigned fury. Her face was aflame. "Get out of my house immedi- ately!"

"Madame, you still haven't heard our proposition," the young man insisted, trying to appease her. But Shula wouldn't give him a chance to placate her.

"Get out of here at once before I call the police! I'll scream so loudly that all the neighbors will come running. You have some nerve! Now get out!"

The expression on her face convinced the men that this was no idle threat, and they turned and left. She slammed the door behind them and stood there trying to catch her breath.

She hurried to tell George about the incident, as well as about Awad and Shawab.

"If they really were Egyptians, they won't try to turn you in," he said, trying to calm her. "After all there's no cooperation between our intelligence services and they could hardly go to the police in Beirut—that would be tantamount to admitting that the Egyptian secret service is operating openly in Lebanon. But you'll have to be very careful. They might try to silence you, or worse."

Her run-in with the Egyptians made Shula nervous for several days, but when nothing dreadful happened she began to relax. She even tried to persuade herself that the intelligence men might have been convinced by her outraged denial.

But a few nights later, as she was coming home from Abu-Sa'id's casino, she had another brush with danger. She had just left Abu-Sa'id's car, getting out as usual at the entrance to the Wadi to avoid unnecessary gossip and was making her way cautiously through the dark and empty street. All of a sudden a car's headlights flashed in her eyes and she heard the deafening roar of a motor. Before she had time to realize what was happening, a car lunged toward her. She raced to the entrance of the first house she saw, reaching the door-step just as she heard an explosion, then another. Something whistled past her in the air, and fragments of stone flew everywhere. One grazed her arm, and the bruise stung with pain. Dazed but safe, Shula stumbled home, unsure whether the attack had really happened or if she had only imagined it.

During the coming days George tried to find out who was behind the attempt on Shula's life. His inquiries came to nothing. He reached the conclusion that it was the Egyptians, smarting under her rebuff and hoping to intimidate her before they made another attempt to buy her services. He warned her that they would be back, but he was mistaken. The Muhabarat people never tried to contact her again.

With the coming of autumn the political tension eased slightly, as the world adjusted to the fact that Nasser had indeed nationalized the Suez Canal and allowed the Soviet Union to make its presence felt in Egypt. Then the Israelis launched a harsh reprisal raid against Jordan, attacking a police station and an army camp just outside

Qalqiliya. The rest of the world waited for war to break out between Israel and its eastern neighbor.

On the twenty-ninth of November Israeli paratroopers landed in the heart of the Sinai, and Israeli artillery began cutting through the entire peninsula. Two days later the French and British decided to join the war to "protect the Suez Canal." A fleet of aircraft carriers that had been secretly amassed lay at anchor at Port Sa'id.

The attack went smoothly, according to a plan that had evidently been outlined weeks before. The Arabs were taken completely by surprise. While the Egyptians were still boasting of their "impressive victories," the Sinai campaign came to a quick end. The Egyptian army was defeated in four days, and Israeli troops laid their camps ten miles away from the Suez Canal.

Champagne toasts were raised at the Olympia Casino in celebration of the defeat of the *rais* Nasser. In the Falangist-controlled Christian quarter of Al-Ashrafiyah the people were saying scornfully, "If one-eyed Dayan managed to defeat the entire Egyptian army in four days, imagine what he could have done if he had two eyes!"

Gathering Clouds

16 Despite Egypt's military defeat in the Sinai and the subsequent jokes made in certain Beirut nightclubs, Gamal Abdel Nasser emerged as the true victor of the Suez War.

The *rais* became the undisputed leader in the Arab world. Even Jordan's pro-Western King Hussein was forced to appoint a radical prime minister, Suleiman Nabulsi.

Only Lebanon—alone among the Arab regimes—maintained a pro-Western stance. As a result Beirut quickly became the principal target for Egyptian-Syrian sabotage.

At first, the Lebanese government did not dare to respond to such a powerful threat. Abu-Sa'id was heard to complain in the Olympia Casino, "The symbol of Lebanon is the cedar, but a twig of parsley would be a more appropriate emblem for our government." But when the president's residence was bombed and several of his personal guards were injured, Lebanon could no longer sit idly by. George Anton was given a free hand, and within twenty-four hours more than thirty Egyptian agents were arrested, and Hassan Ali Halil, the Egyptian military attaché, was deported.

Syrian security forces were hard at work in their own country as well. A plot to overthrow the government had been uncovered, resulting in massive arrests. Many of the country's top military officers had been rounded up for their part in the subversion. Colonel Saraj, who had by then headed the secret intelligence forces for over a year, publicly accused Adib Shishakli of masterminding the plot with the aid of the Lebanese government. With that, Shishakli's presence in Lebanon became too great a burden, and he soon packed his bags and slipped out of the country, not to be heard of until several years later, when he was assassinated by a Syrian agent in Argentina, where he had subsequently taken refuge.

A few weeks after Shishakli's disappearance it was announced in Damascus that Burhan Adham had been recalled to his country's service, at the rank of lieutenant colonel.

George went white with fury when he heard the news. "That scoundrel!" he exclaimed. "He bought that rank by turning in his superior—Shishakli. Most of the people arrested in Damascus are his victims too!"

Muhammed Awad, however, was overjoyed by his friend's new position, and at Madame Bianca's brothel he ordered drinks for all, in honor of Adham's promotion.

Early in January of 1957 another crisis shook Wadi Abu-Jamil. Dib Sa'adia, a prominent leader of the community, was kidnapped.

The reasons for the abduction were shrouded in mystery. Sa'adia had taken a cab to a business meeting, accompanied by another Syrian Jewish refugee who had established himself in Beirut. When they passed the Basta quarter, the old Moslem section in the center of town, their cab was stopped by four armed men. Sa'adia and his friend were pushed out of the taxi and forced by their captors along the side streets and alleyways.

News of the incident reached the Wadi and confusion spread through the streets. After two days, when no ransom note arrived, the confusion changed to panic. No one knew why the men had been seized, or by whom. Rumors sprung up about desperate Palestinians taking revenge on the Jews.

Several leaders of the community finally approached Shula with the request that she use her various sources to unravel the mystery of the disappearance of the two Jews.

George investigated and came up with nothing, but Awad was more successful. He returned in a few days with the unhappy news that Sa'adia and his friend had been kidnapped by the Syrians and were already in Damascus. Shula paid him a thousand Lebanese pounds for the information, even though he was unable to discover the motive behind the abduction.

No one knew how to get the men out of Damascus. When Shula spoke with Abu-Sa'id he offered no hope. He did, however, put her in touch with Pierre Gemayel, leader of the Christian Falanges, with whom he maintained very close relations. Gemayel agreed to help.

"I have an attorney whose specialty is dealing with the Syrians," he said. "I'll see that he does his best to help you. But I have to warn you that it will be quite expensive."

Shula never actually met the lawyer, nor was she informed of his identity. Nevertheless, forty days later, when the kidnapped Jews were released and arrived safely in Beirut, everyone assumed that Gemayel's lawyer had done the trick. Shula went to thank Gemayel, bringing an envelope with the lawyer's fee.

On her way to deliver the payment she stopped off to see the kidnap victims. Sa'adia had been badly beaten. His scarred face and body testified to the torture he had undergone in the Syrian jail.

He was clearly ashamed to face Shula. "Forgive me," he pleaded. "I couldn't hold up under their torture. I told them about you."

"What exactly did you say?" she demanded.

"I told them you were in charge of smuggling Syrian Jews from Beirut to Israel."

"That doesn't matter," she sighed, relieved. "They knew that anyway. Don't worry. But if you cooperated, why did they beat you?"

"Because they wanted to know who's behind the operation to get the Jews out of Syria. I couldn't tell them, since I don't even know myself."

"Why did they choose to kidnap you, of all people?" she wondered.

Sa'adia didn't have an answer. The Syrian investigators had led him to believe that someone had named him as one of the people involved with helping the Jews out of Beirut and into Israel, hardly an accurate accusation. True, he did lend a hand to Abu-Jacques from time to time, but his participation was with only the most menial tasks. He used to collect contributions for the illegal immigrants, and he might have been spotted in the vicinity when the refugees left for the border, but his role in the operation was small indeed.

Shula was deeply concerned: there might be an informer in their midst. She wasn't nervous for her own sake, for she still believed she was being guided by some lucky star. But she was becoming more and more tired, and the kidnapping made her seriously weigh the possibility that one day her star might dim.

Encouraged by their success in removing Shishakli from Beirut, the Syrians increased pressure on the Lebanese government to sign a mutual defense pact and agree to the stationing of Syrian troops on the Lebanese-Israeli border.

Shula was called to Tel Aviv in February, 1957, and instructed to concentrate all her efforts on Major Talal Abudi.

"He's very important to us, Shula," Shimshoni had said, "now even more than ever. We have information that president Chamoun has decided to leave the decision of stationing the Syrian troops at the southern border to a military committee in the chief-of-staff's office. We're not sure whether this is simply a ploy to stall for time before he rejects the Syrian plan outright, or whether Chamoun merely wants to put the blame on the army for succumbing to the Syrians' demands. At any rate, Abudi serves at G.H.Q. so it's vital not only that we establish contact with him, but that we do it as quickly as possible."

Shula played with the idea of getting in touch with the major directly. She had heard rumors that he was beginning to frequent the Olympia Casino once again. But she decided instead to use the services of Muhammed Awad. After all Abudi viewed him as a friend and confidant, so a request that the major collaborate with Israel might be met with fewer moral objections if it came from Awad's lips.

Just as she expected, Awad demanded a special fee for the operation. He pointed out that serving as go-between was not part of the routine work for which a monthly salary was being deposited in his Swiss account. She couldn't argue with his logic. After the inevitable bargaining she agreed to pay Awad five thousand pounds if he would arrange for her to meet Abudi at the Pigeon's Cave restaurant facing Raucha Rock.

Shula chose a stylish light-green English tweed suit for the occasion, knowing it brought out the steel-blue of her eyes. Her hair had been cut short, and two long curls crossed her cheeks, giving her the look of an exotic Spanish dancer. Her hairdresser had worked more than an hour that morning to achieve the effect, and it was worth it; she was both fashionable and elegant when she entered the restaurant that afternoon, and the patrons, men and women alike, followed her curiously.

The major, dressed in his uniform, was waiting for her. He got to his feet when he saw her walk in.

"My dear major," she began as she sat down, "I believe we have something in common."

Talal Abudi was by nature a somber man, and the seriousness of the step he was about to take only added to his somber mood. He answered with bitter sarcasm. "That's like comparing two artists who paint with the same kind of brush."

"Don't they paint the same landscape as well?" she smiled.

"My God," he said, slamming his fist on the table, "I've been wearing this uniform for the past thirty years, and I never dreamed that one day I would be sitting with such a beautiful woman exchanging ideas on art."

His remark buoyed her confidence. "If the subject intrigues you, I'm sure my art teacher could provide you with more interesting ideas and opinions than I. It would be worth your while to meet him."

Abudi minced no words. "Where and when?" he asked.

His directness caught Shula off guard. She knew that Awad had laid the groundwork for her request, but she hadn't expected it to be so easy to add a major from the chief-of-staff's office to her list of collaborators.

"I'll have to arrange a meeting between you," she replied. "I'll let you know when."

"I hope you will join us," Abudi said.

"We'll see."

*　*　*

In the report she relayed to Tel Aviv, Shula stressed that for personal reasons she preferred not to leave Beirut at the present time. Having ignored Joseph's complaints for so long, her sudden desire to remain at home surprised even her, yet the request was now important to her. The instructions from Tel Aviv complied; the Israelis decided that Awad would accompany the major to the meeting. Abudi would have to invent some pretext to go to London, but that would not be much of a problem. The Israelis directed him to fly with Alitalia and change planes at Rome, sure that the major's decision to spend a night in the Italian capital would not arouse any undue suspicion. Abudi was told to stay at the Excelsior on the Via Veneto, while Awad would sleep at the Quirinal. Epstein, whom Awad knew from his previous trip, would contact them in Rome, where Awad would make the necessary introductions.

When Awad returned from Rome he told Shula that Abudi had demanded fifty thousand Lebanese pounds for his services and that the Israelis had agreed—which made Awad extremely happy, for he was to get his cut from both. She had no further official contacts with the major, although she met him a few times at the Olympia Casino, once even stopping at his table to congratulate him on his latest promotion. A short time afterward George informed Shula that a committee appointed by the defense minister had recommended against stationing Syrian troops on Lebanon's southern border. George said that the Syrians had been outraged by the decision, adding that at a joint meeting he had attended, one of the Syrian intelligence officers had complained about the Israeli agent who "had the entire Lebanese government and army dancing to his tunes."

The comment flattered Shula. "My God, that intelligence officer is right," she told herself. A top-ranking intelligence agent, the scion of one of the leading families and now a G.H.Q. major. But what would that Syrian say if he knew that the "Israeli agent" was a woman and the mother of seven children—although still not bad-looking for her age. She glanced in the mirror, admiring her smiling reflection. She was enjoying her success, and it seemed that nothing could stop her. If only she could find a way to make peace with Joseph.

The dizzying pace of political changes continued in the Middle East. Conditions were ripe for Jordan to join the radical pro-Egyptian camp. But when Prime Minister Suleiman Nabulsi publicly declared his readiness to accept Soviet aid in April, 1957, King Hussein made one final, desperate attempt to stave off Russian influence and dismissed the prime minister—despite threats of a military revolt being made by his chief-of-staff, Ali Abu-Nawar. In a dramatic move the king flew to Zarka, the largest army camp in Jordan, where he called together all the officers and demanded their allegiance. Assured of the army's loyalty, he returned to Amman and announced that he had uncovered a plot to overthrow his government and that the chief-of-staff was behind it all. Abu-Nawar fled to Damascus, taking with him Jordan's foreign minister Abdallah Rimawi, and the chief of police.

A few months later the scandal repeated itself when Abu-Nawar's replacement as chief-of-staff also escaped to Damascus. It was only in July that the young Jordanian monarch regained full control of his kingdom.

With Damascus the new center of all the King's enemies, it was natural for Hussein to accuse the Syrians of collaborating in subversive acts against him. The two ex–chiefs-of-staff were sent to Beirut to round up a number of daring Jordanian dissidents there who would be willing and able to sneak into the country and assassinate the king. But from the moment they entered Lebanon, the Jordanians were under constant surveillance by both George Anton and Awad. Each had his own ax to grind, but both informed Shula about the activities of the chiefs-of-staff, giving detailed lists of the people they met. As Shula composed her intelligence reports to Israel, she couldn't help but wonder at Awad's sources. How could he know so much about the connections of the Jordanian exiles with the Syrians?

While the Syrian leaders busily schemed against their neighbors, the earth began to tremble under their own feet. Trouble was developing in the shaky coalition that held the government afloat. Although it enjoyed only a single representative in parliament, Syria's communist party had become increasingly popular since the Suez war. After Foreign Minister Haled El-Azam and several high-ranking army officers joined the party, the communists rapidly became a serious force to be reckoned with. Communist candidate Afif El-Bizri was appointed chief-of-staff, an arms deal was signed with the Soviet Union, and Russian military experts began arriving in Syria. President Shukri al-Kuwatli was frightened. He searched for an issue to cement his position, some concern that would have more appeal to the hearts of the masses than the radical line being offered by the communists. His answer was the formation of a united Arab state, joining Syria and Egypt.

At the end of October, 1957, a group of twenty children arrived in the Wadi from Syria without their parents. Nervous about the insecure atmosphere in Beirut and the entire Middle East, Shula decided to expedite their immigration into Israel. She didn't want them in Beirut even long enough to arrange for false papers from Mahmud Hoj. She summoned Mussa's son, Fathi, from El-Hiam. He parked his truck in an alley not far from the entrance to the Wadi, and the refugees' baggage was loaded on. The prospective passengers themselves gathered outside their hiding place, a small pension, waiting for the signal to move.

Suddenly Abu-Jacques came running. "Two police cars have just pulled up," he whispered sharply. "The Wadi is full of detectives! Someone has informed on us!"

For a long time afterward Abu-Jacques marveled at Shula's composure in coping with the scare. "She didn't even stop to think, she just knew what to do," he would say admiringly.

Her reaction was indeed instinctive. "Go tell Fathi," she ordered. "Ask him to move the truck to the rue de France in front of the jewelry shop."

She dashed into the pension and confidently, as if she had planned her maneuver in advance, turned to the owner. "Where do you keep the candles?"

The confused man pointed to a closet next to the door.

"Come here, children!" she called. She placed a candle in each child's hand and quickly lighted it. "Get in line! Now, what prayer do you all know?" There was a chorus of mixed responses. "It doesn't matter," she said, silencing them. "Does everyone know 'Rock of Ages'? Yes? Then start singing. You," she turned to the owner, "get to the head of the line. Lead them out of the Wadi to the rue de France where the truck is waiting. I'll show you the way. No, wait a second. Where is your prayer shawl? Put it on!"

They marched down the street, joining together in the ancient hymn they would sing for Hanukkah a number of weeks later. Two detectives came toward them as they trooped out of the courtyard, but the sight of the religious leader directing a chorus of praying boys with lighted candles made them stop reverently in their tracks, for like everyone in the Middle East they had a deep respect for religious belief. The holy parade continued through Wadi Abu-Jamil, inviting the astonished glances of Jewish passersby until it reached the teeming rue de France. The truck, parked by the sidewalk, could be seen from the distance.

"Now, start running!" Shula cried. The children obeyed her orders, and the truck was soon off.

Shula stood in her tracks. The sangfroid she had demonstrated had now vanished, and her legs could barely support her weight. She was forced to lean on the wall behind her, and she waited there until her heart stopped pounding.

"You're getting old," she sighed. But it was a fleeting thought, and a moment later self-confidence again flooded through her as she headed home, gleefully reconstructing the details of her latest deception.

Isaac's Bar Mitzvah was celebrated that December. Joseph wanted to compensate for missing the Bar Mitzvahs of his two eldest sons by making sure that Isaac's party would be an unforgettable occasion in the Wadi. Shula spared no effort in complying with her husband's wish, and Isaac's coming of age was indeed the event of the year for the community. Magen Avraham Synagogue was filled to the brim as Isaac was called to the Torah, and when he finished reciting the last blessing, he was showered with sweets from the women's gallery. Shula sat in the gallery, looking like any other Jewish mother in the Wadi, with thankful tears streaming down her face.

After the services the entire congregation was invited to the house for wine, arrack, and cake. As head of the Jewish community of Beirut, Dr. Attia was there to toast the occasion, and Abu-Sa'id raised a toast to the family. All the Mussas arrived, and Fathi presented Isaac with a special gift in the name of the clan: an Israeli army battle-dress uniform he had obtained on his last trip to Metulla. Abu-Amar was on hand, as was Awad, who of course acted as if he were the guest of honor. Even Pierre Gemayel arrived, trailed by an entourage of men. The high point of the day, however, came when a black limousine pulled up in front of the house and a uniformed chauffeur stepped out, carrying a gigantic wreath of flowers with the compliments of the Lebanese president.

Joseph was elated. Long after the final guest had left, he continued to walk contentedly through the house, patting Isaac on the head
whenever he passed him and talking and smiling to himself. He came
to a hesitant stop before Shula and said quickly, "A thousand blessings for this wonderful day."

Shula knew that, finally, the estrangement between them had been
healed.

A few weeks later when she informed Joseph that she had to make
a short trip, he offered no protest.

Her assignment was to bring Nagi Aslan to a meeting with Shimshoni's men, but it wasn't easy to persuade the spoiled playboy to
cooperate. Shula planned her course of action carefully and cun-
ningly. While in the past she had always paid handsomely for every
piece of information Nagi supplied, trying to encourage him and win
his confidence, she now began to complain that her "friends" were
displeased with the quality of his material. A few times she even
returned some documents to him, explaining that it simply wasn't
worth passing on such paltry information. The next time she cut her
price.

Awad was furious. He warned her that Nagi was losing patience
with her; he had only agreed to cooperate with them in the first place
for money, and now he wasn't even getting enough of that. Awad
suggested that the young playboy might go off in search of a new
client, but Shula stood her ground.

"I told him from the very beginning that I'm willing to pay for
valuable information but not for the junk he's been giving me."

"How can he know what is valuable and what isn't?" Awad insisted.

"I've already proposed that he speak with my friends in person.
They're the only ones who can tell him what they really want. But he
doesn't want to deal with them." She looked at Awad innocently. "If
there were some kind of direct contact between them, Nagi might
even be able to bargain with them for better pay. I don't have the
authority to raise his fee."

Shula's ploy seemed to have convinced Nagi. A few days later
Awad announced that he had finally agreed to see Shula's friends.

The orders from Israel were to bring Nagi to Geneva, but Nagi
opposed that suggestion, complaining, "Geneva is teeming with

Arabs, and I'm well known there. My family has a villa on the lake. It would be too dangerous."

A week later Tel Aviv decided upon a new destination: Lucerne. Nagi agreed but insisted that Awad accompany him to Switzerland. Shula assumed the idea had come from Awad, who undoubtedly wanted to benefit from more "broker's fees." She confronted Awad with the accusation and they quarreled. Awad reminded her that it had been he who had established the initial connection between Shula and Nagi, and he could break the contact in the same way should he want to. "Israel isn't the only customer in the intelligence market," he threatened. Shula stared at him evenly and told him about the photographs that had been taken of him in Tel Aviv.

The news didn't seem to faze Awad. "I wasn't sure of it, but I suspected as much," he said. "But remember, if they put me on the fire, I won't burn alone." The cold look in his eyes made Shula shiver inside.

Shula introduced Nagi and Awad to the two Israeli agents who knocked on the door of her Lucerne hotel room and afterward proceeded straight to the airport. On the way she thought about the same intermediary role she had played years before with George Anton in Rome. She remembered the anger and frustration that had overwhelmed her when it was made clear to her that she had completed her part of the operation and was free to go. This time she felt only relief.

She tried to convince herself that this meant she had become more professional. She realized now that her role was to bring other agents together, and she could only perform her mission to the best of her ability. She likened herself to a runner in a relay race, passing the baton on to the next athlete and then leaving the race. Yet the truth kept creeping into her mind, and she had to admit that in all honesty the feeling of relief that filled her now was not merely a reflection of her professionalism.

Shula Cohen was tired.

The Tiger

17 Egypt and Syria announced their unification in February of 1958.

Syrian President Shukri al-Kuwatli was invited to Egypt to serve in the post of vice-president of the southern section of the confederation, while Field Marshal Abdul Hakim Amar was sent in Syria as Vice-President of the northern sector. Abdul Hamid Saraj stayed in Damascus, where he enjoyed even greater power and influence than ever before.

One immediate result of the union was a closer working relationship between the secret services of the two countries. Demonstrations broke out again in Jordan, and a military coup was secretly planned by Iraqi army officers.

In Lebanon the latest agitation focused on the upcoming elections and President Camille Chamoun's intention to introduce a law in parliament to enable his serving a second term. Propagandists from the United Arab Republic reiterated the claim that Chamoun was nothing more than a lackey of the West, but now they also accused the Lebanese leader of trying to maintain his power indefinitely. The latter charge did not fall on deaf ears. Six years with one president were more than enough; there were others waiting in line, after all.

Those waiting in line joined the anti-Western forces supporting Pan-Arabism. Together, they formed an impressive coalition, uniting most of the larger Moslem clans with the Druze under the leadership of Kamal Jumblatt, and with the former followers of Bishara al-Khuri, who now were aligned with the Frangié family, the largest Christian clan in the Tripoli area. Chamoun's opponents warned that they would regard any attempt by the president to change the law as an insult to Lebanese democracy, and they threatened to protect that democracy by armed revolt, if necessary. Such a move was not impossible, for they were well supplied with weapons that were delivered to them from across the Syrian border.

Early in 1958 George's agents stopped a car bearing diplomatic license plates, registered to Louis de Saint, the Belgian Consul General in Damascus. In the trunk of de Saint's car they found thirty-eight machine guns, twenty-eight pistols, a full stock of ammunition, and a letter ordering the assassination of a number of Syrian political exiles who had taken refuge in Beirut. The consul was called back to Belgium and dismissed from the foreign service at once. But apart from this unusual find, the flow of weapons across the Syrian-Lebanese border went entirely uninterrupted.

Chamoun's forces were as hungry for arms as their enemies. They bought whatever military equipment they could from whomever they could. Abu-Sa'id became one of their major purchasing agents. Although Abu-Sa'id generally didn't mix politics and business, he made an exception to help Chamoun's cause. He explained his involvement to Shula, saying "I cannot abandon my own origins." Abu-Sa'id stopped a large arms shipment he had bought on behalf of one of the Persian Gulf emirates and turned all the equipment over to the Falangist forces.

One of the people who benefited from the increasing conflict was Shukry Mussa. President Chamoun, anxious to curry favor with the Shi'ite community of the south, took into account the influence of the Mussa clan and pardoned the old man in April, 1958, after he had served half of his prison sentence. Mussa left Lebanon, but not without making a special trip to see Shula and to explain why he couldn't stay.

"I'm finished here," he reasoned. "My connections with Israel are known, not only to the Lebanese secret service, but to the Syrians as well. If I stay, the Syrians are bound to have me murdered sooner or later."

He went to France, but a few months later his nephew Nabil told Shula that Mussa had made his way to Madagascar, where he bought a cinema in Tananarive. Although his letters were filled with nostalgia for his village in the southern Lebanese mountains, he was convinced that Tananarive was the ideal place for him to live out the rest of his days in peace and comfort.

The removal of the old man from the scene had no effect on the excellent relations that Shula had built up with the rest of the Mussa family. Nabil opened the Star nightclub, and it enjoyed great financial success from the very first day. The club was located on the border of the Moslem section of Beirut, and its clientele came mostly from the Moslem middle class. As the political struggle increased, the Star became known as a meeting place for the militant opposition to Camille Chamoun, second-level government officials, and lower-ranking officers of the military command that was being established in the Basta quarter under the aegis of the Carameh and Salam families. Nabil would wander past the tables, keeping a sharp eye on the waiters and hostesses he imported from Germany and a sharper ear on the conversation, gathering bits of useful information which he rushed to report to Shula.

Mussa's eldest boy, Fathi, also moved to Beirut. He managed a beach chair concession and spent his days working at the seashore and his evenings helping out in the nightclub.

The younger son, Mahmud, remained in El-Hiam, cultivating the family's apple orchard and occasionally smuggling groups of illegal immigrants into Metulla. Syria's Jews had almost entirely abandoned the country by now, so the number of refugees arriving in Beirut had diminished dramatically. The Jews of. Lebanon were also beginning to emigrate, but their points of destination were mostly Europe and Canada, not Israel.

Shula's ties with Nagi Aslan were severed after her trip to Switzerland. She guessed that as a result of the Lucerne meeting Nagi had been given a direct line to his contacts in Israel, but she never made any attempt to verify her assumption. At this stage she was completely satisfied in the knowledge that she had supplied Israel with an important source of intelligence, and she no longer felt she needed full control of that source, as she had in the past.

Muhammed Awad was still a regular visitor to her home, and the reports he brought came primarily from the Moslem Basta sector. Awad's information, combined with the bits of gossip she heard from Nabil Mussa and the news from George Anton and Abu-Sa'id, clearly indicated that it wouldn't be long before Lebanon would deteriorate into a bloody civil war.

By the beginning of May, 1958, the violence grew to such proportions that life in Lebanon was entirely disrupted.

The diverse pro- and anti-Chamoun camps had fortified themselves in the various quarters of the cities, towns, and villages, dividing the country de facto into a series of autonomous cantons. The Lebanese army refused to interfere. General Fuad Chehab, the Christian commander-in-chief, was not among Chamoun's supporters. He claimed that the divisions were political and should be dealt with at a political level, not by force of arms.

Fighting broke out between Christian and Moslem neighborhoods in Beirut and rivalries pitted ethnic villages throughout the country against each other, but there was no government force capable of restoring law and order. The sniping effectively paralyzed life in Beirut and prevented parliament from acting to stem the crisis.

Wadi Abu-Jamil was within firing range of Beirut's two rivaling sections, the Christian al-Ashrafiya quarter and the Moslem Basta quarter, and that summer of chaos the quiet Jewish ghetto was transformed into a no-man's-land. It was sometimes impossible to leave the Wadi for days on end because of the heavy shooting, and a committee had to be formed to make sure that the supplies remaining in local stores were justly divided among the hungry families who had run out of food. Luckily, in between the days of warfare the city settled into sporadic periods of relative quiet. During these breaks the people of the Wadi would rush to their businesses to check if they were still standing or would visit their Moslem or Christian friends to replenish their dwindling food stocks.

The strife that was tearing Lebanon apart in 1958 was a reflection of the unrest spreading across the entire Middle East. Throughout the Arab world rival factions lined up to support either Nasser and the new Arab radicalism or the traditional order, the *ancien régime*.

In the middle of July rioting in Jordan reached a climax, putting King Hussein's rule in grave danger. On July 14, a bloody revolution ripped through Iraq, and Brigadier General Abdul Karim el-Kassem successfully carried out a military coup. Young King Faisal was murdered by the enraged masses, slaughtered along with his uncle, Prince Abdul Illah, and Prime Minister Nuri Sa'id. The Hashimite monarchy, which had ruled Iraq for thirty-seven years, crashed to an end, leaving only Lebanon and a shaky Jordan on the side of the Western democracies.

Only then did the West awaken from its apathy and rush in to preserve whatever could be saved in the Middle East. On July 15, U.S. Marines from the Sixth Fleet landed in Beirut. Transport planes from the R.A.F. were permitted to cross Israel's air space, and paratroopers landed the next day in Amman and Zarka.

The Marines didn't interfere with the street fighting in Beirut, but their very presence, and the presence of the British paratroopers in Amman, was enough to demonstrate to the world that the West was definitely unwilling to let these two pro-Western regimes fall. That alone proved a sufficient deterrent to more bloodshed.

The shooting eventually died down in the Lebanese capital. The city remained divided, but armed guards from both the Falangist and Moslem sides protected the uneasy truce, searching any civilian or car that passed from one part of the city to the other. Finally a compromise was worked out with American help: in September Camille Chamoun, who had already been elected to a second term in a parliamentary session that lacked a quorum, resigned, and General Fuad Chehab took his place as president. Saeb Salam headed the government. Only then was the army called out from its barracks to start taking down the street barricades.

The High Holy Days that September were the hardest ever for the residents of Wadi Abu-Jamil. Once the fighting stopped, demonstrators took to the streets of Beirut. Among them, in rapidly increasing numbers, were the Palestinians who were called from their camps to protest against President Chamoun and his "American masters." As they marched toward Cannon Square, where the American Marines were stationed behind their posts, surrounded by sandbags, they would sometimes sing out their old war cry, *"Falastin baladna waelyahud klabna"*—"Palestine is our land and the Jews our dogs." A few of the Palestinians would get carried away and try to break into the Jewish ghetto. A small group of demonstrators managed to enter the Wadi once or twice, but they only succeeded in breaking a few windows before the "flying patrol" of Falangists and local self-defense groups chased them away. With each incident the tension in the Wadi increased. Jews began asking themselves if Beirut would ever be the same and wondering if it was time to pack their bags and seek new horizons.

The most serious attempt to break into the Wadi was made on Yom Kippur during the chanting of the closing prayer of that most solemn day of the Jewish calendar. Magen Avraham Synagogue was overflowing with worshipers fatigued from their day-long fast and eager to finish their prayers and return home for their holiday meal. Suddenly the peace of the synagogue was broken by the sound of glass being smashed, and the praying stopped. A crowd threatened loudly beyond the doors.

Shula ran down from the women's gallery. "Don't let any of the children out!" she screamed. The young men of the self-defense corps were already making their way to the house where the guns were stashed, and moments later shots were heard in the street.

It was never determined who began the shooting. The self-defense group swore that the first bullet came from the mob of demonstrators numbering several hundred and that they merely returned the fire. Whoever started it, the shooting ended as suddenly as it had begun; both sides fired only in the air, and no one was injured. As soon as the protesters realized they were facing a community ready and able to defend itself, they retreated.

When the first shots rang out, one of the congregation clutched his chest, groaned, and fell to the floor. He had suffered a heart attack. The man died four days later on the Jewish holiday of Sukkoth. The next day he was taken to be buried.

It was the first day under the army's restored order, and curfew had been imposed on the city, so a regular funeral couldn't be held. A quorum of ten men was assembled so that the kaddish, the mourners' prayer, could be properly recited. The man's son was the only family member in the procession.

By nightfall, when the men still had not returned, their worried families began to congregate in the courtyard of the synagogue. The Jewish cemetery was in the southern end of the city, past the Palestinian refugee camps, and the families feared the procession might have met with trouble there.

By seven o'clock the courtyard was filled with anxious people. Some of the women were becoming hysterical.

Dr. Attia went to speak with Shula. "Can you do something?" he pleaded. "Can you find out what's happened?"

If anyone could help, it would be Muhammed Awad. She phoned Awad, and in less than an hour he called her with news.

"I'm at police headquarters at the Saraya," he said with characteristic brevity. "There's someone here who can help you. Come immediately. He'll send a police car for you, so wait at the entrance to the Wadi."

Awad was waiting for her at the entrance to police headquarters. Without a word he led her to one of the offices on the ground floor.

"Captain Hafif, Um-Ibrahim," Awad introduced them. Turning to Shula, he said, "You may speak freely with him. He wants to help." Then he left the room.

"Has Awad told you?" she asked directly. "Eleven Jews have disappeared and I want them back."

The captain pointed to a chair and she sat down. He dialed a number and began speaking.

Finally he announced to Shula, "You have to go to the Basta." When he saw the frightened look that came into her eyes, he added, "You have nothing to fear. I'll send you in my Jeep with my driver. He's well known there."

"And Awad?" she prompted.

"You won't need him. I'm sending you to a man named Abu-Mustafa. His word is law in the Basta. Deal with him. If you have any trouble, come back to me."

Only as the Jeep began wending its way down the dark and narrow alleys of the old Moslem section did Shula realize the extent of the risk she was taking. The streets were dark; all the street lamps had been broken during the fighting. Most of the apartments were darkened as well. Every so often the driver had to stop the car to remove a barbed-wire barrier that had been placed in the middle of the road. Heavily armed sentries in civilian clothes eyed them suspiciously, but the driver was obviously a familiar figure, and no one even questioned them.

The Jeep came to a halt in front of a pharmacy that was well lit despite the late hour. A group of armed Moslems stood at the entrance. She glanced at the sign: Hamda Pharmacy.

"This is it," the driver whispered.

As they entered, Shula saw that the pharmacy was being used as an infirmary for the wounded. Three injured people were lying on stretchers on the floor while medics attended to them. Another wounded man with a bloodstained bandage on his shoulder was leaning against the counter, waiting for attention.

The driver approached one of the medics and whispered in his ear. The man looked in Shula's direction and nodded, gesturing toward a chair next to the wall. The driver turned back to her and said, "You'll have to wait. Abu-Mustafa is expected in a little while." With that he left.

Shula sat watching the parade of wounded for about an hour. Two of the injured men were carried to a car waiting outside, and every so often she heard a single shot or a burst of submachine gun fire echoing in the distance. The longer she waited the more frightened she became. A lone woman in the heart of the Moslem quarter—and even worse, a Jewish woman! She was afraid she had put her head in the lion's jaws, but she tried to calm the mad pounding of her heart by repeating, "There's nothing I can do but wait."

Finally a great hulk of a man came into the pharmacy, wearing a European suit and tie. He wasn't armed, nor did he bear any military insignia, but from his effect on the medics Shula realized he had to be *somebody*. He looked around, spotted her, and came straight to her, crossing the wide room in three long steps.

"I am Muhammed Arnaut," he said simply. When he saw the name made no impression, he quickly added, "I'm called Abu-Mustafa. Are you Um-Ibrahim?"

She got up at once. Abu-Mustafa was about thirty-five years old, tall and healthy looking, and when she stood before him his broad shoulders cut everything else from view. She noted that he was well shaven, without the slightest trace of a moustache—something very strange in a Moslem.

"Yes, I am," she replied. "I've been referred to you for information on the disappearance of eleven Jews. I've been told you can help me."

"I have them," he told her quietly. "They've come to no harm."

"Why were they abducted?" They've done nothing wrong. They were on the way to the cemetery—"

"There's been a mistake," he explained without the slightest apology. "They aroused the suspicions of my men. If you'll come with me, I'll show you that they are alive and well."

As they left the pharmacy two shadows broke away from the wall and began following them at a distance. Shula could see that the figures were carrying machine guns and she could make out the shape of hand grenades hanging from their belts. They walked silently to the end of the street and turned into a dim alleyway.

They continued down the dark path until Abu-Mustafa suddenly said, "Aren't you afraid?"

She thought she heard a note of mockery in his voice, and she answered defiantly, "Why should I be? Captain Hafif put me in your hands." But his question aroused the fears she had been trying to suppress.

Abu-Mustafa didn't speak again, and they soon reached an old apartment building. A single bulb lit the staircase as they climbed to the second floor. The two bodyguards remained outside in front of the building. Abu-Mustafa stopped at a door and removed a key from his pocket.

He turned to Shula and said, "My mother lives here. She's prepared some coffee for us."

"But you promised to lead me to the eleven Jews," Shula protested.

"Are you in a hurry?" he smiled, his voice set in the same mocking tone as before.

"I'm not, but their families are terribly worried."

"Let them worry a little longer. We'll have some coffee first."

The shabby building and poorly lit stairway had made her assume that the interior would be equally shabby, so the luxurious apartment surprised Shula. The living room was spacious and elegantly furnished, and a plush carpet covered the floor. There were touches of wealth and good taste everywhere. Copper vases and a burnished copper coffee table shone as if they had just been polished. Across the heavy table, the tablecloth was meticulously starched and ironed, and the white curtain on the single window gleamed. A small old woman dressed in black, her white hair peeking out from under a black scarf, sat in an armchair next to a radio. Her face was uncovered. She rose as they entered the room.

Even more startling than the beauty of the apartment was Abu-

Mustafa's behavior toward his mother. The husky man rushed up to the tiny woman, towering over her, and led her gently back to her seat. He then leaned over and kissed her hand.

"Mother," he announced politely, "this is Um-Ibrahim. She is from Wadi Abu-Jamil."

She inspected Shula carefully, from the hem of her dress to her forehead. When their glances met, Shula was struck by the power and life she saw in the old woman's eyes, and she had to restrain her impulse to look away.

"Have his boys harmed you at all?" asked Abu-Mustafa's mother. Like her eyes, her voice was that of a much younger person.

Shula hesitated, encouraged by the old lady's eyes to speak frankly. "They've taken some Jews," she replied.

"It was a mistake," Abu-Mustafa was quick to interject.

His mother paid no attention. She looked at Shula again. "Were any of them close to you?"

Shula hesitated again. One of the men was a relative of Joseph's by marriage, although aside from family celebrations such as birthdays and Isaac's Bar Mitzvah, she had very little contact with him.

"One is a member of my family," she said softly.

The old woman turned to her son in expectation. Abu-Mustafa announced hastily, "He'll be freed this very evening."

Shula shook her head. "I wouldn't consider returning to the Wadi with just my own relative. I didn't come only because of him. I'm here to see that everyone in the funeral procession is released." She softened her harsh tone with a plea. "I'm sure they're all terribly concerned, Abu-Mustafa. Please let them go. Just name a price."

"I don't want your money," he shot back angrily. Then he rose and went toward his mother. "I promised Um-Ibrahim you would have coffee with us," he said.

The old woman got up and went into the kitchen and returned carrying a copper tray with an antique coffee pot, three tiny cups, three glasses, and a pitcher of cold water, which she placed on the copper table. Shula was quick to include her in the conversation.

"Ya Um-Muhammed," she said, "here I am offering to donate money to the wounded and your son refuses to accept it."

Abu-Mustafa took the feenjan, the Arab coffee pot, and began to pour. He divided the akmak, the black foam from the boiling liquid, equally among the three cups and then filled them with the steaming coffee.

His mother sat back in her armchair, weighing her words before she finally spoke. "You're a good woman, but my son is right. If he were to take your money, everyone would say that the men were kidnapped for a ransom. Your son, Um-Ibrahim, how old is he?"

"Nineteen."

"A man. Allah grant him long life. Is he your only son?"

"No. I have three daughters and three other sons."

"Allah has graced you."

Abu-Mustafa didn't interrupt their conversation, and as Shula kept up her polite chat with the old woman, she thought to herself, "This is mad! Here I am, sitting in the heart of the Basta, in the middle of the night, in the house of a man who could just as easily be a mass murderer, lightly conversing with his mother over a cup of coffee. Who's going to believe it when I get back to the Wadi?"

When she sensed that the rules of etiquette allowed her to interrupt, Shula said at last, "Ya Abu-Mustafa, it is already late and you promised that I could see the men before I left."

He stood up. "All right, I'll show them to you on the condition that you don't try to speak with any of them."

When they said their good-byes to his mother, the old woman extended both hands to Shula and urged her warmly, "Come back and visit me again, after all this madness ends and the world returns to normal."

When they came out to the dark alleyway, Abu-Mustafa's bodyguards fell into step again at a safe distance. They walked for a few minutes and then stopped in front of a wall. Shula noticed a barred window beneath her, leading to a basement. She could hear the sound of men's voices coming from the cellar.

Abu-Mustafa leaned down and aimed a light through the window with a flashlight that seemed to appear in his hand out of nowhere. Shula could see frightened faces huddled together, and she recognized the eyes squinting in the sudden light as those of the abducted men. Abu-Mustafa moved the light from one to the next, and she counted them slowly: eleven. One man groaned and another sobbed, "How much longer?" They lay there miserably on the dirt floor, but none of them bore any signs of beating or maltreatment.

Abu-Mustafa switched off the flashlight and took her arm. He didn't say a word until they entered the pharmacy. Then he dialed a number and asked for Captain Hafif.

"Um-Ibrahim is ready to be taken home," he told the policeman. "Send your car."

Shula turned to him and said, "I have to go home empty-handed? What about those poor men? When will they be released?"

For a brief moment she thought that he might say, "Immediately." But he seemed to reconsider.

"We'll see," he murmured. "Tell your people not to worry."

He didn't wait for a response but disappeared into the back room of the pharmacy.

Captain Hafif himself arrived in an armored police van. When he saw her sitting alone, he groaned, "It didn't work, I see. Where is Abu-Mustafa?" One of the armed men pointed to the back room and Hafif disappeared. He returned minutes later.

"Let's go!" he said curtly.

They walked out to the car but just as Hafif opened the door for Shula, she turned around and went back to the pharmacy.

When Abu-Mustafa saw her coming toward him, a look of fury came over his face. She had a wad of money in her hands.

"I already told you I don't want your money!" he shouted.

"The money isn't for you," she protested. "It's for the wounded."

His expression didn't change, but he didn't complain when she handed the pack of bills to the pharmacist, who folded it and dropped it into the pocket of his white jacket.

"You make me angry," Abu-Mustafa mumbled as the pharmacist disappeared into the back room. "But I respect you for not agreeing to return home with only your relative. We won't talk about money again."

Shula refused to change the subject. "And what about the men?"

"We won't discuss them tonight either. Maybe tomorrow. Phone me here in the morning."

She jotted the telephone number of the pharmacy in her book and went toward the door. As she started to leave, Abu-Mustafa called out, "It might be better if I phoned you. What's your number?"

"Don't," she replied mechanically. "My wire is tapped." Only later did she realize that her instinctive response might serve another purpose, besides keeping this dirty business away from her home; if her phone was being tapped, Abu-Mustafa would take it as a sure sign that she was a woman to be contended with. Shula was pleased she'd reacted as she had. It wouldn't hurt if he was aware of her importance.

Abu-Mustafa accepted her answer unquestioningly. "All right. But if you can't find me here, there's another way you can contact me. Do you know Hasan El-Badri's bakery at the far end of the Wadi? If you tell him you want to see me, he'll know where to find me."

She knew El-Badri's name well. Everyone in the Wadi called him Hasan the Baker. He was a jolly fifty-year-old whose corpulent body was forever covered with flour dust, and he wore the smell of fresh bread like perfume. Who would have believed that friendly Hasan the Baker was a secret agent, working for Abu-Mustafa in Wadi Abu-Jamil?

She returned to the Wadi disappointed by her lack of success, but she managed to smile happily at the crowd in the synagogue courtyard.

"Not tonight," she shook her head, mustering up all her confidence. "It's too late. But tomorrow for sure."

Each of the relatives of the abducted men cried out the name of a loved one. Had she seen him? How was he? Was she sure he was unharmed? She repeated over and over that she hadn't spoken with any of the men and had only seen them briefly.

The crowd finally dispersed and Shula returned home, weary and upset. The rest of the family was asleep. She brewed herself a cup of tea and sat drinking it slowly, her mind blank from fatigue. Long after midnight she finally slipped into bed, but just as she was about to close her eyes, she heard a loud noise in the street. She rushed to the window in time to see a truck screech to a halt in front of the synagogue and a group of men jump out from the back. She couldn't identify their faces, but she recognized their voices.

It was the eleven abducted Jews! Abu-Mustafa had released them after all.

The report about the disappearance of the eleven men and their wondrous release by Madame Shulamit Kishak-Cohen reached George Anton's desk the following morning. He immediately phoned her at home.

"Madame Cohen," he said in an official tone, for the sake of anyone listening in, "this is George Anton speaking. Do you remember me? News of your interesting little adventure last night has reached our office. We would enjoy hearing some further details. Could we perhaps meet and discuss the matter in about an hour, say at the coffee shop near your home in Wadi Abu-Jamil? Yes? Well, *au revoir*."

Except for a brief meeting in a coffee shop on the rue de France, Shula had not seen George for three weeks. She dressed excitedly and dashed down the street, evading her neighbors, who were eager to talk about last night's events. George was already there when she arrived. From the expression on his face she knew that he was no less excited than she.

"It was a crazy thing you did," he rebuked her before she even had time to sit down. "But you succeeded, and no one can argue with success. Tell me, tell me all about it!"

She began the story. When she reached the part about Captain Hafif, a serious look replaced his grin, and he recorded the name in his little notebook without saying a word. She went on without commenting, describing the events at the Hamda Pharmacy. George shook his head in admiration. "I couldn't penetrate that place with an entire army!" But as soon as she began to tell of her meeting with Abu-Mustafa, he gritted his teeth and spat out, "The Tiger!"

"What did you call him?" she said.

"The Tiger. Muhammed Arnaut. Abu-Mustafa. Don't you know who he is?"

"He's one of the gang leaders in the Basta," Shula repeated. "I saw his men."

George nearly jumped at her. "One of the gang leaders in the Basta —Shula, you kill me! The Tiger is the Syrians' main hit man in Beirut. Some street gang leader! He's directly in command of an army of at least three hundred men, and he could enlist more than twice that amount if he had to."

"Actually, he looked very nice to me," she said, feigning lightheartedness. "You should have seen how gentle and respectful he was with his mother."

"For your information that gentle, respectful man of yours is personally responsible for at least a dozen Syrian-ordered murders in

the Beirut area in the last few weeks alone! He may even have committed them with his own two hands!"

"Tell me more."

He eyed her suspiciously. "You're not attracted to him, are you?"

"No," she said coquettishly, "but who knows? I may want to see
him again. He interests me. What else do you know about him?"

"A great deal, but hardly anything, if you know what I mean. He
was born in the Basta and was a street gang leader in his youth. In
nineteen forty-eight he fought against Israel with Adib Shishakli, and
that's probably how he got involved with the Syrians. In the beginning he was put in charge of street demonstrations. Then they raised
his rank and made him a hit man. Now he's much more than that."
George took a breath. "Remember the arms cache we discovered in
the Belgian consul's car? That was being delivered to Abu-Mustafa's
forces. But for every carload we've intercepted at least three have
reached him. Are you still interested in this nice, gentle man?"

She looked at George's worried expression, her eyes glancing over
his dark brown hair, now laced with gray. "How old he's become in
the past few months," she thought to herself.

After a momentary silence she led the conversation back to the
Tiger. "What do you know about the man himself? They call him
Abu-Mustafa; is he married?"

George laughed nervously. "Don't get any ideas in your head.
Yes, he's married. To a Christian woman, in fact; the foolish thing
fell in love and ran off with him, though she probably regrets it now.
Between his work and taking care of his mother he has no time for
his wife." He paused. "Abu-Mustafa? Well, that's his sore point. It
would be more appropriate to call him Abu-el-Benat, the Father of
Daughters, because his wife has given him only daughters, but no
one would have the nerve to call him that to his face. He wants to be
called Abu-Mustafa. If he ever had a son, he would call him
Mustafa."

The Trap

18 The next day Shula made a trip to Beirut's posh rue Weygand, where she bought a beautiful Czechoslovakian coffee service, the most expensive she could find in the most exclusive of all the stores. On her way home she stopped off at Hasan El-Badri's bakery. She waited for the crowd of shoppers to clear before she approached the baker.

"I want you to arrange a meeting for me with Abu-Mustafa," she told a surprised El-Bardi. "Please let him know that Um-Ibrahim would like to see him."

She returned to the bakery the following morning. El-Badri wrapped her bread, and as he counted her change, he whispered, "Tomorrow at one o'clock, at the Ezram restaurant on M'amari Street, near the American University."

The area around the American University had become a no-man's-land in the divided city of Beirut, since it was quite close to the Basta quarter yet within the boundaries of the city's commercial center. Shula could reach the restaurant without having to pass through the Moslem section, which was still heavily barricaded.

Abu-Mustafa was waiting for her inside. Dressed in a European suit, and without his gun and armed bodyguards, he looked like any of the professors and Moslem businessmen who were still loyal to the famous Aleppo restaurant they had frequented before the storm that had ravaged their beautiful city.

She placed the gift-wrapped package on the table and said, "It's for your mother. I wanted to thank you personally for releasing the Jewish prisoners."

"My mother will be pleased," he said with a smile. "She liked you very much. She's already asked when I'll bring you around to visit her again."

The waiter brought an array of hors d'oeuvres and they ate in silence. After a few minutes Shula looked up from her plate and asked curiously, "Why do they call you 'the Tiger'?"

His hand froze in midair. "Why do you ask, Um-Ibrahim? Would you prefer 'the Hyena'?"

Shula was mystified. Could he be referring to Awad?

"I'm wary of all animals," she answered, careful not to betray any emotion with her voice.

"And I live among them," he said tersely.

"As a predator?"

"When I have to be."

Shula and the Tiger saw each other frequently thereafter.

As time went on, their meetings developed a rather strange character. Abu-Mustafa made no overt attempt to curry her favor, but he made no secret of his eagerness to see her, nor did he attempt to hide the fact that he was collaborating with the Syrians. He often emphasized that he was only in their employ because of the handsome sums they so willingly paid, but he left no doubt about his devotion to his masters, telling Shula on several occasions, "Whoever pays me deserves my unswerving loyalty." His attempts to extract information about Shula's contacts were frequent and none too subtle, and he tried to persuade her to talk about her work as frankly as he discussed his own.

Shula played his game, wondering about its aim. The first time he hinted about her connections at the Syrian border, she said nonchalantly, "It's no secret that I help smuggle Jews into Israel. I was sentenced to prison because of it. It's also no secret that I have people helping me," she went on. "Darwish Baidon was one of them. I'm sure you know him, since he's working for the Syrians as well."

At one of their later meetings, in the beginning of 1959, Abu-Mustafa informed her that he had just come from Damascus, where he had discussed her with his superiors.

"They've known about me for a long time," she shrugged, unimpressed.

Abu-Mustafa returned from his next trip to Damascus with a present for Shula: a Jewish family of five from the Syrian capital that he had personally smuggled across the border.

She laughed when he brought her the news. "It looks as if you want something from me. Be honest, tell me exactly what it is."

"All those others you work with want to use you, to make money from you. I, on the other hand, only want to give you something. . . ."

She cut him off. "But what do you want in exchange?"

He took a heavy drag from his cigarette before replying. "I want to make a deal with you. I'll give you all the Jews left in Syria, without you having to endanger yourself by smuggling them across any borders. I can even arrange it so they'll go straight into Israel through the Golan Heights if you like. Then you won't have to rely on your collaborators in Syria. They're the ones we want," he explained, "the traitors in Syria who are selling their homeland out of greed." He glanced at Shula, sensing her hesitation. "What do you care? You'll be getting your Jews and you won't have any further need of the Syrian traitors."

She laughed softly. "You flatter me," she said. "How can I hand over the names of these so-called traitors when I don't even know who they are, or if they really exist? You know exactly how I operate. Syrian Jews arrive in Wadi Abu-Jamil. I simply help them on their way, so they don't become a burden to our small community."

But Abu-Mustafa refused to be dissuaded. He was even more daring when he raised the subject a second time, offering to provide her with information from Syria in return for the name of the Israeli agent handling things in Damascus.

"We know there's an extensive network of Israelis working in Syria doing more than just smuggling Jews," he said. "Your role in the network is secondary and of no great concern to us. We're interested in the agents in Damascus." He paused, then went on conspiratorially, "To tell you the truth, my superior is under considerable pressure to expose the Syrian traitors, and he's putting pressure on me. I'll tell you what: I'll even agree to take the place of your Damascus contact man. Just give me the name of the head of the network."

"All that for one name?" she teased.

"No," he admitted, "I also want money. I know what the Syrians are willing to pay for information about Israeli intelligence, and I imagine the Israelis would cough up the same amount for Syrian intelligence. I want a quarter of a million pounds."

She drew in her breath. "That's a great deal of money."

"Are you willing to bargain with me?" he grinned. "Does that mean you're interested?"

"No," she laughed, "all it means is that I'd also like a slice of the pie."

She was confident she had put him off the plan. Yet when they parted, she felt her eye twitch nervously, as it often did lately whenever she was tense. She vowed that from that point on she would see less of Abu-Mustafa.

But the twitch remained, even after she stopped meeting the Tiger.

By 1959 everything was running smoothly again in Lebanon, at least on the surface. The political crisis was gradually abating. General Fuad Chehab was sworn in as president in February, and a new government was formed under Saeb Salam, leader of the anti-Chamoun coalition. Under Chehab's rule, Lebanon's foreign policy began to follow the Egyptian-Syrian line, which improved relations between Lebanon and her eastern neighbor and established a basis of cooperation with the northern half of the United Arab Republic. Beirut was no longer a divided city, and the capital gradually returned to normal, becoming, in fact, even more lively than ever. Vast sums came pouring in from the Persian Gulf oil emirates, and signs of prosperity abounded. The population increased rapidly, and high-rise buildings sprouted up everywhere, transforming both the skyline and the atmosphere. Beirut quickly grew into a bustling metropolis—crowded, noisy, and dirty for sure, but full of life.

As Beirut developed, Nabil Mussa's nightclub became even more popular. Abu-Sa'id's casino continued to attract the important local and foreign dignitaries, whose numbers had multiplied. Between the two sources Shula had a steady supply of information to include in her reports to Israel. The smuggling operation was revived, and the air route once again transported the refugees efficiently. Two new routes, via Nicosia and Athens, were added to the Istanbul line.

Even though her many operations seemed to be moving like clockwork, Shula was under constant stress and the nervous twitch reflected the strain. Her relationship with George Anton was the primary reason. With Camille Chamoun's resignation George had lost his power, and with it his self-confidence. He constantly complained that, unlike Chamoun, the new president neither relied upon nor trusted him. One by one his principal aides were transferred to other positions, and George was no longer allowed to choose their replacements personally. He suspected that the rival secret service agency, connected to the Ministry of the Interior, was conspiring against him and planned to take over his office.

But it was not only the new president that upset George. He was also unhappy with the Syrian-Lebanese cooperation that had been forced upon him. The brutal techniques of the Syrian agents with whom he now had to work disgusted him, and he kept an extensive file on their activities. Naturally the pressures that plagued him at work affected their relationship, causing them to exchange bitter words. Shula often found herself on the verge of tears as she left him.

Summer passed and winter arrived earlier than usual. The northern winds began blowing in October and the rains came at the end of the month.

One night late in October Shula sat by herself, listening to the rain beating against the closed shutters, sealing the apartment from the sounds of the street. She could barely hear the pealing of the church bells at Saint Joseph's marking midnight.

Joseph had already gone to bed. Seven-year-old Dudik and eleven-year-old Carmela were fast asleep. The last television program had ended, and she had managed to persuade Arlette and Isaac to go to bed as well.

Huddled on the sofa next to the heater in the living room, Shula sat reading and rereading the most recent letter from her daughter Yaffa, thinking that Yaffa's handwriting was perhaps the only thing about the girl she really knew anymore. Her twenty-one-year-old daughter was now a grown woman, about to be married. Shula thought sadly, "What do I know about her secret dreams? Is she happy? Does she really love this young stranger, or is she just looking for the home that I never gave her?"

She remembered her last hasty trip to Jerusalem four months earlier, and Yaffa's image flashed into her mind. The girl had been terribly withdrawn, and Shula had been unable to melt the ice between them during her brief visits to her mother's house. "I'm a stranger to her," she said silently, accepting the truth with regret.

And what about Bertie and Meir? Hadn't they also become strangers to her? Didn't they, too, resent her for depriving them of a home and the love of their parents?

Shula had been disturbed by such thoughts for quite a while, and she tried to ease her conscience by telling herself she sent the children away for their own good. Only in Israel could they grow up to be proud, independent Jews. Yet there was no escaping her remorse and doubts, and she had lately begun to toy with the idea of giving up everything and joining her children in Israel. Maybe they could plan their arrival in time for Yaffa's wedding?

She knew even before discussing the subject with Joseph that he might have several objections, despite his desire to see the children. What would a sixty-year-old textile merchant do in a country whose language he didn't even know, except for his daily prayers? She thought about herself and her network of spies, and her mind jumped to George, but she forced herself to consider Joseph instead. Would he want to go? Would he be willing to start a new life in a new country? A picture of her father appeared in her mind: her last memories of him were of an embittered man, a man who had failed in life.

She hadn't reached any decision before she lost her train of thought. "I'm tired," she said, almost out loud, as she turned off the heater and went to bed.

But visions of Israel kept her from falling asleep, and she was still awake when she heard a knock at the door. "Who could it be at this hour?" she wondered. The knocking persisted and she clambered out of bed, thinking, "I hope it won't wake the children."

She hastily grabbed her dressing gown and ran to the door, snapping on the light in the living room along the way.

"Just a minute. I'm coming!" she called impatiently as the pounding grew louder.

Buttoning her robe, Shula looked through the peephole. She let out a cry of astonishment.

Abu-Mustafa and two of his bodyguards were standing in the hallway.

She unhooked the chain with a mixture of surprise and anger. Abu-Mustafa had never been in her house, and she had always made sure not to reveal her address when they were together. How did he find out where she lived? Had he been following her?

She opened the door, but the rebuke she had prepared was forgotten when she saw the look of absolute horror that came over his face.

His eyes bulged and he opened his mouth to speak, but the only word that came out was an incredulous "You . . . ?"

"Who else did you come to wake up in the middle of the night in my house, if not me?" she demanded.

Abu-Mustafa stared at her, mesmerized. *"Allahu Akbar!"* he cried. "Good God, it's you!"

Only then did she notice the gun in his hand. His two bodyguards were armed as well.

"What's going on here?" she asked sternly. Then, softening her tone, she gestured toward the living room. "Why are you standing out there? Come in. I want to close the door. It's cold."

"Wait for me downstairs," Abu-Mustafa ordered his men. He followed Shula into the house, and she shut the door quickly, unsure of what to do next.

"Do you want some tea?" she asked, forcing herself to sound polite but unconcerned. Although the gun he was still holding and the unusual hour meant that something was seriously wrong, she tried to act as naturally as possible, as if she always received uninvited armed visitors at two o'clock in the morning.

But Abu-Mustafa hadn't come for tea. "Just a minute," he interrupted, "Um-Ibrahim, are you Shula Cohen?"

She turned to him in surprise, realizing at once that she had never introduced herself to the Tiger by her real name. He had known her only as Um-Ibrahim.

She was overcome with fright, but she managed to muster up enough self-assurance to reply, "Yes, I am Shula Cohen. What of it?"

His face had become deathly pale, and the words came out slowly. "I received orders to bring Shula Cohen to Damascus tonight."

She stared at Abu-Mustafa. He looked terribly alarmed.

"Why?" she mumbled hoarsely.

"I don't know. A special envoy was sent to tell me to deliver Shula Cohen to Damascus tonight, dead or alive."

"But you can't—"

"I have to," he said, shaking his head. "It's an order. If I don't do it, they'll come after me." He sounded so confused and upset that it was as if he were pleading with Shula to try to understand his position.

Her legs almost gave in, but her mind was remarkably clear. She hung onto that note of confusion in his voice for dear life.

"Sit down!" she commanded with such authority that he immediately obeyed. She pulled up a chair in front of him. "Now start again from the very beginning. What exactly did they tell you to do?"

"I have to bring you and three other people to Damascus tonight," he stuttered. "Mahmud Hoj, who works in the Ministry of the Interior; Dib Sa'adia, the mukhtar of the Wadi; and Albert Iliya, the secretary of the Jewish community."

"Were you told what they want with us?" she asked quickly.

He mopped his forehead with a handkerchief. "No. I was only ordered to bring you immediately. And your name was at the top of the list. Are you that important?"

She knew by his hesitant voice that there was only one possible route of escape. There was only a slight chance that her plan would work, but she would have to take the risk.

"Yes," she said threateningly, desperately trying to project a dangerous and cold expression with her eyes. "Yes, my friend, I am that important. And you, my dear friend, are in a lot of trouble."

Only the realization that her entire life was hanging by a thread kept her from laughing at the horrified look on Abu-Mustafa's face.

She continued, encouraged, "The other three aren't connected with me at all. I have nothing to do with them. But if you bring me to Damascus, you'll be wiped out."

"What do you mean?" he gasped.

"Quite simply, you'll be finished." She lowered her voice, speaking to him now as a friend. "Listen, *Ya* Abu-Mustafa, I'm a woman, a very important woman, just as you guessed. If you bring me to Damascus . . . well, you know how the Syrians work. They'll torture me. I'll have to tell them everything. What other choice would I have? Wouldn't you talk if they applied a burning cigarette to your skin? Wouldn't you tell them everything if they ripped out your nails with pliers?

"I'm not a hero." She smiled coldly. "I'll break down under pressure and I'll spill everything. I'll tell them all about you, the way you helped me, the way you brought five Syrian Jews for me to smuggle into Israel, the way you offered me the rest of the Jews in Damascus. And what about your promise to sell me information about Syrian intelligence? Remember that? You wanted to make a deal for a quarter of a million pounds. I don't know whether you received orders to make such a deal, but I think not. I'd guess that the whole affair was your own idea." Her eyes didn't move from his ashen face. "Of course it was. You wanted to please them by giving them the name of the Israeli agent in Damascus, right? But how will they take it when I tell them? You can deny it, of course, and they'll continue to torture me and I'll simply repeat the story, over and over again. I won't have any other choice; it's the truth. What do you think they'll do to you then?"

She spoke softly but forcefully. "Don't you understand? You can't afford to bring me to Damascus. Now shall I get you a cup of tea? Or maybe you'd prefer a glass of cold water?"

She got up and moved toward the kitchen. He made no attempt to stop her. She put the kettle on the stove and poured him some cold water. Placing the glass before him, she asked quietly, "What are you going to do?"

Abu-Mustafa rubbed his face. "You're the devil, *Ya* Um-Ibrahim. Or should I say Shula Cohen?"

"It doesn't matter. The important thing is that we both know you can't let me go to Damascus. It would mean the end of both of us."

"Then what can we do?" he whined.

Shula had already laid out a plan.

"First, go down and tell your men to pick up the other three on your list. Let them pack some clothes and take their passports and money. Then bring them to the airport. Come back to pick me up at five."

He was about to say something but she interrupted him. "Let me finish. You take me to the airport and with the others I'll catch the first plane leaving the country. But you'll be given a document verifying that we left Beirut the day before yesterday. That will convince your superiors in Damascus that it wasn't your fault that we slipped out of your hands. In fact, they'll probably even compliment you for having such good connections with the airport authorities." She gave him a few moments to digest her words before she went on. "You have no other choice, my friend."

He sat down, holding his head in his hands. The vein on his forehead was throbbing. At last he lifted his head.

"How do I know you won't cheat me?" he asked, squinting at her. "How can I be sure you'll really give me that paper?"

"My fate is entirely in your hands, Ya Abu-Mustafa. Or maybe you have a better plan to save both our lives?" she said sarcastically.

Abu-Mustafa was speechless. The discovery that Um-Ibrahim was none other than Shula Cohen had him in a state of shock, and he could hardly think. The same woman who had been his prisoner only a few short moments ago was now dictating his actions, and he could not stop her.

"Look," she added hurriedly. "I'm leaving my husband and children here in Beirut. Would I do such a foolish thing if I planned on deceiving you? We're in the same boat, my friend. We have to trust each other."

Abu-Mustafa made his decision. "I'll be here to pick you up at five," he said quietly. He stood up and left the house, shutting the door behind him. Shula sat alone in the silence of the room. The only sound she could hear was the rain beating against the shutters.

She collapsed at the table in a weak mass. All the life had been wrung out of her. Her left eye twitched slightly, independently.

She remained motionless for a few minutes and then gathered her strength into a whirlwind of activity. She rushed to her room and opened her closet, but as she started to pack, she realized that she still didn't have any idea where she was going or for how long. Examining her dresses, she made an instantaneous decision: Istanbul first, then on to Israel. Afterward she'd decide . . .

She grabbed a light-blue suit, a print blouse, and a pair of low-heeled shoes from the rack. These would be her traveling clothes. She took down a large handbag and threw in some underwear, a sweater, and a kerchief. That should be enough, she told herself. I can buy whatever else I may need.

She checked the papers she kept in her traveling bag: a valid passport with a six-month visa for Turkey and an undated letter from a renowned Beirut gynecologist describing the details of a disease she supposedly had and referring her to a specialist in Rome. She had carried the letter for more than a year, but had never needed to use it before.

Removing a packet of one-hundred-dollar bills from a drawer of her dressing table, she counted over two thousand dollars. Joseph frequently reprimanded her for keeping so much cash in the house, but she had always known the day might come when she would urgently need the money. That day had arrived.

She dialed Fahed Hamouda's number. She had to wait a minute or so before his sleepy voice came on the line.

"Fahed," she said forcefully, "you know who this is. I'm sorry about phoning at this hour, but I have an emergency. Can you meet me at the airport at six this morning?"

Hamouda yawned that he was due there anyway at that time because his company had a flight scheduled to leave at seven.

"That's perfect," she cried. "It wouldn't be to Istanbul, would it? Yes? I need to book four places on that flight. Will it be possible? Wait, that isn't all. I have to ask you to arrange something else. My name and the name of three other people have to appear on the passenger list for the day before yesterday. Can you handle it? Fahed, you have no idea how grateful I am!"

Shula showered, dressed, put on her makeup, and packed her makeup case. Then she went into the living room and peered at the clock: it was quarter to five.

She put the kettle back on the fire and opened the door to her husband's bedroom. Shaking him gently, she said, "Joseph, it's time to wake up."

He stirred and squinted in her direction until his hand found his glasses on the night table.

"You can't sleep?" he asked when he saw her standing above his bed fully dressed.

"No," she whispered. "I have to take a trip. Something's come up. First get washed and then we'll talk."

He didn't argue.

Shula poured two cups of coffee and set them on the coffee table in the living room while Joseph washed. Then she tiptoed into her daughter's room. The gentle kiss she planted on Carmela's cheek almost awakened the child. "Shh, go back to sleep," Shula cooed. Carmela turned over and moaned something incomprehensible in her sleep. Shula crept into the boys' room and tightened the blanket around Dudik. Glancing at the mess in the boys' room, she felt the anxiety drain out of her body, and a warm smile replaced the frightened look on her face.

Joseph was already sitting in his bathrobe, blowing into the hot coffee, when she returned to the living room and sat down beside him, disconcerted again.

"I have to go away for a few days," she began somewhat nervously. Her voice triggered his suspicions.

"What happened?" he demanded.

"Nothing important. We've had some minor complications. If anyone should come around asking about me, I've gone to Rome to see a specialist."

"Whom do you expect to come around asking?"

"Anybody. The police. Maybe no one. But don't worry about me. Everything will be all right. Take care of yourself and the children."

"Do you have enough money?" he asked. She nodded.

"God be with you," he said huskily. "The children and I will pray for you. And if you can, write us."

Shula heard the blast of a car's horn coming from the street and she went to the window, opened the shutters, and looked outside. An enormous black American car was parked in front of the building. She shut the window.

"That's for me," she announced sadly to Joseph, who was gazing silently into his coffee cup. "I have to go now. Tell Arlette to take care of Carmela and Dudik. She's old enough now. And have Nazira cook for you all. Good-bye, Joseph."

She kissed him on the cheek and walked quickly out of the house.

Abu-Mustafa called out to her from the driver's seat, "You're right on time."

"So are you," she said, climbing in. "Is everything all set? Are the other three waiting at the airport?"

"Only the Jews," he grunted, turning the car away from her house. "Hoj wasn't at home. It wasn't exactly easy with the other two either. They're pretty scared, but they're waiting at the airport. My men are guarding them." He glanced at Shula. "What now? Are you sure everything will be all right?"

"I told you it would be," she snapped, purposely adding an air of impatience to her voice.

The car made its way through the streets of Beirut until they reached the windy Corniche, still empty at that early hour. The towering new high-rise hotels rose off to their left, and on their right the stormy sea was raging. Shula gazed at the surf, following the rhythm of the waves breaking on the rocks, until the car turned left and headed for the airport.

Neither one spoke until Abu-Mustafa parked the car in the airport lot. He opened the door for her and growled menacingly, "Don't forget, you still have to give me that phony passenger list. And don't try to fool me." His hand went to his vest in an unmistakable threat.

"Are we back to that?" she scolded. "You'll have to trust me, Abu-Mustafa. You have no other choice."

They walked through the gate without another word.

The departing passengers scattered here and there couldn't fill the emptiness that pervaded the massive departure hall. Shula immediately picked out Dib Sa'adia and Albert Iliya, hunched mournfully over their suitcases. Two other men were sitting beside them. Iliya raised his head in recognition as she approached, but she hurried past him, praying that he wouldn't talk to her. Her prayers were answered. He lowered his head again without speaking. She charged toward the line of public telephones with Abu-Mustafa trailing at her heels.

He watched her drop some change in one of the phones and dial, but he couldn't make out what she was saying. She emerged from the phone booth moments later.

"Everything's all right," she informed him. "We have to go to the cafeteria. The document will be brought to us there."

Assured that things were now under control, Shula wanted to calm Abu-Mustafa's nerves. She turned to him after the waiter set down their coffee. "How is your mother?" she asked.

"Fine, thank you," he replied tensely. "She sends her best."

"And your wife and daughters?"

"*El Hamd Ul Illah*—Thank God."

They waited in strained silence until a short young man in an airlines uniform approached their table. He leaned over to Shula, left an envelope on the table, and disappeared.

Shula emptied the envelope onto the table. Three airline tickets fell out. She took one for herself and passed the remaining two to Abu-Mustafa. She unfolded the other piece of paper, a carbon copy of a passenger list, and skimmed through the names, making sure Fahed Hamouda had followed the instructions she had given him a few minutes earlier on the phone and removed Mahmud Hoj's name from the list. With a satisfied smile she handed over the counterfeit passenger list.

"Here are the names of the people who flew to Rome via TMA the day before yesterday," she told him. "That ought to convince your bosses in Syria." She grinned. "They'll be going crazy trying to pin down the traitor who tipped us off in advance!"

A weak smile flickered across the Tiger's lips as he looked over the names of the passengers. Shulamit Kishak-Cohen was number seven on the list, Dib Sa'adia was twenty-two, and Albert Iliya was twenty-six. His smile broadened.

"Do you always manage to get what you want?" he asked admiringly.

Shula shrugged her shoulders. "There are no traffic signs in our profession," she replied.

Although he now had what he wanted, Abu-Mustafa stayed at Shula's side until he heard the loudspeaker call for the passengers to board TMA Flight 331 from Beirut to Istanbul and Frankfurt. Then he rose and shook Shula's hand solemnly.

"Good-bye," he said. "It's been quite an experience knowing you."

"You're talking as if we'll never see each other again," Shula answered.

Abu-Mustafa's eyes widened. "Are you thinking of returning to Beirut?"

"What else? My home is here, and my husband and children."

He cleared his throat uncomfortably. "And what about Damascus?"

"I'll cross that bridge when I come to it," she smiled. "I'm counting on you to see to it that they'll never again be able to surprise me in the future. You mustn't forget that we're both in the same boat."

He didn't respond. Shula stepped toward the gate, turning to him before she walked through. "Send my regards to your mother," she called out. "I'm very fond of her."

A stewardess showed Shula to the first-class section as she boarded the plane. She assumed that this, too, was the handiwork of Fahed Hamouda and she thanked him in her heart. The other seats were empty and Shula could kick off her shoes and surrender to her growing fatigue without being disturbed. She fell asleep at once and didn't wake up until the stewardess gently tapped her on the shoulder.

"We're landing now, madame," she said quietly, apologetically. "You were sleeping so soundly that I didn't have the heart to wake you for breakfast."

"That doesn't matter," Shula smiled. "I wasn't very hungry anyway. I preferred to sleep."

Shula still hadn't said a word to her fellow exiles, and only after the airplane landed and the passengers were filing out toward the customs desks did she find a chance to whisper to Albert Iliya, "Collect your bags but don't pass through customs until someone makes contact with you."

As soon as they entered the arrivals hall she pulled out the two Turkish coins that she always kept in her purse and went directly to the public phones to call Epstein.

She was relieved to hear his voice.

She identified herself curtly. "It's Shula. I'm at the airport. I had to escape from Beirut unexpectedly and there are two others with me."

"Wait for me," he instructed. "I'll be there on the double."

It took him over half an hour to arrive, giving Shula plenty of time to retrieve her small suitcase and clear customs. She was sipping a glass of cognac, casually flipping through a French magazine that had been left on the table, when she saw him arrive. Epstein wore a tweed suit and carried a black umbrella under his arm, apparently trying to achieve a British effect, but it didn't match his manner or his round Slavic face. He was accompanied by a man Shula had never seen before, a younger, taller fellow with short black hair cut military-style.

Epstein didn't bother to make introductions. He shook her hand and sat down, anxious to deliver his news.

"I've already contacted Tel Aviv and informed them that you're here. They want to see you. There's an El Al flight to Lod this afternoon."

He removed an Israeli passport from the inside pocket of his jacket. "This is for you," he said, smiling. "Use it when you pass through customs again so you won't have a Turkish exit stamp on your Lebanese passport." The routine was familiar to Shula, and she followed it whenever she traveled from Istanbul to Tel Aviv, but for some reason Epstein found it necessary to explain the procedure again each time. "In fact," he added, "just to be safe, give me your Lebanese passport. I'll return it to you when you get back to Istanbul."

She handed him the passport. "What about the people that came with me?"

"Who are they?" he asked. Shula explained, telling him they were waiting in the arrivals hall. Epstein signaled to his assistant, who strode toward the customs station.

He returned shortly.

"The lawyer, Albert Iliya, wants to go back to Beirut," he announced. "The other one is willing to go to Israel." He glanced at Shula. "That is, if you'll promise that his family can join him there soon."

Epstein looked at her. "Do you think it will be all right? I mean about the other one returning to Beirut."

"Maybe," she answered uncertainly. "He has many friends to protect him."

"All right then," Epstein said. "Check when there's a return flight to Beirut," he told his young companion, "and get him a ticket. Reserve two seats on the El Al flight as well. Shula, you have four hours to kill until the flight. Do you want to wait here, or shall we go to the city?"

She gazed out the window at the cloudy gray sky. A slight drizzle was falling steadily, and she imagined there must be a brisk cold wind in the air. "I never did like Istanbul in the winter," she sighed.

Her mind jumped to the first winter's night she had spent in Istanbul.

"No," she replied. "I'll stay here. I'm tired."

Early that evening the plane carrying Shula Cohen and Dib Sa'adia landed on the rainy runway at Lod. One of Shimshoni's men greeted them.

"We've reserved a room for you in Tel Aviv," he told Shula after she passed through customs. "I'm sure you'd like to rest. Shimshoni is expecting you tomorrow at nine."

"If we can change it to eleven, I'll save you the expense of a hotel," she said. "I want to go to Jerusalem, to my mother's house."

Shimshoni's man didn't object. She handed Dib Sa'adia over to his care and walked out to the line of taxis waiting in front of the airport.

The Eclipse

19 The following morning Shula told Shimshoni about the attempt by the Syrians to abduct her and her subsequent escape. She related the events dryly, trying not to boast. But recalling the entire incident was like reliving it, and she could feel her heart pounding as if she were face to face with Abu-Mustafa all over. Shimshoni listened without interrupting, his eyes never leaving Shula's face.

When she finished speaking, he said, "You acted very wisely. Let me congratulate you." In all the years they had worked together Shimshoni had rarely complimented Shula. "The question remains, however, what are we going to do now?"

"What do you mean?"

"Even if we assume that you managed to convince the Tiger that it's in his best interest to keep you out of Damascus, and even if the Syrians actually believe you left Beirut because you had prior warning, it still doesn't change the fact that they're after you. Your escape will make you even more valuable in their eyes, especially if they think you were warned in advance. Now they'll want more than ever to get their hands on you, to find out who the informer was. Don't you understand? They'll only try to kidnap you again and this time they may not use Abu-Mustafa to do it." He drew in his breath. "You can't return to Beirut."

Shula felt the color drain from her face. Only three hours earlier her daughter Yaffa had said almost the very same words.

Yaffa had not been home when Shula arrived at her mother's house from the airport. She and her fiancé had gone to visit some friends, and Shula was too tired to wait up for her. They didn't see each other until the next morning, when Yaffa was already dressed and ready to go to work. She tiptoed into her mother's room and woke her with a kiss and then served her some coffee. Shula sat sipping the hot beverage, and Yaffa perched on the corner of the bed, tossing off eager questions about her father and younger brothers and sisters.

"And how is Abu-Jacques?" she inquired. "Does he still come to visit so often?"

"Yes." Shula replied. "Why do you ask?"

"And old Mussa?"

"He isn't in Beirut anymore. He's joined some relatives in one of the African countries. Why?"

"Mother, he didn't just decide to go to Africa, did he? He had to escape from Beirut, right?"

"What are you talking about, child?" Shula scoffed.

Yaffa continued impatiently. "Mother, stop treating me like a little girl! Do you really believe I don't know what you've been doing all these years? How else can a Jew from Beirut just happen to visit Israel every few months? But how long do you think it can last?" She paused, lowering her voice. "Look, I don't resent your sending me away, or Bertie and Meir either. It was all for the best in the end. But did you ever think what would happen to daddy and the little ones if you ever got caught? Mother, haven't you done enough? Don't return to Beirut. Stay here with us. Daddy will bring the others and we'll all be together again, and I'll be able to sleep at night without worrying about you!"

Yaffa exploded into great, uncontrollable tears.

Shula was still upset by her daughter's outburst when she traveled from Jerusalem to meet Shimshoni in Tel Aviv. And now here he was, telling her the very same thing: you can't go back to Beirut.

Ignoring Shimshoni, she lost herself in a dream for a moment: to come home to Jerusalem, this time with her entire family. They might even be able to buy back the old house on Alfandari Street that her mother had had to sell after her father's death. But she immediately had second thoughts. What about Joseph? And what about her work? Would she be able to settle into the quiet life of a Jerusalem matron after all these years? Would she be satisfied with keeping house and filling her evenings with parent-teacher meetings at the Evelyna de Rothschild School discussing Carmela's progress?

She eyed Shimshoni levelly. "I think you're wrong," she said. "Now that I'm aware of the danger I can be on guard. They won't be able to surprise me again. Anyway, how can I not go back to Beirut? My home is there, and my family."

Shimshoni studied her for a moment.

"Whatever happens," he finally responded, "you'll be staying here for a few days; you could use a rest. In the meantime we'll investigate the situation in Beirut."

Her vacation lasted a week and turned out to be quite pleasant. Yaffa never again brought up the subject of her mother's return to Beirut. Shula became acquainted with her future son-in-law and grew very fond of him. Naomi, her favorite sister, came to her mother's house to visit, and Shula spent time as the guest of her eldest brother in Tel Aviv. She filled her days with sightseeing in and around Jerusalem, and she was pleased to see that the barren countryside of her youth was now covered with forests of evergreen trees, picturesque despite the winter rains.

At the end of the week she went back to Shimshoni's office.

His report was encouraging. "We've checked, and everything seems to have been restored to normal in Beirut, on the surface at least. Abu-Mustafa is in town and has come to no harm, and life in Wadi Abu-Jamil is running smoothly as well. Albert Iliya returned safely, and no one has bothered him. If you want our opinion, you should stay away, but the final decision is yours, of course."

Shula didn't hesitate a second. "I'm going home," she said resolutely.

Epstein had been advised of Shula's arrival and was waiting for her at the airport in Istanbul. He took her Israeli passport and handed her the Lebanese one and stayed with her until the TMA flight to Beirut took off.

The plane flew over the familiar rooftops of the capital, and Shula breathed a sigh of relief.

Everything went well when she landed in Beirut. The passport inspections officer gave a cursory glance at her passport and then stamped it. The customs officer peeked into her traveling case and waved her through without problems.

Shula used Fahed Hamouda's small office behind the TMA counter to phone George. She counted on him to recognize her voice. "I'm back," she declared.

"Yes, I know," he remarked. "I received a report ten minutes ago, just after you landed."

"Has anything happened that I should be concerned about?"

"I don't think so. Everything is relatively quiet. I've put some men on your house." Shula understood from this that the attempt by the Syrians to arrest her had not passed unnoticed in the Wadi. Just as she suspected, George had been duly informed of the incident.

"I have a lot to tell you," she said. "Can we see each other tomorrow?"

Joseph was full of questions about Bertie and Meir, and wanted to know all about Yaffa and her fiancé. He didn't ask Shula to explain her sudden departure from Beirut and went to bed at his usual time, right after the eight o'clock news. Shula couldn't get past Isaac quite so easily, however.

Isaac had been suspicious of his mother's activities for quite a while. His interest was first aroused one night when he overheard her conversation with Abu-Jacques. Shula had assumed the children were fast asleep, but she later discovered that Isaac had been hiding behind the door, listening to every word. As soon as Abu-Jacques left, Isaac had emerged, demanding to know what was going on. Shula had tried to dismiss his questions with a casual joke, but the wounded look on the boy's face told her she couldn't deceive him. So for the very first time she had treated her sixteen-year-old son as if he were a grown man. She spoke to him seriously, explaining that she was involved with smuggling Jews into Israel. Isaac was relieved to have the riddle solved once and for all; the adolescent boy had often wondered about the strange men who visited his mother at night when no one else was around. And now that he understood what was happening, Isaac's imagination was fired by the adventure. Shula had to promise to allow him to help before he would agree to go to bed.

From then on Isaac had taken care of a variety of errands. He would deliver her packages to Shlomo Adut's pharmacy, and if she ever had to see Abu-Jacques or Nabil Mussa urgently, the boy would rush off to notify them, proud to participate in his mother's wonderful, dangerous secret.

It was natural that Isaac now felt that his part in the operation earned him the right to know about his mother's unexpected and mysterious journey. He demanded to hear the truth behind the rumors circulating around the Wadi about the men who tried to kidnap his mother.

Shula had no choice but to tell him, although she attempted to minimize the danger so as not to frighten the impressionable boy. Thinking about it later, she was even happy to have had an opportunity to remind Isaac of the importance of keeping a secret. She emphasized that her son should refrain from answering even the most casual inquiries from strangers concerning his mother. She also told him about his sister's upcoming marriage, and about his older brothers' life in Israel. Isaac had decided awhile before that he wanted to go to Israel and serve in the army as soon as he finished high school, and now he was more excited than ever about the Jewish state.

She saw George the following day. With his declining status under President Chehab, George was no longer entitled to the apartment in the officers' club, and they had no choice now but to meet in public. They would wait for each other in front of the new Starco office building in the center of town, and later George would drive her to a restaurant in one of the half-empty hotels on the Corniche.

As soon as they were alone, she began the story, and George listened carefully. When she mentioned that Abu-Mustafa had been ordered to bring four people to Damascus, he interrupted her. "Who was the fourth?"

"Mahmud Hoj, from the Ministry of the Interior," she replied. "But he wasn't home."

Shula thought for a moment. "He left Beirut the day after we did. And the night before, Abu-Mustafa couldn't find him at home. That can only mean that someone tipped him off in advance. It would be interesting to know who warned him."

"You'll have to go to Ghana to get your answer," George replied. "That's where he's gone. Unless maybe Awad can tell you. He knows a little too much for his own good about the Syrians. But go on."

When she finished the story, George said bitterly, "A year or two ago I wouldn't have allowed Abu-Mustafa to walk the streets after a move like that. But now? His superiors are too friendly with mine. They'd have him released in a matter of hours." He sighed, shaking his head. "At any rate let this be a lesson to you. Your security in the Wadi is assured. My men are watching your home. But I can't guarantee your safety outside the Wadi. I hope you'll put an end to your visits to the Basta."

"Why should I?" Shula cried. "I want to go and talk with Abu-Mustafa."

George stared at her. "You're crazy. If the Syrians get wind of the fact that you've been seen in his company, they'll murder him. Not that it would be any great loss!"

Shula decided to phone the Hamda Pharmacy the following day anyway. The voice at the other end informed her that Abu-Mustafa had left town for a few days.

The tension Shula felt after the kidnapping attempt slowly faded, and once she finally arranged to meet with Abu-Mustafa, it disappeared completely.

The Tiger was even more amiable than usual and didn't seem to hold a grudge against her for forcing him to cooperate in deceiving the Syrians. In fact, he was almost gleefully conspiratorial.

"I reported that you had already slipped away," he explained, "and I sent them the passenger list as proof. I must admit I was a little worried when I was ordered to appear before my superiors in Latakia, but they didn't suspect a thing. It was just as you predicted —they even complimented me."

"Good," Shula nodded, "but the affair isn't over yet. When they find out that I'm back in Beirut, they'll try again, won't they?" She eyed him coolly. "What was true two weeks ago still holds true, Abu-Mustafa. If I should fall into their hands, it will be bad for you as well."

A troubled look came over his face. "You're right," he stuttered. "If I should hear anything, I'll notify you."

"I'd be grateful if you would," she nodded. "In the meantime, for both our sakes, it would be better if we don't see each other. Imagine what would happen if someone reported to the Syrians that they saw us together."

"Don't contact me anymore then," Abu-Mustafa replied. "If I ever have a message for you, I'll be in touch now that I know your name." He glanced around. "By the way, how does Darwish Baidon know that I tried to kidnap you? He said something the last time I saw him that led me to believe he knows all about the affair."

Shula couldn't answer, but it didn't concern her greatly that Baidon knew.

"Who could have told him? Maybe he heard that I escaped, and he just put two and two together. Or he might have heard from Damascus. Actually, what difference does it make?"

But a few weeks later she remembered what Abu-Mustafa had said, and suddenly she wondered if she hadn't been too quick to dismiss his question about Baidon. What if the informer came from her own camp?

Shula's relationship with Muhammed Awad had become strained again, and although there was no single definable reason for her suspicions, something about Awad made her recall the conversation with Abu-Mustafa. Awad was visiting her house as frequently as before, and he still supplied the lion's share of secret information. Yet he was so greedy that he even tried to sell her news already published in the city's daily papers. George repeatedly urged her to be cautious in her dealings with the old man, and Shula's trust in him began to waver. It got so that every time she was in his presence she found herself boiling inside, trying to restrain a desire to lash out at him.

That August a group of right-wing Syrian exiles in Beirut formed a sabotage ring to overthrow the government in Damascus. A Syrian intelligence officer managed to infiltrate their ranks, and after he identified most of the members of the group and the time to expose them arrived, the Lebanese security forces were called into the picture.

George related the details of the affair to Shula, unable to hide his anger. "It isn't enough that the Syrians have turned Lebanon into their own private battlefield! They leave all the dirty work for us."

"So why do you have to do it?" Shula asked, hoping to encourage him to continue talking.

"Why? Because the president has decided we have to cooperate with our 'sister Arab nations.' Some family! It was only yesterday that the Syrians tried to swallow up Lebanon, and today we're the best of friends." As George's authority diminished, his resentment toward Fuad Chehab had multiplied.

Shula tried to console him. "At any rate it's better for your people to carry out the arrests themselves than to have the Syrians send their own men to Beirut."

He knew she was right, and that only made him more angry. "For two lousy cents, I'd even warn the conspirators that we're on their trail," he muttered.

"Do you want me to do it?" she asked cautiously.

"No," George sighed miserably. "What difference would it make? They're all Syrians anyway. . . ."

That same evening Awad visited her at home. "I've made contact with a group of right-wing Syrians," he told her. "They're very well organized and they have plenty of support in their country. A number of important people are behind them." He drew in his breath dramatically. "They want to overthrow the present government and disband the United Arab Republic."

Shula forced herself to appear nonchalant. "What does that have to do with me?" she asked.

He gave her a startled look. "What do you mean? These men could be the next leaders of Syria! That should be of great interest to you! If we can establish contact with them today—if we help them toward their goal—we'll have them in our back pockets. Think of the power you'd have over them if you could threaten to reveal to the world that Israel financed their revolution!"

She eyed him narrowly. "And what do you expect to get out of the deal?"

Her provocative tone put him on his guard, but he replied with an element of surprised innocence in his voice. "What do I expect? Well, I certainly expect a large piece of the pie, as always. A very large slice at that. I think I deserve it."

"And I think," she spit out angrily, "I think I'm sick and tired of your greed! I'm sick and tired of paying you for all kinds of nonsense that has nothing to do with me!"

He straightened up and stared at her indignantly. "If you're not pleased with our partnership, we can always go our separate ways."

Shula was too angry to notice the veiled threat in his words. "Our partnership is based on the money that I pay you," she declared. "I'm the one who decides when to dissolve this so-called partnership."

He stormed out of the house without replying.

The saboteurs were apprehended the very next day. Only the ringleader, Abu-Sa'id's old friend Salah Shishakli, escaped arrest. He was already in Amman by the time the Lebanese security men broke into his house and discovered a large arms cache.

Awad returned to Shula's apartment with his tail between his legs.

"You were wiser than I," he admitted sheepishly. "Or perhaps you knew of the upcoming arrests?"

Shula didn't reply, but she couldn't help thinking, "Perhaps you knew as well, my friend!"

At the end of September George learned that Taufik Jalabut, the head of the general security forces in Lebanon, had left for Damascus on a secret mission to discuss further cooperation between the intelligence services of the two countries. As far as George was concerned, this was the writing on the wall, the proof that his own security force had completely lost its power. The rival security force of the Ministry of the Interior was run under the aegis of Abdallah Mashnuk, Prime Minister Saeb Salam's right-hand man. Both men were Moslems, and they shared a belief in Lebanon's prospective role in a united Arab world.

"This is the beginning of the end," George announced gloomily. "The market has become too big for my taste. I've decided to retire." He turned to her sadly. "I'm going to hand in my resignation very soon, and I suggest that you also give serious thought to quitting the game."

"But why?" she mumbled incredulously.

"I'm burned out," he sighed, rubbing his tired eyes. "Finished. If they've tried to kidnap you, they won't have second thoughts about murdering me."

She gasped. "Because of me?"

George waved his hand, dismissing her implication. "No one suspects us. No. It isn't because of you. It's because of everything I know about the people in the present government. They won't be able to sleep at night as long as I'm still alive."

"What are you going to do?" Shula asked, afraid to hear the answer.

"I'm leaving the country."

"Where will you go?"

"To South America maybe," he said flatly. "What difference does it make?"

"What about us?" she cried. "It will be all over between us!" Her voice trembled.

George's expression softened momentarily, and the melancholy look disappeared from his eyes.

"What we've had together will never end," he said quietly. "It will simply become a closed chapter in our lives, a beautiful memory to hold onto forever."

"Does that mean we may never see each other again?" A sharp pain ran through her chest.

George spoke softly, with no emotion in his face. "We always knew it would have to end sometime. We each have our own families. You have your country, and I am about to leave mine in search of another. Our paths have to separate."

She heard his words, but refused to listen.

"I don't want it to end!" she shouted like a spoiled child. "I won't let you leave me!"

"You're not listening to me!" George cried angrily, impatiently. "I'm leaving the country. Don't you understand that? You'll never see me again."

Shula sobbed uncontrollably, and his anger cooled with her tears. "Shula, please take my advice," he continued soothingly. "The time has come for you to get out as well. Things here are getting too rough. And this is only the beginning."

Tears streamed down her face as she stumbled blindly out of the café.

Shula tossed and turned the entire night, unable to sleep and afraid to believe it was over. She tried to convince herself that George would change his mind. After all his work was his whole life. How could he give it all up? She couldn't accept the urgency of his intentions. She was sure they would still see each other, and she would persuade him to remain with her in Beirut.

When a week passed without a word from George, she called his office.

"The colonel is no longer here," an unfamiliar voice replied.

"When will he be back?" she inquired hopefully.

"The colonel is no longer here," the stranger repeated. "Perhaps someone else can help you?"

She slammed down the phone.

The next evening Abu-Sa'id dispelled whatever illusions Shula still had that her eight-year relationship with George Anton was not over.

"You knew Colonel George Anton from the military intelligence service, didn't you?" he said casually. "Well, he's resigned. Left Lebanon quite suddenly. He's been appointed by Nikola Khouri to represent the family's interest somewhere in South America. A lot of people are interested in Anton's old job."

Shula was devastated, convinced she would never recover from her loss. But after a few days she saw that life went on despite George's absence. Nothing really had changed. She did miss him, however, and particularly missed his guidance. Whenever Awad turned up with one of his complicated jumbles of gossip and rumor, she would say to herself, "If only George were here to unravel the mess!" She threw herself into a whirlwind of activity and rushed from one meeting to the next, allowing herself little time to indulge in sentimental nostalgia.

In November, after the flow of illegal immigrants from Syria and Iraq slowed for the winter, Shula found a pretext to go to Israel. She spent several days with Yaffa and her husband in their new apartment and bought them a lovely wedding gift. When she was ready to leave she went to Tel Aviv to tell Shimshoni, but he wasn't in town.

"Well, I'll be going now," she informed his assistant. "Would you notify Epstein in Istanbul?"

Shimshoni's aide promised to send a telegram that same morning, but something went wrong. Epstein wasn't waiting for her at the airport and there was no answer when she phoned him.

"Damn! What bad luck!" Shula cursed. Epstein had her Lebanese passport and she had only an Israeli passport with someone else's name on it. She wondered what she should do. Should she just go into town and knock on Epstein's door? Perhaps something had happened to him? What if his house was under surveillance? She thought of going to the Lebanese consulate and reporting that her passport was stolen. But the consulate officials might not issue a new one. They might even want her to report the theft to the local authorities. Then the police would want to know under what circumstances the passport was stolen and the name of the hotel where she had been staying for the past week . . . Shula refused to allow herself to worry.

Not wanting to have another possibly unnecessary entrance stamped in her Israeli passport, she chose not to pass through the border inspection. She took a seat in the arrivals hall and phoned Epstein again. There still was no answer. Now she was truly frightened. The arrivals hall was quickly emptying out, and she felt the clerks casting suspicious glances in her direction.

It took five agonizingly long hours before she finally reached Epstein.

The new arrivals who poured into the hall gave her some respite from the wary glances of the passport officials. The tired officials were replaced by new ones as the shifts changed, but the newcomers soon began to notice Shula and eye her curiously.

As she went through passport control, the officer took more time than usual inspecting her Israeli passport, checking all the visa stamps carefully before he stamped it himself and allowed her through. She fell on Epstein's awaiting arm.

"What happened?" he asked quickly. "I wasn't expecting you at all today!"

"They promised me they'd send you a telegram!" she fumed. "Now I've missed my flight to Beirut!"

"Don't worry," he said. "There'll be another flight at six. But we can't stand here any longer. That passport officer hasn't taken his eyes off us for a second. Let's get your luggage and go to the restaurant. You must be famished."

She was in fact quite hungry, but she was too irate to think of food. Epstein tried to calm her, repeating over and over, "These things do happen."

It took a long time before Shula relaxed enough to enjoy her meal.

As they ate, Epstein surreptitiously removed the Israeli passport from her purse, replacing it with the Lebanese one.

She spent another half-hour or so with Epstein, and then the passengers to Beirut were called to board the plane. He took her suitcase and walked her to the departure hall. He gazed at the row of passport inspection booths, but when he couldn't find a familiar face, he opted for a friendly one.

That turned out to be an unfortunate choice.

The inspector leafed through the Lebanese passport until he came to the Turkish entry stamp from the previous week. He stared at Shula for a few moments and then checked the date on the passport a second time.

"Didn't madame arrive this morning?" he asked in halting English.

Epstein answered quickly in Turkish, and the inspector replied sternly. Epstein raised his voice, but the inspector lost his temper and asked to see Epstein's papers as well. Shula stood by in silence, feeling more and more uncomfortable by the minute. If the inspector were to call his superior, the entire affair could end badly for all of them.

But the document Epstein handed the clerk pacified him enough to bring the encounter to a close. He stamped Shula's passport and handed it back to her angrily.

Epstein glanced at the stamp and noticed the error at once: the inspector had placed another entry stamp alongside the first, instead of a departure stamp. He brought the error to the clerk's attention. Cursing, the inspector grabbed the passport from Shula and stamped it again properly. Epstein nodded satisfied at last.

"Stay well," Epstein called brightly as she proceeded to the gate.

But despite his cheery farewell Shula couldn't rid herself of the ominous feeling that had unsettled her since the moment of her arrival in Istanbul. While she waited impatiently to board her flight, she worried about her arrival in Lebanon. There were now two entry stamps in her passport. If the border guards should inquire about that in Beirut, would they believe it was only a clerical error? And she no longer even had George there to iron out all these infuriating complications!

The more she thought about it, the more anxious she became about having to face the Lebanese border officials, although there was no rational explanation for her growing anxiety. "It's merely a clerical error," she whispered. "I've already gotten myself out of more serious situations." But she couldn't suppress the fear, and when the Turkish stewardess arrived to open the boarding gate, Shula decided to follow her intuition.

"I've changed my mind," she told the startled stewardess. "I'm not taking the flight. Can my baggage be retrieved from the plane?"

Shula had to wait about ten minutes for her luggage. She headed toward the farthest passport control booth, trying not to arouse any attention on her way. She greeted the surprised clerk's gaze by saying, "I forgot my jewelry case in the hotel."

He opened her passport and affixed a fourth Turkish arrival stamp. Then he motioned for her to pass through.

Shula hurried to the Palace Hotel. She phoned Epstein from her room. He answered immediately this time.

"It's me again," she announced. "I decided not to go. I was afraid of the extra entry stamp."

"Where are you calling from?" he asked tersely.

She gave him the name of the hotel and her room number. "I'll get in touch with you," he replied and hung up.

Epstein phoned later that evening and instructed her to meet him at a coffee shop in Taksim Square quite near her hotel. They sat in the farthest corner of the dimly lit café, watching the stylishly dressed teen-agers dance to rock and roll music.

"I contacted Israel," Epstein whispered. "They want you to go to Rome, where your passport will be 'cleaned'."

"Cleaned?" she repeated blankly.

"They'll erase whatever is unnecessary," he explained. "They have experts there for that kind of work."

There were further complications with the experts, however.

A telegram from Epstein preceded her to Rome. Minutes after she checked in at the Impero Hotel on the Via Minale, one of his men knocked on her door. He examined her passport and said that it would have to be sent to Israel. He estimated that Shula might have to wait as much as two weeks before her passport could be returned.

Shula immediately cabled home, saying simply, "Further tests necessary. Return delayed." Later that day she wrote a letter apologizing to her family for having to stay away so long. She jotted down several suggestions for Arlette, who was running the house in her absence, and she expressed concern for young Dudik, whose asthma attacks were sure to become more severe with the onset of winter.

Despite her protests to her family to the contrary, Shula accepted her fate in good spirit, and she was even secretly pleased about the delay. She still could not explain that sudden, illogical fear that overcame her in Istanbul as she was about to board the plane that would have had her in Beirut in less than two hours, but she knew that something was holding her from wanting to go home.

Conveniently for Shula her unconscious unwillingness to leave for Beirut matched the wishes of her superiors in Tel Aviv. They had repeatedly but unsuccessfully tried to persuade her to remain in Israel, and now that they had managed to detain her in Rome, they decided to keep her there as long as possible. Two and a half months passed before Shula's passport was finally returned.

As the weeks dragged on, Shula's life in Rome became increasingly lonely and boring. She instinctively avoided making new acquaintances, for she was haunted by a vague sense of danger that made her suspicious of her surroundings.

She spent her time on safe, predictable sightseeing tours: Naples, Sorrento, the Pope's summer retreat in the mountains at the Castel Gandolfo, cold and empty at that time of year, and Frascati. She decided on the tours so she could be with other people, but as soon as the buses returned to Rome, she would slip away from the group, lest any of her new acquaintances invite her to dinner or to the opera.

Whereas in Beirut she had always been exhausted by the stress of too much to do, now Shula had trouble filling her free time. Her friends in Beirut knew her as forever rushing around, usually managing to be late for her appointments. But in Rome she had no appointments to keep, and time stood still, like a broken clock.

She knew she wasn't happy in Rome, and she told herself she would be happy to leave. Nevertheless, when her altered passport finally arrived, something intangible held her back. It was then that Joseph sent a special messenger to see her in Rome.

His name was Milad El Korah, and she learned that he was a secret agent in the security police of the Ministry of the Interior, as well as Muhammed Awad's latest "find." Awad had given him a letter of introduction which said, "He's willing to work with us. He can be trusted. I've got him well in hand."

Awad had met Milad quite by chance at Madame Bianca's, and the two became great friends. Only later did Awad learn how carefully planned their chance encounter had been.

Awad had long been under the surveillance of the security police. The suspicions about the mysterious treasury official were confirmed when the heads of Lebanese and Syrian security met. They exchanged notes on the old lecher, and the Syrian officer revealed that Awad often sold intelligence information to his country. But the high standard of living the old reveler maintained indicated that he had to be working for others as well, and the Lebanese agents decided to maintain constant surveillance of Awad's activities and keep an extensive open file on him. Milad El Korah was the man chosen to head the investigation.

El Korah was an efficient investigator. He soon became a regular client at Madame Bianca's and in no time was one of Awad's favorite drinking companions. He never tried to conceal the fact that he was working for the security police. On the contrary, he emphasized his position, knowing it would provide an irresistible lure to the greedy old lecher.

His plan worked, and Awad inevitably succumbed to temptation. One evening, feigning drunkenness, El Korah began to complain about the disappointing pace of advancement in his job, and he let slip his interest in making his fortune more quickly, any way he could. Awad observed the younger man for several weeks, testing him patiently before making his first proposal. With Mahmud Hoj out of the picture, blank Lebanese passports were scarce. Perhaps El Korah could arrange to sell the documents? Delighted, El Korah agreed without hesitation.

He supplied Awad with three passports, openly but not obstinately expressing his disappointment when Awad postponed payment by explaining that the person who controlled the funds was temporarily out of Beirut. El Korah agreed to wait.

Awad then made his next move. He brought his new friend to the Star nightclub and arranged a lavish spread of food, drinks, and women, all in El Korah's honor. When he thought the time was ripe, he made his second request: more passports, but at least twenty this time.

He hinted that the passports were destined for Israel and that the market was unlimited. Encouraged by El Korah's response, he offered to buy any and every Lebanese passport his friend could supply.

"I can make you rich on passports alone," Awad boasted, "but they're only a drop in the sea. There's no end to the Israelis' supply of dollars, nor to the things they're willing to buy."

When El Korah recovered from his "drunken stupor," he learned that he had agreed the night before to work for the Israelis. "I taped our conversation and you were photographed with Israeli agents," Awad warned him. "You're in now. You have no choice."

El Korah grumbled that he had been tricked but admitted sadly that, indeed, there was no way out.

Awad was tremendously proud of his latest accomplishment, but with Shula out of the country he couldn't translate his victory into money, the only language he understood. He began, therefore, to take an urgent interest in getting her home. Awad didn't know the reason for Shula's prolonged absence, and although Joseph couldn't tell him much, he did confide that she was in Rome, and that for some unknown reason she seemed afraid to return.

Joseph's admission was exactly the kind of news Awad was waiting for.

"I have a friend who's involved with the Ministry of the Interior's security police," he said. "We can ask him to find out if there are any grounds for Shula's fears. He has access to the most confidential files, and he can tell us exactly what the security people know about her."

True to form, Awad didn't miss an opportunity to feather his own nest, and he took two thousands pounds from Joseph as his friend's fee.

He soon reappeared in the Wadi, bringing Milad El Korah along. "Tell *hawaja* Kishak what you've discovered," he suggested.

El Korah then repeated the story that had been carefully prepared for him. "It's true that Shula Kishak-Cohen has a file in the security police," he began, "but it's been closed for years. It goes into detail about her trial in nineteen fifty-three, and there are a few other entries regarding the illegal smuggling of Jews across the border, but the last entry was made in nineteen fifty-six."

Joseph was overjoyed. He could now prove to Shula that there was nothing to fear, and he could categorically demand that she return to Beirut. He would send off a letter at once!

But Awad had another plan. "If you write her," he said cagily, "she won't believe you. After all, how would you have gotten confidential information out of the security police's closed files? But if Milad here were to go to Rome to persuade her, that would be a different story."

Awad convinced Joseph that for another seven thousand pounds he and El Korah could go to Rome and convince Shula it was safe to come home. Joseph agreed eagerly, but in the end El Korah had traveled alone, presenting Shula with letters of introduction from Joseph and Awad.

Until that point the Lebanese security services had no real suspicions about the nature of Shula's activities. They were probably aware that she headed a ring which smuggled Syrian Jews into Israel, and they must have been informed by their Syrian counterparts about the Jewish woman who had so many highly placed connections in the government. But George Anton had always made sure that these charges were never recorded in any confidential file. It was Milad El Korah's daily reports that instigated the extensive secret investigation that eventually proved to be Shula's downfall.

Like Awad, Shula immediately trusted Milad El Korah. The handsome twenty-eight-year-old was the man she imagined George to have been in his youth. Furthermore, El Korah's timing was right; after three months of alienation in Rome Shula was at last ready to go home.

Shula reported El Korah's arrival to the Israelis, and an agent was sent to speak with him. After observing Awad's messenger at great length he, too, was favorably impressed. El Korah had been well coached for his meeting, and he had been equipped with a number of state secrets that his superiors knew would interest the Israelis. His performance was convincing, and the Israeli came away believing that he was indeed a secret agent who would be willing to betray his country out of greed.

On February 22, 1961, Shula set out with Milad El Korah for the airport in Rome. She was on her way home.

But once again her intuition frightened her, and she almost canceled the flight at the last minute. As they checked out of the hotel, she noticed the morning newspaper lying on the reception desk. She scanned the headlines and her eye hit a small item announcing that there would be a lunar eclipse that day. She recalled an old saying the women of Jerusalem used to repeat in her youth: "The demons of destruction come out of hiding during an eclipse."

"It's an unlucky day," she said to El Korah with a weak smile. "If my mother were here, she would insist that we delay the flight."

He gave her such an incredulous look that she swallowed the lump rising in her throat. "It's only an old wives' tale," she laughed, and followed him out to the airport bus.

Shula didn't mention the superstition again, but as their Pan Am flight landed in Beirut, the ominous feeling of approaching danger swept over her once more. When the border official took longer than usual to inspect her passport, she was sure he had discovered that it had been tampered with. The thought echoed in her mind, and she felt herself becoming pale.

Her fears increased when the official motioned to his superior. Shula was sure she had seen the tall captain before, but she couldn't remember where they had met. He bowed and introduced himself, "Captain Gabriel Lahoud, at your service, madame," he said gallantly.

Captain Lahoud gave a cursory glance at her passport while Shula held her breath. Extending the document, he bowed graciously. "Welcome back to Beirut, madame."

Once she had freed herself from her children's insistent embraces, Shula felt as if she had never left Beirut. The news of her homecoming spread quickly through the Wadi. Abu-Jacques was the first to welcome her, and Albert Iliya stopped by the following day. That evening Abu-Sa'id called, saying, "I missed my translator very much."

Within a week Shula managed to revitalize the entire espionage network. She phoned Nabil Mussa, who reported to her house, proudly displaying the accounts from the Star. He told her that a wealthy Egyptian patron had approached him with an offer of partnership in a similar nightclub in Cairo. She resumed her appearances at the Olympia Casino, promenading through the halls on Abu-Sa'id's arm.

Shula's faith in Awad was restored as a result of his coup in finding Milad El Korah, and she approved their passport deal, giving Awad a generous bonus that was more than enough to satisfy even his lofty demands.

El Korah became a frequent guest in her home. Joseph was grateful to him for bringing Shula back, and he enjoyed Shula's full confidence as well. She allowed him to work with Awad and even suggested that he make a trip to Israel.

Her life seemed as clear and as untroubled as the Beirut sky, and when she recalled the inexplicable fears that had haunted her after her last visit to Israel, she found the lapse unforgivable. Her behavior in Istanbul and her escape to Rome had been capricious, unworthy of an experienced professional!

Life continued its peaceful course until Wednesday, August 9, 1961. Wednesday was laundry day at the Kishak-Cohen house, and as usual the children had been sent out of the house. They spent the morning on the beach, and Arlette had been entrusted with money to buy a light lunch for everyone, with enough left over for a trip to the matinee at the local cinema. Joseph had gone off to work; with Shula busy with the wash he would have to be satisfied with a cup of coffee, a roll, and a hard-boiled egg at the shop.

Shula helped the Arab laundress carry the bundles of clothes to the roof and light the small gas stove to heat the water. While the laundress scrubbed one pile, Shula rinsed the other in clear water and hung it out to dry.

By the end of the day she could barely move, and when Milad El Korah appeared at the door, she could scarcely hide her displeasure. He sensed her mood and left after a few minutes.

Late that night, after she had fed her family and they had read Bertie and Meir's letters aloud, she assembled the laundry that had dried since the afternoon and prepared to iron the clothes. Joseph and the younger children had already gone off to bed, and Isaac and Arlette were lying on the couch watching the last television program. Shula had to muster all her authority to get them off to sleep after the show ended.

She brewed herself a cup of mint tea and sat down to rest. A sudden ring at the door woke her from her drowsiness. Isaac quickly appeared in his pajamas and rushed to the door barefooted, saying, "I'll get it." She glanced at her watch: it was twelve thirty.

He unlatched the lock, and all of a sudden the door was thrown open. The room filled with men in uniform. Shula recognized Captain Gabriel Lahoud among them, and Milad El Korah was standing beside him, his arms locked in handcuffs. A man in civilian clothes, a neighbor from the Wadi, followed them cautiously into the house.

Isaac recoiled in fear and Shula sank down on the couch.

"What happened?" she said softly.

"They caught me! I didn't say anything," groaned El Korah. He began to struggle with the policemen.

"Quiet!" shouted Captain Lahoud. "No talking!" He turned to Shula. "Where's the radio transmitter? The invisible ink? The letters?"

He called to his men, "Search everywhere! Turn the house upside down if you have to!"

Isaac glanced at the coffee table and noticed his brothers' letters lying there. He eased his way backward and slipped them stealthily into his pajama pocket. Moving toward his mother, he whispered, "I'll go make sure the children aren't frightened."

Captain Lahoud didn't even notice him. A moment later Shula heard the sound of water running in the bathroom. Carmela and Dudik were now wide awake. Dudik burst out crying, and Carmela stuck her head through the doorway and called out in a timid voice, "Mommy!"

One of the policemen shouted at them, "Get back into your room and don't cry!"

Joseph appeared in the hallway, also barefoot and in pajamas. He shakily put on his glasses.

"What's going on?" he asked in a sleepy, bewildered voice.

Lahoud spun around. "Are you Joseph Kishak-Cohen? I have a warrant to search your home. Where's the bedroom?" He ordered two of his men to follow Joseph. Pointing to Milad El Korah, he yelled to two others, "Take him down to the station!"

Shula sat frozen on the couch, completely numb. Only the sight of a weeping Arlette coming into the room with a policeman on her heels shook her from her apathy.

"Quiet!" she screamed at her daughter. "If you don't stop crying I'll slap you!"

Arlette slumped down next to her mother in stunned silence, watching the policemen tear the living room apart.

The search lasted two hours, and when the policemen finished, the contents of the living room closets and shelves were strewn all over the floor. Shula shuddered to think what they must have done to the other rooms.

One police officer collected all the bottles in the medicine cabinet and on Shula's dressing table, shoving everything into a sack. The clatter of broken dishes rang out from the kitchen. Carmela and Dudik curled up next to Shula and whimpered. Isaac stood aside, silently clenching and unclenching his fists.

At last the turmoil ended. Joseph was brought in to sign the search report, and the officers forced him to approve a list enumerating all the items they had confiscated. The frightened representative from the Wadi was also told to sign as a witness.

Captain Lahoud turned to Shula. "Get dressed," he ordered. "You're coming with us. And take some money."

"Why?" she taunted recklessly. "Are you so sure I won't be returning?"

He didn't bother to answer.

Shula's mind was a blank, and she dressed mechanically. Only one thought kept repeating itself over and over again, like a broken record: "They didn't find anything! They have no proof!"

She removed a handful of bills from Joseph's wallet and stuck them into her purse without counting them. Throwing on her coat, she walked slowly toward Joseph. She kissed him on the cheek, but he was too shocked to feel a thing.

She clutched each child to her bosom and whispered to Arlette and Isaac, "Take good care of daddy. Be good children," she told the little ones.

Then she left the house.

Despite the early hour a small crowd had gathered in front of the building. Nazira was among them. As soon as Shula appeared, the old woman ran over to embrace her.

"God bless you and keep you!" she called out as the policemen pushed her back.

They shoved Shula into a small car that had been stationed a short way down the street. Behind it a police van was parked. Shula peered into the van. Milad El Korah was sprawled along the back seat with a sarcastic, triumphant sneer over his face. His hands had been freed of the cuffs.

Day of Judgment

20 Stunned by the suddenness of her arrest, Shula didn't notice where the police were taking her. The car stopped after a short ride and she was ordered to get out. She found herself in a paved courtyard in front of a two-story building and guessed, from the armed sentry who snapped to attention at their arrival and the whitewashed curbstone alongside the path, that this was an army base. A few days later her suspicion was confirmed: she was being held prisoner at the army intelligence camp in southern Beirut.

A clerk in uniform recorded her name when they entered the building, and another soldier led her to her cell. She was asked if she wanted anything, and she replied that she was thirsty. Ever since Captain Lahoud and his men had burst into her apartment, she had been struggling with a parched throat.

The soldier locked the cell and returned a few minutes later with a large tin cup full of steaming tea. The door slammed behind him.

Shula felt a sharp pain pierce through her abdomen, and then another. She rose to stretch out on the iron bed in the corner. As she reached out to smooth the coarse army blanket covering the cot, she caught a glimpse of her shoes. With horror, Shula realized they were covered with blood. The terrifying arrest had precipitated an unusually heavy menstruation. She fell on the bed and burst into tears.

She cried more out of disgust for the blood than out of desperation, for the severity of her situation had not yet hit her. With her usual optimism she was convinced that her influential friends would come to her aid as always, and that her release would be arranged discreetly and efficiently.

By the time the investigator arrived the following morning at seven, Shula was her old confident self again. His appearance encouraged her belief that she wouldn't be held for long. She had met the investigator, Joseph Freiha, on several occasions at the Olympia Casino, and she was sure that as soon as the news of her arrest reached her friends there, Abu-Sa'id would quickly intervene in her behalf.

Freiha began to record her testimony, asking the routine questions: name, father's name, address, marital status. He had barely finished the preliminaries when she complained of nausea. She explained her condition to him, clearly embarrassed. Freiha stopped the interrogation immediately and inquired politely whether she would be in need of a doctor. Shula mentioned a few medications, saying they would be sufficient. He asked her to spell the names for him and promised to send for the supplies as soon as the pharmacies opened.

Later that morning, after the medicine was brought in, Freiha informed her that he had decided to postpone his investigation for a day or two, in view of her condition. He ordered the guard to allow her to wash and promised she would be left undisturbed.

Shula considered this a good omen. It could only mean that Abu-Sa'id's influence was already at work.

In reality the decision to postpone the investigation was made not in deference to Shula's feelings, but because Freiha and his assistants were too busy examining the other members of Shula's espionage network. Milad El Korah had provided the police with the names and addresses of most of Shula's accomplices, and that same night the police had arrested Albert Iliya, Muhammed Awad, Fathi, and Mahmud Mussa. Only Nabil Mussa managed to escape arrest. He had returned to the family farm in El-Hiam for a visit, and his lover, Marilyn, phoned him there to warn him of the police raid on the nightclub and the arrest of his brother and cousin. Nabil crossed the border to Metulla at once and reported the arrest. A few days later, however, confident about the protective influence of his powerful family, he returned to Lebanon. The police apprehended him as well.

The suspects broke down immediately. Muhammed Awad sang for more than thirty-six consecutive hours, and the astonishing record of his testimony filled 319 typewritten pages.

Locked in her prison cell, Shula was unaware of these developments. She spent three relatively relaxing days undisturbed in solitary confinement. The medication worked, and the bleeding was under control. The guards were extremely polite to her, and she felt her optimism returning, along with her strength. The only thing that disturbed her was the fact that none of her family or friends had managed to contact her.

Although Joseph hadn't been arrested, he had been brought to police headquarters in the Saraya and interrogated for several hours. The authorities wanted to know the reasons for Shula's prolonged stay in Rome and Joseph kept insisting his wife had gone to Italy for medical reasons. However, the police had confiscated the letters they had exchanged during her two-and-a-half-month absence, and these strongly refuted his claim. Joseph seemed to change his mind. Sacrificing his pride, he claimed that his wife had left him after an argument and he had tried desperately to bring her back. He stuck to his story and eventually the investigators were forced to release him. Only afterward, when the extent of his financial assistance to his wife's work became known, was Joseph Kishak-Cohen charged as an accomplice to Shula's crimes.

Isaac was also questioned by the police. The boy denied any connection with his mother's activities, even when the police played the tape of a telephone conversation he had had with his mother from the Mussa family farm in El-Hiam. Isaac heard himself relate happily that he had caught a glimpse of Israel from afar. The tape played on and he spoke of "seventeen bolts of cloth that had been delivered to their destination." Isaac adamantly defended his claim that they honestly were discussing rolls of cloth. The investigators taunted him, saying that the entire population of El-Hiam couldn't use up seventeen bolts in a year. The boy refused to budge, and the police finally released him because of his age, even though they didn't believe his story. They had much more important suspects to deal with anyway.

On Saturday, August 12, Shula was interrogated for the first time. The investigation was conducted by two young lieutenants, but two senior officers in civilian clothes, Joseph Freiha and Joseph Barody, were sometimes present as well. Their very first questions told Shula that she was in far more trouble than she had dreamed.

The lieutenants took turns interrogating Shula and recording her answers. They would flip through the thick file that was placed before them and then aim their questions at her. Each question indicated an intimate knowledge of the inner workings of Shula's spy network. And only one person was capable of supplying such an abundance of information: Muhammed Awad.

The investigators made no bones about the fact that Awad had talked at great length. "This entire package, almost four hundred pages, is Awad's testimony," Freiha informed her, gesturing toward the file. "It's the result of two days' and three nights' work. So there's no point in your playing innocent. We know everything."

"Awad is an incurable liar! All of Beirut knows that!" Shula shouted, enraged. "He never did a full day's work in his entire life, let alone two days and three nights!"

The officers were amused, but they didn't give up. Their investigation continued, even more intensely.

From the very beginning Shula followed a simple rule: to admit to the least of her crimes, and also the easiest to prove—the smuggling of Jews. She emphatically denied the more serious charges of treason, espionage, contact with an enemy state, and smuggling gold.

"Awad told you all that and Awad is a liar," she repeated obstinately. But she had little hope of persuading them.

At the end of the day Shula was ordered to pack her few things. Accompanied by four armed guards, she was driven to the Saniya women's prison in the southwestern section of Beirut. There she was placed in a solitary cell in the bloc for suspects awaiting trial.

For the first few months in solitary confinement she had very little contact with prison life. Every morning she was taken for questioning, either at the Saraya or at the army intelligence base, and she wasn't brought back until evening.

Although she had to admit the fact that her position wasn't good if she was being held in prison, she consoled herself with the thought that every evil has its compensation, and at least the prison allowed her to have visitors.

Isaac was the first to come, on Monday, August 14. Ever since his mother's arrest, the sixteen-year-old boy had been saddled with all the responsibilities of the household. Joseph had not recovered from the shock of Shula's arrest, and for many months afterward he wandered around helplessly, not caring about anything. He fell into his own private world of silence, neglecting his business and avoiding all human contact.

Not wanting his mother to know how difficult life had been in the five days since her arrest, Isaac put on a courageous air in the presence of the prison officer who was supervising their visit. He reported that both he and his father had been interrogated by the police and subsequently released, and that everyone was well. Their only concern was that she be freed.

Shula, too, put on a brave front. They needn't worry about her, she assured the boy; she was being treated well and had everything she needed except cigarettes. Isaac had anticipated that, he explained with a smile, and produced a box of her favorite brand. The guard inspected the carton of Viceroys and Isaac passed it to Shula. Shula began to discuss Isaac's studies, and the boy realized at once that his mother was trying to tell him something without alerting the guard.

"Your private tutor," she said, "the one who helped you prepare for your examinations . . ."

"Yes," he nodded, understanding. "What about him?"

"He has a lot of important material. It'll be worth your while to get hold of it."

"I'll do my best," he assured her.

For a boy his age Isaac displayed a great deal of resourcefulness. He began to investigate the trial procedure, and when he learned that his mother was to be judged by a military tribunal, he made friends with one of the clerks in the archives and bribed his new friend to give him a copy of the prosecution testimony, paying "per page" at the same rate fixed for all the lawyers. But even though Isaac managed to get a copy of Muhammed Awad's testimony before it was brought before the court, his work didn't help his mother's case very much. Awad's testimony only showed Shula's lawyer how tough the case would be.

The day of Isaac's first visit to the jail the newspapers broke the story of the Israeli espionage ring captured in Beirut. The Lebanese, Jordanian, and Syrian papers had a feast with the event, competing among themselves for the most provocative headlines about Israeli connections in the "highest circles of Beirut society." They reported breathlessly the Israeli attempt to dominate Lebanese politics by establishing a daily newspaper in Beirut, and they emphasized the "two thousand confidential documents" Shula had supposedly passed on to Israel and the "twenty million Lebanese pounds" she had paid out in bribes. Muhammed Awad was accused of having "Jewish blood," and the business proposition to open a nightclub in Cairo similar to the Star was interpreted by the press as "an attempt to spread the ring all the way to Egypt." Jordan's daily A-Dif'a tried to drag the as-Sulh family into the ring and hinted that a "certain Arab embassy" was also involved in pro-Israel espionage activities, while another newspaper revealed that Awad was a relative by marriage to Lebanese Prime Minister Saeb Salam. If the press were to be believed, there was hardly a name among the leading families of Lebanon that was not connected to the spy network.

The investigators and lawyers alike swore that the Lebanese security services were not interested in blowing the affair out of proportion. Yet somehow the most intimate details of the investigation made their way into the newspapers, as if the press had been given copies of that day's testimony. Someone with access to such highly confidential information was obviously divulging the news, and Joseph Barody was heard to remark to the other investigators that Syrian intelligence agents were probably responsible for the leaks.

"It would serve their interests nicely to embarrass the Lebanese government," he said bitterly. "Syria would love to present us to the public as people who would sell themselves to the highest bidder."

The people who suffered the most from the exaggerated coverage given to the "Israeli spy from Wadi Abu-Jamil" were, of course, the members of Shula's family. It was as if a wall had suddenly been built around them, and they were ostracized even from the Jewish community. Isaac's girl friend tearfully ended their relationship when her parents forbade her to see him again, and even Carmela's and Dudik's friends abandoned them.

At the Suk Sursuk accusing fingers pointed to the Kishak-Cohen brothers' shop, labeling it "the store of the *gasusa,* the spy." There were so few customers that Joseph no longer had reason to keep the shop open in the afternoon, but he didn't really mind. His heart was no longer in the business. He would stumble home at noon, defeated, and nibble at the meal Arlette had prepared, murmuring, "Poor child, who will marry you now?" Then he would lock himself in his room for the rest of the day.

Shula was kept unaware of the boycott her family suffered on her account. Every day she was taken for questioning, and each time the pattern was the same. The more she stood her ground and refused to confess, the more difficult and unpleasant the questioning became. The investigators would shout accusations at her, not even taking time to record her answers. They repeated the same questions over and over again, and her weary replies never changed. Shula understood their strategy and knew they were hoping to exhaust and weaken her. After each nasty session she thought they might just succeed the next time.

Shula steadfastly held her ground nonetheless, obstinately admitting to nothing, save for the smuggling of unfortunate Jewish refugees out of the overburdened Wadi Abu-Jamil.

When their first strategy brought no results, the investigators tried a new ploy. Joseph Freiha would play the "bad guy," insulting and abusing Shula almost to the point of tears. Then Joseph Barody, the "good investigator," would step in to protect her from Freiha, begging her to cooperate "before it's too late."

But this also failed, so they began to bring in the newspapers and read the exaggerated reports aloud. On September 13, Jordan's *A-Dif'a* wrote, "Once her husband discovered her adultery, she was forced to flee." The following day the investigators showed her a full front-page spread with the glaring headline: "Shula Cohen collapses in questioning, incriminates accomplices."

"It's going to get even worse," Barody warned her. "The only way you can keep them from printing such lies is to confess, and then we can publish an official statement."

Shula was adamant. "I've already told you the truth. I helped Jewish refugees on their way to Israel. All the rest is a lie, a lie."

Barody and Freiha next decided to set up a confrontation between Shula and Awad. Even though Shula had every reason to hate the old man, when they brought him in, she almost felt sorry for him. Awad's skin had turned a sickly gray and he looked exhausted and ill. His week-old beard was totally white. The investigators motioned to him and he launched into a description of how Shula had arranged for him to go to Istanbul to see an Israeli agent named Joseph Epstein, who sent him to Tel Aviv. He told how he had helped her enlist the services of Colonel Talal Abudi in the Israeli plot. As he spilled the story, betraying her with every word, Shula felt her pity for Awad quickly dissolve. She turned to him angrily and shouted, "You filthy liar." She was so enraged by Awad's part in the destruction of her network that she didn't give a thought to her own false accusation.

After six weeks of intensive probing Shula had nearly reached the breaking point. More than anything, the fact that none of her influential friends had come to her aid weakened her spirit. The first time Joseph visited her cell, she demanded, "Why don't I have a lawyer?" She listened impatiently as her husband explained that she would not be allowed to see an attorney until the investigation ended and the trial began.

"What does Abu-Sa'id have to say about that?" she asked.

Joseph shifted uncomfortably and bit his lip. Isaac, who had accompanied his father, cleared his throat. "Abu Sa'id's too busy," he said hoarsely. "I tried getting in touch with him a number of times and I keep getting the same answer."

One evening, soon after she was returned to her cell in the Saniya prison, a visitor was admitted. He was a handsome, silver-haired man of about fifty, and his elegant suit and suave appearance made Shula even more conscious of her own wretchedness. She had the impression they had met somewhere before, but she wasn't sure, and he didn't identify himself.

He waited for the guard to leave them alone. Shula knew that was a violation of prison rules, and her mouth fell as the guard quietly walked off. Only then did the stranger speak. "I'm a lawyer. I know who you are and what you've done—and with whom. I'm coming to you in their name."

Shula had had a particularly trying session that day with the investigators, and she was numb with fatigue. All she wanted was to be alone and to stretch out on the bed. She gazed at the stranger without responding.

"I understand," he said. "You probably think I'm from the police and that this is a new ploy to make you talk." He smiled. "I assure you that isn't the case. I'll do all the talking and you just sit there and listen. That way you can be sure you don't incriminate yourself in any way."

She asked for a cigarette and he brought out a Viceroy.

"That's your favorite brand, isn't it?" he asked. "I left a carton for you with the guard. But let's get to the point. It cost me a fortune to see you and we shouldn't waste time." He lit her cigarette with a gold lighter, and then his own. Inhaling the smoke deeply, he began, "The man who turned you in was El Korah." Shula looked up. "Did you know that?" He went on, "Of course, Awad talked a great deal. In fact, he told the police absolutely everything he knew. Were you aware of that, too? The three Mussa boys are also talking, but they have their family to protect them."

The lawyer eyed her levelly. "As for your case, well, there are several avenues open to you. If you were to mention the names of some of the people you were involved with, it would only constitute a partial confession and it wouldn't help you in the least. If, on the other hand, you were to reveal all your former contacts, the police would never believe you. They'd say, 'She's mad. She has delusions of grandeur.'" He paused. "The best thing for you to do is to maintain the story that you only helped Jews emigrate to Israel. And the people whose names you won't be mentioning will remain very grateful to you—"

"So as a sign of their gratitude they'll do their best to forget me as soon as they can?" Shula cut in sarcastically.

"Or perhaps they'll try to help you," he suggested. "When the time comes. By exposing them now you won't make matters any better for yourself."

After he left, Shula considered what the lawyer had said. She also thought about the things he hadn't said. He didn't mention, for example, who was behind his visit, and she never managed to learn who sent in the silver-haired lawyer. She understood one thing, however. Whoever it was who called in the lawyer wouldn't be intervening in her behalf, at least not for now. Perhaps the smooth-talking attorney had been right when he said that mentioning names wouldn't improve her situation in the least. It would probably make things even worse for her. If she kept her secrets to herself, perhaps one of her old contacts could be useful when she was finally brought to trial.

Shula considered the possibility of confessing to some of the more serious charges, such as enlisting Talal Abudi's help for the Israeli cause. She knew that Abudi was no longer in Lebanon, so he could not have been the one who sent the mysterious stranger to see her. She wondered if an admission of Abudi's role would speed up the proceedings, making it easier for the anonymous benefactor to step forward and help her.

Then she remembered the lawyer's warning that the authorities wouldn't be satisfied with a partial admission of guilt, and she quickly dropped the idea of confessing. Her pride and strength of character were at stake, she told herself resolutely. She would not admit to anything more than smuggling Jewish refugees into Israel.

But after another month of brutal questioning Shula had to wonder how much longer she could hold up. The investigating techniques had become more violent in the past few weeks. The young and inexperienced lieutenants who had first been assigned to the case had been replaced by older, more hardened investigators. They grilled Shula mercilessly for twelve hours a day, day after day. It wasn't hard to guess that they had received orders from above to expedite the investigation and obtain a confession, but that wasn't the only reason for their zeal. Quite simply, Shula's obstinacy frustrated them, and they were determined to get at the truth by breaking her spirit.

"Why are you being so stubborn?" the new investigator finally yelled in desperation. "After all, the others have already said it all. We have more than five hundred pages of testimony against you!"

"None of it's worth the paper it's written on!" Shula spit out disdainfully. "It's a pile of goat dung!" He slapped her across the face.

Shula's mouth fell open. This was the first time in her life anyone had laid a hand on her.

She touched her swollen cheek in amazement. Looking the officer straight in the eye, she cried out defiantly, "Pig!"

He slapped her again, even harder this time. She fell to the ground with the impact of the blow.

"If you don't show some respect," he shouted, looming above her, "it'll get even worse! And this is nothing compared to what we'll do to you if you don't start talking. You have long, lovely nails, and it would be very easy to rip them out with pliers."

As if on cue, Joseph Barody entered. The scene was simply too well timed, and Shula was positive the entire incident had been carefully staged. Barody helped Shula off the floor, brushed the dust off her skirt, and sent the other investigator out of the room.

"Forgive him," he said quietly. "He's been working on criminal investigations, and he's not used to having his questions answered like that."

"Then why does he ask such questions?" Shula demanded, rubbing her cheek. "Stupid questions invite insolent answers."

Barody grew serious. "Madame Cohen, perhaps you don't realize the severity of your situation. Even without your confession we have enough proof to put you away for at least two hundred years. Why don't you cooperate with us? It can only help you."

"So then I'll only get one hundred years?"

He sighed. "I don't even know why we're bothering with you. The Syrians are dying to get their hands on you. They won't put up with any of your games!"

With that Barody touched Shula's sensitive point. She knew all about the "methods" of investigation in the El-Maza prison in Damascus, and the thought of being sent there brought chills to her spine. But she refused to consider that possibility and stubbornly said no more.

By the time the frustrated investigators gave up, three months later, there was barely an inch of Shula's body that hadn't been injured and bruised. Her jaw had been dislocated, and four of her teeth had been knocked out from the vicious beatings. Yet the police got nothing more at the end of the probe than they had at the start. Shula had confessed to only one activity, the work she had originally planned to admit: the smuggling of Jewish refugees into Israel.

It was a rather miserable consolation, in view of her sorry physical state, but it filled her with pride nonetheless.

With the close of the investigation, Shula was taken from solitary confinement and thrown into a ward for prisoners awaiting trial. She had prayed for the change, but when it came she found it insufferable. In her single cell, after the torturous questioning, she had at least had the luxury of privacy. Now she was surrounded by thirty-one other women for twenty-four hours a day, and what kind of women! Hashish smugglers, pickpockets, unmarried mothers who'd murdered their newborn infants to escape their families' wrath, women who'd poisoned their husbands or domineering mothers-in-law, and the lowest level of streetwalkers from the harbor district. Shula found them all, regardless of their religious and ethnic back-grounds—Christian, Moslem, or Druze—frightfully ignorant, filled with superstitions, coarse, vulgar, loud, and primitive. Worst of all for Shula, the other prisoners were very easily excitable, and the "Israeli spy" became a natural target for their venom.

The evil woman in charge of the bloc was Fauzia Harshite. At thirty-five Fauzia might easily have been considered attractive if it were not for the cold, cruel look that scarred her features. She ruled the bloc with an iron hand. As chief guard, she had total control over the prisoners. She instigated arguments among them and turned one woman against the next. Fauzia maintained a solid corps of in-formers who received small favors in return for prison news, and she soon tried to recruit Shula to her inner circle of obedient servants, but Shula managed to escape her clutches. When Fauzia tried to take revenge by curtailing Shula's visits, she complained to Joseph Barody. The investigator reprimanded the guard, warning her to leave the Jewish prisoner alone.

But without Barody around all the time to intervene, Fauzia could do what she pleased. Now she was angry with Shula not only for refusing to join her gang of admirers, but also for crying to the authorities. Shula found herself assigned to latrine duty twice or three times a week, and on more than one occasion her family's visits were canceled at the last moment. Yet she was afraid to complain, since a word from Fauzia was enough to incite the wrath of the other prisoners against "the Jewish spy who sold out our country."

So Shula remained silent about the evil prison guard. When she was allowed to see her family she pretended that all was well so they wouldn't worry. Besides, she told herself bitterly, what good would it do to complain? What could Joseph do to help her anyway?

Once Shula was assigned to the ward and the preliminary inves-tigation ended, Joseph was finally free to hire a lawyer. He consid-ered the matter carefully and consulted with Albert Iliya before making his choice. Iliya had been released a week after his arrest, but he still wasn't sure whether he would be tried for his part in the smuggling operation, an offense to which he had promptly confessed.

Iliya recommended Nasri Ma'alouf, one of the most renowned— and expensive—Christian attorneys in Beirut, but when Joseph approached him, Ma'alouf wasn't overjoyed at the prospect of taking on Shula's case. His fame and steep fees were a tribute to the high degree of success he enjoyed in the courtroom, and he didn't want to endanger his favorable record by taking on Shula's doubtful cause. He asked Joseph to give him three months in which to investigate the case privately, to determine whether there was any point in establishing a defense.

After the three-month period Nasri Ma'alouf agreed to take Shula's case. Joseph saw this as a favorable sign; it could only mean that Ma'alouf believed that there was a chance. The lawyer stipulated one condition, however. The judge for the trial still had not been assigned, and there was always the possibility that a Moslem might be selected as chief magistrate. Therefore, he demanded that he be joined in the defense by a Moslem attorney, suggesting a costly and famous one, at that: Farid Abu-Zayit, his Moslem counterpart in the top legal circles of Beirut. Joseph agreed, even though he knew that the combined fees of the two attorneys would rapidly consume all the Kishak-Cohen savings.

Time passed at a maddeningly slow pace for Shula. Autumn petered out and winter rolled in. Tortured by Fauzia and her band of vicious puppets, Shula could barely withstand the long hours in her cell. The only ray of light left in her life was visiting time, and she found it increasingly difficult to pretend with her loved ones.

Shula's desperation did not escape her family's watchful eyes, and whenever they returned from their visits, they would spend the night in an emotional family consultation.

"She's so thin and pale," Arlette complained after an especially difficult visit.

"Why don't they at least let us give her some food?" Isaac cried. "She hasn't even been brought to trial."

He went to see Dr. Attia, but the old man only raised his arms helplessly and shook his head. "What can we do?"

Still, Isaac would not give up, and he continued his unsuccessful attempts to contact Abu-Sa'id.

Only one of Shula's powerful friends stayed with her in her desperate hour. One rainy evening the family heard a knock on the door. They opened it curiously; no one had ventured to visit the home of the "notorious spy" for weeks. They didn't recognize the tall man standing in the doorway. He introduced himself simply. "I'm called Abu-Mustafa. I've come to ask about Um-Ibrahim."

They had heard of the Tiger and were frightened by his reputation, but invited him to come in all the same. Arlette prepared a cup of tea.

The look on their faces told him everything. "It's not going well, is it?" he asked quietly.

Arlette was the first to speak her mind, perhaps because she knew the least about the stranger.

Abu-Mustafa listened attentively and then turned to Joseph. "As a Jew, she has the right to demand kosher food. Have you consulted a lawyer?"

Joseph hesitated, but Isaac answered bitterly, "The lawyer still hasn't decided whether he'll take the case or not."

"She's still entitled to receive food from the outside," Abu-Mustafa insisted. "Who's preventing it?"

"It's that horrible guard Fauzia! She's making our mother's life miserable!" Isaac cried.

"Fauzia? Not Fauzia Harshite?"

"Do you know her?" Isaac asked.

Abu-Mustafa nodded. "I do. Her husband is Syrian, a good-for-nothing drunk. He owns a garage on the Beirut–Damascus highway. And there's a way of getting to her." He looked at Arlette, embarrassed. "Mademoiselle, would you please excuse us? What I am about to say is not fit for a young lady's ears."

Arlette reluctantly went into the kitchen and Abu-Mustafa turned to Isaac. "Fauzia Harshite has a lover, a questionable character they call Bonaparte. She would do anything for him. I think I can find a way to put pressure on him."

Shula's redemption came in part from Abu-Mustafa's threats, and in part from the monthly fee that Joseph offered Fauzia's lover if he would only convince the sadistic guard to change her behavior toward her prisoner.

By their next visit the improvement was noticeable. Fauzia led Shula into the visitors' room personally. Smiling, she asked softly, "Why didn't you say you were Jewish? You have the right to have kosher food brought in. Tell your husband to arrange it."

Shula was so surprised that she couldn't find a suitable reply to Fauzia's remark. She stared as the guard strolled back toward the door.

Prison life quickly began to change for the better after that. Fauzia didn't pretend to like Shula, but at least she concealed her hostility toward her. The other prisoners, ever sensitive to Fauzia's moods, automatically stopped abusing their Jewish cellmate. The abundant food packages that started to come in for Shula each week transformed her almost overnight into one of the "rich" prisoners, giving her the means to purchase services and favors, as well as the goodwill of her fellow inmates.

As soon as Nasri Ma'alouf agreed to defend Shula in court, Isaac brought him a copy of Muhammed Awad's testimony. The lawyer read the hefty document with astonishment.

"Allah preserve him," he cried, "this man's a fool! He has put a noose around his own neck!"

Awad's testimony was unusual indeed. Isaac managed to conceal a copy of the police report among the few things he took with him when he emigrated to Israel several years later. Even from a distance of time and space, the testimony he reread from time to time was an amazing collection, the ramblings of a spy who served many masters, plotting intrigues and counterintrigues with masterful acrobatic skills until finally, through his lies, he became a victim of his own deception.

Ma'alouf scratched his head and reread the testimony from the start, as recorded by Lieutenant Yousouf Nasser of the investigations department of the security services: "I, Muhammed Sa'adallah Awad, manager of the contracts division of the Ministry of the Treasury and a native of Beirut, do hereby swear that I have never been tried for any criminal offense, and that everything I shall say here, of my own free will, shall be the truth.

"I know the Kishak-Cohen family. I was told about them by Darwish Baidon. Shulamit Kishak-Cohen is acquainted with many important people in Beirut, among them: Emir Farid Shihab, the former head of the Lebanese security services and the current Lebanese ambassador to Tunisia; Mahmud Hoj from the Ministry of the Interior; Darwish Baidon; Abu Sa'id; and Riad and Sami as-Sulh. She would meet such contacts at the Pigeon's Cave restaurant near the Raucha Rock.

"After I learned that Shulamit Kishak-Cohen was working for Israel, I went to Damascus, where I spoke with Hisham Midani, the head of the Syrian security services. I informed him what I had learned. I preferred him to the Lebanese security services because I knew that Shulamit Kishak-Cohen had connections within the Lebanese security, and I was afraid that she would be told about my statement from her contacts there.

"Midani informed me that he had a file on a Shula Kishak-Cohen. I offered to infiltrate her espionage ring, and it was agreed that I would receive a monthly salary from his offices, as well as special payments for whatever information I would supply.

"At that point I received instructions from Mrs. Kishak-Cohen to go to Israel."

Awad proceeded to tell how he was ordered to go to Istanbul, where Epstein instructed him to set up a meeting between Major Abudi and some Israeli agents and pulled out several photographs which had been taken of Awad during his visit to Israel.

Awad returned to Israel in connection with the Abudi affair, and on that occasion he was taught the use of invisible ink.

Upon his return to Beirut he opened a post office box, number 3486, in which he received monthly notices from a Swiss bank that his salary from Israel had been deposited in his account.

When Abudi returned from London, he spoke with Awad and agreed to meet with some Israeli agents in Rome.

Awad mentioned Abudi's beautiful mistress in Rome, because of whom the major had cancelled his first appointment with the Israelis. When Abudi finally saw the Israelis, he extracted a promise from them of a payment of fifty thousand dollars in three installments, in exchange for his services.

Awad returned from Rome and approached one Alfred Shawab, a former sergeant in the Lebanese army's signals corps, to serve as radio operator for the transmitter he had been promised by the Israelis. Shawab suggested they also contact the Egyptian espionage service.

"Shawab provided me with the telephone number of the Egyptian military attaché in Beirut, Captain Hasan Ali Halil," Awad wrote. "I contacted him and we set a date to meet. Our appointment took place at Hasan's residence on rue Clemenceau. An Egyptian major by the name of Muhammed was also present. From Halil's residence we went to the Realini restaurant, where I proceeded to repeat everything I knew about the Abudi affair, Rome, Epstein in Istanbul, and Shula Cohen. I mentioned the excellent relationship she maintained with Sami as-Sulh.

"We agreed that the Egyptians would pay me a monthly salary of one thousand pounds and would provide a written confirmation stating that I had joined Shula Cohen's spy network on their orders, for my protection should I ever be captured."

Awad explained that he was in need of a large sum of money because his ambition was to become Lufthansa's agent in Beirut, and he believed he might have to prove to the German airlines that he had sufficient capital to open an office in Beirut.

A little while later he went to Germany to negotiate with Lufthansa, and on his return home he stopped in Rome, where he received four hundred dollars from the Israelis.

The Lufthansa deal fell through in the end, but Awad recovered financially by selling Shula Cohen blank Egyptian passports that he obtained from Hasan Halil. The Egyptian military attaché also supplied him with blank Lebanese passports, issued by the Lebanese embassy in Cairo.

Eventually both the Israelis and the Egyptians stopped paying his monthly salary, leaving Awad in difficult financial straits.

"I met a Palestinian by the name of Hamis Bamiya, who knew of my connections with Hasan Halil. He proposed that I work for the Jordanians and introduced me to the Jordanian military attaché in Beirut, Colonel Radi Abdallah. I told Radi everything I knew about my other sources. When I went to Radi's house for the second time, I was introduced to Gazi Arbiyat, the head of Israel's department of Jordanian intelligence. He invited me to Amman to meet King Hussein."

Awad arrived at the Philadelphia Hotel in Amman and was told to wait there, but as it turned out, a series of border incidents with the Israelis took up all of the king's time, and he had no time to speak with the spy from Beirut. Awad returned to Lebanon, having accomplished nothing in Amman.

Several weeks later he managed to be invited to Amman for a second time, and this time he met the Jordanian chief-of-staff, Ali Abu-Nawar, at the bar of the Philadelphia Hotel.

"Whiskey was brought to the table, and Gazi indicated that I shouldn't drink too much. I assured him that I knew how to hold my liquor. Later Abu-Nawar produced copies of some letters he claimed were part of a secret correspondence between Israeli Prime Minister Ben Gurion and Gamal Abdel Nasser. When I expressed some skepticism, the chief-of-staff assured me they were genuine and told me to keep them as a souvenir.

"The following day I was received by King Hussein for a twenty-minute interview at his palace. He was quite charming. He revealed a great interest in the Lebanese intelligence services.

"On my return trip I made a stop in Damascus and told the Syrians everything that had occurred in Jordan.

"When I arrived in Beirut, I went to see Hasan Halil and gave him the latest news as well. I showed him the copies of the letters Abu-Nawar had given me, but he maintained that they weren't authentic. He took them from me, nevertheless, and sent them to Cairo."

The testimony continued in the same vein—319 pages of rendezvous, lies, deals, and back-stabbing.

But Nasri Ma'alouf's prediction did not come true. Awad's testimony did not put a noose around his neck, as Shula's attorney had hoped. The old man was never even brought to trial. One morning in July of 1962 he was found on the floor of his prison cell by one of the guards. Muhammed Awad had died of a heart attack.

Just as the trial was finally set to begin, Albert Iliya suffered a heart attack. The chief magistrate decided not to postpone Shula's case any further and instead ordered a separate trial for the lawyer. In the end, however, the secretary of the Wadi was never brought to court.

When the trial opened at last on November 5, 1962, only four defendants stood accused: Shula Cohen and the three members of the Mussa family, Nabil, Fathi, and Mahmud. Muhammed Awad had died, Mahmud Hoj had fled, and Albert Iliya had been hospitalized. Joseph's name also appeared on the indictment, but everyone assumed that to be a clerical error.

Orders came from some high authority that the trial was to be played down. In the scandal that had resulted from Shula's arrest, several names from the cream of Beirut society had been linked with the operation. By now the fuss of the investigation had already subsided, and the powerful people pulling the bureaucratic strings were not anxious to revive the negative publicity all over again. As a result, the press was severely restricted. While the trial was open to the public, entrance to the courtroom was by signed invitation only, and the chief magistrate made sure that no more than two or three press passes were issued each day. The month-long postponement on the very first day of the trial helped further to dampen the public's interest.

Shula viewed these events as favorable omens. The abuse of the head guard had come to an end with Joseph's generosity, and the year that followed had been one of comparative rest and tranquillity for her. Her nerves had calmed down and her health had returned to normal. With that her feeling of optimism was restored, so that when she was brought into the court and the chief magistrate nodded in her direction after she bowed before him, she was convinced that he not only remembered her, but that Abu-Sa'id or one of his men must have already established contact with him.

Consequently, Shula was quite arrogant as she sat facing the bench. When the prosecutor began his opening speech by saying, "Your Honor, the woman you see before you has been called the Mata Hari of the Middle East," Shula immediately sprang to her feet. Without waiting for the judge's permission to speak, she called out, "Your Honor, isn't it strange that the prosecuting attorney is comparing the qualities of one woman he has never even read about to another woman about whom he knows even less?"

The judge banged his gavel angrily and ordered her to be seated. A few moments later the prosecution again brought up Mata Hari, calling Shula yet another woman who spied against the very country that granted her refuge and citizenship. She jumped up a second time. "Your Honor," she shouted, "why doesn't the prosecution compare me with Madame Curie, merely because the police confiscated some medicine from my private bathroom?"

The magistrate reprimanded Shula harshly. Nasri Ma'alouf ran over to silence his client, whispering that her outrageous behavior would only hurt her case. But Shula wouldn't listen, and a short time later she was on her feet again.

The prosecution had just reeled off a long list of Shula's alleged crimes. "The prosecuting attorney may say anything he pleases," Shula hollered, "but he has no right to add years to my life. To have committed all the crimes I have just been charged with I would have to be at least forty years older than I really am."

Shula's self-confidence finally began to waver when the prosecution called its first witnesses. The names of those who were unable to appear personally were recited, and the prosecution started to read their damaging testimony. The first affidavit was that of Farid Shihab, Lebanon's ambassador to Tunisia and the former chief of Lebanese security services. Shihab stated that ten years previously he had received information that Shulamit Kishak-Cohen was a foreign agent.

"I ordered a secret investigation," he wrote, "but the amount of information uncovered was insufficient to formally charge Madame Cohen. Years later I met Muhammed Awad in the home of Sami as-Sulh. At the end of nineteen fifty-seven, Awad came forward to tell me that Shulamit Kishak-Cohen was an Israeli spy. He offered to keep her under his personal surveillance, and I agreed. I even paid him an advance on the salary he would receive. Since that time I have neither seen nor heard from Muhammed Awad."

More written testimony was presented before the court. Captain Hasan Halil, who had been interrogated at the Lebanese embassy in Cairo, stated that Muhammed Awad had also approached him to volunteer to follow the activities of Shulamit Kishak-Cohen, whom he called "an Israeli spy."

The third affidavit had been taken from Burhan Adham at the El-Maza jail in Damascus, where the former colonel had been imprisoned after the latest military coup.

But the most damaging statement of all was, of course, Muhammed Awad's masterpiece of skulduggery. It took more than three full-day sessions to hear the bulk of the heavy file. The judges listened attentively, not varying the serious expressions on their faces, and Shula sat hypnotized as the prosecutors described one scheme after another.

But nowhere in his unabashed and incriminating ramblings did he mention one of the key figures in the network: Nagi Aslan.

The trial progressed, and all the witnesses were heard and the reels of telephone conversations that had been taped from her home telephone were played, but Shula was surprised that another important name never surfaced. No one ever implicated George Anton in the conspiracy.

Could he still have so much power and influence, even today? Shula wondered. Or were his friends simply more loyal than hers? Oh, if only George could be here now!

As the trial drew to a close, Shula's nervousness grew. Yet when it was her turn to take the witness stand, she put her fears aside and stood proud and erect, looking directly at the chief magistrate.

She spoke with unshakable confidence. "Your Honor, the prosecution had many aides and assistants to collect the false charges that have been brought against me, while I, after months of enjoying the company of prison lice, have only the truth on my side, and the knowledge that I am innocent. I am guilty of one charge only, and I have never attempted to conceal my guilt. I have confessed to the smuggling of Jews. That is my only crime."

Three hours later the persistent prosecutors finally wound up their cross-examination. Nasri Ma'alouf sprang from his chair and kissed his client's hand. "Excellent testimony!" he congratulated Shula. The court announced a further postponement, and when Shula was led back to prison, still flushed with her victory, Isaac and Arlette were already waiting for their weekly visit.

"Everything's all right," Isaac whispered reassuringly. "Whoever had to be bribed was bribed."

Shula allowed herself to feel more and more hopeful.

Monday, March 19, 1963, was Shula's day of judgment.

It began like any other day as she opened her eyes in the predawn darkness that filtered through the small barred window. From the damp chill on her cheeks she could tell it was raining outside. And there was nothing quite so dismal and repugnant as Beirut on a wet winter morning when the stinging sea wind blew sheets of rain under umbrellas and down the brims of hats, whipping at faces with sharp, painful lashes.

Even so, at that moment she would have paid any price to be out, walking down the promenade of the Avenue de Français, without umbrella or rainhat, abandoning her face to the slashing rain, letting the whistling wind tug at her clothes as though trying to rip them off

and strip her naked; perhaps the wind would flush away the foul
prison stench that permeated her being.

She raised herself slightly on her elbow and looked across the dark
dormitory with its thirty-two beds arranged in two rows. The sounds
of sleep filled the room—a grinding, rhythmic snore, the choked
mutterings of a painful dream, the rattlings of a spring as an inmate
turned over in her bed. None of the others was yet awake.

The rustlings of sleep had a hypnotic effect and her eyelids grew
heavy. Telling herself that sleep was the best state for a prisoner, she
turned on her side and tugged the rough horse blanket around her.
Only as she felt herself dozing did her mind flash in protest: "Today
is the day!"

She was not excited. She felt only a tremendous sense of relief.
"The nightmare is coming to an end," she told herself. And she was
certain it would end well. After all, hadn't Arlette and Isaac whispered that all the obstacles had been removed, that everything had
been arranged? Those who had to be bribed had been bribed; the
sentence would be light. Her lawyer had assured her that she would
be given no more than a three-year term, perhaps less. But even if
she were given the maximum, she had already served nineteen
months; and if the "third" for good behavior was deducted, it was
altogether possible that the prosecutor would stand up and, with a
broad smile on his face, point with his finger to the door, the *main*
entrance this time, and she would pass through, a free woman on her
way home.

Shula tried to visualize the scene in her mind. She deliberated on
whether it would be proper for her to smile gratefully at the judges.
But she found it more pleasant to ponder that moment when she
would be walking through the wooden gate to the other side of the
courtroom, where she would fall into the loving arms of her children
and her husband. The thought of Joseph stirred warm feelings deep
within her. How faithful and patient he had been all these years.
How loyal. He deserved some special reward, some special gift. But
even while contemplating what the special gift would be, her mind's
eye was roaming the courtroom, searching hopefully for George.

The door at the far end of the corridor clanged open, cutting short
her imaginary voyage. Even before the familiar figure of Fauzia
Harshite appeared in the rectangle of light in the doorway, her

hoarse voice could be heard bellowing: "Up, you animals! Get moving!"

All at once the cellblock came to life with cursing and yawning of inmates attempting to hold onto the threads of rapidly vanishing dreams. Some already stood by their beds, their hair disheveled, the dresses they slept in wrinkled. Others still basked under the warmth of blankets, scratching their underarms, resigning themselves in advance to the downpour of abuse that would spew from Fauzia's lips. Two of the on-duty inmates had already gone out to the hall and returned, setting a heavy bucket by the door.

Shula washed meticulously. She removed her pajamas, the only pair in the cellblock, and with a soapy washcloth scrubbed her neck, arms, and shoulders. As usual her first contact with the icy water sent shivers down her spine.

By the time she had finished washing, Fauzia had brought in her "court clothes."

The suitcase containing her street clothes—which Arlette alternated with the seasons—had been impounded by the prison authorities. The evening before each day in court Shula would go to the storeroom, carefully select an outfit, and place it on a hanger to remove the wrinkles. Fauzia would bring it to the cell the following morning.

This time Shula had chosen a black suit—modest in hue, but attractively tight—and a white blouse with a touch of lace that buttoned up to the neck. Despite its severe and matronly color, this suit accentuated her tall, slender figure and gave no hint of her forty-three years or the seven children she had borne. Even more important, however, was the fact that in Beirut, as in the entire Middle East, a black suit was considered proper attire for a married woman of good social standing. Even before her attorney had instructed her on this point, Shula had instinctively realized that it was of paramount importance to counteract the impression created by the prosecution.

Breakfast was brought into the cell. Shula contented herself with a cup of coffee and a piece of stale bread. She sat on the edge of her bed sipping the tasteless liquid. Then she ran a comb through her wavy hair. She would have liked to polish her nails, to put on lipstick, but neither was permitted. She consoled herself with the knowledge that her faint pallor would heighten the impression she was trying to create—an honest, decent woman who was the victim of unfortunate circumstance and her own naïveté.

By now a number of inmates had finished eating and were gathering around Shula, curiously studying her movements. Every so often, one would withdraw from the group to make her bed or to attend to some other task—but never before bidding Shula the accepted prison farewell: "Let's hope we never see your face again." And Shula would reply: *"Inshallah"* (God willing).

Finally Fauzia approached and motioned to Shula that it was time. The two women walked down the long corridor. Once out in the courtyard the guard revealed the ugliness of character which had inspired her nickname.

"They'll probably give you twelve years at least," she said, rejoicing in anticipation of Shula's misfortune.

Shula remained silent.

They stopped at an armored, bullet-proof van with an overhead window and two parallel benches within. A Lebanese army lieutenant greeted her with a nod and motioned her to the back door. She sat, and four soldiers sat opposite her. The door was sealed from the outside and the officer took his place next to the driver. They were off.

From the moment the lieutenant had sealed the door, Shula could think of nothing else than that this might be her very last trip to the courthouse. She was gripped with excitement. Over and over again she reenacted the scene when the judges would pronounce her a free woman, when she would fall into the waiting arms of her children, her husband. . . . She was startled, even annoyed, when the back door opened and the lieutenant signaled her to step out.

As usual, they had parked inside the walled yard of the Place de la Justice. The people standing about, soldiers and Justice Department employees, stopped their conversations in midsentence to gape at the "notorious spy." Seeing no one she knew, she continued swiftly toward the main entrance. The soldiers had to move quickly to keep pace.

They marched the length of a dim and empty corridor and turned right to a block of four cells. She entered one and the door slammed shut behind her.

She sat on an iron bed that hung from the wall by heavy chains.

A few minutes before eight thirty two gendarmes appeared and escorted her to the courtroom.

The court clerk took over at the entrance and led her to the dock, a small cubicle surrounded by a wooden railing and located directly in front of the as yet unoccupied judges' bench. She tried to comport herself erectly, but soon she found her eyes darting to the left, scanning the spectators' gallery. Joseph was sitting in the middle of the third row, his balding head hunched between his shoulders, his face void of expression even as their eyes made brief contact. Arlette and Isaac sat next to him, smiling at her encouragingly. Two of her neighbors from Wadi Abu-Jamil were there, too, and even made a small gesture as though to wave. Much to her surprise Abu-Jacques sat directly behind them. She had not seen him since her arrest nineteen months ago. And although he had never before come to court, she had never reproached him for this. He had a family to protect, and she could well understand his disinclination to exhibit any affiliation with the Israeli spy whose trial was stirring up Beirut. But today, the day the verdict would be read, Abu-Jacques had put caution aside and come. Without looking at him she bowed her head in deep appreciation.

She entered the dock and nodded to her lawyer, who sat at the defense attorney's bench to her immediate left. He rose to shake her hand. From a second bench the prosecuting attorney, Michel Talhameh, nodded his head to her in greeting. Throughout the several months of the trial he had behaved quite courteously toward Shula. This, however, had in no way deterred him from hurtling the most severe accusations at her while court was in session. Beside him sat one of his aides, Joseph Barody. Shula recalled that he had treated her with more respect than any of the other pretrial investigators. "They haven't sent out the bastards today," she told herself in consolation. Barody's presence encouraged her; it was further confirmation that the verdict would be in her favor.

Her three codefendants sat in a dock at the other end of the defense table. They caught her eye and smiled warmly. She returned their smile and turned toward the large portrait of the Lebanese president, Fuad Chehab, hanging directly behind the judges' bench.

The voice of the court clerk cut through the air:

"All rise!"

The entire hall stood as the door leading from the judges' chambers opened and the justices entered. The president of the court, Colonel Hussami, led the procession. He walked to the tallest chair on the rostrum, seated himself, and opened the file before him. Only then did he deign to raise his head and let his eyes sternly sweep the courtroom. He glared at Shula with the same harsh expression, but her optimism was undaunted. She had known Colonel Hussami for many years, had met him socially on numerous occasions. Even when she first met him, Shula knew instinctively that the colonel could be bought. For some reason, she was now convinced that it was the colonel to whom Isaac had been referring when he said that "those who had to be bribed had been bribed."

The deputy magistrate, Major Aadel Chehab, a Christian, smiled at her briefly. When he took his seat to the right of Colonel Hussami, under the picture of the president, Shula noticed again how closely the Lebanese major resembled his famous uncle.

Three additional judges, none of whom Shula was particularly familiar with, entered the court. Two were civilians and she assumed that one was a Christian and the other a Moslem. Rarely at any point in the long trial had all five judges been present concurrently. Hussami and Chehab were always in attendance but the subordinate judges rotated. Today, however, was different; it was her day of judgment.

Colonel Hussami nodded toward the court secretary, who in turn stood up from his chair beneath the rostrum and turned to Shula: "Does the accused, Shulamit Kishak-Cohen, daughter of Meir Cohen, wish to address the bench before the reading of the verdict?"

She was prepared for the question. For several weeks now her attorney had been impressing upon her the impossibility of a total acquittal; the trial had simply received too much notoriety for that. She would have to confess to some of the charges, the lighter ones. "But don't worry," he repeatedly encouraged her, "your friends outside are extremely grateful that you have not mentioned any names. They'll help you." Together they worked out what she would say to the judges when the time came.

In a calm and dignified voice, Shula began to speak.

"I have been accused of smuggling Jews into Israel. I admit to this. I helped poor, unfortunate refugees from Syria and Iraq continue on their way so they would not become a burden here in Beirut. But this is all I confess to having done. As God is my witness

—and the prosecutor knows this as well as I—I am innocent of all the other charges that have been brought against me. I place my fate in the hands of the court and in the hands of God."

She stood in silence. The judges conferred quietly. Then Colonel Hussami motioned to the court secretary and whispered in his ear.

"Court will recess for half an hour," the secretary announced.

The recess seemed endless. She had no watch but she knew that the half-hour had long since passed. Suddenly she was gripped with ominous fear.

When the guard arrived after about two hours she knew, even before he spoke, that her fears were well founded. He whispered to her, "Your son asked me to tell you that things are bad. The promises that were made cannot be fulfilled."

She wanted to flood him with questions but she knew it would be pointless. He certainly would know nothing more than the brief message he had been paid to deliver. But what had happened? What was going to happen? Her heartbeat quickened and she thought she was going to faint.

She was brought directly to the dock and the judges entered immediately. She did not even have time to look for her children.

The court secretary stood holding a piece of paper.

"The verdict of the court," he read aloud, "is that all charges brought against defendant number one have been proved beyond any shadow of a doubt."

Her legs buckled and she had to lean on the wooden railing for support, but only for an instant. She immediately regained her composure and stood erect. The court secretary continued:

"The court is convinced that Shulamit Kishak-Cohen is a dangerous spy who has worked in the services of an enemy state and that she has greatly harmed the Republic of Lebanon, the country that granted her citizenship. The court is further convinced that the actions of the accused have damaged the interests of all the Arab sister nations. Using financial and other forms of temptations, all of which have been proven to the satisfaction of the court by the prosecution, she deceived and corrupted the morals of many people in the name of her egotistical endeavors. Furthermore, she has been employed as a spy and has smuggled valuable state documents out of the country. The court accepts the prosecution's claim that, by means of the great sums of money placed at her disposal, it was the accused's intention to overthrow the Lebanese government. Through the introduction of recordings of the accused herself, and on the basis of the testimony heard in court, the prosecution has succeeded in proving to the court the great danger this enemy agent poses to the state of Lebanon.

"Therefore, the Lebanese Military Court unanimously sentences the accused to be hanged. The court hereby declares a recess."

The clerk's cry of "All rise!" was drowned out by the commotion in the spectators' gallery. Arlette fainted and the people around her began yelling for water. Others were shouting, "Long live justice!" Still others were calling for silence and order.

The reporters in the first row knocked over benches as they rushed to the corridors to phone in the news to their papers. In less than an hour the first evening editions hit the stands. The newspaper vendors barked out the headlines at the top of their lungs:

"ZIONIST SPY SENTENCED TO DEATH!"

Shula heard none of this. While the court secretary was reading the verdict, she was overcome by a wave of dizziness. She held onto the wooden railing with all her strength, and then everything went black. She was not aware of the two policemen who escorted her back to her cell. She sat on the bed in a state of shock, staring at the wall. Only one thought pounded in her brain: "It isn't possible. It just isn't possible. . . ."

She was still in shock an hour later when she was brought back to the courtroom. She did not know why she was there. Perhaps it was to hear the sentencing of the other three defendants.

The court clerk stood up and without preamble or explanatory remarks stated: "To continue the verdict against Shulamit Kishak-Cohen."

Upon hearing these words, Shula's lucidity returned and she stood attentively, listening to what would come next.

"The Military Court has carefully weighed the arguments of the defense and has decided to take into consideration the fact that the accused is the mother of seven children. In view of this the court has seen fit to commute the death sentence and in its place to sentence the accused to twenty years of hard labor. The court declares a recess."

She was in full control while being led back to her cell for the second time since her sentencing. Once alone, however, she broke down. Twenty years! Twenty years away from her children! Twenty years locked up with prostitutes and drug peddlers. . . .

The new verdict seemed even more horrible than the first. Twenty years! She would be a worn-out, wrinkled old woman by the time she was released.

She had no strength left. She lay down and buried her head in the coarse blanket on the bed and cried in bitter desperation.

When the guard came to take her to the courtroom for the third time, she had already regained some of her composure. She told herself how absolutely impossible it was that all the efforts of her influential friends had come to naught, that there must have been some mistake, and that now everything would be rectified. If they could lighten her sentence once, they could certainly do it again.

Feeling encouraged, she asked the guard to wait a moment while she washed the tear stains from her face and combed her hair. She was pale but proud when she entered the court for the third time. She stared directly at the portrait of the Lebanese president while taking her place.

She had not heard the court secretary's opening words but soon enough she pieced together what was happening!

". . . although he was not among the formal defendants tried here, his name was included in the original bill of indictment. The charges brought against him still stand. The court finds these charges to have been sufficiently proven in order to convict defendant number six as an accomplice to a crime against the Lebanese state. Therefore, the court sentences him to ten years in prison. In consideration of his advanced age and poor state of health, the sentence is hereby reduced to two years' imprisonment. . . ."

Suddenly whatever remained of Shula's world caved in. They were talking about Joseph. They were going to put him in prison. What would happen to the children? Who would take care of the two little ones? What would become of them?

She was bereft of hope. The situation could not be worse. The thoughts swam madly in her head. Only later did she realize that she must have fainted. She was taken out of the courtroom before the verdicts of the other three defendants were read.

Later she found herself seated in the armored van on the way back to Saniya Prison. A prison guard was with her this time.

He spoke to her quietly and she could not tell whether he was speaking out of provocation or compassion: "The sun has set, Shula Cohen, hasn't it?"

She instinctively sat up straight and heard herself say without thinking, "Don't turn on the lights. It isn't night yet."

And life returned to her eyes.

Behind Prison Walls

21 "Don't turn on the lights. It isn't dark yet." The words echoed from the far-off days of her youth in Jerusalem. They were her mother's words, repeated over and over again as she followed her father from room to room, curbing expenses by turning off the lights he had turned on as soon as he came home in the evenings.

However, in Shula's mouth the words assumed a different meaning, became a shout of defiance, an attempt to hold back the despair which was spreading and filling her heart.

She had no time now to think of the sentence. She was too concerned about the fate of her children to worry about her own future. With Joseph sentenced to prison, the children were all alone now.

Her lip trembled for a moment as she realized how alone she, too, really was. Returning to jail had been a humiliating experience. She was stripped of her civilian clothes and all her possessions and then pushed around by the guards as they searched her, dressed her in a filthy prison uniform, and shoved her into the ward with the other convicted criminals. Fauzia understood instinctively that her prisoner no longer enjoyed the protection of those nameless outside forces and she was quick to make Shula painfully aware of the grue-some future awaiting her. Shula bit her lip and suffered silently. She thought only of seeing her family and learning about her children's fate.

The children drifted back to the Wadi, downcast and dejected after their heartbreaking separation from their father. They were terribly concerned about their mother's sentence, and yet another blow was awaiting them at home. Joseph's brother, Chaim, and his wife announced that they had no choice but to separate the children. The two little ones, Carmela and Dudik, would be taken in by a great aunt who lived at the end of Wadi Abu-Jamil Street. Arlette would move in with another relative, an aged, childless woman, who could benefit from the young girl's presence around the house. Isaac would live with Uncle Chaim.

The four children cried all night and appeared before their uncle the following morning with a resolute decision: they would remain together as a family and continue to live in their own apartment.

"And how will you support yourselves?" the old man snorted.

"I'll work," Isaac replied. "I'll stop studying and take my father's place in the shop. Arlette will manage things around the house."

"But you're only children!" Uncle Chaim cried, raising his hands in dismay.

The children wouldn't be budged, and Uncle Chaim had no choice but to give in.

The day after the verdict was read Nasri Ma'alouf came to visit Shula.

"Your husband sends his regards. He's being held in Dir El Amar, in the mountains, a small prison for first offenders. It's quite com-fortable, and he even has a Jew for a cellmate. He'll be all right." He smiled confidently, holding out a piece of paper. "But I haven't come to speak about him. Here, sign this."

"What is it?" she asked glumly.

His smile broadened. "Power of attorney, to appeal. What did you think? I'm not going to allow them to get away with such a ludicrous sentence! They don't know Nasri Ma'alouf!"

The appeal was heard on July 23, before a completely different set of judges. Both Shula and Joseph were brought to court, but neither

was called to testify. The appeal centered entirely around complicated legal points of procedure which Shula didn't even attempt to
follow. She couldn't take her eyes off Joseph, and her heart was filled
with pity for him. How disastrous his months in prison must have
been! How thin he looked! Joseph was indeed emaciated; for three
weeks he had eaten nothing but oranges, until the authorities at last
allowed kosher food to be brought in. He was exhausted and had
aged a great deal. His hands shook as he put on his glasses, but when
he saw her watching him, he smiled and waved bravely.

Two weeks later Nasri Ma'alouf received the results of the appeal.
He came to Shula first with the news. "Your sentence has been reduced to seven years," he announced happily. "I have to run to see
your husband at Dir El Amar now. I'm going to bring him home.
He's been acquitted!"

She was so overjoyed at the news of Joseph's release that
Ma'alouf's good news about her own sentence didn't fully register.
That night she lay in her cell, savoring every word the lawyer had
said. Suddenly she sat up. Taking a hairpin, she scratched a faint
mark on the wall next to her bed. She promised herself that she
would make a similar mark on the twenty-third day of every month,
until the entire wall was finally covered and she would at last be set
free.

The months dragged on endlessly; some were bad, others were
worse. The years immediately following her appeal were the most
difficult. Nasri Ma'alouf continued to visit her in prison and one day
he arrived with the bad news that the Syrians were attempting to
have her extradited. He told her that her friends and family were
frantically working behind the scenes to foil the Syrian plan, but
Shula spent many sleepless nights worrying nonetheless. Finally
Ma'alouf reported that the Syrians had been sent a friendly but negative reply, explaining that Shula was a Lebanese citizen and thus
could not be extradited.

Shula's old struggle with Fauzia Harshite flared up right from the
start, making her early months of internment pure hell. Fauzia's
lover had left her, and Shula bore the brunt of the guard's bitterness,
unable to protest.

But thanks to Isaac, Fauzia's abuse again came to an end. At
Passover time in 1964 the boy was enraged when the guard wouldn't

permit Shula's family to bring her special food for the holiday. Against his father's protests Isaac went to the Ministry of the Interior and refused to leave the building until the minister's aide agreed to see him. He protested forcefully about the cruel treatment his mother was receiving in prison, and a special order permitting Shulamit Kishak-Cohen to receive a Passover holiday meal was immediately cabled to the prison authorities. Fauzia was so frightened by the intervention of the ministry in the case of a prisoner she had assumed to have been deserted that she started to handle Shula with kid gloves.

Their relationship gradually improved, and Shula eventually began to purchase little favors from the prison guard. She was allowed to use perfume, and Fauzia didn't stop her from wearing clothes brought in from the outside, as long as they resembled the prison uniform. Soon Shula arranged to have an additional family visit every week. But even when her bribes paid off, Shula never forgot Fauzia's sadistic abuse. A new doctor was assigned to the prison, and when he got wind of the tyrannical methods employed by the head guard, he was horrified. He swore that if even one of the inmates had the courage to speak out against Fauzia, he would have her tried and put behind bars. Shula was the only prisoner with such courage, and she got her revenge when Fauzia was sentenced to two years in prison.

News from the outside world penetrated the prison walls. Shula learned that the Israeli-Syrian border had become an open battlefield, and her family informed her that the Palestinians in Lebanon were also beginning to organize increasingly violent actions. They no longer attempted to conceal the fact that they were receiving vast numbers of weapons and they began to launch occasional terrorist raids into Israel. When Charles Hélou succeeded General Chehab as president, he attempted to curb the Palestinians, but he was too late. The Palestinian groups had grown into too powerful a force.

"Everyone is saying there will have to be armed conflict with them sooner or later," Isaac said sadly.

Isaac had his own problems as well. Once his father was released from prison, there was no longer any reason for the boy to work in his father's shop. He went on to become a successful sales representative of an American cosmetics company in Beirut. But as Isaac's career boomed, Joseph's trickled to an end. There was little business now at the shop in the market, and certainly not enough work to fill both brothers' day, so Joseph stopped going to the shop altogether. Isaac became, in turn, the family's chief breadwinner. Shula watched her young son develop into a handsome man. He would drive his Renault recklessly through the busy Beirut streets, casting appreciative glances at the young women promenading down Hamra Street. But as much as he achieved on his own, Isaac never could escape the label, "son of the spy." The worried mothers of Wadi Abu-Jamil prevented their daughters from dating the handsome young man. Isaac felt slighted, but he had no regrets, for he didn't intend to make his life in Beirut.

"As soon as mother is released, we're all going to leave," he would say to his father and Arlette. "We'll start a new life in Israel."

He often discussed his future plans with his mother during their weekly visits, and they even devised a code to allow them to speak freely in front of the ever-present prison guards. "Going to the mountains" meant emigrating to Israel, and Isaac would tell his mother of any of their friends who had gone "to the mountains."

All of Isaac's plans for his own family's "trip to the mountains" focused around August 11, 1967, the sixth anniversary of Shula's internment. Nasri Ma'alouf had developed a warm relationship with the entire family over the years, and they often discussed Shula's chances for release. He informed Isaac that prisoners convicted of treason were not eligible for a reduction of their sentence for good behavior. Still, he had promised to make an appeal for a presidential pardon after six years, and he believed there was a good chance that it might be granted.

Isaac had other ideas about his future as well. He had registered for an accountancy course at the Belgian Academy. His studies were going well, and he had every reason to believe he'd breeze through the final examinations, scheduled for June 5, 1967.

But he never appeared for the tests.

That morning Isaac and his cousin Albert were listening to Radio Cairo announce the outbreak of war with Israel.

Albert turned white. "I'm sure there'll be riots, and my father is at the store all alone!"

They hurried out to Isaac's Renault and raced to the Suk Sursuk, passing mobs of Palestinians carrying flags, banners, pictures of Gamal Abdel Nasser, and clubs. The shops in the market that had just opened shut their doors out of fear.

Isaac and Albert sent Chaim Kishak-Cohen home while they locked the iron gate, closing themselves inside the store.

By eleven o'clock the Egyptians had already announced several overwhelming victories. The cousins realized that if there were to be riots, they wouldn't center around the market. They locked the store and ran to where they had parked the car, but as soon as they reached the main street, they were stopped by a mob of jeering Palestinians. Someone shouted, "Here are the Jews!" Spotting an empty alleyway, they ran as quickly as they could, with the enraged mob at their heels. Somehow they managed to escape.

Catching their breath, Isaac and Albert stumbled toward the other end of the alley and charged straight into another mob of demonstrators. Realizing there was only one way to escape, the boys fell in step with the rioters and began shouting the praises of the Egyptian leader and calling for the destruction of Israel. At last they managed to slip away from the crowd and make their way to Wadi Abu-Jamil. An army unit had already been posted at both entrances to the street.

Shula learned about the outbreak of war when a crowd of noisy, excited demonstrators passed the prison walls. Several inmates heard the slogans being chanted and returned to the ward, repeating the war cries at the top of their lungs. Shula listened wordlessly as they chanted the slogans over and over, and suddenly a barbed-wire fence of hatred dropped to separate the Jew from the others in the ward. Only yesterday Shula had been chatting with her fellow inmates, reading their fortunes in tea leaves. Now even the friendliest inmates cast hostile glances in her direction. She armed herself with silence, afraid for herself and terrified for the Jewish state.

By nightfall she knew that Israel was on the road to its startling victory. One of the guards had heard an Arabic newscast from Monte Carlo and Shula heard her exclaim, "The Jews are winning, the sons of bitches!"

Shula called the guard and asked to be removed to another ward. The guard's eyes narrowed into flashing slits and she spun on her heel to find the officer on duty. Shula was immediately taken to solitary confinement.

A month passed, and Beirut settled into a grudging acceptance of the Israeli victory in the Six-Day War and the strange new political realities in the Middle East. The demonstrations gradually subsided, but the fury and humiliation remained. At the Suk Sursuk, Jewish storekeepers refrained from opening their shops, fearful of the wrath of a defeated people.

In the Saniya prison, Shula continued to wait out the storm in solitary confinement. She had not seen her family since the war began, and she missed them terribly. Still, she knew it was better for them within the safely guarded Wadi at a time like this. Once the emotions died down, they'd be able to visit her again.

Shula perceived little connection between the war and her own fate. Still, she couldn't help but worry that in light of the brilliant Israeli operation it might be difficult for President Hélou to grant a pardon to his Jewish prisoner. But she forced herself not to think of that possibility, and focused all her hopes on the eleventh of August, waiting for salvation to come through the official channels.

She was surprised, therefore, when a guard unlocked her cell and told her she was wanted in the prison office because a representative of the Red Cross was asking to speak with her.

Shula headed for the office and was introduced to Alain Modoux, the Beirut representative of the International Red Cross.

As soon as the guard left them alone, Modoux turned to Shula and explained the reason for his visit. "Madame, Israel wants you. I have been instructed to discuss your release with the Lebanese government." He gave her a moment to catch her breath. "However, before I do so, I must ask you a simple question: are you interested in going to Israel? If not, we can arrange to send you to some other country, provided, of course, that the Lebanese authorities see fit to release you—and I must warn you that I have not received any assurances to that effect."

Modoux didn't reveal the details of the Israelis' interest in her freedom, but once she returned to Israel, Shula pieced together the events leading up to her release.

When the Israeli defense forces captured the Old City of Jerusalem, many Lebanese citizens, including the Lebanese consul and the entire staff, were still in the city. A few days later when the Israelis seized the Golan Heights, they captured a great deal of heavy equipment the Syrians had planned to use to construct a channel to divert the Jordan River. The equipment, which was worth millions, belonged to a rich Lebanese contractor.

Israel placed the Lebanese citizens on the bargaining table, along with the costly equipment. In exchange the Israelis demanded the return of an Israeli pilot who had parachuted into Lebanon after his plane was hit in battle above Syria, and another soldier who had crossed the Lebanese border by mistake prior to the war. At the last moment they added Shulamit Kishak-Cohen to their list of demands.

When Modoux first approached the Lebanese authorities with Israel's offer, he received a categorical refusal. Shula Cohen was, after all, a Lebanese citizen, and it was unthinkable that one Lebanese citizen should be handed over to the enemy in exchange for another.

But Modoux concluded quite correctly that Lebanon's refusal was a mere formality and that if the question of Shula's citizenship could be cleared up to allow a way out, there would be no further objections. He reported this suspicion to the Israelis.

The response from the Jewish state was direct and clear-cut: Shula Cohen may have received Lebanese citizenship after marrying Joseph Kishak-Cohen, but she had been born in Jerusalem and was therefore a citizen of Israel. They argued that citizenship by birth is a stronger claim than citizenship by marriage.

Modoux returned to Beirut with the Israeli solution, but he decided to present the idea to Shula before bringing the question back to the Lebanese authorities.

Shula was thrilled with the plan but also a bit concerned. It had been so many years since she had lived with her family—perhaps too many.

"I can't answer you immediately," she told Modoux regretfully. "I'm ready and willing to return to Israel today, but you must speak with my children. I don't know how they'd feel about the matter."

Modoux agreed to speak with the rest of the family and said his good-byes, warning Shula not to reveal the latest developments to anyone connected with the prison.

The following Saturday when her family arrived for their first visit since the war, Shula broached the subject cautiously. "A man from the Red Cross was here to see me," she said. "He'll be in touch with you as well. He wants to invite all of us to go to the mountains."

Two weeks passed before a secretary from the Red Cross telephoned the Kishak-Cohen home and asked Isaac and Arlette to meet

Monsieur Alain Modoux at the bar of the Riviera Hotel. Modoux informed the children that negotiations involving their mother's release had been going on for more than a month, but that only now did he have the privilege to confirm that all the obstacles had been removed and Madame Cohen would be freed in ten days.

"Your mother is ready to return to Israel, but only on the condition that you agree as well," he continued. "It may be possible to arrange that you all cross the border together. If not, however, your mother will be escorted across the border at Ra's an Naqurah and the rest of the family will have to fly to Nicosia and from there to Israel. How do you feel about the plan?"

Isaac replied that he would have to consult their father before making any final decision, and he and Arlette rose to leave. As soon as they got out of the hotel, they hugged each other and began to dance in the street. The uniformed doorman stared at them as if they were mad.

They raced home to give Joseph the news, and the family stayed up all night discussing the move. In the morning Isaac called the Red Cross and jubilantly announced his family's approval.

Two days later Modoux contacted them again. "Wednesday, August twenty-third, is the day," he said, "but as I suspected, the Lebanese government won't permit the entire family to cross over at Ra's an Naqurah. The rest of you will have to fly to Nicosia."

Their last days in Lebanon were spent furiously preparing the few things they could take with them on the plane. Dudik opted for his stamp collection; Isaac, the camera he had received from old Shukry Mussa for his Bar Mitzvah. Joseph chose an old *shofar*, a ceremonial ram's horn that had been passed down in his family from generation to generation for more than two hundred years.

Because of the secrecy surrounding their mother's release and their emigration to Israel, the family couldn't sell the rest of their belongings, so the night before the trip their relatives crowded into the house and fought over the remains of the Kishak-Cohen household in a scene that resembled a Greek wake. But the bulk of their possessions, the furniture and housewares, had already been discreetly handed over to old Nazira. It was a small token of their gratitude for her loyal care of the family throughout the six years of Shula's imprisonment.

The preparations went smoothly until a slight complication

cropped up at the very last minute. Everyone in the family had a valid passport except for Joseph, whose passport had expired years before. When they realized the documents were not in order, Isaac began running from office to office in a fruitless attempt to speed up the procedure. Finally it occurred to him to phone Monsieur Modoux, who in turn contacted the Ministry of Interior.

A new passport was issued to Joseph Kishak-Cohen in unheard-of record time. Isaac received the documents at eleven thirty in the morning and rushed to the airport, where the rest of the family was anxiously awaiting their twelve thirty flight.

An hour later they landed in Nicosia.

Shula was informed of the date of her release the Saturday before the event, and between Saturday and Wednesday she only managed to sleep two hours a night. When she finally did drop off to sleep, her dreams were more vivid than ever before. Sometimes she had terrible nightmares, but at other times her dreams were so pleasant that she forced herself awake so as not to forget them.

Wednesday finally arrived.

At six thirty in the morning someone knocked at the door of the solitary cell where Shula had lived since the Six-Day War. She had been awake for hours, and she had dressed carefully in a seven-year-old, too narrow skirt and a blue jacket that had long been out of fashion. She looked up when she heard the knock and was surprised to see Joseph Barody, one of the two investigators who had so brutally questioned her for months on end years before and had aided the prosecution during her trial.

He laughed at her expression.

"The Red Cross has arranged for us to escort you to Ra's an Naqurah at four thirty this afternoon," he smiled. "Your husband and children will leave for Cyprus earlier. But before we say our good-byes, Madame Cohen, we have prepared a special going-away present for you: a tour of Beirut." Shula could scarcely believe this was the same Joseph Barody, addressing her so politely. "This will surely be the last time you will see the city, and we wanted your final parting to be a pleasant one. It is my honor to have been chosen as your personal escort. Oh, and your daughter has asked me to give you this." He held out an envelope. Shula opened it and found 150 Lebanese pounds and a note: "*Au revoir*. Arlette."

She asked Barody for a few minutes to arrange her hair, say good-bye to the friends she had made, and divide her belongings. She gave the last of a dozen bottles of perfume that Abu-Sa'id had once bought her to one of the nicer prison guards.

They finally set out for the gate, stopping at the prison office where the watch, rings, and money that had been confiscated the night of her arrest were returned to her. Barody lifted her suitcase and walked her to a car parked in the prison courtyard.

"What's the first thing you'd like to see?" he asked, settling in behind the wheel. "Wadi Abu-Jamil?"

"Anyplace but the Wadi," Shula thought automatically. Now that her family was no longer there, she felt as alienated by the Jewish ghetto as she had when she first arrived there thirty-one years before as a young bride.

"It doesn't matter," she told Barody. "Let's just ride around."

Beirut had not quite awakened. The stores were still tightly shut, but the streets were beginning to fill with people. As they drove through the familiar streets, Shula found herself staring at the faces of the passersby, searching. She was so involved with the people that it was moments after they drove by an empty building that she realized, with a start, that they had passed the spot where the Star nightclub used to be.

Barody brought the car to a stop in front of a restaurant and asked her whether she might like to have breakfast. A table had already been prepared for them in the back. Shula picked at her food, too excited to have much appetite. She wished Barody had arranged for a seat by the window, where at least she might observe the people in the street.

They went back to the car and rode down the Corniche and then turned and traveled the length of the city once more, to A-Nahar in the northeast and then to al-Ashrafiyah. They made their way up the mountain to an observation point from which the entire city could be seen, but when they reached the top, Shula asked to return. It was the people she wanted to see, not the view.

As Barody headed toward the city again, Shula finally admitted to herself that in truth she was interested in seeing only one person. Was he still alive? Had he come back to Beirut? She didn't dare ask Barody about him, but she couldn't help thinking, "What a miracle it would be if he passed us on the street!"

At noon Shula remarked, "You paid for breakfast, now it's my turn. But on one condition: that I choose the place. Let's go to Abu-Amar's restaurant. I'm in the mood for fish."

Barody gave her a bemused, knowing look. "Now Madame Cohen, we have no interest in your seeing him, or any of his friends," he said pleasantly but firmly. He turned the car instead onto a road Shula knew well and headed for the Pigeon's Cave restaurant, so strongly tied to so many memories.

Once again everything had been prepared in advance. A waiter who had served her many times in the past took their order, avoiding Shula's eyes and pretending that he had never seen her before. As they sipped their coffee, Shula asked for the bill, but the waiter averted his glance and told her, "The patron says it's on the house."

Shula didn't know whether this gracious final gesture was made in her behalf or because of the man who was accompanying her.

After lunch they went for another short ride around the outskirts of Beirut. There was much more traffic and noise now than Shula remembered. She took a last lingering look at the towering sky-scrapers that had been built in the years of her imprisonment, and they drove down the Corniche again, past the row of elegant luxury hotels. Heading south, they came to the large Palestinian refugee camp; that, at least, had not changed. The car continued southward on the coastal road in the direction of Sidon.

Shula sat in silence, gazing at the passing landscape. She told herself that she should be either happy or sad, for the longest chapter of her life—for better or for worse—was now coming to an end. But she felt only a deep void and a touch of disappointment.

The car stopped before the Lebanese border station a little after four o'clock. Barody looked at Shula and said, "We promised to arrive at four thirty so let's be punctual. We'll wait here for a few minutes." He shifted in his seat, eyeing her levelly. "Madame Cohen, I wonder if I might ask you something. You've already been tried and convicted, and you've served your sentence. Now that you're leaving us and everything belongs to the past, please tell me the truth. Did you really work for Israel, or have you just been a hapless victim of circumstance?"

Shula looked at him for several minutes, and then a wide smile spread across her face.

"If you're merely interested in satisfying your own curiosity, I've already declared in court that I was never an Israeli spy. But if you're interested in establishing contact with the Israelis, I'd be happy to see what I can do!"

He stared at her in surprise and then burst out laughing. "My God," he cried, "even at the very last moment!"

They parted, laughing.

A customs officer carried Shula's suitcase and walked beside her the three hundred yards until they reached the Israeli border station. Off in the distance she could see the blue and white Israeli flag flying atop a low building. As she approached, an Israeli officer stepped out of the station and marched toward her. He stood at attention and saluted.

He hesitated for a moment, not knowing in which language to address her. Then he smiled and said in Hebrew, "Welcome home, Madame Cohen."

"*Shalom,*" Shula replied.

He led her to a waiting car and they drove southward. Shula peered out the window, fascinated by the passing panorama and impressed by the abundance of green. She whispered the names of the Jewish settlements as they rode past the signs, comparing them to her distant memories.

"We'll be in Haifa in half an hour," the officer said, breaking into her thoughts.

Shula pulled herself back to the present. "Aren't we approaching Nahariya?" she asked. "Do you think we could stop there and find me a hairdresser? I don't want to arrive in Haifa looking like this!"

The young officer turned to the woman at his side in astonishment and admiration. Her eyes brightened and she blushed slightly.

Despite her ludicrous, unfashionable attire and the streaks of gray running through her long, windswept hair, Shula Cohen was still very much a woman.

AFTERWORD
Where Are They Now?

WINKLER, whose being smuggled off the *Transylvania* at the beginning of 1948 opened the door to Shulamit Kishak-Cohen's espionage career—Shula's mystery man remains a man of mystery. In the great confusion that accompanied the establishment of the state of Israel, his story was somehow lost. "Winkler," obviously a pseudonym, is not to be found in the archives of that period.

ABU-JACQUES, Shula's faithful aide. When Shula was arrested in 1961, Abu-Jacques put an end to his own smuggling work. In 1970 he emigrated to Israel with his entire family and they live there today in a suburb of Haifa.

NAZIRA, the neighbor who saw everything and guessed the rest. In 1975 Nazira moved to Israel with her family. She lives in Bat Yam.

GEORGE ANTON, the man who said to Shula, "You have the nerve, and I the experience." George's experience didn't betray him, and the instinct that told him when to retire was right. He was last seen in 1965 in South America, serving as the commercial representative of one of Beirut's richest families. In a moment of candor Shula mused, "I wonder what he'll say when he reads the book."

ABU-SA'ID, the "Prince of Thieves," went on pulling strings and managing his diverse and often dubious affairs until one day in 1975, when he was found hunched over an easy chair in his private office on the third floor of the Olympia Casino. Abu-Sa'id was wearing a white suit with a red carnation in his lapel when his heart stopped beating.

DARWISH BAIDON. The Baidon family declined but still retained its wealth. Darwish died in 1970. It was said in Beirut that he "succumbed to his obesity."

FAHED HAMOUDA. When Shula was arrested and Mahmud Hoj disappeared, Hamouda felt the earth shaking under his feet. He escaped to one of the Arabian Gulf emirates, where he still works in the field of aviation.

MAJOR TALAL ABUDI. His obsessive hatred for Lebanese President Camille Chamoun caused him to be discharged from the army even before Shulamit Kishak-Cohen's spy ring was exposed. The major emigrated to Spain, but on the basis of Muhammed Awad's detailed testimony he was tried in absentia in Lebanon and convicted of treason. He died and was buried in Malaga.

COLONEL GABRIEL LAHOUD, the man who arrested Shula. The uncovering of Shula's spy ring expedited Lahoud's promotion, and in 1970 he was appointed head of the *Deuxième Bureau,* the Lebanese intelligence agency. With the election of Sulieman Frangié to the presidency in 1974, the entire upper echelon of the intelligence force was found guilty of destroying important confidential files "related to elections and other important matters" at the Syrians' behest. Of the eighteen men accused, four found political asylum in Syria. Another five, Gabriel Lahoud among them, escaped to Spain. He, too, was tried in absentia and sentenced to ten years' imprisonment.

NAGI ASLAN, the "Playboy of Beirut," landed on his feet again. His influential family sent him off to Europe, and even though his name was not mentioned at Shula's trial, Nagi decided not to return to Beirut. Today he is still leaving his mark on the European "jet set."

MUHAMMED ARNAUT, ABU-MUSTAFA, "THE TIGER." Various regimes came and went in Damascus, but the Syrian hit man remained —not forever, however. When Hafez al-Assad took power in November of 1970, "the Tiger" was summoned to report to the new heads of the Syrian secret service. He left for Damascus and hasn't been seen since.

ALBERT ILIYA, secretary of the Jewish community in Beirut and Shula's codefendant until his heart attack. Iliya was eventually acquitted on all charges of participating in Shulamit Kishak-Cohen's spy ring but his acquittal didn't remove him from suspicion, particularly in the eyes of the Syrians. He disappeared in 1975. The rumor spread through Beirut that he was abducted to Damascus. In any case, he hasn't been seen since.

DR. JOSEPH ATTIA, head of the Jewish community in Beirut. Dr. Attia died of old age before his beloved city was to become a battlefield once more in 1975. After his death the entire Attia family emigrated from Lebanon.

SHUKRY MUSSA. The old head of the clan died in Tananarive without ever returning to his beloved Lebanon. His son Fathi and his nephews Nabil and Mahmud were last seen by Shula on the day of their sentencing. Nabil's nightclub and Fathi's beach chair concession were both confiscated by the Lebanese authorities. The three men served their prison terms and returned to their farm in El-Hiam. When Israeli forces entered southern Lebanon in the summer of 1978, Shula inquired about them but was informed that they were no longer living in the village.

NASRI MA'ALOUF, Shula's attorney, served a brief term as Lebanon's defense minister in 1974.

For the Kishak-Cohen family there was a happy ending.
After an emotion-laden reunion with Bertie and Meir, whom their father had not seen for fifteen years, and with Yaffa, who was al-

CODE NAME THE PEARL

ready married and a mother, Shula and Joseph settled down in Jerusalem in the elegant Rehavya quarter. There they brought up their other children who, one by one, married and began their own families—all except Dudik, who is still a bachelor and lives with his parents.

Once a year, on the anniversary of their mother's release from prison, they all gather in Jerusalem (except for Isaac, who is abroad with the Israeli diplomatic corps) to celebrate the occasion. At their last reunion, in 1977, thirteen grandchildren were present.

But between the yearly reunions Shula and Joseph are on their own. Joseph busies himself as the volunteer treasurer of a neighborhood charity fund. Shula is still much too active to be satisfied with the humdrum existence of a housewife. When she was fifty-five years old, she became the manageress of an antique shop near the King David Hotel—at the exact location where, forty years previously, had stood the florist shop from which Joseph ordered the bouquet that announced his engagement to sixteen-year-old Shula Arazi-Cohen.

None of the employees or regular customers at the antique shop suspected that the blue-eyed, placid matron with light brown hair sprinkled with white, was once known as "the Mata Hari of the Middle East." Then, in January, 1979, Shula Kishak-Cohen was invited to the presidential mansion, not far from her home, where the president of Israel officially awarded her a scroll expressing the state of Israel's gratitude to her for services rendered.

Temple Israel

Minneapolis, Minnesota

IN MEMORY OF
HELEN BOHM
FROM
PHIL & BEVERLY BERMAN